Dr. Gary Andrew Dresden

ARPress
ILLUMINATING IDEAS.
EMPOWERING VOICES

Confessions of
a *Gynecologist*

ARPress
45 Dan Road Suite 5
Canton MA 02021

Hotline: 1(888) 821-0229
Fax: 1(508) 545-7580

Ordering Information:

Quantity sales. Special discounts are available on quantity purchases by corporations, associations, and others. For details, contact the publisher at the address above.

Printed in the United States of America.

ISBN-13:   Paperback   979-8-89356-042-8
             eBook   979-8-89356-043-5

Library of Congress Control Number: 2024903163

Confessions of

a Gynecologist

TABLE OF CONTENTS

For my parents, Ruth and Arnold who gave me the spark of life, for my wife Trudy who keeps that spark burning strong and true, and for my children who make it all worthwhile.

PROLOGUE

Many of the events portrayed in this novel are true. They actually occurred. Painstaking care has been taken in order to prevent any relationship between events described in this book and people who were actually involved in those happenings. Names and locations have been changed. Settings have been altered. The chronology of events has been purposely modified so that there is no continuity or relationship to occurences. Fictional incidences have been developed so that it is impossible to separate the truth from the tale. Any recognition of similarity between real life events and episodes in this story are completely coincidental and without intent.

Nevertheless, this story was purposely written in the fiction format in order to give me latitude of expression and the ability to describe actual real life events without fearing retribution.

By changing names, locations, settings and chronology, and by mixing truth with fiction, I could avoid accusations of libel or, at the risk ofbeing paranoid, criminal prosecution by some over zealous prosecutor bent on self-promotion. Ironically, by taking the fiction format, I could more accurately maintain the thread of actual events.

The purpose of the story is twofold. First it is to tell an exciting story. Next and more importantly, it is to disclose the decay, injustice and inefficiency that exists in the delivery of medical services and the training of our physicians.

This story is many years in the writing. I started back in nineteen seventy to write the story line for events that were fresh in my memory. Although I was constantly busy and frenzied in my residency training program, I occasionally stole a few moments to jot things down as I felt them and experienced them. When I started practice in nineteen hundred and seventy three, I had almost half the story written. My full attention was then diverted to building a large and successful practice and the book was placed somewhere on a back shelf to gather dust. Somehow, I discovered the hand written pages a number of years later and had my office typist painstakingly transcribe my miserable handwritten prose onto the printed page. Again, in the pursuit of greater deeds, I put the half-completed book aside on the top shelf of my closet and forgot about it. Many years later, my son Bryan discovered the text and read through it. He asked me why I didn't complete the novel, since it was a great story to tell and I obviously had a gift as a storyteller. This spurred me on to read- dress the issue. I had the book successfully scanned into my computer and went from there. Upon completion, I asked Bryan ifhe would take care of the mundane and laborious task of getting the book published. As ususual, he rose to the occassion. I hope that you enjoy the result. Most of all, though, I hope that you learn something about the decadence and injustice in our medical system. Awareness gives us all a better chance to address the problems before they get totally out of hand and, hopefully, the people can raise enough of a voice to force government to do something about it.

THE DEVELOPING YEARS

My first subconscious recollection was that of battering my head against the wall. The quarters were confining. Later on in life, through a long process of deductive reasoning, I was able to discover the locale of those first experiences. The Uterus!

I was battering my head against a goddamn pelvis that was too small to accommodate it. Damn inconsiderate to say the least. The problem seemed unresolvable and with a deep sigh, I resigned myself to life in utero. At that moment, when all hope was lost, a sliver of blinding light stole in from above. Over me, I could see the razor sharp edge of a knife plummeting through the opening and I hunched myself back into a corner. Too late! The blade nicked my scalp, and a sensation I later learned to call pain shot through me. With the help of a long pair of scissors, the sliver spread to a quarter moon. "Careful you bastard," I thought. Then a hand grabbed me roughly around the head and twisted me around, as another fell on my rump and pushed hard, with an extreme lack of consideration for my private parts. Of course, at the time I didn't realize that I had any parts at all that were private. The sliver, which changed to a quarter moon, took the shape of my head and then, "snap." My head shot up and there was light all around and I could straighten my legs for the first time.

What followed afterward was a bit hazy to say the least; the feeling weak; the necessity to suck in what I would later learn to call air; the complete violation of all my orifices with a ball sucking at my mouth, a tube in my nose, a fingertip in my rectum, drops in my eyes, and this god awful pain right smack in my penis.

Never had I seen such commotion. One minute I'm alone, and then they wouldn't leave me alone. Being too busy learning how to breathe, I didn't get most of the repartee. But I do remember the voice saying. "The pelvis wasn't big enough, and the head was turned around posterior and would not come out that way."

"Of all the gall", I thought. "They were blaming the whole episode on me. How the hell was I supposed to know which way to turn."

1)I resolved that I would become the helper of feti in distress and

2)I forgave my mother.

My initial intentions were good, but along the way my environment warped me and soon detoured me from my goal. I learned all too quickly that life was a system of rewards and punishments, and that my actions were geared to predicted outcomes.

For good marks I got a pat on the head and a smile. For scoring touchdowns I got laid. In either case room and board were provided. Obviously the quest for orgasm prevailed.

There was one conflict. Eventually I had to endure quite a bit of punishment before I got through the maze and got my just desserts. Don't let anyone fool you. Football is a dangerous game, but to coin an old adage. "You must risk a lot to gain a lot."

I made up an accounting sheet placing all my physical characteristics into an asset and deficit column, attempting to find the formula that would insure the greatest number of orgasms and secondary pleasures for the least amount of sacrifice.

My computer mind came up with quarterback. In prestige and glory the position was number one; in pain it was third from the bottom, just in front of holder and kicker. Besides, I was lithe, agile, coordinated, and fairly fast; attributes most essential to the position, while my lack of strength and weight had the least detrimental effect. At five feet ten inches, I was just borderline with regard to height.

With fierce determination, I set about my goal. Each day in school I would diagram plays in class like a general directing an army and try and appreciate, in three dimension, the flow of motion on the field for each given play and the time intervals at which spots in the defense would be weakest. The permutations and combinations were infinite and my total being was devoured by the problems at hand. There were temporary setbacks, such as chastisement by my teacher for not listening or for doodling. There were even occasional trips to the principal's office for creating disruption and showing indifference in the classroom. Even my parents got into the act, but their words of wisdom fell on deaf ears. The little pear shaped kid with glasses, sitting in the corner with his nose in a book and his 96 average, got laughed at and abused. The captain of the football team, acne, cracked teeth and all, got laid.

My father warned me.
"That roly-poly is going to surpass you and enjoy greater success."

But at fifteen, with each day a relative eternity, planning ten years in advance seemed like an absurdity. For effort to be persistent it must be coated with sugar and there were no immediate and few imminent rewards in view by pursuing the hard and tedious line of study, study, study. After school I practiced with the freshman football team. Me and another guy were battling it out for the first string quarterback job. He was bigger and tougher and could throw further. I was smaller, smarter, and faster but I knew it wasn't enough. Intelligence helps, but all the brains in the world can't make a football arrive at point X in Y time. That takes a natural arm, good vision, good timing, and depth perception.

I used all the sorcery at my command. After practice I threw balls into a tire for two hours before dinner and two hours after. I ate and

ate and ate, and prayed that I would grow. Most of all I prayed that the first string quarterback would break his leg or something.

God heard me. On the fourteenth play of the third game of the season, their middle linebacker did what our coach had been telling our middle linebackers to do for two months.

"I like sportsmanship boy, but come up with that elbow under the shoulder pads. Catch him in the Adam's apple. Let him know he's in a ball game." Pointing a finger for emphasis, he added. "Good, clean, hard fun. That's what I like."

Our quarterback sailed backwards, eyes bulging, and fell in a lump. An accommodating defensive end sat on his extended leg and snapped it cleanly.

Thank heaven for prayer. With forehead furrowed, frown across his face, and tears welled up in his eyes, the coach resonated with conviction.

"Get those bastards, an eye for an eye." All that lacked was a bible. The whole team was sad, but now determined to get revenge. Secretly I was elated. Second string quarterbacks don't get laid.

Confusion, fear, and occasional abandon characterized that first game experience. Nevertheless, repetitive practice paid off, as reflex predominated over cerebral function. My mind was clouded but, almost instinctively, I knew what to call and my body carried out each task with mechanical precision. The end result was a 14-13 victory. My efforts, as viewed by others, while certainly not distinguished, were definitely not deplorable. Rather, despite my mental confusion, I came across as competent, methodical, and capable. From that day on I was number one. With each game I gained confidence. No longer were there many surprises. My mind caught up with my body and, within the framework of basic reflex action, I was able to develop a degree of flexibility that makes for surprise and excitement. My arm grew stronger, my body more relaxed but most importantly I acquired game experience. I could sense tacklers on my right or left or behind me. I could throw blindly to a spot and complete a pass more often than you would think. Some called it a sixth sense. The explanation though was simple enough. With repetitive exposure, you learn the basic flow of traffic during a play. You know where each player is at different time intervals, not because you see them, but because you have seen the same play hundreds of times before, and you have had a pass intercepted, or you have been creamed from the blind side to taste a mouthful of dirt, and to nurse sore ribs for a week or two. By my sophomore year a gap had developed between me and the unfortunate quarterback who broke his leg that could only be bridged if he were given equal playing time. While potentially he might have surpassed me, at the moment I was better and, since the varsity needed a quarterback with some experience, I would play and the gap grew greater until it was not negotiable. His friends called me lucky, but to me luck is when "preparation meets opportunity" My chance came and I was prepared. I used it to full advantage and because of that I remained number one.

With each game, I continued to strengthen my position, and I learned one important lesson. Prepare and be ready and when opportunity or surprise confronts you, you will be able to grab hold of it and perform creditably until experience permits you to stand apart and above.

That first time, though, you must hold on or you may drown and never get a second chance.

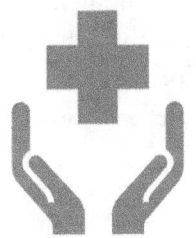

INTERNSHIP-PARKER MEDICAL CENTER

The headlines should have read "January 1st, Hell Freezes over." At least it seemed that cold as I walked the hundred yards from the parking lot to the doctor's entrance with the cold, biting wind ripping through my overcoat." It was a foreboding of the nightmare that lay before me. Thank God I was as unaware as the lamb going to the slaughter. Otherwise, I don't think I would have taken those last strides through the doors of the medical center that would be my home for the next year. I found my way to the office of the director of medical education and presented myself to his secretary.

"Please make yourself comfortable," she said, pointing to a row of chairs across from her desk. She never even lifted her head. I found a seat next to another fellow who was engaged in conversation with a girl sitting to his left. He looked about my age and was probably another intern. She looked stumpy of body and fleshy of face, common qualities found in a female Doc. Somehow, there seemed to be a direct correlation between ugly and smart, especially when it came to females. I sat down and introduced myself to them.

"Hi," he replied, "I'm Bob. Bob Norris and this is, Sheila?" He paused for a moment. She filled in.

"Canter."

"New interns too," I asked.

"I'm afraid so. Seems nobody but you, Sheila and I have arrived yet.

I looked at my watch. It was 7:30 AM. We were supposed to arrive at eight.

"We're early, I guess."

"Where are you from," Sheila asked.

"Bologna."

"Where?" she asked with a confused countenance. "Bologna, Bologna Italy."

"Oh," she replied in a supercilious tone that would typify the physician response upon finding out that someone was a foreign graduate. "I'm from Flower Fifth, you know, the jungle. Bob and I were at school together."

She was referring to Metropolitan Hospital in the heart of Manhattan where Flower Fifth students trained. They dealt almost exclusively with welfare dependent and poverty stricken Puerto Ricans and Blacks.

"I bet you got a lot of experience dealing with the variety of illness that you must have seen there."

"Are you kidding me," Bob cut in. "I got to the point where I could tell the difference between a man cut by a nigger and a spic. The nigger stabs but the spic carves."

Right away I couldn't stand Bob. Those racial epithets made me sick. "How about you Sheila. Did you have an opportunity to get your fingers wet?"

"Of course. In all American medical schools your last year is practically an internship. I'm used to taking care of people, writing all their basic orders, starting the IV, drawing blood and doing the CBC, urinalysis, EKG, etc. by myself."

Her reply startled me. I knew about those things but I had never done any of them. I hadn't even performed a history and physical, which is the basis on which the physician forms his working diagnosis.

I had to learn it all from scratch and it became evident that I was way behind. I hoped that my lack of experience would not be taken for stupidity. I was willing to learn. All I needed was a helping hand. As we made small talk, the room began to be filled with would be house staffers, mostly foreign graduates. Most America graduates began their internship on July 1st right after graduation in June. Sheila and Bob were exceptions because they chose to do six months of research after graduation. Foreign graduates usually finished school in July, August or September and, therefore, had to wait until January to begin their year of internship. At eight o'clock sharp, we were all ushered into the office of the director of medical education and, following his indication, took seats in the various accommodations spread throughout the room.

Dr. Gardner was an imposing figure. He addressed us all as a group, as his gaze swept across the room. I felt disappointed that he didn't offer me a wink of recognition. He had been so friendly at our luncheon engagement in Bologna last January. It was essentially that impression that convinced me to sign the contract to intern at the Parker Medical Center. Under him, I felt that he would offer concerned supervision and an empathetic ear to my individual needs. Speaking to me now, he seemed so disconcertingly distant. Little did I know that this posture was an omen of things to come. His major job was recruiting and he stretched the truth as far as he had to in order to recruit his quota of interns. Just like in college athletics, once signed, the rules changed. You were an indentured servant and there wasn't anything to do about it.

Dr. Gardner opened on a positive note.

"I'm glad to see you all here this morning. I know that you are all anxious to get started and therefore I won't make you to listen to a long speech. Let me just say that I wish you all luck and am looking forward to a successful and fruitful year. Now, if you'll all speak to my secretary outside, she will give you your floor assignments and direct you to the laundry section where you can sign out for your uniforms.

Let me just add that I am proud to have this group here with me today. You were all hand picked and I am looking forward to a rewarding year both for you and for the Center."

With a nod of his head, our meeting had come to an end. I wouldn't speak to him again until the graduation ceremony. We all got up and picked up our assignments from his secretary's desk. She didn't even lift her head.

After signing up for my uniforms, I headed to my on call room. They told me that it would be at least a week until we had our uniforms and, blood or no blood, we would have to make it with our own clothes until then. The on call room was small, aseptic and bare except for two beds, a phone, wall lamp and a chest. I deposited my belongings and left to find the medical floor that would be my home for the next three months. I approached the nurses' station and introduced myself to the nurse behind the desk.

"Good morning. My name is Dr. Robbins." It seemed funny sliding the doctor in front of my name. After all, until I learned something, I was just an imposter.

"Good morning, Dr. Robbins," she replied and returned to her work on the desk. I fidgeted with my thumbs for a second and then spoke up again.

"Um uh, I'm the new intern on the floor." She looked up and said with a somewhat twisted smile on her face.

"Well Hallelujah," and returned her eyes to her work.

I milled around for an uncomfortable thirty seconds and then started to walk down the hall. I couldn't help but let out a just audible, "Well thanks for all the help," as I turned away from the desk.

The hallway was short and blind and I had to retrace my steps back toward the nurses' station. I slipped unobtrusively behind it and found a chair in the small glassed in office in the back. The nurse behind the desk got up from her busy work and caught me with her left eye as she started toward the corridor. She changed direction and, with a determined step, approached the office, never removing my face from that icy penetrating gaze. I avoided her eyes, but nonetheless felt naked and vulnerable. "What the hell are you doing in my office?" she shouted, finger pointing, the whole bit. I waited for her to stomp her feet. I wanted to tell her to suck but, instead, I just returned a refractory stare. "I asked you a question," she shouted, hands on hips, her face menacingly near mine. I looked about, ostensibly to see if anybody was watching. The softness of my voice magnified the intensity of her own. I bent over and whispered, faces almost touching.

"I'm sure I made a mistake. This must be a psychiatric ward?"

"Listen," she shouted again. "I don't have time to play games. You have no right to be in here. Now get out!" I stood up slowly, obviously not intimidated by her diatribe.

"You might even be pretty if you smiled," I offered, trying to find another way to break the ice. She managed to control her mouth and eyes, but most red heads can never control their skin. The blush came out blood red, and no matter how menacingly she tried to act, the cover was off. "You almost made it that time," I added. The smile took full bloom but her voice, although less intense, defied it.

"Will you please get out of my office?"

"Under one condition."

"What's that?"

"That somebody tell me what I'm supposed to do around here."

"You don't know," she asked incredulously?

"Nope, I've never been an intern before."

"So what; you've worked under them."

"Nope to that one too."

"Where did you go to school?"

"Italy, University of Bologna."

"Oh no, not another foreigner," she said shaking her head in disbelief. I can't take another one." Her tone rang with sarcasm.

"You know, I can't tell you how appreciative I am of all the assistance and support being offered here."

"Listen here smart ass!" she retorted. "I'm not going to be your nursemaid. You're going to have to do your own work."

"I'm willing to but I hope that you'll be of some help. Exposure to hospital wards is new to me but I'm willing to learn and I learn fast."

"We'll see. Why don't you just start by picking up those thirty charts and get the hell out of my office."

"Thirty charts," I responded although somewhat overwhelmed.

"You heard me. We have a very busy floor. "I nodded my head and walked out to the nurses' station and picked up the first chart. I didn't have a good start with Nurse Sutton, but I knew that I would try to do what I needed to do to get her off my back.

Forty five minutes later I was still stuck in the first chart trying to familiarize myself with the format let alone the diagnosis and treatment. I had never seen a patient chart before and didn't realize that so much organization and thought had gone into its preparation. They seemed to leave nothing to chance.

The front sheet contained the admitting diagnosis as well as the discharge diagnosis, which of course was not filled in yet. This was for a triple purpose. It offered easy reference, easy comparison, and an easy method for compiling statistics for retrospective studies. Also included on the front sheet was all the pertinent data necessary for filing, billing, and further correspondence; i.e. name, address, phone, hospital number, insurance, admission date, discharge condition at departure, procedures and operations etc.

Behind the front sheet was the order sheet. Each medication or test, that the patient received, was ordered here by the physician. Occasionally, a busy practitioner might forget that he ordered a narcotic or antibiotic and forget to discontinue it. Therefore, as a matter of hospital policy, all medications needed to be reordered every week by the physician of record or they were discontinued.

Most doctors bitched about the added paper week. But a great percentage of them, if occasionally embarrassed by conflicting medications, were saved from medical malpractice suits. Conflicts and duplicated medications, as well as unexpected deletions were caught at a surprising frequency when two or more doctors wrote orders on a patient. More often than not, a busy consultant either failed to read or could not read the prior orders of another physician and, in haste, would occasionally duplicate or conflict with them. Occasionally, one physician would blatantly cancel out the order of another physician only to find it back on the chart. The renewal system was a check and a good one. It was here to stay. Behind the front sheet lay the "Heat" sheet with the records of the patient's temperature and other vital signs

(BP, pulse, respirations) taken at prescribed intervals. In back of this, the history and physical was recorded. This was usually dictated and typed out by secretaries located in the Medical Records department. Their job was a tedious and a monotonous affair. On arrival they went right to their desks, located in a windowless bare room in the basement, inserted their earphones, snapped in a tape, and began to type dictation. They could control the flow with the foot pedals. Each day they had to do so many pages of dictation. In an eight-hour day an average typist had to apply herself diligently to her task for at least six and a half-hours to finish her quota. In that time she had no contact with the outside world. There was no way in hell that I could do that job. Nevertheless, their contributions were individual. Lastly comes the medication sheet, another check on the order sheet itself. Here, all drugs administered are marked and their times of administration noted.

In essence, the chart is crammed full of information. Its preparation is methodical and usually complete and affords a full description of the illness of that individual. Even without the patient there, a complete chart should paint the picture of a person's illness, its severity, its course, its outcome, and its prognosis. From it the patient should spring to life, insuring the availability of an invaluable permanent record. I had only waded through the first chart before my stomach got the better of me and I went off to lunch. I had no idea how I was going to familiarize myself with all those patients, as well as the daily new admissions, but right now I was hungry and I was going to eat. The line moved at a snail's pace and I fidgeted nervously waiting for the people before me to be served. With food steaming on my plate, and my stomach growling with excited anticipation, I found a seat at an empty table and was just about to bite in when I heard my name paged. Reluctantly, I stood up and moved toward the phone and called the operator, who told me to call my floor. Sutton answered at the other end.

"Dr. Robbins. Mrs. Brown is having difficulty breathing doctor," she said hurriedly. "I think you'd better come up and see her."

I responded in the affirmative and made my way out the door toward the elevators. My mind churned over the possible causes of shortness of breath as I ascended to the 6th floor. Everything seemed confused and a sudden fear rushed through me that I wouldn't know what to do. Reluctantly I pushed toward my first confrontation with a patient in acute distress. Praying silently that emergency heroics would not be necessary, I rushed into the room. Sutton was administering oxygen by mask to Mrs. Brown, who was gasping for breath. I moved around to the other side of the bed and placed my stethoscope under her gown and began to listen to her heart. The sounds were jumbled, with interference coming from her noisy breathing and the gown rubbing against the tubing of the stethoscope. I couldn't make out a thing. I listened to her lungs, the bases of which were filled with bubbling noises called rales. Her pulse was rapid and irregular. "Do you want me to start an IV, doctor.?" I paused before responding, weighing the possibility in my mind. I didn't know if it would help, but certainly it couldn't hurt. I knew that in case she went into shock, with an IV, a vein would be available for intra venous medication.

"Yes and what's her blood pressure?" The other nurse in the room responded.

"100/60, doctor."
"Maybe you'd better lie her down, I don't want her to go into shock."

My hands were clammy and my thoughts were still confused, but like a vice, I crunched out all the noise and commotion around me and willed a clear-cut summation of the facts that I knew.

Her pressure was 100/60, slightly low. I grabbed her chart and saw that normally she ran 160/100. For her, the pressure was very low. Her pulse was rapid and irregular indicating a rapid irregular heart beat. Her lungs were filled with basilar rales. I quickly glanced at the impression in the History and Physical. It stated congestive heart failure. I looked at a previous EKG tracing. I couldn't read them well, but the diagnosis below stated regular sinus rhythm with left ventricular hypertrophy. The rate was easy to read. It was slow and regular, differing from the rate today. Like the sun bursting through a sea of clouds, the diagnosis hit me. The patient was in congestive heart failure, probably as a result of atrial fibrillation, a cardiac arrhythmia in which the heart pumps inefficiently. This leads to back flow of blood in the lungs and, when real severe, frothy pink sputum. Sutton cut into my trance. "Do you want any medication Dr. and do you want me to call your resident?"

"Yes, give her a 1/4 grain of morphine IM," I said hesitantly," and sit her back up. And yes, get the resident." Mrs. Brown began to gag violently and, as I helped her sit up, she expelled a large mass of frothy sputum on my forearm. I swallowed hard and again listened to her heart. This time I pulled her gown up and held it away from the stethoscope. With intense effort, I tried to block out all the extraneous sounds around me including the gurgling noises, worse now, coming from her lungs. The heart sounds, somewhat distant, came through. Lub dub, lub dub, lub dub. The rhythm, always irregular, was rapid with a varying intensity of the first and second heart sounds. "Please get an EKG," I said to the other nurse standing beside me. My neck was wet with sweat and a fine tremor ran through my limbs.

Mrs. Brown seemed to be getting worse. I prayed the resident would get there.

The resident walked briskly into the room, a halo of confidence around his head. With his arrival I sighed with a gasp of relief and moved inconspicuously to the foot of the bed. The responsibility was off my shoulders, but for the first time I noticed my heart was pounding loudly in my chest. He listened briefly to Mrs. Brown's heart and lungs, making sure that her gown was removed before attempting auscultation. He felt her neck, liver and extremities swiftly, and, at the same time, ordered medications as he went along.

"Rotating tourniquets, Lasix 40 mg. IV." His crisp commands sharply contrasted with my own hesitant behavior.

"Has she been on Digitalis?" he asked. Sutton leafed through the chart to the medication sheet and responded with a curt,

"No."

"Give her 0.8 mg. IV of Cedilanid and add 500 mg. Aminophylin to the bottle." He then looked smilingly at Mrs. Brown. "Don't worry sweetheart, you're going to be alright."

As Mrs. Brown responded miraculously before my eyes, I felt a deep sense of elation and relief. But I was also wrought with frustration and inadequacy. Everyone was moving busily about, giving medications, running the EKG, and administering oxygen. I felt like a third wheel at the foot of the bed, unneeded, and totally discarded. I seriously doubted whether I would ever be able to synthesize and analyze the symptomatology as rapidly as Dr. John Belli did that day and institute an effective method of treatment.

As Mrs. Brown improved, I walked out of the room and moved back to the nurses' station with her chart. I started to read through it, hoping to learn something and look busy at the same time, when the other nurse, who was in the room, approached. She was slim and blond with a cynical smile on her face. The name A. Hartung was written across her nameplate. "Excuse me doctor, Dr. Belli needs the chart."

She placed her hand out to take it, not expecting a refusal. I gave it up without a battle. That was the crowning blow. My reading it was of no real importance. The despair that accompanies the sensation of uselessness is difficult to describe. Let it suffice to say that tears welled up in the corners of my eyes and I wished only to vanish from the spot, never having to face these people with their critical stares again.

Belli came out of the room five minutes later and approached me at the nurses' station. "You the new intern I assume?"

"Yes," I responded, trying to get myself together.

His tone was serious and belligerent. "Well what the hell were you doing in there? That lady almost died."

"Trying to take care of her."

"Well let me tell you something doctor," he said, pointing his index finger in my face "We are not going to tolerate incompetence. You'd better find out how to treat congestive heart failure and find out fast, because you are going to see an awful lot of it." He made no effort to lower his voice and the aides and Hartung were all listening. I felt undressed and terribly small, but I refused to be bullied and intimidated.

"I did the best I knew how."

"Well that's not good enough. Now make sure Mrs. Brown continues to do well. Write some orders and then learn the rest of your patients. I'll be back at 5:00 PM to make rounds with you." He took off down the hall. I watched him disappear and then turned toward Hartung and asked,

"Where is Mrs. Brown's chart?"

"I think it's in the room doctor."

The disdain in her voice, when she said doctor, cut through me like a blade. I ignored it and, since she made no effort to get the chart for me, I started off toward Mrs. Brown's room. I found the chart at the foot of her bed and then walked over to her side, lifted her gown off her chest and listened again to her heart. The rhythm, though still irregular, had slowed. I concentrated on just the heart sounds and I was amazed how well I could hear, now that her gown was no longer interfering with the tubing on the stethoscope and the peripheral noise in the room had diminished. I vowed then never to let concern for modesty interfere with a physical exam and, if need be, I would insist that everybody shut up and stand still while I listened. Her respiratory rate had slowed considerably and the intensity and level of rales had diminished.

I picked up the chart and walked back to the nurses' station, busily running over the orders given by Belli and actively committing them to memory. I made a note in my small pad to look up emergency treatment and management of this disease. For the meantime I looked up the drugs Belli had ordered in the Physicians Desk Reference that I accidentally saw lying before me. Time made it impossible for me to check them all in detail so I chose to read about Lasix and how to order it. Fifteen minutes later I wrote my first orders in the chart: 1st, Lasix 40 mg, po (by mouth) qd (once a day) and 2nd, electrolytes qd. I chose to order them later since diuretics can alter the electrolytes significantly. I then gave the chart back to Nurse Hartung and indicated that I had written orders. "What do you want me to do with the IV, doctor?" Doctor rolled off her tongue like she had a mouthful of shit and had to spit it out before it made her sick.

"Uh," I paused, not anticipating the question. I could see no harm in keeping it open as long as I gave her only sugar water and no salt, slowly.

"Keep it going and run it slowly."

"How slowly?" she said disdainfully.

"What's usual?" I had no idea. Hartung smiled, realizing she had scored her point.

"I'll keep the vein open at about 20 drops par minute, Okay?"

"Okay," I'd said relieved. "And thanks, your the first one to help me since I've been here." She smiled sympathetically and I was grateful.

In an atmosphere of hostility, that small sign shone like a light from heaven. I turned back to the charts and began to review all the others I had missed before lunch. My stomach was knotted and I moved through them without any thought of food. Time flew and I just managed to familiarize myself with all the names and their illnesses when Belli appeared on the floor. I looked up at the clock. It was 5:00PM on the nose.

"Let's go," he said and started down the hall. I rose quickly and caught up with him. Rounds that first day were an indication of the living hell that he would put me through for the next couple of months. Belli made it clear to everybody that would listen that I was an absolute idiot and that he didn't know how I would ever be smart enough to be an orderly, let alone a doctor. No matter how hard I tried, it was impossible to please him. I just didn't have the time to study the things that he wanted me to know and still take care of all of my responsibilities.

Things went from bad to worse. There was nothing I could do to make Belli or the attending physicians happy. I was working at a feverish pace, fourteen hours a day on my nights off and thirty-eight hours in a row on my nights on call. Every other weekend I worked from Friday morning until Monday night with less than ten hours of cumulative sleep. I was a walking zombie and nobody cared. I was constantly harassed by Belli and the attending physicians and, despite my efforts, I never heard a kind word.

The educational system at a foreign school was different, and although we were adequately trained in academics, it was becoming increasingly obvious that our practical training was totally inadequate. Things they expected me to do readily I couldn't do without their help and getting them to help me was like pulling teeth. They never gave me credit for my academic knowledge, because they assumed that, if I couldn't do all the practical tasks, I must not know my medicine. That was because American teaching relies heavily on pragmatics and statistics, repetitively bombarding the American student with the key diagnostic tests and treatment regiments for all of the most common diseases. These diseases, which may comprise only ten percent of medical knowledge, still comprise probably eighty percent of the diseases that patients get, so that the American trained intern can at least look good on eighty percent of the patients. Furthermore, they emphasize emergency training, which allows the American graduate to function at a decent level in the face of disaster.

Italian training was different. We were taught an overview of all diseases, but not a systematic approach to their diagnosis and treatment. The assumption was that if you have the overview, then the rest can be taught rapidly to the student and, in the end, you would have a better understanding than the pragmatically trained individual. To better understand, it would be like bringing a person with a master's degree in finance into a bank and expecting him to know the procedure for dispersing money at the teller's window, or for securing the vault at night. The tellers and security officers that work there may know all the pragmatics about everyday bank functions, but they really don't understand how banks work and how they get such high internal rates of return. On the other hand, the finance major, that would look like an idiot if asked to disperse money, would eventually learn the bigger picture and, in a short time, be much more valuable than any of the technicians. Unfortunately, no one had the patience to help the Italian trained intern through the early stages of clinical exposure. As a result, the period of paralysis became longer, leaving the residents and attendings with a choice; either roll up your sleeves and help, or shake your head in disbelief over the so called incompetence of the Italian graduate. Most chose the latter course of action and, for the Italian graduate, the result was inefficiency, waste, and sometimes danger in the first few months of training.

At the end of the first month I was reviewed by the chief resident in medicine, an Indian named Mohatma Nehri. He told me, in no uncertain terms, that my performance was disappointing and that I had better improve if I wanted to continue in the internship.

When I left the review, I was devastated. I thought that I had made great progress and that my stamina, dedication, and improving knowledge were self-evident. I didn't know what to do, but resolved to work even harder the next month.

Despite my efforts, the next month's review was bad and the one after was even more devastating than the last. Dr. Nehri informed me in his supercilious tone that I was incompetent and lazy and that I was the worst intern that he had ever seen. With as much disdain as possible, he said. "Why can't you be like your friend Desarco? He's got the right attitude and we are rewarding him by giving him a month's rotation in coronary care. Against my better judgement, I am giving you one more month to show that you really want to be a doctor. Now, get out of here."

As I left the room, rage and frustration boiled inside me. I had no idea what he wanted from me. I couldn't try any harder or put in more time. I knew, as a foreign graduate, that I had started behind the American Medical students, but Nehri's evaluation shocked and surprised me. I didn't know what to do.

I decided to confide in Desarco and, as a last gap measure, ask him if he had any insight into what the problem was. I had been helping him learn to read cardiograms through vectoral analysis. The irony of course was that he was being rewarded with a rotation through coronary care, because I was reading his cardiograms, and my developing skills went unrecognized.

His response was blunt. "Are you sure that you really want to know."

"Of course," I said. "This guy really wants to get rid of me and I have no idea why."

Tony turned to me and looked me straight in the eye. "I'm gonna tell you but your not going to like it"

"Tony," I said despondently. "I'm hanging by a thread and I really don't understand why. Tell me," I said impatiently. Taking that for the green light, Tony shot out criticisms unmercifully.

"To begin with, you ask too many questions on rounds."

"What do you mean by that," I resisted. "You know as well as I do that none of us know the information that I am asking for and that the right answer can sometimes save us hours of research."

"Not the point."

"What do you mean it's not the point?"

With hands in the air, Tony sighed with frustration. "I just told you that you wouldn't listen." Trying again, he leaned forward in his chair and spoke pointedly. "It's not about logic or efficiency; it's about image and illusion."

"What?"

"You heard me."

"What are you talking about?"

"The impression that you make on other people. It stinks!" "You mean just because I ask questions?"

Tony shifted in his seat to face me more directly. "Partly."

"What are the other parts?"
"I'll get to that. Let me deal with the questions first," he said with a hint of irritation in his voice.

"Fine, the floor is yours."
Leaning over, Tony enunciated clearly to emphasize the point. "For one, when you ask a lot of questions, you expose ignorance."

"But you guys don't know that information either?" I interrupted. Slapping his hand on his thigh, he shot back. "But they don't know that. You expose yourself with the questions and we all get the benefit of the answers without ever appearing ignorant."

"So what you are telling me is that I should stop asking questions even if it means that I will learn less."

"In a nutshell, yes!"

"That's stupid," I retorted, throwing my hands up in disgust. We're here to learn."

"Wrong!"

"What do you mean wrong?"

Shaking his head with frustration, Tony sighed and stood up getting ready to leave. "I knew that you wouldn't listen."

"No, wait Tony," I pleaded. "I'm having trouble understanding but I'm trying."

Tony resigned himself to another go round and sat down. "What I'm saying is that you are disrupting the rhythm of the residents and the attendings. They want you to get certain mundane tasks taken care of for them and, for the most part, they are willing to trade off a few moments of teaching. Most of them are really not interested in facilitating the learning process for you, and some even derive a sadistic pleasure in knowing that the road will be paved with uncertainty and misinformation. They want you to suffer just as they did. In essence, your questions irritate them and expose your lack of knowledge."

Somewhat confused, I looked at Tony and asked him to continue. Tony took the cue and jumped in unmercifully.

"Look! You are here to serve the needs of the people above you and if, in the process, you happen to learn a few things, count yourself lucky. The residents are overworked just like us and their recommendations will be based on the amount of relief that we give them, not the amount of our esoteric knowledge."

Tony looked at me as I sat quietly and decided that I was finally listening. "You need to get all your histories and physicals done, all your basic lab work ordered and all the basic medicinal orders in the chart in order to save work for the residents and the attendings."

Before he could continue, I responded with venom.

"There's not enough time in the day. Everything is new to me. I order a sleeping pill and I need to look it up to find out the side effects as well as the vehicle through which it is eliminated. Otherwise, I could give, for example, Seconal to someone who has liver disease instead of using Phenobarbital that is excreted by the kidneys."

"Come on," Tony said disdainfully. "What are the chances of hurting someone?"

With disbelief, I asked. "Are you telling me that I have to take chances in order to get the job done so that I can please these people?"

Realizing that he was getting through to me, Tony sat back in his chair and sighed in relief. "Exactly!"

"And if I kill someone?"

Tony threw up his hands and said in a supercilious tone. "What are the chances?"

"That's not the point."

Tony leaned in for the kill. "Sorry, but that is just the point. Your chances of doing damage are remote and, if god forbid you do, you can always stand on the fact that you're just an intern. They expect an occasional bad decision on the part of an intern, but they will not accept that intern being a daily source of extra work and irritation for them, because he works too slowly.

"What else?" I asked, not expecting more.

"Learn the few physical tasks that you have to do on patients without fanfare and without calling a resident for help every time you do something."

"Such as?"

"Putting in a Levine tube. Last night you called the resident to help you. By now you should be doing it alone."

"Tony," I retorted with conviction. "Two weeks ago one of the interns shoved a Levine tube into a nose with an obstruction and caused some significant bleeding."

"So what."

"So what?" I asked in disbelief. "That patient was put at risk unnecessarily, not to mention the pain and inconvenience."

"And if the resident were there, what would be different."

"Maybe he would have anticipated an obstruction after the first try and looked in the guy's nose."

"A lot of maybes. Maybe one time in fifty you have a problem that he could have solved, but the other forty-nine times you saved the resident from having to stop what he was doing and come help you, when he doesn't have enough time in the day to complete his own tasks."

"Jesus, is there more."

Tony was now on a roll. "Yes there is more." He paused for a second to gather his thoughts and see if I was still giving him my full attention. "You don't prepare well for presentations at conference."

"How can I? Prior to the last conference, Mrs. Wakefield had signs of congestive heart failure that I needed to treat immediately. I couldn't prepare."

"And if you just ordered a diuretic and prepared for the conference and then treated her later?"

"Then I would have compromised her care and put her through some unnecessary discomfort and danger."

"The only one that would have bitched about that would have been the nurse taking care of her if she knew that doing more could have resolved the issue more quickly. Remember, you could always have told her that you were treating conservatively to see what level of response you were able to attain before you added medicines to the regime."

"But that's wrong."

"Wrong? On the contrary. Your way, you piss off forty doctors at a conference who are shaking their head in disdain while you fumble through your presentation. My way, you make everybody happy and no one's the wiser."

"So, in a nutshell, you're telling me to compromise my patient care in order to make a better impression on the residents and attending physicians."

"If you want to put it that way, in selected situations, yes. You got to use common sense." Tony turned in his chair. "Look! If you weren't such a decent guy, I wouldn't be telling you this. You hear a different drummer than the rest of us, and, unfortunately, it just doesn't fit the system well. You adapt or you die."

Tony got up to leave and I thanked him perfunctorily. I was definitely confused and bewildered. Everything I thought was backward. I was an intern who expected to be taught by a mentor with enthusiasm. Instead, I was there to save time for the people above me and, in return, they would throw me a few morsels of information. It was clear, that if I wanted to remain as an intern, I would have to conform to the system or perish. I would have to learn less, do more risky things on my own, and occasionally compromise patient care. I was hoping Tony was wrong, but in my heart, I knew he was right.

With fanatical conviction, I followed Tony's plan for my last month on the medicine rotation. I kept my mouth shut and never asked a question. Although I learned very little medicine, I did improve my manual skills by jumping in and trying to do the IV's, catheters, spinal taps, Levine tubes, cut downs and E.K.Gs. etc. that saved the resident's time. Miraculously, I didn't hurt anybody badly, although I wasn't so sure that I wouldn't during the learning process. I made it a point to avoid calling the resident for help when I was not sure about what to do, and only once did I expose a patient to undue discomfort, when, while doing a spinal tap, I poked at his arthritic spine more often than I should have, before I called for help. I also diligently prepared my conferences so that my presentations were flawless, although at least two patients suffered undue discomfort because of the delay in their treatment. Another one got his antibiotics three hours later than he should have in the face of septicemia, and could well have died because of the delay. But as Tony said, "What were the odds?"

I went for my final fourth month evaluation from Dr. Nehri, somewhat resigned to the fact that medicine wasn't really for me and maybe he was right; maybe I didn't belong. After all, this month was definitely my worst. I learned very little and had exposed some patients to danger and discomfort that could have been avoided.

Nehri's comments threw me for a loop!

"Doctor," he said, as he enthusiastically moved me into his office. While offering me a seat, he smilingly added. "I don't know what to say." I sat there silently waiting for him to continue. "I am extremely surprised to see this kind of reversal. I have to admit that I doubted your skills and attitude but obviously what I told you at your last evaluation caught your attention. Your residents and attending physicians have all informed me that you have done a miraculous job this last month, once you decided to focus and take your work seriously."

Inside, I felt the rage and frustration building. "What do you mean focus? Are you saying that I didn't focus before?"

"Well, isn't it obvious? You should be proud. You did well."

I shook my head in confusion. My world was turning upside down. I learned less and exposed patients to risks that should have been avoided and now, I was being lauded and praised for it. With anger and intensity, I blurted. "I learned nothing this past month and did not service my patients as well as I did in the last three months. I thought you were going to criticize me again, and instead you laud me for incompetence?"

Walking behind his desk and taking his chair, Nehri responded.

"What's the matter with you?"

The rage inside me surged! "What's the matter with me? What isn't the matter with me? I thought that I was here to learn under expert guidance, so that I wouldn't expose my patients to danger during the learning process. Instead I'm rewarded for negligence, carelessness and bravado. Don't you see the irony in that."

Nehri got up from his chair and pointed a finger at me. "Don't you take that kind of tone with me," he ordered. "Maybe I didn't make a mistake in evaluating you."

I slapped his finger aside and stared disgustingly into his eyes. "Don't you ever point a finger at me again!"

"That's it Robbins! You're done! Pack your things and get out of here!"

The surging rage inside of me finally exploded. The months of confusion, endless work, sleep deprivation and a new awareness of the compromises I would have to make in order to successfully complete my training program, were more than I could handle. I leaned across the table and grabbed that supercilious little bastard by the shirt and, with my bare hand, pulled him up to me so our faces were only inches apart. "Listen ass hole and listen well. It's a long walk down the tunnel to the parking lot. I'm done with you and your service." Shaking him for emphasis, I added. "You make trouble for me and I swear to Buddha or whoever the fuck you pray to, that I will take care of you. I shoved him back, and as he slumped into his chair, I leaned over the desk, and whispered threateningly. "You make trouble for me you stinking little piece of shit and I promise you that I will slit your throat from ear to ear." I reinforced the words by running my free index finger across his throat and, after shoving him back into his chair, I turned to leave with the picture of a speechless, pale white, and frightened little Indian etched indelibly in my brain.

With four months of internship under my belt, and the situation with Dr. Nehri over with, I was ready to tackle the surgery rotation. I knew that since the American graduates had two years of exposure to the clinic and hospital environment and that I had only four months of medicine, it would again be like starting over. But I knew, even if I didn't like it, what I would have to do to keep the dogs at bay, while I tried to learn my trade. I had seen the progress I had made in medicine, not necessarily week by week, but over the entire four months. Now I could do a thorough History and Physical, record progress notes, order appropriate lab tests and X-rays, order medications and treatments and dictate a complete discharge summary. I figured that the more I did for the residents and surgeons, the more they would teach me. How ironic! The more you knew, the more they would help you. It seemed to me that it should be the other way around.

Again, there was no time to ease into a new situation. As luck would have it, I was assigned to share a room with an Egyptian intern, right after the war between Israel and the Arab world in 1967. Needless to say, we faced each other with one eye open as we fell off to a restless sleep that was constantly interrupted by calls from the surgical floor and circumspect fear of each other. After three weeks of exhaustion, I finally confronted the situation with Samir Kalabani and, after a thorough exchange of outlooks and philosophies, it appeared that Samir and I both thought alike. He was from a ruling family and very well educated. He knew that people are the same all over the world and that greed, fear, ignorance, jealousy and/or hunger motivate them to do physical violence. He saw justification on both sides and was frustrated by the fact that no significant effort had been made to resolve the crucial issues diplomatically. I felt the same way. I was proud of my heritage and proud to see that the persecuted Jews of the world had founded their own state and made it thrive. I also felt sorry for the Palestinians who were forced to leave their homes and property because they felt that they couldn't live under the Israeli government. There is no fair or reasonable resolution to this conflict and the only hope lay in a willingness on both sides to compromise significantly.

Once our politics were out in the open, our friendship flourished. Samir had practiced surgery in Egypt and was only an intern again because the rules and regulations of being licensed to practice medicine in the United States of America required foreign graduates to repeat their training. For the first time, I had someone who would patiently answer questions and call me to watch him do something that he thought that I would have to do during my surgery rotation. Most importantly though, from that day on, Samir and I slept just a little better.

Adjusting to the surgery rotation was just a little easier than medicine. I already had a background in most of the things that I needed to do to satisfy my resident and the surgical attendings. They needed me to do the same chores that I did on the medical floors as well as assist in surgery, which really boiled down to holding a retractor so that the surgeon could have greater visibility. Nevertheless, I was still behind the average American graduate and had to spend the few minutes of spare time that I had tying knots and learning how to improve my skills in the simple hands on procedures like Levine tubes, IV's, cut downs, and removal of superficial skin lesions. Thank God for Samir. He facilitated the process of learning, occasionally letting me see something that he did so that I could follow the credo "see one, do one, teach one," instead of what appeared to be my credo, "do one, teach one." Predictably, with my added value, came more voluntary instruction from the residents and the attendings so I learned at an even more rapid pace.

In spite of the fact that I was a little better prepared to take on this rotation, my first day on surgery was the nadir of my medical experience. I had been assigned to be the second assistant in a cholecystec- tomy, a surgery involving the removal of the gallbladder. Since I knew that holding a retractor was a boring experience, I asked one of the residents how long a case like this would take. He told me, "about an hour and a half," and with a sigh, I walked to the scrub area wondering how I would make it through the next hour and a half. I watched the general surgeon, who was on the case, scrub and tried to follow his lead, with the nailbrush first, and then the betadine sponge.

After I scrubbed, I put on my mask, and walked into the operating room, only to be told by the nurse that I must put the mask on before I scrub and that I had to scrub again. Twice more she found something wrong with my technique and sent me back to scrub again as I listened to the derisive comments of the surgeon, 1st assistant surgeon and other operating room personnel. As I came back into the room, she scolded. "Now don't do anything or touch anything. I will put your gown on and tell you what to do!" Holding out my gown, she said, "Now hold your hands out in front of you." I did as I was told and she slipped the gown over my arms. This time I didn't try to anticipate how to help her. Instead, I stood perfectly still until she gave me the next set of instructions. "Now turn slowly around so that I can tie you up." I twisted slowlywaiting for her to scream in disgust for something that I did wrong. But nothing happened and she told me to hold out my hands so she could glove me. This procedure required a little bit of timing on both our parts and, since I had never done it before, the process was awkward. While she tried to correct the application of the gloves to my fingers, she shook her head and said sarcastically for all to hear. "You're a beauty." True to form, the ensemble behind her echoed support. Moving me to the side of the table next to the assistant surgeon, she added. "Don't touch anything or scratch anything." The surgeon stuck a big retractor into the incision and without looking up said.

"Hold this firmly." Since I was above the incision, I couldn't see much and, after five minutes, which seemed like an hour, my arm began to tire. I relaxed just a tad on the retractor and that helped for a minute, but my arm started to cramp again. My nose began to itch relentlessly and there was nothing that I could do about it. I was soaked with boredom and an ever-increasing ache in my arm. Again, I released some of the tension on the retractor and, without warning, the surgeon whacked the back of my hand with the handle of the scalpel and yelled. "Hold that so I can see!" I pulled harder and found a way to switch to my left hand to give my right a rest, but now I could see even less of what was going on in the incision. Minutes passed and it seemed like hours and finally I got up the courage to ask,

"Excuse me Dr. Johnson, about how much longer do you think this case will take." Johnson never looked up? Instead, he mumbled to the first assistant without taking his eyes off the incision.

"Can you believe this guy, Lew?"

Shaking his head in disdain, Lew responded. "No sir." Nothing more was said and I stood there quietly, impatient and tense, switching arms every minute or so to prevent the cramping pain from getting worse. Looking up at the clock, forty-five minutes had passed, although it seemed like a day. I noticed that my nose didn't itch any more and that I had forgotten about it only to have it start itching again when I realized that it had stopped. I was no longer trying to watch the surgery, because I had to lean over in a very uncomfortable position to see what was going on and, since nobody was explaining anything, I had no clue about what they were doing. After what seemed like an hour, I looked up at the clock again, and saw that only eight minutes had passed. Based on his first response, I was afraid to ask the surgeon how much longer the case would take. Instead, I suffered in silence, letting my mind wander, occasionally being brought back to reality by a sharp sting on the back of my hand when I let the retractor relax too much. With trepidation, at the hour and forty five-minute mark, I finally got up the courage to ask again. Ripped from his total focus on the incision, the surgeon tersely said.

"We are just getting started," and looked up at the resident for a confirming nod. "Now just hold the retractor and shut up."

"Not having any idea how much time was left, I started to panic. I wanted so badly to get out of there and, each time I'd look at the clock, only seconds or minutes had passed. One moment began to drift into the next and my mind wandered from daydream to daydream. As time moved on, my senses dulled, although I could feel a slight ache in my back and the sensation of my bladder filling up. I functioned by reflex and am sure that, for short periods, I fell asleep at the side of the table. Finally, I was just numb all over, and suddenly I woke up at the side of the table to see Dr. Johnson, arm slung over Lew Kolec's shoulder, walk out of the room, and say.

"Lew, I love this! I could do it all day long."

"Me too Dr. Johnson! Me too!" said Lew.

I was still in a daze. I looked around the room and saw that everybody had removed their gown. I started to take off my gown and felt stiff and sticky everywhere. My legs felt swollen and I could smell the stench of nervous sweat under my arms. My gown off, I felt as if I'd been freed from a dark, dank, solitary confinement, except with the dampening effect of knowing that I was going to have to go back in that cell again. Despondent, I moved slowly to the surgeons lounge, emptied my cramping bladder, fell back into a recliner and sighed with relief just to be off my feet. I looked up at the clock and saw that it was nine thirty at night. We had been in there for thirteen and one half-hours. I started to sob very softly as I replayed the comment in my

mind that the surgeon made to Lew, the resident assistant. "I love this Lew! I could do this all day long."

And his response! "Me too Dr. Johnson! Me too!" I couldn't believe what I had heard. It became poignantly clear to me that either these people were nuts or there was something wrong with me. In either case, I knew that I couldn't compete with them and, after all these years, it became clear that I had chosen the wrong profession. I remained in the recliner, numb and dulled, for a half-hour before I summoned the strength to get up, shower, and dress for the short walk home. I'm sure that my wife had expected me for dinner, although by now she was used to being disappointed. The surgery lounge was eerily empty as I finished getting dressed. As I walked out the door into the chill of the night air, I looked back again, resigned to the fact that, after I quit, I would never be back again.

After returning home, I poured out my heart to my wife, telling her that these people were fanatics, and that, in my wildest dreams, I could never hope to compete with them. "Thirteen and a half-hours of abject torture and they left the room with a smile," I complained. "I just can't do this."

My wife took it all in and, in a perfunctory and sweeping statement, summated. "Forget it, you'll feel better in the morning."

I called Samir to talk it over with someone who knew the ropes, and he said. "Yes, I heard about the case. It was a Whipple."

"What's that," I asked naively.

"It's a modified autopsy," he answered. "You do it for pancreatic cancer. You take out just about everything and the patient lives six months, whether you do the surgery or not."

"But I thought it was supposed to be a gall bladder?"
"Yes," Samir said, "but when they got in, they discovered the cancer"
"So why do they do it if the result is the same?"

Samir responded in the irritating supercilious tone that seems to be monopolized by well-educated third world country English colonists.

"Because the abdomen was already open, because they are surgeons and because there is always the hope that surgery may remove all of the cancer, although, in this disease, the statistics don't bear this out."

"Samir," I said pointedly. "Forget the prognosis. How can anybody stand thirteen and a half hours of surgery?"

Samir responded with patience and compassion. "Listen," he said. "It's a very unusual case. It should take six hours, but this was the first time that Johnson has done one of those and you just got unlucky. Besides, I guarantee, when you are the first assistant, the case gets much more interesting, and when you are the surgeon, you are concentrating so hard that the time flies by quickly." He let that sink in and then emphasized. "Nothing is more boring than second assisting on a case in which you have no idea what's going on. But in time you will. Just be patient and you will begin to like it more, and I can almost promise you that you will never again have this type of experience." Thanking him, I hung up the phone and went off to bed, resolved to turn in my resignation in the morning.

There is nothing like a good night's sleep to rejuvenate one's energy and resolve. I woke up refreshed, and ready to give it another shot. Samir was right. Never again did I have to live through such an ordeal. As I learned more anatomy and some practical skills, like sewing tissue and tying knots, I began to lose myself in the case and found that, sometimes, an hour would pass without notice. Sometimes, I felt as if I made a contribution and, sometimes, I even liked what I was doing. It also helped that three hours was the longest case that I had for the rest of my surgery rotation.

The rest of my internship was relatively uneventful. Having started in January, I was being compared to the intern that started in July of the prior year and, given the fact that I had no clinical experience to think of, I fell far short of expectations. But by July of my internship year, I already had six months of intense and continuous experience that seeped into my skin, let alone my brain, and I was well ahead of the new group of interns. My last two months on surgery were fun, as some of the attendings appreciated the help I could give them on the floor care of their patients and, in return, they let me do a few simple surgeries from closure of the abdomen to appendectomies.

After surgery, I had two relatively easy months on pediatrics and followed that with two delightful months on obstetrics and gynecology, where I was taught even more because I could do so much more than the new interns. This was a happy rotation. For the most part, the patients were young and fun to talk to. Also, most of the time, I was dealing with happy events. I liked the concept of a little medicine and a little surgery. At the time, the longest gynecology case that I had been on was two hours. The surgery was confined to one area of the body and it seemed as if this amount of surgery could be mastered without too much difficulty. I didn't yet know about exenterations, which were done in OBGYN oncology, that could take many hours, and required very special surgical training. Lastly, as said before, I was now a better intern so that my relationship with the people on the OBGYN service was positive. I had come through a difficult ordeal and, despite the scars, had survived. I was ready for the next step and choosing OBGYN as my choice of specialty seemed like the natural thing to do.

THE DEVELOPING YEARS

My sophomore year was characterized by a developing sense of self-importance and extreme confidence, which expressed itself as charisma in the eyes of others. I did not have to search out friendship. It found me. My manner became reserved; I commented little, went my own way and was followed. Because of my image, a grunt from me was considered a word of wisdom; an articulate soliloquy by a brilliant but non-athletic classmate on any topic of national importance, a hunk of horse shit. They made the rules and I followed them.

Another important segment of my character was carved in the year of the wise fool. My upbringing, while not of a religious nature, was one of a sound upper middle class background. The basic rules by which we lived were simple and could be summarized in the Bill of Rights and the Ten Commandants. Compromise or convenience usually resolved any conflict between the two. Flexibility and elasticity were permitted, though, in thought and action. My peer group usually derived from a similar but more religious, fixed and inflexible home life. Their attitude toward sex was then an admixture of paradoxes; exciting but dirty; cavalier for the man, disrespectful for the girl; semi-permissible if propagated on the basis of love; lewd and wrong if for the purpose of sex alone. But you did not screw a girl you loved for you respected her too much. You only screwed girls that generated nausea, girls who you could disrespect with a justifiable passion.

Somehow it all left me confused and at age fourteen I knew that I had many questions to ask and many beds to share before I could form some firm commitments on the subject of sex.

After our first game of the year, a winning effort to the tune of 27-13, (I played well running for 65 yards on 14 carries and 1 touchdown and completing 5 passes in 12 attempts for 65 yards and another touchdown,) I was approached by Bob Knudel, fullback and president of the student body.

He was of stocky build, standing five foot eleven inches, and weighing about 195 pounds. The jaw was square; the teeth strong and white, with nose small and slightly upturned. His eyes, blue and twinkling, were buried in well-excavated orbits; his hair blond and bristly, styled in the brush cut of the day. He walked with shoulders square and legs apart. The latter contributed heavily to his overall "rock of granite" appearance. I suspected his feet were kept apart, not to improve stability afoot, but rather to avoid friction from constant rubbing of chafed and tender inner thighs, a condition generated by the combination of dirt, friction, and a plastic athletic cup. Nevertheless, his physical appearance reflected solidarity, strength, simplicity, and confidence and mirrored the same characteristics in his personality.

His actions were positive in nature and governed by good common sense. Over the years he had made many tangible contributions to the school. In the beginning no job was too small. He would help paint sets for school plays, sell tickets for school functions and so on. He was patient and able to wait for acclaim without blowing his own horn. He avoided petty conflicts and the expression of opinions that did not concern problems of a practical and immediate importance. Therefore, when he did comment, his words were listened to with refreshing interest; his slow, simple tongue, expressing sensible ideas, was easily followed and understood. Having, over the past few years, built up his reputation as a fine athlete and a solid, interested, hard working and sensible member of the student body, he had all the ingredients for the assumption of leadership; respect, friends, and few enemies.

He ran for president of the student body against a brilliant, skinny, four-eyed radical with brash liberal ideals and a subtle, enthusiastic and expressive delivery that was way above our heads and therefore labeled as suspicious. Needless to say, our fullback won in a landslide, the contender being booed into oblivion. And I began to learn another lesson. People can evaluate others only within the level of their own capacity. Brilliance detached from understanding is not only unappreciated but defamed. Simplicity, with which most of us can identify, is rewarded.

Bob placed his fingers lightly under my elbow and directed me to a corner of the locker room. "Come're, I want to talk to you for a second." We sat down on a corner bench and then he continued.

"We're having a little gathering tonight. Id like you to come with me." I was elated to receive such attention and feel that Bob wanted me to pal around with tonight.

"I'd love to but," I apologized, "I don't have a car."

"That's okay, I'll pick you up at seven thirty."

He was fifteen minutes late. I waited anxiously at the door and, on seeing his car arrive, my fears of desertion dissipated. I yelled goodbye to my mother and trotted out to the car. The routine greetings were dispensed with by a wave of the hand on both our parts. Of notable absence was an apology on his part for being late. Number one never apologized. I was just happy that he showed up that time. As the car, a 1949 Morgan, dragged away from the curb Bob commented. "Someone is going to have to show you how to dress." I was wearing black chinos with a short-sleeved clinging, black sport shirt and I thought I looked pretty tough. "You look like something out of a fascist movie. All that lacks is the stick." I was confused, disheartened and not quite ready to taste the first big brother lecture that Bob was going to make a habit of giving throughout the year. At first I was thrilled that he took such an interest. As the year wore on and I began to develop an individual identity, a position of importance, and an air of superiority in being in with the "in group," I began then to resent his all knowing attitude.

By the time I had digested my first lesson on dress, consisting essentially in coordination of colors and patterns as well as styling, we had arrived at our destination. Up to this point, all Bob had told me is that we were going to a small gathering at Barbara Rush's home. Barbara Rush was a dynamic, lithe redhead with blue eyes and an endless supply of energy. She was bright, witty, and carried herself with a supercilious air of supreme confidence, typical conduct for an attractive young heiress. She was president of the senior class, head cheerleader, and in charge of numerous other clubs and committees. As were all the boys in my class, I was infatuated with her, although I knew that she was beyond my reach. I considered just a hello from her holy lips to be a major triumph. I really didn't think that she knew that I was alive. Her father was vice president of Town Bankers, a large suburban chain with a tradition of ninety years. Her grandfather was still the acting president of the firm, which had been originated by her great, great grandfather just after the civil war. It was said that she was the image in looks and personality of the old man. Her father, as so often is the case, was a stymied, subdued, and suffocated individual who had not been given the opportunity to develop his own individuality. Instead, the old man had attempted to stamp his son with the indelible ink of his own mold. Continued rebellion, which was squashed in a systemic efficient manner, resulted not in an imitation of grandpa, but rather in an amorphous, lackluster, and no longer assertive individual that held a title of position in the bank hierarchy without effective responsibility. Fortunately the institute could afford the window dressing, but disappointment in his one and only son, accompanied by a suspected sense of self guilt, left a void in the rich fulfillment that he derived from all other segments of his life. He tried to fill this void with Barbara and, realizing his prior error, he allowed the pendulum to swing the other way and encouraged her to be as stubborn as he and insured her license to do as she wished.

Bob deftly slid his Morgan along the gravel driveway winding around the thickly wooded hillside.

"Wow, what a house." I couldn't hold it in.

"Impressed?" he said smilingly.

I nodded positively. As we drove out from under the trees, a massive, large, white pillared structure loomed at the top of the hillside. The circular driveway swept up toward the front entrance and, with a little imagination, one could easily conjure up the image of Jefferson Davis riding up the driveway for dinner at the home of Robert E. Lee in pre-Civil War days. The home, with all its landscaping and adornments, instilled in me a feeling of serenity. In the four minutes that it took to navigate that long winding driveway, I felt as if I was inexplicably removed from the bustling, pressured world without and thrown into one with luxurious calm. What a retreat!

We parked, approached the door, rang and entered. Barbara answered herself. It seemed out of context that a servant did not answer the bell. She gave Bob a brush kiss and smiled at me. I didn't know what to say so I just smiled back. She took Bob's elbow with her arm and absently took mine with the other and guided us through the hall up the winding staircase, addressing her conversation and responses to Bob. I felt like a piece of added baggage she was dragging up the stairs. We settled into a large, comfortable dimly lit den with thick, overstuffed, black leather furniture. A bear rug lay before the fireplace, which was glowing, brightly. Barbara dropped our arms and told us to make ourselves comfortable and wandered over to Larry Castillo standing at the bar. Larry was a junior, tall, slim, with dark curly hair, and classic Roman features. A tremendous all around athlete, he was a second team All County end in football, and an honorable mention All State forward in basketball, and first team All County in baseball. Personality wise he was smug and egocentric and not very popular except with his own small clique of followers. He didn't make friends. They found him and tagged along. The ones that didn't, he didn't appear to miss. I didn't like him.

Two other junior girls and one other junior boy were there. Ralph Stone was the other guy. He was average height, cute, blond and built beautifully. He was a good football halfback with lots of guts and dedication and an all state wrestler in the 155-pound division. He was friendly, but not particularly endowed with Betz cells. Nevertheless he was thorough and determined in everything he attempted and, despite his mediocre academic capacity, still managed to find himself on the honor roll more often than not. In high school you don't have to be smart to do well; just steady and somewhat motivated.

The two junior girls were Gail Norris and Karen Brown. Gail was the most luscious of the three girls. Blond hair and blue eyes nicely accented her creamy white skin. Bodily, she was over endowed with curvaceous hips, succulent thighs and large D-cupped breasts. In ten years she would probably run to fat. But right now, slithering down the beach in a bikini, she was "instant hard on." She never said much, but she never had to.

Karen Brown I knew well and was surprised to see her there. Her folks and mine were very friendly and she had always treated me as a kid brother. Once, we had gone on a skiing vacation together and rented adjoining rooms in a hotel. I was twelve and a half and she was fourteen with budding hips and breasts. The rooms had a vent high up on the common wall. I remembered climbing up on the dresser and sitting precariously over one of the rafters for hours looking through the vent. I had observed Karen while she was resting on the bed and reading a book. Our folks had gone to a show and we had retired early. I waited anxiously for what seemed an eternity and then she stirred and slipped off her robe. She started toward the bathroom wearing her pajamas and a sensation of total letdown shot through me. Something caught her gaze and she stopped in front of the mirror, smiled at herself and brushed her hair back with a soft sweeping hand motion and a flick of the head. She placed her hands under her chest, lifted her small breasts and turned sideways. A look of disappointment shot across her face. I watched in astonishment, heat spreading through my fledging loins, with an intensity that I never before conceived oflet alone imagined possible. I edged closer to the vent.

She slowly unbuttoned the top ofher pajamas and then began to act a pantomime love scene. Her head shook "no" as she lightly pushed away her imaginary lover. He appeared to persist as her hand slipped to the button below and she slid her body onto the bed. One arm wrapped the pillow; the other groping for the remaining buttons. She twisted from side to back and rolled over the pillow, kissing it frequently. In between kisses she whispered just audibly, "Marlon, I love you, I love you," referring to the steamy male movie star, Marlon Brando. She shifted out of her pajama top, pillow pressed against one arm, as the other crept slowly down into the warm cleft between her legs, her head nodding only token resistance to the pillow. Her body gyrated backwards on the bed, friction causing her pajama bottoms to slide down over her hips, exposing her hand with middle finger moving rhythmically into the depths. "Marlon, Marlon" she repeated clutching and scratching the pillow, hips rolling with counter resistance to the finger. She rolled over, chest thumping, finger clutched between her thighs like wood in a vise, and bare cheeks, stark white and tensed, pointing toward the vent. As she fell again to her back, thighs spread and legs lifted she let the pillow fall to her side and began to stroke her pink tender nipples with her free hand. Her breath was as heavy as was mine. My nose and eyes were plastered against that vent like a prisoner barred from the sweets of life but able to see and smell them. With increased intensity and speed, her hips rolled up and down against that finger and she moaned again "Marlon, Marlon."

A key in the lock made my head snap away and, with a palpitation in my chest, I jumped down to the dresser and cat quick from there to the floor with a thud. My parents entered the room and my dad asked crossly. "What happened?" I explained that I had been doing exercises and with the excuse accepted I went into the bathroom to wash the beads of sweat from my face with cool water.

My genitals were heavy. I could hear Karen talking to her mother next door; her mother's voice at least a decibel louder. I couldn't make out the words but she was certainly scolding. Her father's voice was strangely absent. I learned the following day, while my mother and hers were making small talk, that her father had found something to read before coming up to the room. That accounted for his conspicuous absence the night before. Thinking back, lucky for Karen. Her mother was a liberal, forgivable sort. Her father was a straight arrow. He never would have understood or forgiven and her mother knew well enough what to and what not to disclose to him.

Comparing her then to now, she was like a budding rose with a hint of hidden beauty that finally bloomed. Her complexion was smooth and olive, her eyes twinkled, and her smile was toothpaste commercial class. Shoulders were square and regal, breasts firm and full, stomach smooth and long with lithe hips and long shapely legs. She was one gorgeous girl.

She was interested in music and drama and desired to pursue a career in acting. She had run the yearly shows in every sense of the word from director to stage setter, and lead actress to ticket seller and she laid forth a professional production. She had played the piano at numerous local concerts with a skill and sensitivity beyond the reach of most musicians. She read extensively and thoroughly and was well informed in a cultured as well as academic sense. In school she led her class, but knew nothing of touchdowns and homeruns. With the rest of the group she had no common ground except for one. She represented "par excellence" in what she stood for and so did we.

Everybody moved easily with each other and acted as if they were right at home. I felt uncomfortable and exposed. To me, these people represented the elite and I felt outclassed. I kept repeating to myself again and again that, although younger, I was just as good looking, just as cool, just as confident. I probably wasn't succeeding, as Karen, on gazing over, seemed to pierce my outer armor and sense my basic insecurity. She walked over to engage me in conversation and make me feel more a part. "Hi little tiger." She always liked to call me that.

"Hi," I replied softly. In moments like these, when I felt naked and vulnerable, I took one of two defensive measures. Either, I conducted myself with a quiet reserve or I covered up by allowing my multiple comments to be colored by a light, detached sarcasm, as if I were just observing and not really participating.

"At ease", she said, "you don't have to stand at attention."

That pierced me like a sharp knife in the gut and I blushed obviously. With a last ditch effort for cover, I stated matter of factly. "Isometrics keep the body in good shape."

Karen didn't let that deter her. She became serious. "Listen, I felt the same way the first day that I moved into this group and it was tougher for me. You'll learn to understand that later. Just relax. We're here to have fun together and we invited you because we want to share it with you. You're accepted." She shook her head and sighed. "I shouldn't really be telling you this. It's too premature and it's not my place but I've always felt a little protective toward you." I didn't fully follow what she said but my tense muscles softened and after a deep breath I smiled. "That's better," she said.

I shrugged and accused. "You read me like a book, don't you."

"Never mind little tiger. Just be yourself and don't force a thing. You won't have to make apologies to anyone. They need you, you don't need them as badly."

"Okay big sister," I replied.

"Okay," she finalized and skated away.

I moved toward the bar to pick up a soft drink, feeling more comfortable and at home, but still conspicuous, as there were four boys and three girls present. I was the fourth and youngest and still felt as if I should have been the neuter mascot. That sensation was readily relieved when a sophomore classmate of mine walked into the room. She had apparently been in the bathroom freshening up.

Sharon was a soft featured, sensually beautiful little girl. She stood five feet two inches tall and gave off a doll like aura. She looked like someone you would like to cuddle, not fuck. Her personality crystallized that first impression. She was soft toned, sweet, and well mannered. She was also semi-sheltered and naive in outlook.

I walked over toward her and broke into conversation. We spoke for fifteen minutes over cokes, closing out the threatening room out around us. We didn't notice Bob and Barbara as they approached. Bob asked Sharon if she would like to go for a walk and she eagerly agreed. I looked around and my heart skipped a beat. I was all alone with Barbara.

I looked back at her and she smiled and my instinctive fear melted away. She took my hand and silently led me toward a love seat angled toward the fireplace. She spoke softly, intently, and I responded spontaneously without contrivance. In contrast to the cold disinterest I had sensed on arrival, she seemed concerned and preoccupied with me. We spoke of small things, then big things and, as time passed, I became more relaxed, confident and expansive in response. She reacted with pleasant surprise.

As we talked, her knee touched my leg and I could feel electricity shooting up my thigh. No overt move seemed to be made, but somehow our hands fell together, first finger tips, then fingers. Our thighs touched and her head rested against my arm. Her face turned toward mine, the smile still marking her lips. I moved just a fraction of an inch and then, in what seemed like hours, our lips finally touched. Her tongue flashed out and, recovering from surprise, I responded, wildly flashing my tongue over hers. "Gently," she whispered, "gently." Feel, sense, search out." With deftness she controlled the tempo and modified the action. She slid my fingers to her breast and my heart burst with excitement. This could not be happening to me, but it was.

"Why me," I kept asking myself, "why me?" But suddenly I didn't care anymore. It was me or so I thought.

With expertise she guided my fingers and, with gentle abandon and complete caprice, explored my body with her own. With combinations of pressures, strokes, and surface of her lips and fingers, she drew forth all the glorious body sensations I could imagine. Our clothes fell smoothly to the floor, piece by piece, without interruption of the progressive sequence.

She slid her body below mine and a haven of wonders opened its pleasures to me. Our bodies began to move in unison, she at my mercy but in control. I dazed in the glorious satisfaction unfolding below; the pace grew faster, our arms tightening, making us one, culminating in an incredible surge ofbursting ecstasy, settling in a bowl of sweet contentment.

Her voice shattered the silence. "You're good, much better than I suspected."

"You're better than that," I replied with mock envy.

"Experience my boy," she teased, "experience."

For some reason all of this seemed weird to me. That first statement, as if she had preplanned the event and expected less; Her rather nonchalant attitude toward me earlier in the night; the supreme confidence and expertise she displayed in making love.

All my life I was taught that girls didn't screw unless they are crazy about you and then it's a long hard hassle. Not only did she play a dominant role in the event, but I had the distinct nagging feeling that she was emotionally unattached. For the first and only time in my life I felt like a whore. "You make me feel like a statistic," I said.

"Does that bother you?"

"Yes," I replied, surprised that she might think that it wouldn't.

"Why?" She was serious, deadly serious.

I figured I'd change the tone with a little light sarcasm.

"Nah, it really doesn't, I'm not hard to make," I said in resignation. emphasizing the point with a shoulder shrug.

"It does bother you," she said sitting up.

"This is ludicrous."

"What is?"

"This is, the whole thing," I said exasperated.

"What do you mean?"

"Why?" I figured I could move from the defensive by using her technique of question and command and avoidance of answers.

She moved toward the edge of the couch and leaned over toward me. "Because it may help you and me better understand ourselves," she said softly, slowly, and with conviction.

I thought about that and decided to be open. "Okay, you asked for it. Here goes. "Point one." I liked to categorize. It seemed more professional and impressive. "A young boy is ignored by the school queen. Point two. One hour later, in a complete about face, she seduces him. Point three, through her actions and words she expresses continual indifference toward him as a person. In summation, that is a basketful of paradoxes."

"By whose standards, yours?"

"Yes, mine. Whose else do I have to go on?"

"What makes you think they are logical?"

They are.

"Why?"

"Because," I thought for a second, "That's the way it is! I mean that's the way it was."

"Be logical," she pleaded. "I hardly know you. How can you expect me to be involved with you on a personal basis?"

"Oh god," I said exasperated. "That's just the point.' Things follow in order. First you're supposed to get to know me, to like me, to love me and then shower me with your physical love."

"Who says?"

"I don't know," I intoned, opening my hands in frustration. "I give up. "At least that's a start."

"Well anyway, one point of logic."

"What?"

"It's cold in here. Let's put on our clothes or warm each other up."

"I vote for the latter," she said smilingly.

"Me too," I retorted, grabbing her to me. I was already aroused again and ready for another round. Besides, I needed out of that conversation fast.

That year opened up new worlds to me. I experienced my first sensations of charisma and power. On the football field I slowly and insidiously took command, as is the natural right of the quarterback. Although not the best player, I played the most publicized position and therefore received most of the press.

Football is a team game. A quarterback's success depends heavily on his front line, running game and pass receivers. But the fault or the glory belongs to him. I accepted it philosophically and, since we won the conference championship with a 7-2 record, I tasted mostly glory.

My relationship with Barbara and the role she was to play in my life began to take on full meaning. With repetitive exposure to the group, I soon learned that Barbara was not my girl at all, but our girl. When with me she could be all encompassing and totally involved. When with any of the other guys, she could be the same. On our third party together, I caught her making out with Larry on the same couch we had christened our first night together. This aroused confusion and jealousy in me. Karen came quickly to the rescue, psychologically and physically. She listened to my laments and then soothed them in a bath of strokes and endearments. I responded with a sense of vengeance and excitement. Karen was also good, less polished perhaps, but more natural and less contrived. She loved with abandon and aroused in me a sense of physical supremacy and control. The excitement of the moment assuaged the jealousy that I felt, and I learned to transfer some of my possessive instincts and affections toward Karen.

Miraculously, each time that I caught a glimpse of Barbara making out with one of the other guys, Karen came to the rescue, and each time I caught a glimpse of Karen making out with one of the other guys, Barbara came to the rescue. Soon I learned to make love to Barbara or Karen without expecting more than was offered at the moment. As time passed and I became innured to their transgressions, they became more blatant in their physical entanglements with the other boys, Larry, Ralph, and Bob and, as more time wore on, their activities with the others ceased to arouse jealousy.

One night, I found myself alone with Gail and, if insipid in personality, sexually she epitomized the sensuality of Venus. Just the thought of burying my head in her large sumtuous breasts, so pillow soft, stamped with large, round, light pink areolas, topped so perfectly with prominently thrusting pink nipples, was so wonderfully arousing. The curve of her abdomen, the flair of her hips, and her succulent thighs, parting tenderly to her open warm wet womb of pleasure, engendered pure ecstasy.

I found myself accepting each experience more easily, without involvement, just for the sake of momentary pleasure.

Gail, Karen, and Barbara now took license in front of me to flip their affections to another one in the group and I became more detached as I found myself seeking pleasure with the one who became available to me. Soon it became commonplace to catch one of them fornicating behind a sofa with one of the fellows. At first I was embarrassed and fumbling. Later on I just excused myself or watched, whichever caught my fancy.

Once I found myselfin bed with Karen, about to reach the height of orgasm, and Barbara and Ralph walked into the room stark naked.

I tried to move but Karen held my buttocks to her and I lay there feeling awkward and uncomfortable with by bare ass open to the sky.

"Karen," Ralph's voice pierced the ecstasy.

My woody had wilted.

"Where are the cigarettes?"

"On the table," she mumbled nonchalantly and half disinterestedly and continued to move her hips and kiss my lips until I found myself hard again.

"Thanks," Ralph said as the door closed.

She ignored them and I tried to. Soon we regained our rhythm and crystallized the act with simultaneous climax. The light shot on and I was up and tensed, adrenaline pouring, ready to react.

"Very good," Barbara said clapping her hands.

I thought they had left but apparently they stayed to watch. I turned to Karen, confused and embarrassed, but again Karen shocked me by her indifference. "Let's see you do better," she dared.

"Okay," replied Barbara accepting the challenge.

"But first I have to get little Ralph's attention." She knelt to the ground and with quick flashes of the tongue aroused the fire in his loins. Karen watched amusingly; I watched in semi disbelief.

They were wonderful and synchronous in all their movements, nothing dirty, all so pure and open. Their bodies melted into one and their lovemaking took the form of artistic purity. They were masters and their performance seemed to be so natural and spontaneous. To my surprise, they aroused in me a sense of envy for the skills at their command.

What would have been inconceivable, horrifying and disarming to me, only months before, seemed picturesque. And then I understood it all! I had been conditioned. From the first night with Barbara, I was being taught to detach the act of sex from love. The seed was nourished over the next few months; gently, systematically, incessantly my mind was stretched and teased until it became flexible enough to appreciate sex for its pleasures alone without emotional entanglement; to observe the art of lovemaking on a critical level just as I might observe a quarterback and second guess his decisions on a Sunday afternoon. I looked at Karen. She stared back and she knew. "Now you understand, don't you?"

"Yes," I said, feeling I should be disturbed, but emanating contentment nevertheless.

"Usually it takes longer."

"Did it take longer for you?"

"Of course silly," she said shaking her head. She gave me a quick brush kiss on the, lips. "Don't you know that girls have many more barriers to break down?"

I hadn't thought of that and suddenly felt pretty stupid. It showed. She said. "For me it was very difficult. I went through months of turmoil in a continual state of confusion, anxiety and guilt." She shuddered for a second, the discussion bringing up old wounds. "Of course I was taught more gently and more slowly. It was well planned and my tolerance was very carefully measured. Each inhibiting move that was broken and redirected required an extreme degree of patience and understanding, combined of course with controlled prodding. Fortunately, the fellow that trained me was an empathetic individual. He was fully aware of my background and problems and never once forced me beyond a level that I wasn't ready to accept."

"I suppose that's what Sharon is going through now."

"Yes."

"Do you girls help her," I said genuinely concerned.

"Of course," she said sternly, a little disappointment crowding out her natural smile. "We're not cruel. What we are offering to you and Sharon is complete freedom from one of the most warped social enigmas in the history of civilization. With birth control as effective as it is today, there is no reason not to pursue sexual pleasures just as you would culinary ones, social ones, athletic ones, et cetera. Society isn't ready for that but we are not going to lose our best years waiting for it to change." She paused for a moment, took a drag on her cigarette and continued. "Freedoms come hard, especially when you are not used to them and especially when their limitations have been printed on your mind almost from birth. As we all did, Sharon is going through a trying period but, with support from us and proper training from Bob, she will make it. Your sexual freedoms, being a boy, were not so greatly limited and therefore your adaptation was quick and sure. I'm afraid, with the double standard as it is, that girls are not so lucky. Nevertheless, they are just as entitled to the same liberties and rights."

"Touché," I said, "with that kind of conviction all you need is a podium." I wanted to be sarcastic but somehow, in the saying, it lost that meaning. "How am I to take that crack?"

"Not as a joke," I said seriously. "You are a wonderful and convincing speaker," I said meaning every word. "No guy could want more in a girl."

"Thank you," she said appreciatively. "That's a very encouraging thing to hear."

"Your welcome. Now let's fuck."

"Oh, is that your coolest line?" she teased.

"It's my very best and I'm sticking to it. Now open wide! Make believe you are at the dentist."

The school year, in its inception marked by turbulence, anxiety, insecurity and new frontiers, ended smoothly with a note of accomplishment.

I had nailed down the job of first string quarterback and they were expecting an all-county performance from me next year. I worked my way up to sixth man on the basketball squad and made a valuable contribution to the team's moderate success. In baseball I was the starting shortstop and did an excellent job in the field and a creditable one at the plate.

Most importantly, though, I was firmly entrenched as a member of the group and equally impressed with my growing importance in school affairs.

My grades were not up to par but they had been relegated to secondary importance in my own mind. I passed and that was enough. It seemed that schoolwork was just a necessary evil that was a prerequisite for participation in the other forms of pleasure. Somehow, I wished they would cut out formal classes and examinations and just permit us to play ball, make love, govern ourselves, and read whatever caught our fancy, in that order.

Barbara and Bob would be leaving the group for college, with Bob off to one of the Ivy League establishments and Barbara off to one of the elite eastern finishing schools. We would all have a reunion during Christmas and Easter vacations but for all practical purposes they had left our lives and were no longer a part of the group.

The nucleus was formed by Larry, Ralph, Gail, and Karen as well as Sharon and myself. We had the job of selecting next year's pair of sophomore girls and boys to join the group. We met out at Larry's father's beach house. I was first to arrive.

The home was Spanish in style and looked more like a stockade than a villa. A ten-foot high stone wall protected the three land vulnerable sides of the property. The open side looked to the bay separating Atlantic Beach from the mainland of Long Island. A spotlight shone out over the water, which leveled about seven feet below the seawall. I felt as if I was in a fort.

It was rumored that Larry's father had some strong Mafia connections. This of course could never be proven. I was anxious to meet his old man and see if he really fit the stereo type of a Mafia warlord. Much to my surprise, he was very warm and friendly when he was first introduced, although he was dressed in a typical, gaudy, Italian

American fashion, a dark blue mohair suit, white silk tie and black and shiny leather loafers. His dark black hair was slicked back on the sides, where strands of shiny silver hair began to shine through. "Hey," He greeted me with a slap on the back. "How you doin' kid. Heard a lot about you. You're some kind of quarterback."

"Thank you sir," I replied.

"Hey," he said, hands open to the sky as ifhe were holding a pizza pie in one hand and spaghetti in the other, "here we don't use no sir's. Call me Frank, eh?" It was really an order, not a question.

"Okay Mr. Castillo."

"I said Frank. You hear me!"
"Sorry Mr. Cas…, I mean Frank. I'll try to remember."

"Don't try," he castigated."Do it!" That done, he turned to Larry and said. "Listen, you make your friend comfortable; eh? Give him what he wants to drink and eat. Mary's in the kitchen making some sandwiches for me and the boys. We got a little meeting upstairs. Ask her to make some for you kids too."

"Don't worry poppa, I'll take care of it."

"Okay, just make sure your friends get what they want."

"See you later kids," he said and started up the stairs. He stopped midway, looked down and said with an afterthought. "When the girls come, I don't want no screwin' around though," he warned pointing a finger at us.

"Don't worry," Larry replied with a discarding wave of the hand.

"Don't don't worry me in that tone of voice. In your mothers house, god rest her soul, there will be no fucking around. I don't want her turnin' in her grave. You want to play, play outside, not here, I owe her that."

"Okay Poppa."

Seemingly satisfied, he ascended the stairs. Larry's mother had been shot violently to death when Larry was five years old. His father had been shot too. The doctors had pulled four bullets out of his leg, one out of his belly and one out of his shoulder. Although it had been rumored that Tony Jerello had been the assailant, Larry's father had professed complete ignorance of any enemies that should want to kill him and firmly insisted that Tony Jerello was not one of the murderers. Frank spent three months in the hospital. Three days after he was discharged, Tony Jerello was found dead in one of the waterfront warehouses. His body was mutilated. Before being shot in the head he was beaten savagely to a pulp. Both testicles had been shot off and his penis was sliced in half. The rest of his body was marked with numerous skin slits. They never found out who did it but the Jerello gang, up to then the chief competition of Frank Castillo, was now extinct.

Larry led me into the sunroom and out to the patio overlooking a sixty-foot free form pool. "Don't mind my old man," He apologized, "he's sometimes crude and sort of a ham."

"I don't," I replied. "I thought he was kind of down to earth and nice."

We moved through the sunroom out to the patio. Larry pressed the button on the intercom and asked Mary to bring out some sandwiches and cokes. Her assent was muffled but easily heard at a distance through the speaker. Turning back toward me, he asked with what appeared to be a condescending tone. "Want to take a swim?"

"I didn't bring a bathing suit."

"Get one in the cabana," he said pointing toward it.

"We have all sizes." "Are you going in?"

"No, I've had enough for the day."

"I think I'll pass then," I said. I really wanted to go swimming but I didn't want him to think he was doing me a favor.

We made small talk until the rest of the kids filtered in. This was our first occasion together since school closed in mid June and we greeted each other with enthusiasm and scrutiny.

Gail looked as voluptuous as always, her body accented by the five pounds she had put on over the summer. Karen carried herself like a countess and, although no feature was classically beautiful, she was as attractive and desirable as ever. Sharon appeared to be more mature and more confident in her actions. This I speculated would be a fun year for her, the metamorphosis from the innocent to the aware and responsive having taken place last year. The scars would remain but they were small and well healed.

Ralph looked a little thicker and a little tougher, in his quiet firm competent way. He would now handle the bread and butter plays this fall and would probably be an All County selection. The glory would be mostly mine, but I knew that I would rely on Ralph heavily during the season and that our success would depend almost as much on him as it would depend on me.

Larry changed the least. Still good looking and lithe. From the conversation, I had changed the most. My body had begun to take on more of the character of manhood leaving the child behind. My muscles were thicker with more depth to my chest and midriff. My yellow peach fuzz took on the bristly nature of a beard and I had to shave at least four times a week. Even my gun appeared to sling a little lower like an experienced western marshall. But that of course the girls didn't know yet.

We gathered around the table and Ralph began to talk while the others gobbled up the sandwiches and cokes. None of us knew what the word diet meant. (Thinking back in envy how great it was to be a human garbage can and not suffer the embarrassment of obesity as a result.) "All of you know that today we must select four new members of "The Group." For the benefit of Sharon and Dodd, who were not at last years meeting, each of us may list five boys and five girls in order of preference. A point score ranging from five to one will be given to each candidate, five for the first preferred, four for the second and so on. In the case of a tie the votes of group members of the same sex as the candidate are discarded and the three members of the opposite sex must choose among the candidates."

He paused, methodically structuring his next sentence. Surprisingly his slow rhythmic monotone was appealing and authoritative. Prior to this occasion I had never heard Ralph speak before a group. In fact, by nature, he was reticent and withdrawn. But in having the patience to allow the natural order of things take their effect, he obviously assumed, that, as the oldest member of the group, it was his duty to lead just as he knew that it was his duty to follow in past years. All in all he was quite impressive. "I can't emphasize," he continued, "how important each and, every vote is, not only for the continued survival of "The Group," but for the life long effect that membership will have on the selectees. We wish to insure that quality persists and, to do so, each and every individual studied must score well in your own minds in each of the following categories:

1) Personality-he or she must be likable, self-confident and flexible enough to accept change.

2) He or she must be attractive.

3) He or she must have skills that will permit them to stand out within the hierarchy of the school's social structure."

"Cut the shit, Ralph," Larry butted in. "What we want are good looking cocks and cunts."

"Is that your only criteria for acceptance?" Karen offered.

Larry lounged back in his chair with his hands folded behind his head and a smirk on his face. "No, they must shower every day. That's why we pick the jocks. With you girls we have to gamble."

Sharon and Gail giggled. Karen and I didn't think that was so funny and countered with frowns. Ralph turned toward Larry and glared icily. "This group has meant more to me than a quick lay. By breaking down the barriers of sexual inhibitions, many other doors were opened to all of us. For myself, Larry, I move more easily with people, I understand their actions and words better, and I know how to make women happy, not only on a physical plane, but on a psychological one as well." Ralph paused to regroup his attack. "Here Larry," he said, leaning forward in his chair and raising his voice just a fraction in intensity, "I learned to communicate, to empathize, to reflect, to meditate, and to relate." He paused again, leaned back in his chair, lowered his voice to almost a whisper, and shook his head slowly from side to side as he spoke. "And all you can say is that you learned to fuck. Hallelujah!" The last was just audible.

"Listen," Larry retorted, "don't pull that philosophy crap on me. That first night we left the group together, all you could talk about was big thrusting tits and pussy."

Ralph's face flushed as Larry sat back triumphantly. After a second, he looked up, again shaking his head, but having regained his composure. "That's just the point Larry," he said, returning the disdain that Larry projected in his voice. "I've changed from a kid with a warped and dirty concept of life and love to a man with a more balanced understanding of what its all about."

"Horse shit," Larry summed up.

I appreciated what Ralph had said for I had followed the same route. Sure I loved sex, but it was only a part of what the group had offered to me and I felt as enriched by my participation as Ralph had by his. It was my turn to butt in and I addressed Ralph.

"Since Larry will never understand anyway, I think that we should get to the discussion of the candidates."

Larry got up from his chair, leaned across the table and shook a finger in my face. "Who the fuck do you think you are? Watch your mouth ass hole or I'll close it."

"The truth bothers you," I retorted. I was a little afraid of him but my pride wouldn't let me show it.

Karen got up and grabbed Larry's hand. "Come on, this will get us nowhere. Everybody's entitled to their opinion."

Larry sat down reluctantly but added, "All right, just so that cocky little bastard understands that he's not running this show."

I didn't want to fight and Karen had cooled things down, so I let well enough alone. Larry wasn't that tough. He was a calculator, the worst kind of coward. He would never threaten Ralph, for he knew that Ralph would tear into him and break him in half. But he definitely thought that he could kick my ass and wouldn't mind trying.

We got down to a brief analysis of all of last year's freshmen who were now sophomores. We easily eliminated 80% of them on the basis of mediocrity oflooks, lackluster personality or lack of participation in school athletics or clubs. There were one hundred in all, so that we were now down to twenty, ten boys and ten girls. Ralph read off all the names. Any individual who did not receive at least three affirmatives from us, (an affirmative meaning they would be placed in one of the five positions on our card,) was eliminated. That left us with fourteen candidates, eight boys and six girls.

Despite what Ralph said, six of the eight boys were jocks and the other two were good looking, talented individuals who happened not to enjoy playing ball. They got in by the skin of their teeth by am affirmative from Karen, Ralph and me. The girls were all attractive. At this point Ralph spoke again. "Remember, your decision must be based on all around merit combined with adaptability of the individual to the club. I would like to point out that Kurt Henessey is a religious kid who attends mass every morning. He's a nice kid, a good student and he's going to be a great halfback, but his convictions are such that membership in this group will only generate in him persistent anxiety and guilt. Janet Lawson is gorgeous but dumb."

Larry blurted in again. "Cut the lecture. We all know the kids. Now let's vote."

Before Ralph could respond, Gail had her say. "I'm afraid Larry's right Ralph, although he's always so undiplomatic about it. We all know what we want in the kids we accept and we all have a right to our own opinions."

Ralph nodded his head and ballots were handed out. I chose mine carefully, trying to remember the strife that I, to a minor degree and Sharon in excess, had to suffer the year before. It was important for me to choose kids that I felt could hold up to the pressure, especially the girls, and come out the better for it. My list went as follows:

Boys	Girls
Terry Stone	Ellen Wallace
Bob Jeniter	Jane Eliot
Alan Coen	Denise
Joe Capricelli	Kim Golden
Sean Ellis	Janet Lawson

Except for Janet, they all had three things in common; good looks, at least average intelligence and no fanatical religious affiliation. All the boys I chose were excellent athletes with the exception of Terry Stone. I had met Terry through Karen at the theatre club. He was destined to take over for her as top producer, actor, singer, sales manager and scout. He loved show business and was a walking encyclopedia with regard to its history. He brought to the rehearsals a dynamic exuberance that was contagious to all. He had the appeal and charisma that could one day make him a star.

Ralph accepted the ballots and tallied them. Terry had gotten in by the skin of his teeth with thirteen votes, five from Karen, five from me and three from Ralph. Sean Tillis topped the male vote getters with seventeen. He was tall, six foot one, and lanky, with blue eyes, blond hair and cute Irish features. Personality wise he could best be described as one of the boys. Larry and Ralph liked him for his clean looks, athletic prowess and humble and respectful attitude. Gail and Sharon liked him because of his clean fresh innocence that they would delight in corrupting. Gail would no doubt assume the task as his instructor as Barbara had assumed with me the year before. Karen would take Terry who, in being a more intelligent, worldly, and sensuous individual, would probably learn quite spontaneously.

The girls selected were Ellen Wallace and Kim Golden. Ellen vibrated with enthusiasm and energy. She participated in a number of school functions and whatever task she was assigned to do got done. She was petite and cute with light brown hair and a fair complexion.

Kim was a more moody and aloof type. She had the classical beauty of a love goddess with large, blue almond-shaped eyes, a straight, perfectly proportioned nose, high cheekbones and moist pouting lips. The curves to her body were sinewy and lithe and she moved with the grace of a mountain lion. She emanated self-confidence and independence. She aroused not lust but worship. She would be a problem. I half pitied, half envied he who got to instruct her. She breathed individualism. She was not given to infatuation and her successful adaptation to the group would be a monumental achievement. Although she was the most desirable of all the sophomore girls, I had placed her fourth on my list, for I feared that she might jeopardize the successful continuity of the group. Apparently Ralph and Gail had similar misgivings as they had placed her low on their ballots too. Ralph spoke up interrupting my train of thought. "Our choices then are Terry, Sean, Ellen and Kim. Are there any suggestions on how they should be handled and who they should be assigned to?"

"I'll take Terry," Karen stated gaily with delightful expectancy. "That is if it's all right with Gail," she added quickly.

"Then Sean shall be mine," Gail followed agreeably.

"I'll take Kim," Larry stated with finality.

Karen countered quickly,

"I don't think you should."

Larry looked wounded. He said angrily. "You got who you want. Now mind your own goddamn business and leave this to Ralph and me." He looked expectantly toward Ralph.

"It's okay with me," Ralph offered trying to maintain harmony.

Karen continued obstinately. "I still think that it's very impractical. Kim can be a special problem. She is independent, opinionated and stubborn. Larry is egotistical, bullish, demanding and prone to quick temper. They will grate at each other like rubbing two pieces of sandpaper together and we may lose her."

Larry was angry again. "Who are you to judge. It's already settled anyway. Ralph agreed."

"It's not settled," Karen continued, "and I think we should all discuss it and vote."

Gail spoke up apologetically, "I'm afraid I agree with Karen, Larry. I like you. I think we all do, but we also know you well and understand why you act the way you do. Kim will not. If you are insistent and demanding, she will respond with equal and opposite determination. To make her bend will require flexibility. That is not your strong suit."

I was impressed. I had always thought that Gail was a voluptuous shell with an internal vacuum. Now, I was in the process of learning another lesson. People are complex and inconsistent and they cannot easily be categorized into stereotypic behavioral patterns. What,in the past, was probably reserve on her part may have been misinterpreted by me as stupidity. She sure made sense and I made a note to be less premature and sweeping in my evaluation of character in the future. Larry slouched back in his chair, resigned to the fact that there was too much resistance to his handling Kim. "All right, if you think Ralph can do a better job, she's his."

I don't think that he's the answer either," Karen said. The group fell silent and all eyes turned toward me. There was electric tension in the air, as everybody moved toward the edge of their seat. It had been the practice that the senior boys trained the new girls. Karen had threatened tradition.

Larry jumped to his feet and leaned menacingly over the table, looking at Karen and pointing at me. "Him," he burst out in defiance, his eyes boiling with hate. "Ralph yes, but him over my dead body."

"Yes him," Karen shot back.

Larry slammed his hand on the table. "I am sick and tired ofhearing about him from you every time we're together. What does he have that's so special, an electric vibrator on his dick?"

At another time that would have been funny but there was menace and tremor in his voice. Larry looked toward me, his body keyed and ready to spring, his eyes begging me to make a move. A wave of combined pity and hate ran through me. But, like all else, I smothered it and controlled the tremendous urge I had to strike out; to smash that mouth that was the source of a year's worth of disregard and insult. I was too much in control though to permit my body to satisfy its impulses. The satisfaction to be derived was just not quite enough to offset the potential pain and danger that existed in defeat. Larry was sadistic and hateful enough to try and maim me for life. I let my muscles relax just a little bit, but sill sat on the edge of my chair with the balls of my feet on the ground, ready to spring if necessary.

Ralph's voice cut through the tension like a knife. "We're not animals. Cool it Larry and let's listen to what Karen has to say."

Larry hesitated for a split second as I tensed, prepared to react. For that moment, at that time, he decided to retreat and, after offering me an icy stare, he moved back to his seat. We all waited expectantly for Karen to continue. "I believe that Kim presents an explosive problem that, if not handled properly, could result in the disruption of this group."

"That's not possible and you know it," Larry burst in disdainfully. "What do you mean it's not possible," Karen challenged.

"Just what I said. We all know that our method of induction and adaptation has built in safeguards. If she decides to pull out, she will effectively know of the group only that which she has accepted for herself as well as the one step she refused to take. Since we take them one light step at a time, it is fairly obvious that she will not threaten our existence."

"Yes, but her loss will destroy the balance of the group."

"So we'll replace her."

"Not so easily done. At any rate I think it's obvious that we should do the best we can to adapt those we've selected and not concentrate on the risk. With Kim, I think that Dodd would limit that risk more than either you or Ralph."

"Why," Gail asked, taking the words right out of Larry's mouth.

"Because she's infatuated with him. Going with Larry or Ralph and seeing him here, so close, yet so unreachable, would only be a distraction and make her more resistant to either of you two. With him, the affair would be natural and spontaneous. The only difficult task would be for him to determine when to attempt to detach the concepts of love and sex,"

She paused, waiting for agreement. Nobody was committing himself or herself yet.

Ralph said sarcastically. "No kidding, that's the whole ballgame. The rest is pretty easy."

"I know." Karen replied. "And I firmly believe that Dodd is equipped to handle that too. He is kind, gentle and empathetic. He has a natural ability to sense a woman's needs and desires, something you Ralph have had to work to acquire and you Larry don't seem to even care about. He has the capacity to be not only a lover but in the same instant paternally protective. Paradoxically, "she said smiling, breaking the serious tone of her voice, "he even aroused the mother instinct in me." To my surprise and embarrassment Gail and Sharon nodded in agreement. Karen continued. "It is rare that a man can represent a father, son and lover."

They all fell quiet and it was obvious that they agreed. Kim, breaking tradition, would be mine and I was excited by their faith and determined to meet the challenge with complete preparation and dogged tenacity. Besides, Kim was a piece of ass and ass turned me on.

Clump, clump, clump, clump, clump went the cleats as they echoed through the corridor on their way to the locker room. You had to open your eyes and look to really believe that there were bodies attached to those shoes.

We filed into our musty smelling confined quarters and littered the floor in front of the lockers with our sore sweaty bodies. Everybody grabbed greedily for the oranges. There wasn't much else that was positive to think about.

The mumbling abruptly fell to silence as the coach stormed into the room. Sounding like a cross between Bogart and Col. Sanders ofKentucky Fried Chicken, he expanded his stomach, flexed his diaphragm and bellowed menacingly. "You guys want to know how to bust ass, I'll show you." His foot lashed out and caught Bob Norrick in the rear. Bob went flying back against the locker with a resounding thud. He whimpered more from fright than from pain and fell to the floor with a thud. The rest of us scattered away from that wayward foot. The coach jumped up on the bench that lay between the row oflockers and paced up and down silently for what seemed an eternity.

"What do you think your doing out there, playing hopscotch? Dancing? What? Are you afraid to hit those guys because you think they'll break, or are you just a bunch of pansies?" His foot lashed out again, kicking the orange out ofTom Hooper's hand, which was moving toward his mouth. "What do you need that for. You just stood around and watched the first half. I'm surprised you didn't wave bye-bye as they ran past." Hooper held his head down, ashamed. He had great natural talent but occasionally relied on that alone. He didn't have the killer instinct Coach Burton respected. "Now I'm not gonna give you guys any fancy lectures, any stop gap defenses, any new sensational plays. We've got all we need. What it boils down to is guts. Block and tackle and guts." He paused letting that sink in. His voice softened as he resumed. "I can't tell you how to hit. That you gotta feel inside. A man comes at you and your pride has got to tell you to stop him." His voice rose to a crescendo. "Stop him! Stop him! Because you're better and tougher than he is." Again the soft, tender tone returned. "If you haven't got any pride in the fact that you're men then I can't teach you a thing. Now sit there and think about that."

The room fell quiet. The guys were moved and they kept their heads down in pensive silence. They were moved and ashamed. I myself couldn't understand what being a man had to do with wanting to hit somebody hard. But I followed trend and kept looking seriously at the floor. The coach's voice floated softly through the room like a pillow like cloud. "You guys know what you have to do. Don't let them walk away thinking they played a bunch of faggots." Directing his attention to Hooper he said, "I heard their quarterback's laughing at you Hooper. He said, any time they need yards, they just have to run right and you'll let them run right over you. You got ten minutes to show me that they are wrong. I want that loud mouth asshole to know who you are Hooper. Simply put, he's out or you're out." Returning to us he stated, with extreme reverence. "Now bow your heads and ask him for the strength to do what must be done." And then we prayed. Hypocrites had nothing over on that man.

Once out on the field, things happened fast. On the second play from scrimmage, their quarterback rolled right, looking for the left end to come across on a flood pattern. Hooper got outside their right tackle and exploded toward the quarterback. Before he knew it, Hooper, at full stride, had him in his grasp, lifted up and drove him to the ground, shoulder first, snapping the collarbone on his throwing side. That was it for his season and for that matter, the hopes and aspirations of our opponents. Fueled by the shift in momentum, we struck like lightning, scoring five unanswered touchdowns to win going away. There was joy in Mudville that day and Hooper was at he center of it. He had been the catalyst and we all were the recipients. We would get better and better as the season wore on and I would fulfill my dream as an All County selection. But I would never forget how fleeting fun and glory could be; just one collar bone away; just one scheming asshole hell bent on upsetting the apple cart; just one fateful accident away. I learned to take things with a grain of salt and not let myself get so full of myself that I was set up for a fall. I appreciated the fun and attention, but I knew, deep down in my heart, that it could be fleeting and that I had to eventually plan to do something more substantial.

My junior and senior years in high school were the best. I was on top of the social and sports world. In school, I was the center of attention and, at the end of my junior year, I ran for the class presidency for the following year. I never said anything brilliant and avoided all controversy. I stood behind everything that was popular and I won in a landslide. In class, my teachers gave me the benefit of the doubt and were loath to give me a bad grade. I didn't study much and, thank God, I didn't have to.

My dating life was confined to the group. Kim was of course my first real test in manipulation and, although I prevailed in the end, it was not without trial and tribulation. In the beginning she was extremely infatuated and awestruck with me and I was able to get her to do things before she was ready. When I attempted to break away, she went into extreme depression and had great difficulty adjusting to doing anything with the other guys. Larry almost pushed her over the brink, but with support from Karen, Gail and Ralph, she was able to ride out the storm and accept the changes in sexual mores that she was observing about her. Each time I spent the evening with her, she left, anticipating that we would be an item, only to find out at the next visit that I had betrayed her emotions by being with another girl. Each time it was devastating, but just as we were about to give up hope, she finally responded to Ralph and opened the door for some relief. As time moved on, she learned to distance herself from me, first with total rejection and then with grudge fucks with Larry who she knew that I didn't like. Finally, she began to understand and with mixed love and hate, again shared my bed. Eventually, the love and hate were replaced by cool detachment and I knew that she was there. She had made the transition, never to go back to the innocence of youth, the purity of singular love. Although I was happy being where I was, I was never sure with Kim. Sometimes, I thought that she fully appreciated the level of sexual sophistication that she had achieved, but wished in her heart that she could reclaim her innocence. I never knew for sure, because I was afraid to breach the subject with her. Her silence and cool detachment on the matter always left me in doubt. Sometimes, I would look into her eyes for answers, but she would turn quickly away, never allowing me to see what she really felt. Maybe that was her way of getting back at me for causing all that pain. To this day, I still don't know.

While I flourished athletically and socially, I did have a few incidents of note that affected my character and development. I recognized early in the game that I was extremely smart in math and science and, in these disciplines, I could perform brilliantly with very little effort.

In my sophomore year, I took Geometry with a teacher whose most defining characteristic was that she was ugly. In a moment of combined bravado and boredom, I wrote a note to a young girl that I was trying to impress. It said, "Ms. Greaby plus Geometry equals horse shit." As proof, I added, "the whole equals the sum of its parts."

The teacher caught me handing the note to the girl and told me to bring it up front. Defiantly, I tore it up into a thousand pieces before

I reached her and I dropped the ripped up paper over her desk like I was dropping confetti in a parade. The class laughed raucously as she frowned and ordered me back to my seat. I just turned, smiling widely, as I shrugged my shoulders, and ambled to the back of the room, where I could retake my seat and lean back against the wall. The teacher stared angrily after me, as she pulled a manila envelope out of her desk. Then, she swept the little pieces of paper on the desk into the folder. To ice the cake, she bent over, still staring at me with fixed anger, and swept all the pieces of paper, that had fallen like snow flakes to the floor, into the envelope, as the class uttered a universal "oooooooh." She then announced that she would see me tomorrow, and I knew that I was in trouble.

I went home, and, for the first time all year, I decided to do my homework. It was early November and I realized that there was no way I could do the work until I learned the eighty five pages that led up to it. I stayed up all night, doing two months work in ten hours, and got the homework done perfectly. Exhausted, I went to school and, at second period, I turned in my geometry homework.

She never even looked at it. She tore up the sheets, and then announced to the whole class. "You, young man, are a disgusting individual, and I don't want you in my classroom. For all I care, you can spend the rest of the year in the library and take the Regents exam on your own. With a sweep of the hand, she added. "Now get out of here." Without hesitation, I was on my way, with intense feelings of ambivalence. On the one hand, I was thoroughly embarrassed. On the other, I was relieved to be freed from the daily drudgery of a snail crawling, boring class.

The year passed swiftly. I enjoyed my free time in the library, where I could sneak in the back and talk to the girls. I never gave geometry a second thought until the last day of the year, when I realized that I would have to take a Regent's exam the following day.

I went home, somewhat despondent, with an impending sense of doom. With fear of failure as a motivator, I decided that I was going to do everything in my power to get through that exam. I convinced myself that Regent's exams could not be that hard, because they were laid out for the average kid in the state of New York to pass, and that meant the rural kids too.

To compound the problem, I also had a biology Regent's the next afternoon, but I decided that I would spend only a little time reviewing that subject and concentrate on the math. Getting to page eighty-five was relatively easy. Then I sat down to dinner, and my mother spilled a chicken pot pie on my leg and gave me a second-degree burn. Cursing, I went to the doctor, who patched me up and sent me home, with the advice to get a good nights sleep. I nodded my head and, after warning my mother that a failure would be on her shoulders, I returned to the books. I took aspirin to alleviate the dull ache in my thigh and honed in on the math text with a capacity to focus that I had never experienced in my life. By eight in the morning, I had finished the math text, and committed it to a tenuous memory. Without eating, I went to school in the same clothes that I had worn through the night, and sat down to take the exam. After the preliminary instructions, they delivered the test paper to me and I opened up the folder for a quick review. All of a sudden, a wave of numbing fatigue swept over me and, as I looked at the questions, it seemed apparent that I couldn't answer a single one.

I took a deep breath and focused on gathering my thoughts. I convinced myself that I could reconstruct this subject from scratch, since each proof was build on the last. I returned to the first question, slowly, methodically, and logically rebuilding the subject, until I could answer each and every question on the test. Usually, three hours were allotted for each Regent's exam, although I had found, over the years, that I was usually out of there in less than an hour. In this case, I was finishing my last question, when the proctor interrupted my trance, ordering me to turn in my exam. The three hours had flown by and I had no idea of the time. I got up and left the room, knowing in my heart that I had creamed the test.

There was no time for self-congratulations. I had to take a biology Regents and I had hardly studied. I had two hours until it began. I sat down in a quiet place outside the school and leaned back against the wall. I was wound up, no longer fatigued, and I studied effectively for two hours and walked in and took the biology test, finishing in my usual time of just under an hour and a half.

Once done, I felt a wave of elation spread through by body. I had taken on the tiger and won. I had risen to the occasion, sweaty palms and all, and had walked away with the brass ring. It was not the first time in my life that I had that feeling, and it would not be the last.

The exams were graded at the state capitol in Albany and then sent back to the school, bound in wire in reverse order of grade. For the first time since November, I returned to the geometry classroom from where I had been publicly exiled, and took my seat in the back of the room. The teacher entered, greeted the class, and removed the binder from the exam booklets. She then began to read off the names and the grades. "Jansen, fifty seven!" Carl Jansen stood up and walked to the front of the room, retrieved his paper, and, with a shameful awareness that his grade was the lowest, slithered, with head bent, to the safety of his seat. "Berkow, sixty one," she bellowed, shaking her head as he walked to the front of the room. "I expected more of you." She continued the parade, announcing grade after grade.

Nobody paid attention to me until half the class was called. Then, a creeping awareness seemed to take over the classroom, as she called name after name. With each passing announcement, more kids would turn to look at me. I leaned back against the wall, palms against the back of my head, with a wide grin of self contentment plastered on my face. With each name called, the tension mounted. When she got down to the last four names, she looked up and gave me a dirty look each time she called another name that wasn't mine. Finally, she got to the last exam booklet and, with a deep sigh, called my name. As I rose, the applause started, thundering through the room as I approached the desk, wide grin still plastered on my face. I returned to my seat, navigating the gauntlet between kids cheering and standing to slap me on the back. After taking my seat, the teacher called for order and, when the room quieted down, addressed me directly. With a conciliatory gesture, she said. "I must admit, I never expected this."

I couldn't let it go and I gave her no quarter. "Thank God I never listened to you. Otherwise it never would have happened." The muffled giggles followed me out of the classroom as I stood and strolled out the door.

I took two thoughts home from this episode. The first was that no matter how it seemed, no task was too daunting. The second was that I had a streak of insensitivity that had to be addressed.

Another episode in high school pointed out my willingness to get a good laugh at someone else's expense, if they were an asshole, a hypocrit or a pompous ass.

On the first day of solid geometry class in my senior year, in walked a brand new teacher, a man of mass and girth whose math skills were inversely related to his waistline. He stood before the class and bellowed. "My name is Dr. North, and I am here to teach you solid geometry. When I get done, you will all be well versed in this academic discipline. I want you to know, that you will get what you deserve." He paused for effect. "I don't play no favorites and as you will learn, I don't "AK" nobody."

Not a bad beginning, but he couldn't follow up. Everything went south from there. Not only couldn't he teach. I seriously doubted that he knew half as much solid geometry as I did. To make matters worse, he was the biggest brown noser that I had ever met. Despite the fact that the class was filled with smart and attentive students, it was impossible for them to learn from him, and the class was in total chaos. Because I could learn quickly on my own, I was the only one who knew anything, and I was his star pupil. He would always use me for demonstrations, because I knew the process, and, he could delude himself into believing that, since I had learned, the lack of understanding on the rest of the class's part must be their fault and not his. Often he would say out of frustration. "If you don't get this right I am going to jump out that window," but of course he never did.

On teacher parent day, Dr. Salter, the superintendent of the high school system, showed up to monitor his daughter's progress. Dr. North had just made an announcement to the class. "I want you all to know, that this is just solid geometry as usual today. We don't have to put on no shows for nobody." And for emphasis, he added. "No sir, I don't "AK" nobody!"

At that very moment, Dr. Salter's face appeared in the half glass entrance door to the room, and Dr. North waddled quickly over to open it for him, and guide him to a comfortable seat in the back of the room. After making him comfortable, he returned to the blackboard and said. "I am extremely honored to welcome Dr. Salter to our classroom today so that he can observe, first hand, the progress that you students have made. Wanting to make the best impression possible, he took a simple subject from regular geometry for discussion in order to demonstrate to Dr. Salter his teaching prowess. Pausing for a breath, he continued. "Today, we are dealing with alternate interior angles for the first time and I am going to bring up one of our average students for a demonstration."

In his review of basic geometry, he had emphasized the study of alternate interior and complementary angles and he knew that I knew this subject like the back of my hand. Turning his gaze toward me, he said. "Dodd, please step up to the front of the room." I got out of my seat and ambled to the front of the room. As I walked to the front, he drew two parallel lines on the blackboard and dissected both of them with another straight line. He then began to try again to teach the concept, which I already knew. Then, he pointed to one of the angles, and asked. "Which one, son, is the alternate interior angle." Of course I knew the answer, and he knew, from the previous day that I knew the answer, but I purposely pointed to the wrong angle. With patience, he commented. "No son, that is not it. Now take your time and think." After a moment's reflection, I raised my palms, indicating confusion, and he took this as a cue to again explain the concept. "If this angle over here is so many degrees, then this angle over there has to be the same because it just is." With that inadequate explanation, he turned to me and pointed at another angle. "Now tell me young man, which angle in this diagram is exactly the same." I took the pointer and purposely pointed at the wrong one. Nothing was going right. With frustration and impatience in his voice he sighed. "I'm gonna ask you one more time, and, if you don't answer correctly, I am going to jump out that window." There were only two other choices left. I slowly raised the pointer and pointed at the wrong one. Then, without hesitation, I walked over to the window, unlocked the latch, and opened it as far as it would go. With the class bellowing with boisterous laughter, I opened up my palms, giving Dr. North the sign to go ahead to jump. Salter had seen enough. He got up and left the room, leaving Dr. North transfixed to his spot at the blackboard. It was clear that, when the school didn't renew his contract for the following year, the educational system rid itself of an unnecessary burden.

Over the years, I became more aware of other peoples feelings and more tolerant of their self protective actions, but, if there was one thing that I could not tolerate, it was injustice delivered from the seat of power. One such episode involved my Spanish teacher and I went to extremes in order to deliver to her the justice that she so richly deserved.

Upon application to college, she gave me the worst character references possible. The crux of the matter was this. She wore short skirts and sat on my desk with her legs crossed. Rather than concentrate on Spanish, I used to concentrate on looking up her dress, which I might add was an awfully exciting view. One day, while I was focused on the glistening black patch between her succulent thighs, she asked me a question, and I responded as if I wasn't really there. "Why is it, Dodd, that whenever I ask you a question, you seem to be in a daze?"

Instead of answering diplomatically, I answered truthfully. "Because Senora, you sit on my desk and wear short skirts." The room burst out into raucous laughter and red was permanently etched into the senora's face. Needless to say, she never forgave me, and hence, the infamous character references.

Based on this information, and other input, the principle made a judgement that my projected performance in college was unpredictable. A reasonably bright, mature and well disciplined student predictably performed better in university than an exceptionally bright, but immature, and undisciplined student. Therefore, he refused to find me a place in one of the better, more traditional eastern schools, except for Columbia in New York. This school was acceptable to him, because every student wanted to leave town to go to college. Since my high school was located near New York City, nobody wanted to go to Columbia. Therefore, if I performed badly, he didn't care because he didn't need the placement guarantees.

I bode my time and got back at Ms. Celento, after I graduated from medical school. After her school day was done, I walked into the doorway of her classroom. She was sitting at her desk, and had to turn her head sideways to see me standing in doorway. I was wearing ponchos and chains and I had a full beard and long hair. As I stepped through the doorway, I was hit by a halo of sunlight that shone through the windows opposite the door. She squinted in order to see me, and I am sure, in that light, I looked like the rising of Jesus himself. "Yes?" she asked. "May I help you?"

"No," I responded, "but I think that I can help you."

"What do you want?"

I took another step into the room and answered.

"I want to speak with you."

With the sun now less bright as I stepped into the room, she could see my face.

"Wait a minute," she intoned. "Wait a minute." She hesitated for another second and then recognition came to her face.

"I know you, I know you." While pointing at me, she drew deep from her memory. "You're that Robbins boy," she said disdainfully with recognition in her voice. Then assuming a supercilious air, she added. "Look at you. What have you done with yourself young man," she said, thinking that my attire must have some relevant relationship to my achievements.

Coming further into the room and taking a chair opposite the desk, I responded. "I went to medical school. I'm a physician."

Startled, she responded. "My gosh, congratulations. I never would have guessed that."

"I know," I responded soberly, "and that's what I've come here today to talk about with you."

"What?" she asked somewhat confused.

"Ms. Celento," I emphasized in a soft and patient tone, trying to get her full attention. "I have come here today to talk to you about evaluating people and how we can sometimes use the wrong information, so that we judge them unfairly."

"What does that have to do with me?" she asked, somewhat confused.

"When I was here as a student, you had an impression of a number of my classmates, which, I'm sure, you incorporated into their character references. You were so far off in mine, giving emphasis to things that really didn't matter and ignoring the things that did, that I have to assume that you misevaluated all of my classmates. Your character references weighed heavily in the course that a student's life took, and I was hoping that, if I could point out the flaws in your process of student evaluation, I might help you be more fair and accurate in your future evaluations."

"Well young man," she said with a haughty tone. "Everyone is entitled to his or her opinion."

"Please, Ms. Celento," I pleaded in an even softer voice. "I'm not here to criticize you. Only to help. Will you please listen?"

"All right, but I don't see this going anywhere."

"When I was a student here, you gave me the worst character references imaginable based on the fact that I was brutally truthful in response to a question that you asked me."

"Yes, I remember that," she interrupted. "I can't even repeat what you said."

"I admit, that I was not diplomatic and properly evasive in my response. But I was truthful."

"What you were doing was disgusting."

"Categorize it as you wish, but the truth was that most boys are thinking about sex a lot of the time and, at one time or another, most of the boys in that class expressed a desire to have sexual relations with you."

"I don't have to listen to this."

"No you don't, but it is the truth and it is only natural. The difference between them and me was that I was naive enough to be truthful and they had learned not to be." I paused, letting that sink in. "Did you hear me say that they learned not to be."

"I still don't see what that has to do with anything," she responded.

Leaning forward in my chair, I said. "Then let me tell you what it means. At school, these kids learned to say only what sounded right and never to say what they felt. The truth was not important, the end result was. They were rewarded for brown nosing, ass kissing and lying and it was reflected in their character references."

"That's still just a matter of opinion," she said defiantly.

"OK," I jumped in as quickly as I could. "Let's take a few examples of students that you remember and let's see how well your evaluation of them correlates with their accomplishments."

"I don't see how I can remember "

I cut her off at the pass. "Let's just try with a few that had your class for three years; that you thought you got to know well."

"OK," she sighed, resigned to my tenacity not to let it go, and hoping that this whole episode would stop, after she showed that her evaluations were not off the mark.

"Let's take Susan Terell. You thought the world of her."

Ms. Celento's eyes lit up.

"Yes I did. She was a wonderful girl. A conscientious student, very stylish, who was active in school clubs and activities."

"What do you think that she is doing now?"

"Oh I don't know, but, whatever it is, I'm sure that she is very successful at it."

"As a matter of fact she is," I lied. "If you go down to Central Park south near the Plaza Hotel, you will see her walking the streets with the rest of the high priced prostitutes."

"What, she said incredulously."

"You heard me. The very qualities you thought were substantive in her personality were only camouflage. She only did those things because she knew that it made her look good. Also," I continued to lie, "she was so attractive, that she would trade sex for homework or help on exams."

"Well, I am shocked."

"As well you ought to be. But that didn't help Susan. You and this school rewarded her for that kind of behavior because you took her superficial actions at face value, instead of really trying to get to know her. But in the outside world, those qualities that you so cherished here, were obviously transparent. They didn't get her anywhere and, unfortunately, she was never prepared to do things the right way, because she was never made to be accountable for her transgressions."

"I never would have thought," she reflected, but I didn't give her time to digest the information any further.

"What about Marty Angel?"

"Oh yes, I remember him." She paused to get her thoughts in order. "He was not very bright. He was a slow learner and very immature, certainly lazy to say the least. I expected him to have difficulty in college.

He was a nice enough boy, and I only hoped that he had the tools to get through school and do something."

"Suppose I were to tell you that he did do something and that he is financially, one of the most successful students in the class." I paused to let that sink in. "He earned a law degree and now runs the financial planning program for E.F. Houston inc. You just got him all wrong. He matured late. That was all. But his basic character strength was there. He was honest, loyal and fair, qualities that you don't allude to at all but qualities that we should try to encourage in our young people. These are qualities that serve you well as you climb the corporate ladder."

"Gosh, I didn't know," she said, somewhat in a state of shock.

I continued to go on and on, intermixing the truth with a few lies, only to emphasize my points. With each story, she became more and more despondent, until I finally stopped to summarize. "Listen, Ms. Celento. I know that you meant well. I am only here today, not to castigate you for what you have done in the past, but only to try and help you make better judgements in the future. This way, you can help foster the basic characteristics that will serve your students well for the rest of their lives; this way you can reward those who are really deserving with good character references, which will have a profound effect on their college placement."

"But," she objected, obviously devastated by the revelations she had just witnessed. "I am retiring at the end of this year."

Wow! I couldn't have twisted the knife in any better if I had tried. "Then," I said ever so softly as I stood to leave. "I guess there is nothing more that you can do to make amends." I bowed my head and walked out the door, leaving her to ruminate on her new information, and wallow in her newfound despair.

Sometimes, in the pursuit of justice, I let my pride interfere and I'd cut my nose to spite my face. I made college applications to a number

of schools, but lost the opportunity to go to my first choice because of my refusal to accept temporary injustice.

At this Ivy League school, they offered me an acceptance, if I played football. Since a couple of my friends from high school were receiving money for playing sports at other schools, I asked the admission's interviewer if they could offer me some financial assistance. His response was curt. "In the Ivy League, we are not allowed to offer athletic scholarships."

That may have been technically true, but it didn't deter them from offering academic scholarships to mediocre students that were great football players. "Fine," I retorted. "What about an academic scholarship?"

"Are you kidding," the interviewer said with disbelief. "Your grades are not nearly good enough. Get real"

"What if I don't want to play football?"

"Listen," said the interviewer. "Maybe I'm not explaining myself clearly." He paused to choose his words carefully. "You are a borderline applicant. With your extra curricular activity, including football, we see the potential for a well rounded student." What was clear was that their football team was hurting for numbers. Athletes got academic scholarships and there were just so many to go around. They couldn't take a chance on me, since I came from a small high school league, (translated, I was the creme-della-crap.) But, at worst, I would be useful as fodder. I could run the opponents plays in practice without counting as an expense against the football program. At best, I might be a surprise.

"Are you telling me that I must pay full tuition and that I must play football to be accepted?"

A big smile crept across his face. "I think you get the picture."

I knew that I intended to try out anyway, whether I received a scholarship or not. I also knew that, once accepted, if I kept my grades up, I wouldn't have to play if I didn't want to. But I was so incensed by this attempt at extortion that it didn't take me long to burn that bridge.

With the utmost sincerity, I responded. "Kiss my ass," and I was out the door.

After closing the door to this fine American school, I waited impatiently for acceptance to other institutions. Finally I got into a few, but, to my delight, I was accepted at McGill University in Canada, thought by some to be Canada's answer to Harvard and Oxford. I decided to attend. It was a clean start in a new place; a different country with a European flavor. Attending school there would be unusual for an American and a point of discussion at home. I liked being different and I liked being the point of discussion.

My mother took me up and helped me register. The fees were

shockingly low, approximately six hundred dollars a semester. I used that cost savings to manipulate my way into an expensive studio apartment in a luxury building, rather than a dorm room. Once leased, my mother said goodbye and rode off into the sunset. I felt lost and began to walk the streets of Montreal alone. School didn't start for a week and I didn't know anybody. Football player not withstanding, I started to cry uncontrollably. I didn't know why and I didn't care. I just knew that I was going to begin a new chapter in my life and I was scared and alone.

The process of growing up is painful and I paid my dues just like most of us do. I learned how to cook rudimentary meals, clean the apartment, and do the wash, skills, heretofore, I knew nothing about. I learned to get myself up out of bed and to go to class, since there was no one there to wake me, albeit I still missed around a third of the classes. I learned that I was all alone when it came to servicing a car or showing up for a doctor's appointment. Mommy wasn't there to take care of my business. I learned that if I didn't do it, it miraculously didn't get done.

I signed up for football and played on the junior varsity (there was no freshman team.) Although, I was overwhelmed at first with the athleticism and size of the players compared to high school, I soon realized that I could compete. I quickly made it up to second string quarterback, passing two other guys on the depth chart. The first string quarterback, John Percy, was the recipient of the Most Valuable Player award in the Montreal High school system the year before. Still, it was clear to me, that, while he had better coaching, I had the athletic skills to surpass him. For one, I was twenty pounds heavier and much faster in the hundred. We didn't time forty-yard dashes in those days but I killed him in sprints. I could throw the ball just as accurately and much further, but I had to admit that he had a much better pocket presence and exuded supreme confidence in the huddle. By our fifth game, the coach was playing me a lot and, over beers one night (I didn't like the taste, so I faked it,) he confessed to me that he made a mistake, and should have started me. For the last game of the year, I was the starting quarterback and I did a credible job. We won. I completed a few passes and ran for over a hundred yards in the game on fifteen carries.

In my dreams, I aspired to being the first string quarterback on the varsity. But I looked at the depth chart and realized that the uphill battle would be too steep. In Canada, graduate students can play, and we had two former all East players playing quarterback at McGill. These guys had arms like cannons, and might have been borderline pros if they had been so inclined. I knew that I was better than the rest of them, but those two were just unreachable in talent and experience. Rather than being a third stringer, I decided that my college football career was over and, after our last game, I hung up my pads for good.

Starting anew, I had to develop my own social and academic life at McGill. I didn't have the advantage of a mentor or friends from home. I didn't know a soul and I had to build relationships from scratch. I joined a fraternity and went through the rigors of rush, which left a bad taste in my mouth. The week preceding acceptance into the group was a nightmare. This was in an era before restrictions were put on rushing and, although uncommon, serious injury or even death were not unheard of. Basically, a group of immature, superficial and sometimes sadistic individuals were put in a position to torture you unmercifully, ostensibly to see what you were made of, with impunity from retribution.

I was taken, blindfolded, in a car for a one-hour ride up to the North Country and told to get out of the car. I stood, shivering in snow that was almost knee deep and was told to run at full speed with the blindfold still on. The fear level was incredible and, then, when I hit a patch of unleveled land, I would jolt my joints and sometimes tumble into the snow, only to be told to get up again and keep running. Finally, at full speed, one idiot had me run into a parked car and I smacked my kneecap. That was enough! I ripped off my blindfold and went after the asshole that gave me that order. I knew his voice, (he had been taunting me unmercifully since rush began,) and seeing how enraged I was, he started to run. I caught him quickly and drove him into the snow, burying his head face down. He squirmed and screeched with muffled sounds, but I held him there until three other brothers pulled me off him. He got up, gasping for breath and, seeing me held by three other fraternity members, bellowed with newfound confi-dence."Fuck him! He violated the rules by attacking a brother. Throw him out."

Seeing that my arms were held by his cohorts, he mustered up the courage to pick up a wad of snow and rub it in my face. With a super human effort, I broke loose and punched him flush in the face. He went down on his back and I knelt on his chest with my knee, fist raised high and ready to strike. "You ever lay a hand on me again," I strained through gritted teeth, "I'll cut your fucking balls off if you have any."

Surprisingly, the other brothers reacted slowly this time. They walked up and nudged instead of grabbed at my arms. "Come on big shot," one of them said. "We'll see what you're really made of." Surprisingly, they had some sense of rudimentary justice. They realized that the asshole had crossed the line and deserved what he got and, although they continued to hassle me, it was clear that they were going to give me another chance. They walked me back to the car, pushed me in the back seat, drove me back to town, and, after making sure that I had no money, dumped me at the railroad station and told me to wait until they came and got me. Twenty hours later they showed up, expecting that I hadn't eaten or slept in that period of time. In actuality, I was able to explain my story to a couple of sympathetic listeners, who, with hesitation and doubt, loaned me a couple of dollars, which allowed me to buy a sandwich and a coke. They took me back to the fraternity house, where they put me and the rest of the pledges through rigorous exercise. That done, they stood us up in a dark room and made us hold coke bottles up for what seemed like hours and, each time that our arms would drop, someone would slap our hand and tell us to get them up.

All the while, they kept telling us that we were going to get ready for a special banquet dinner to celebrate the beginning of our induction into the fraternity. After being awake for two days without sleep, they told us to shave and shower, because now was the time. With renewed energy, we jumped in the showers and put on our Sunday best, that we had been ordered to bring with us, and they took us out to Keller's, one of the fanciest restaurants in town. We filed into the banquet room, filled with four long rectangular tables. The brothers sat on one side of each table and the pledges on the other. We were all starved and salivating with great anticipation. "Wait until you taste their appetizers," offered one of the brothers.

"Man," said another. "This place always makes my mouth water."

After an agonizing hour of preliminary speeches, they brought out the first course. I waited impatiently as they served the brothers their shrimp cocktail on the other side of the table. After fifteen minutes, they began to clear the plates and we still hadn't been served. Nobody acted as if anything was wrong. Most of us were confused and dazed from our lack of sleep. Another two speeches later, they brought out the salad and only served the other side of the table. It slowly dawned on me that we were going to watch the brothers slowly consume a delectable meal, while we watched in abject agony. The night grew painfully long as we watched the brothers consume course after delicious course, interrupted each time by a long, boring and seemingly endless speech. After the brothers ate a sumptuous dessert of bananas foster and cherry's jubilee, we filed out of the restaurant into the cold, miserable night.

One of the nerdy pledges with me was ordered to strip naked and get in the car. They knew really well who they could intimidate and who might stand up defiantly, and, with this prank, they didn't really want to take a chance. Gordon, the nerd, acceded to their demand with only token objection and sat there, naked, embarrassed and shivering as the car pulled up on St. Catherine St., Montreal's biggest downtown thoroughfare. Across the street was another car filled with fraternity brothers, and Gordon was ordered to get out and run across the street to the other car. He hesitated for a second until one of the brothers barked. "If you want to get into this fraternity, get the hell out of the car. You only have to run thirty feet. Now get the hell out!"

Gordon opened up the door, looked both ways, jumped into the street, and ran quickly across, covering his ass with one hand and his balls with the other. Just as he was about to reach the other car, it pulled away. Gordon, shocked and surprised, turned around and started to run back toward our car as people on the street stopped to watch, pointing at Gordon to inform the others around them what was going on. Just as Gordon reached our door, our driver pulled away, leaving him stranded and naked in the street. We circled the block and came back to get him, everybody in the car still bellowing with uncontrollable laughter. Gordon was no where to be seen. After searching for twenty minutes, we returned to the fraternity house, with the brothers still commenting and laughing about the look on his face. The fraternity house was only three blocks away, and we assumed that Gordon had taken off like a jackrabbit and made his way back. Our assumption was correct. We found him shivering, wrapped in blankets, in a corner of the main salon, with a look of shame and disbelief on his face.

With all of us somewhat dazed and numb from lack of nutrition and sleep, they took us into a room six at a time. They went through some rigmarole that I didn't fully understand. Our group leader said something and then the president yelled out and said. "Oh no! You did it. Now, none of these six can become brothers." I didn't really understand what happened, but I really didn't care that much any more. But one of the pledges, Billy, was the brother of the vice president, the next president to be, who screamed out in protest.

"What are you talking about! We just don't have to say anything!"

Over the months that we pledged, we had seen tremendous friction between the president and the president to be, so this confrontation seemed so natural. It was all part of the set up, though, that these perverted assholes had planned. Instead of spending those precious hours studying or doing something constructive, they spent their time figuring out how to make pledge week end as agonizingly and painfully as possible. The president came forward and loudly confronted the president to be. "What are you crazy?" he yelled. "What would happen if National found out! Are you willing to sacrifice our charter just so your little brother can get in.?" The president was now just inches from the vice president's face as he waited for a reply.

Standing toe to toe, the "president to be" didn't give an inch. "You don't have to put on a show for these people. If nobody says anything, they're in and nobody knows the difference."

Billy, the pledge, was devastated, and you could see the tears in his eyes. All he ever wanted was to be accepted in his father's and older brother's fraternity, and now, through no fault of his own, he was going to be permanently disenfranchised.

Whatever happened next was a blur. The president to be pushed the president and a fight ensued. You could hear the sounds and the moans, but you couldn't see, since the brothers had quickly encircled the two battlers. After a while, all was quiet and a lane opened for us to see what happened. The president to be was laying there on the floor, motionless with blood pooling at his head. "It wasn't my fault," the president pleaded. "He attacked me first."

Billy screamed out in uncontrollable anger and flew at the president. Three brothers intervened and held him as the lights went on and the president to be got up off the floor, all the brothers smiling and back-slapping the pledges, congratulating them that they were now members of the fraternity. At first confused, it now dawned on me that this was a superbly acted out ruse. Billy, more confused than I, finally came around. Realizing that it was over, we all finally reveled in the moment. All that is except Gordon. He still had that look of shame and disbelief on his face.

After this experience, all else that had to do with the fraternity was anticlimactic. I lost my enthusiasm for a brotherhood of individuals that lived to vegetate. Their primary interests were parties, pussies, and perversions. Nobody was really interested in world events, charitable endeavors or knowledge. They were constantly occupied with the mundane and preoccupied with joyfully planning the misery and discomfort of others. I really didn't want any part of that and, in the second year, I quit, before I could be asked to participate in the dehumanizing event of pledge weekend.

Despite the depressing climate, my years at McGill were rewarding. Here, I grew into young adulthood. As mentioned before, I learned to take care of the responsibilities of running a household, albeit a small one. I could deal with the bank, the phone, the rent, the utilities, the car, the food and the laundry. I could make travel arrangements, buy cloths, take care of school responsibilities and budget my allowance. I learned to drive under the worst possible conditions. All these skills allowed me to move with ease wherever the Gods would take me. In the process of working out life's problems, these things, at least, were not obstacles.

Living in Canada, under a different government, among different ethnic cultures, allowed me to open up my mind earlier than most. Almost all of us are brainwashed to some degree. Early in our lives, most of us are bombarded with some type of religious belief, so that without objective reasoning, we feel, at a gut level, that our religious tenets are the right ones. Furthermore, we are propagandized with our version of history. As I emerged from my teenage years, I was still being brainwashed with American self-richeousness. I saw us as a nation of benefactors. We had the right system and we were destined to teach the world the right lessons.

When I went to Canada, my senses were rudely awakened. They accused us of being imperialists, enamored with power and the pursuit of our own interests. I observed the conflict between the French and the English in Quebec, and saw that there were reasonable concerns on each side. I sat at cafés and bars with students from almost every country in the world, listening to their slants on what was happening. After years of exposure to bright and reflective people from other lands, I began to realize that people are all the same all over the world. They need their own space and they have their own value system. They just want to feel safe and secure within that place. Challenge that, and you incur fear and anger. If they are weak, they withdraw with resentment and if they are strong, they fight back. The only cure for peaceful assimilation into a common value system is to communicate well and often and to move ever so slowly, so as to assuage fears. Naturally, the standard of living must be stabile and improve over time for the process to be effective.

While I found that I flourished in the midst of intellectuals and artists from all walks of life, I suffered greatly and was often ostracized by the mass mediocrity. Whenever I challenged their fixed beliefs, they responded with disdain or anger, rather than inquisitiveness. It took me a long time to understand, but to be accepted in this vast group of vegetative Americans, I had to learn their jargon and limit my comments only to what they felt was important. Needless to say, my comments had to be in keeping with their own provincial viewpoint on things. So today, when I mistakenly ask an average buddy of mine how he feel about Boznia-Hertogovenia, and he asks me. "What's his handicap," I usually reply with a number and let it go.

In summary, my college years were wonderful, filled with exploration and independence. Here, I continued to open my horizens. Here, I began to emerge, intellectualy, into a man of the world.

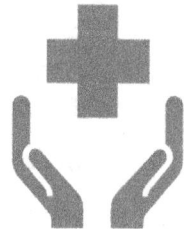

RESIDENCY-CITY
MEDICAL CENTER

The Yankees used to train in St. Petersburg Florida and the area held an aura of romanticism for me. As a boy, I would listen to all the spring training games and imagine Mickey Mantle gallivanting in the sunlight as I froze my ass off in the piercing, wintry wet cold of Atlantic Beach, N.Y.

Despite the fact that the Mets trained there in nineteen seventy, the area had a magnetic charm for me and I applied for a residency in the community hospital. Much to my delight, I was accepted and after completing my internship at the end ofDecember, we packed our bags and moved south with excited anticipation. As Christina and I crossed Tampa Bay over the Howard Franklin Bridge, I was awestruck by the beauty and expanse of the water. I couldn't help but verbalize my enthusiasm. "This is it baby! Our little piece of paradise."

In short order we found a house to rent, on a canal that opened to the bay, for two hundred and twenty five dollars a month. In the New York City area I couldn't get an outhouse for that, but given the fact that my take home pay was about one hundred dollars a week, the rent seemed pretty steep.

I was filled with pride that, at twenty-eight, I would at long last be able to support my family. My mother had a fixed income from her father's inheritance and spent more that a fair portion on her children's education. Now it was time to take a load off her shoulders and carry the responsibility myself.

Since most legitimate programs start in July, I agreed to work on the OBGYN service and the Emergency Room for the next five and a half months, without getting credit toward my residency. I felt that the extra time would serve to help me prepare for the rigors ahead. Meanwhile, the first opportunity I had, I excitedly ran out to the Payson complex to see the Mets in training. Back then, there were no fences separating the practicing players and the public, and I was able to walk out on the sideline and see things, close up. Much to my happy surprise, two of my favorite childhood heroes stood in foul territory down the right field line. I approached them hesitatingly, hoping to get a closer glimpse and maybe exchange a few words, praying that I wouldn't be summarily rejected. Without naming names, the ugly, short, stocky one let out an enormous fart and turned to the godly one and said. "Beat that you fucker" The great one worked up tension in his abdominal muscles and blew one out of his ass that made the first one seem like a polite call for attention. They continued the contest with more farting, belching, spitting and vulgarity After five minutes of watching this melodrama, I turned around and left, my bubble burst, never to return. Somehow, it became clear to me then that these were just two sorry uneducated slobs that happened to have the talent to hit a baseball hard and far but had no business being sanctified. They didn't belong on a pedestal and it would be the last time that I would ever believe that the perception of the public persona had anything to do with the real person.

My first months at the hospital, prior to the start of my true residency were tumultuous at best and I was glad that I had them. I still had lots to learn before I took on the responsibilities of a first year resident. Thank god I did, because the experience that I added to my fragile fabric of usable medical knowledge was barely enough to let me keep from drowning in the vast responsibilities heaped on my shoulders when the year began in July.

The reasons for the pressured, dangerous and exhausting routine were, in the beginning, a mystery to me. I couldn't see why we couldn't be taught in a patient and organized way, in safe harbors, so that we could learn more calmly, more efficiently, and more safely how to care for patients. I never understood why we had to be on call from Friday morning until Monday afternoon every second or third weekend, often getting only ten or twelve hours of interrupted sleep over the full four days. I never understood why we had to find things out the hard way and why we often had to do things we never saw. It took a couple of years of being part of the system before I began to fully understand why things were done as they were.

For one, I thought that the primary purpose of residency was to train and prepare new physicians for their chosen specialties. Although that was a byproduct of residency, it was no longer the primary function, especially in community hospitals.

Teaching hospitals often had a harmony of purpose. The government often financed the beds of indigent patients. Furthermore, full time hospital based physicians were paid to stay there and teach and a good educational program often acted as a magnet for private physicians trying to keep up their level of knowledge. Private physicians meant revenue to the hospital from admission of their patients let alone utilization of outside laboratory and radiology services often owned by the hospital.

To the contrary, in most community hospitals, the purpose of a residency program was not necessarily to provide a place for the indigent and a teaching program for the interns and residents. Instead, its primary purpose was to provide a buffer between the private physicians and the non-paying (service or indigent) patient, so that they could attract more private physicians.

Most city hospitals felt that they had an obligation to care for some of the indigent patients. This was often a condition of their lease with the city or their tax-free status. In order to provide this service, they had to demand that their private physicians provided coverage for these patients on a rotating basis. This discouraged many physicians from joining the staff of a number of hospitals that depended on the physician to bring patient flow and therefore revenue to their hospital.

By providing residents, the hospital could provide a staff of physicians in training to cover the bulk of the indigent care in exchange for a few hours of instruction from the private physicians. Some took their role seriously, but most only performed the task in a perfunctory manner because there was no compensation and it distracted them from their revenue producing practices.

In order to secure residency staff, many community hospitals had a recruiting committee. Volunteer physicians would visit potential interns and residents and give them their pitch. The trick was for each hospital to paint as rosy a picture as they could in order to entice young physicians to join their training programs. Naturally, in the face of competition with the teaching hospitals for interns and residents, most community programs ran chronically short of enough interns and residents to fill their needs.

It was very difficult to switch programs in midstream without losing significant credit and without raising suspicion as to your own dedication to the training program. Despite the skeleton crews, the workload still needed to get done. Therefore, once there, a resident could be exploited to the fullest with a minimum of teaching. This set the stage for overwork, sleep deprivations and selective instruction in an abusive situation. Because the resident was starved for knowledge that he could only receive efficiently from another well trained doctor, especially in the surgical specialties, he was willing to suffer most indignities in exchange for information. When an attending yelled, the physician in training cowed. When an attending mercilessly insulted you, you took it. When an attending said, "jump," you said, "how high."

It was difficult to change programs and if one complained too much, he would not get the recommendations necessary to be accepted into another accredited program. They had you by the balls in a catch twenty-two and they knew it. This attitude filtered right down to the residency staff, so that the low man on the totem pole took the most abuse. It was almost like a four year hazing program in order to get into a fraternity.

On the other hand, the private physicians could resign from the staff, and bring his revenue elsewhere, if they felt that they were overburdened with teaching responsibilities. Therefore, they were allowed great latitude in the interpretation of their service responsibilities. Unfair treatment and over utilization of the residency staff by self-focused private physicians was commonly ignored by the department of medical education. It is a testimony to the great character of some physicians that, in spite of the decadent pragmatics of the system, teaching and training did go on at a level which prepared most residents to competently practice their medical specialties when they graduated from the community programs. But the training was not without its scars.

With this structure in place, I entered my final three years of residency training. The resident above me treated me brutally. No matter what I did, it wasn't enough. In the OR any hesitation on my part was treated with insults.

"If you don't speed it up, the fibroblasts will grow across the wound before you have time to sew it up," was a typical sarcastic remark. Every time I wasn't sure what to do, he would shake his head in disgust and make a big show of it in front of the nurses.

One time, at surgery, he asked me to feel in a certain place and then asked me if that was a tumor. When I responded, "I think that it needs to be biopsied," he had a big laugh at my expense with the operating room personnel.

"It's the tip of the catheter you dope! Even the orderly knows that." I didn't realize that this was the kind of joke they played on everybody who was new to the program. It was a form of hazing.

One time, when I was a second year resident and already attuned to the cruel jokes, I watched as this now chief resident abused the new first year resident. At the start of the operation, he halted the case and told the new resident to put his hands at his side. After he reluctantly did so, the chief resident continued to operate in awkward silence for the next ten minutes. Then, looking up and waiting for the full attention of the rest of the operating room's staff, he turned to the first year resident and said. "See how much better I'm doing since you stopped helping the doctor." The laughter was raucous and in unison. Needless to say, the resident was thoroughly humiliated, and the chief resident reveled in the moment.

In my case, I could have taken the hazing, even though I thought that I was being singled out, if the resident above me was at all inclined to teach or help. Instead, he used me like a slave, making sure that I did all the work that I possibly could while he saved up his energy for moonlighting; that is working for pay outside of the residency program. If there were eight deliveries, I would do all eight and he would scream at me if I didn't rush to finish one so that I could get to the next. He never gave me a chance to digest what I had done or at least finish the paperwork in an orderly manner, so that I didn't forget to order an important test or medication. It got so intolerable that I did something that I had never done in my life. I threatened to go to the head of the department with my complaints if the abuse didn't stop. The resident above me responded curtly. "Do what you want," he said with disgust and walked away.

I went directly to the head of the department of OBGYN and lodged my complaint. While sitting in a lounge chair, I poured out my heart and sole. Standing above me, he listened patiently for half an hour. When I was finished, he turned, looked down at me and said. "Shit runs downhill and you are at the bottom of the pile!" Then, he turned on his heel and walked swiftly out of the room, leaving me to chew on that bit of wisdom. I felt thoroughly defeated, knowing that I had no practical recourse but to do as I was told. The chief resident never asked me what he said. He understood the system all too well. We had only three residents, two-second year and me in the first year. He was ahead of the other second year resident, and therefore crowned as the chief. He knew that the attending physicians needed him as a buffer since he was the only one with Caesarian section privileges and minor surgery privileges. Without him, the private physician on call would have to help us on everything and this could lead to a run on private physicians resigning from the staff. The department head could not permit that. Therefore, he had no other choice but to ignore my complaints and I was now relegated to a term of servitude from which there was no escape. I resigned myself to the injustice, gutted it up, and decided to do whatever it took to graduate from the program.

In contrast with my internship program, where there were no indigent patients, our OBGYN service was overrun with service patients. I learned as I went. In my first year, I did eight hundred deliveries, saw about twenty-five patients a day on rounds, and assisted on at least four hundred major surgeries. I also saw at least one hundred patients a week in clinic and checked at least twenty patients in the ER. I learned through observation, trial and error and osmosis. I survived misinformation and disinformation, often unintentionally offered by an attending physician not quite up on his academics. From a practical point of view, the over work and sleep deprivation were a blessing in disguise. I learned and learned and learned. I repeated things again and again until they became second nature and I learned to grit my teeth and function under the most adverse conditions. One night, I assisted on seven caesarian sections, delivered five babies and assisted on surgery for an ectopic pregnancy, only to be expected to make my rounds the next day, assist in two major surgeries, deliver a couple more babies and see twenty five patients in clinic before I could go home, utterly exausted and unsure as to whether or not I would make it to the bed.

Sometimes, our service caesarian section rate was one to two percent and we were proud of it. It took me till my second year and conversations with residents in other programs to realize that this was practice at its pragmatic worst.

In our program, the presence of a physician with surgical privileges was required in order to perform major surgery. On the other hand, an inexperienced intern could do a forceps delivery on his own. Therefore, it didn't take a genius to figure out that our attendings were going to do everything that they could think of to guarantee a vaginal delivery, albeit a difficult forceps, in order to avoid having to come in to the hospital in the middle of the night to help with a caesarian section. If the resident messed up the forceps delivery, the blame fell on him. Classically, the response from an attending physician, when called about a patient with arrested progress in labor, would be. "Did you pit her?" What the attending wanted to know was whether or not I gave the patient pitocin, a medication that stimulated her contractions. For the most part, in the case of suspected arrest of progress in dilatation and descent from either inadequate contractions or pelvic dystocia (inadequate size of the pelvis with regard to the size of the baby,) you were ordered to bombard the patient with pitocin so that they got strong prolonged contractions. If progress was rapid and the baby delivered quickly, the problem was solved, although the baby might have undergone some ischemic episodes (lack of oxygen) resulting in a lowered IQ or learning disabilities.

But if progress was slow, in the face of repetitive intense and prolonged contractions, you definitely subjected the fetus to ischemic episodes let alone the trauma from a forceps delivery. Also, forceps deliveries sometimes required very special skills that needed to be nurtured and taught and, from time to time, residents were out of their league trying to deal with them. Suffice it to say, national section rates ranged between eight percent and twenty percent depending on the recipe of the day, but never anywhere were they between one and two percent, as we experienced in my residency program, to the detriment of the mothers and their offspring.

A second negative result of the emphasis on the convenience of the attending physician ranking higher than the quality of care offered service patients was that the residents were purposely taught the wrong information. In my first year of residency, I spent about eighty to ninety percent of my time on the obstetrical service. When I took the in service CREOG exam for residents, I scored extremely well overall, but I scored very poorly on the section on obstetrical care since I had been taught a lot of wrong information. Fortunately, in time, through attending numerous conferences over the years of training, I was able to separate the wheat from the chafe and learn the information that was in the patient's best interest and discard that which was contaminated by attending physician self-interest.

Ironically, the often unguided experience with manual obstetrical skills, such as the application of difficult forceps, offered me the tools that allowed me to provide my patients with the best possible obstetrical care. Academics you can get from a book, but manual skills are like diamonds, rare and beautiful. Sometimes, manual skills come with a great price; sometimes the compromised care of one patient results in the physician learning manual parameters that allow him to better treat the next. Such is often the case in the less guided and regulated residency programs.

My first weekend on call with the lame duck chief resident helped set the tone for the attitude that I would direct toward the need for sleep over the rest of my career. I followed him around like a little lamb. We were on call on Friday and Saturday nights and he had invited my family to go to the beach with him on Sunday. After two nights, in which I had a total of five hours sleep, I turned to him at six AM on Sunday morning and tried to beg out of the trip to the beach by telling him how tired I was. He wouldn't here ofit. "Listen," he said intently.

"Don't ever tell another doctor that you are tired." He paused to let that sink in. "Every doctor is tired. When they complain about him playing golf on Wednesday afternoon, it's probably because he was up all night Tuesday. If you use tired as an excuse, you will never do anything."

"And what do I tell my body," I asked exasperatedly.

"You don't tell it anything. You just do the things you would normally do and you ignore the fact that you are tired. Just eliminate the word from your vocabulary and the idea from your head. It is not allowed, period."

Better advice was never given. I refused, for the twenty years that I practiced medicine, to allow fatigue to interfere with what I was doing. I was able, albeit with pain and difficulty in the beginning, to enjoy a full and variable life experience, and get the most out of my only too few free moments. Somehow, in denial, I was able to talk myself into feeling pretty good most of the time in the face of sleep depravation. This reflected well on parts of my home life in which I was able to spend quality time with my children and revel in the effect that I had on their development.

The first year whipped past like a whirlwind and, before I knew it, I applied for and was granted both minor surgical and caesarian section privileges. Now, finally, I was in the OR ready to do a section on a case of fetal distress, in charge, the kingpin. Despite the fact that I was surrounded by six or seven people, I was feeling very lonely and suddenly unsure of my skills. I waited impatiently for the anesthesiologist to give me the go ahead, each second feeling like an hour. Finally, the nod came and I made my incision, fully aware that I had a fine tremor that I struggled to keep under control. I reached the abdominal cavity, pulled down the bladder flap and began tentatively to make my incision into the uterus. I was afraid of cutting too quickly and nicking the baby's head. Instead, I cut so slowly that it seemed as if I would never get there. Finally, in what seemed forever, the amniotic sac began to bulge. I nicked it, got my fingers inside and then, as I was taught, made the incision larger by pulling my index fingers in opposite directions. I reached in with my left hand, but had trouble getting my palm under the baby's head. No matter what I did, I couldn't seem to get the right leverage needed to get the baby's head outside of the incision. I started to panic as I moved my hand frantically inside of the uterus to try and work the head free. It seemed like I was running out of time and I wished that the floor would open and that I could disappear. "I was too young to be doing this," I thought.

But there was no magic. I looked around the room and realized that it was me and me alone who had to do this. I forced myself to focus and grab control of what I was doing and I decided to take a few seconds to extend the incision with my fingers. After doing this, I methodically placed my hand into the uterine cavity again, just as I was taught, and lifted the head upward with gently accelerating pressure. All of a sudden the head sprung free. I quickly sucked out the mucous and then pulled the baby the rest of the way out of the incision. I clamped the cord, cut it and gave the baby to the pediatrician. Blood was pouring everywhere. I removed the placenta and had the assistant hold the uterus under tension as I started to sew. It seemed like an eternity till I heard the baby cry in the background and, with that relief, I painstakingly continued to sew, knowing that the bleeding would ebb just a little more with each added stitch. Finally the uterine incision was closed and I slowly completed the remaining tedious steps in the operation. I degowned and walked back to the nurse's station to dictate my operative note and write my orders. I felt numb as I got up and walked back to the doctor's lounge to change clothes. My scrub shirt was covered with sweat and I could smell me a mile away. I slowly took off my clothes and walked into the shower, letting the warm pellets of hot water wash away the stench and gently relax my tense muscles.

A smile came on to my face, as I began to reflect on what I had just done. My first operation on my own, and I got through it. I had the strength of character to face adversity and deal with it. I didn't choke or get paralyzed. I approached my problem, in the face of tremendous tension, in a logical sequence and came out with a good result. I was finally a doctor, doing a man's job. As the water rushed down, bringing feeling back into my face, I would hold on to and cherish this moment for the rest of my life. I was on top of the world and nobody could get me off.

The third resident on our three-man service was a Cuban exile named Raul Santana. He was in his mid fifties, and although he had been a general surgeon in Cuba, he was forced to repeat his internship and residency in this country in order to get licensed. He chose to do Obstetrics and Gynecology and found a place in our program. He did his very best to keep up, but he was aging and was used to a slower pace of practice in Cuba. He treated patients wonderfully but could only see seven or eight in an afternoon, while I learned to see thirty and the other second year resident who was the chief resident by default (we had no third year resident,) saw fifty. I felt rushed and under pressure all the time, but understood the need to get the job done. The chief resident often whipped through his, often not even saying two words to the patients he was seeing. Occasionally, he would go into a room, listen to the complaints, examine the patient, write prescriptions, hand them to the nurse, and leave the room without a word.

Poor Raul couldn't keep up and he was constantly harassed by the chief resident and the attending staff. They would often make fun of his difficulty in pronouncing the language, not ever realizing that he was at least able to speak some English, while none of them knew a word of Spanish or any other language for that matter. Provincialism can be a nasty thing and, in our hospital, it flourished.

Toward the end of my second year, Dr. Santana was sued for malpractice by a local attorney, Paul France. The complaint was that he had delivered a patient who had to have gall bladder surgery six weeks after delivery, because, when she had her tubes tied at delivery, the plaintiff thought that something should have been done to prevent the gall bladder attack. The accusation was absurd, but it didn't matter. When you are sued, you are sued and you are in the soup, justified or not.

Santana was dumbfounded and frightened. He didn't understand the process and felt personally threatened. I argued the logic of the complaint to the plaintiff's attorney but it fell on deaf ears. I was named in the case because I had assisted Dr. Santana on the tubal liga- tion. When Dr. Santana moved back to Miami to start his practice, he was forced to make the five-hour drive up to St. Petersburg every time we had a conference. He was frightened to death and was afraid to fly in fear that the plane might be hijacked back to Cuba.

With this background, I was irate and frustrated. This poor man was being abused unfairly and I decided to do something about it. It was also my first exposure to malpractice and I took it personally. It was an affront to Santana's and my reputation and we had done nothing wrong.

I painstakingly went through the clinic charts of her visits and found that Santana had written a note regarding her complaint and had referred her to surgery clinic. I followed that up and found out that she had made an appointment at the surgery clinic. Further investigation showed that she never showed up and never rescheduled. Armed with this information and wondering what could have been done anyway to avoid an emergency gall bladder attack, my rage intensified toward this attorney. He was upsetting my life and Santana's life for no reason at all. If he had just done his homework, he could have avoided a great deal of agony for all of us, especially Dr. Santana who was making those long driving trips every few weeks. I hoped and prayed that the attorney would spend a lot of his own money on the case before he came to get my deposition.

Finally, two years later, that day came. We sat down in my office with a court reporter and I responded to his questions. Eventually, he asked me. "Don't you think Dr. Santana should have gotten a consult with a general surgeon when Mrs. Clayton registered her complaint."

I drew my response out, almost like stabbing him with a knife and then twisting it in slowly. "Absolutely." Twisting in my chair, I added.

"In fact, according to the records that I have copied from the obstetrical clinic, he did just that."

"How do you know that!" the lawyer cut in.

"I just read his notes," I offered, handing him the copy of the chart.

He scanned it hurriedly and added. "That doesn't mean anything. He never made the appointment for her to see the general surgeon."

I delivered the "coupe de grace." "I beg your pardon," I said, giving him the copy of the surgery clinic schedule with her name scheduled and then crossed off. "The appointment was made, but she was too irresponsible to keep it. She was a no show and she never bothered to make another appointment. Dr.Santana did all he could outside of taking her by the hand and leading her down the garden path. But he is only her doctor Mr. France, not her baby sitter." I leaned back in my seat, a big smirk on my face.

France looked up, annoyed. "Why didn't you bring this up before?Before we wasted all this time."

I leaned over relishing the moment. "Because Mr. France, it's your job to gather the facts before you waste my time or Dr. Santana's or for that matter, your own."

France got up in a huff, turned on his heal and stormed out of the office, never to hear from him on this case again. Santana was vindicated and France had lost some money by advancing expenses on a contingency case. I was elated. Later, I learned the hard way that you don't burn bridges, let alone brag about it. France would live to have another day.

In my second year of residency, I decided that I would moonlight in the emergency room of a small community hospital to kill two birds with one stone. For one, they were paying ten dollars and hour, more money than I had ever seen in my life and for two, I could learn how to handle emergencies and triage. Thank God that I had done a couple of months in the emergency room before my residency began or I would have been a walking time bomb. Still, there was a lot that I didn't know and would learn on the job.

The job of an emergency room physician is pretty straight forward, once you have it down. It is to treat emergency situations, to treat whatever else you are comfortable doing, to identify whether someone is sick enough for admission, and to refer the patients to the right specialists. This seems easy enough if every one else would cooperate, but, unfortunately, that is not the case. If someone came in with a head injury, you would get a series of skull x-rays. But if the radiologist wasn't in, you would have to read the series of x-rays yourself. When you called the neurosurgeon or neurologist for follow up, you were in for a battle. If the patient had no symptoms and no sign of fracture, they would want you to send the patient home. But if you weren't sure about the x-rays, they would demand that the radiologist come in to evaluate before they saw the patient. When you called the radiologist, he would tell you to just admit the patient for observation and that he would read the x-rays in the morning. When you called back the neurologist or neurosurgeon, he would say that there was no reason to admit the patient if there were no signs of a fracture and no symptoms, and you would go round and round. If you weren't sure of too many things in the various specialties, you would be chastised for making the specialists make too many unnecessary trips to the emergency room. But if you guessed at things that a more trained eye would be sure of, then you could be risking the patient's life. The specialists always pressured you to take the risk and sign the chart so that they didn't have to come in. Your job was to resist the specialist and insist that they come in to see the patient, if you were not comfortable going it alone. Of course each doctor had his or her own comfort level, and by admitting ignorance, you were setting yourself up for gossip.

With this background, I fumbled through my first couple of months in the emergency room. I called for help often and occasionally I was bullied into doing things for the first time that I never should have been doing. In this way, I learned how to put in a posterior nasal pack, sew back a tendon and put in a chest tube for a pneumothorax. So much for "seeing one, doing one and teaching one." Sometimes "doing one and teaching one" became the rule of the day.

I treated all emergencies, sometimes from a book and sometimes over the phone with a specialist giving me orders. But the day that I became a doctor, that is a real doctor, was the day they brought in over thirty patients from a train wreck.

I was the only doctor on call that night, anticipating the usual ten or fifteen patients on my shift and, if lucky, the nurse could stack some of them and give me three or four hours in a row of uninterrupted sleep. Just as I was ready to go to bed, all hell broke loose and they brought in streams of patients through the emergency room doors. One right after another, some moaning on stretchers, others unconscious, some staggering into the room in agony, and others with various complaints but in control. The staff was in chaos, not knowing what to do. They were all running around like chickens without heads. I looked up, startled and paralyzed for a moment, and then all of a sudden it hit me what to do. I got up on the desk and called for everyone's attention in a loud and authoritative voice. They all stopped, turned and listened and I gave my orders.

"I want an I.V. and Hemoglobin on everybody lying down."

That was simple enough. With one fell swoop, I separated all the potentially bad cases from the ones that could wait. A ruptured spleen needed rapid attention. A broken arm could wait. They still have a caricature of me, standing on that desk, issuing those orders, pinned to the wall of that emergency room. I saved a lot of lives that day. I put a chest tube in a patient with a spontaneous pneumothorax, preventing him from suffocating to death. I diagnosed a ruptured spleen, preventing her from bleeding to death. I treated a lady in shock, and discovered a patient with a broken pelvis and a ruptured bladder. I found a sub-dural haematoma in a patient that had been unconcious and got the neurosurgeon to come in and take care of him. I even found a fractured femur and treated the patient with packed cells and plasma expanders, preventing him from going into shock from the loss of blood surrounding the fracture site. I also stabilized a patient with atrial fibrillation that came off that train, another one with a heart attack who was brought in by ambulance and a kid with a severe asthma attack. When I was done with that, I wiped up the mess of cases that could wait; the broken arms, multiple bruises and contusions, and the cuts and scrapes. Everyone came out O.K. and I realized then and there that I could handle the preliminary stages of any emergency, stabilizing the patient and calling in the right specialist to follow through with his or her care. Now, all I had to do was learn all the follow up care in my own specialty and I would be home free, able to step out into the world with the confidence to take on any medical challenge. At least I was on my way.

Learning the specialty of OBGYN was a slow and painstaking process. In any give day or week, I would be overburdened by repetitive simple and boring tasks, only to occasionally fall upon something that

I hadn't seen before. If it was a patient requiring surgery, I could bring her to a special clinic staffed by one of our attendings who would confirm my findings and allow me to schedule her for surgery as long as I could find someone to help me who had surgical privileges. The entire process was a balancing act. Keeping the patient interested and getting approval was one thing; staffing the surgery was another. Fortunately there were two or three attendings that would agree to help as long as you scheduled with their office well in advance and found a hole in their busy schedules. Once the surgeon accepted, you had to make sure that there was operating room space available at that time. If not, you started from scratch. As an alternative, you could reverse the process, that is, set up a few operating times with a resistant O.R. staff, (hospital administration secretly gave them orders to limit resident surgery time for non paying cases,) and hope that there would be an attending physician available to help on the case. If not, you would then have to go back and cancel the times that you set up. If this happened too often, you got the OR unit coordinator mad.

All that done, you then had to, in your spare time, chase down a patient who didn't have a phone, who just moved, who didn't leave a forwarding address, and who probably really didn't care. You could tell them to call you at the hospital, but some how that never worked very well. Most of the time, they didn't call and, if they did, the hospital would page you, but if you were in surgery or in with another patient, nursing staff would often not pick it up.

If you were lucky enough to coordinate all of this, then you hung with baited breath to see if the patient actually showed up the night before to be admitted. If all the x-rays and lab tests were within normal parameters, the case was a go. If not, you needed to cancel the attending physician that was planning to assist you on the case. When you cancelled, you hoped that you did it early enough so that the attending physician wasn't inconvenienced by having to make an unnecessary trip to the hospital. Otherwise, there would be hell to pay, and you might not get him to help you next time.

You also needed to inform the O.R. staff that the case wasn't going to go off. You tried to do every thing to make it happen. Sometimes you were able to slip in another case that you couldn't get scheduled so that it would seem as if there was no gap at all. The down times for the O.R. were always treacherous. Administration would want to know why they are paying staff and nurse anesthesia to sit around doing nothing and they would exert more pressure on the head O.R. nurse to reduce available O.R. time for the residency staff. You spent a lot of time being a secretary and a salesman in order to get just one surgical experience. But somehow, over three years, I got to do and see enough surgery so that when the time came to go out on my own, I felt confident that my surgical skills would allow me to attack just about anything in my field.

The nights in residency were long and lonely. They were filled with disruptions, emergencies and deliveries. I was on call alone for the first two years, except in the few instances that we had a student doing an externship. Many times I made decisions that I shouldn't have been responsible to make. Miraculously, nothing catastrophic ever came of any of those decisions, but at the time I wasn't sure of what the result would be, and I had to balance good patient care against the wrath of the attending physician on call. If you called him too much, you would get bad evaluations. If you didn't call him when in doubt, the patient was subjected to bad treatment. In the early years, there wasn't a night that I didn't agonize over something I did and, instead of going back to bed, I would sit up and wait to see the evolution of findings that would support or contradict my actions. There wasn't a night that I did a difficult forceps delivery, a section or an emergency surgery that I didn't leave the O.R. drenched in nervous sweat.

The fears of doing damage were incessant and there was no relief; no shoulder to cry on. The gap between my wife and myself grew wider. She was not in the field and wouldn't have any idea what I was talking about, let alone any interest. You walk the plank alone and I certainly felt that I walked mine every time I was on call.

In the frenzy of treating an emergency or delivering a baby or doing emergency surgery, there are always a few players that take command; that make it happen. At the conclusion of one of these events, if there is time, those players often sit down and gloat in the accomplishment, giving each other rave reviews and understanding. Only when they have walked a mile in your shoes do they seem to understand the tension and agony. A sensitive ear is very attractive and if it happens to be on an attractive female, who can feel the isolation and fear that you have gone through, then the rest becomes history. There were many nights that ended in an empty room down the hall. Two people entangled in the throws of ecstasy, finding relief and momentary comfort in each other's arms. I had my share of these episodes. I don't try and justify them. That's for someone else to do. I only offer the facts so that you can feel the endless pressure and see how easy it was to succumb to the releases, however fleeting, however short.

During my second year of residency, my childhood friend, Donald Nitlack, came to visit me for a week. At the time, we were going house hunting, so Donald decided to accompany my wife on her various house hunting excursions, while I was working at the hospital. I was earning $7,000 a year as a resident and had just started to take home another two to three hundred dollars a week by moonlighting in emergency rooms and by doing insurance histories and physicals. I figured that I could afford about twenty five thousand dollars for a house, knowing that if we lost the right to moonlight, I could still make ends meet. In fact, the house that I was renting could be bought for eighteen thousand dollars and I was ready to do that and get it over with.

Donald and my wife had different plans. They came rushing home one day with a description of a house on open Tampa Bay that I would definitely have to see. And it was only ninety two thousand dollars.

It could have been a hundred and ninety two thousand dollars for all I cared. I couldn't afford it at ninety-two. Nevertheless, Donald persisted. "It's the chance of a lifetime. Do you know what this house would cost up in New York?" He didn't wait for an answer. He knew that I knew it. "$500,000. That's how much." Leaning over me, he let that sink in. "The taxes alone would be more than your mortgage payment down here."

Christina leaned over his shoulder, echoing every comment with a nod of the head. I couldn't argue with them. The house was a good deal, but I just couldn't afford it. Donald really didn't understand. He ran the financial planning program for a large brokerage house in New

York and was already making six figures. The pressure was too much, and I agreed to go see the house.

All they said was true. The house was like a dream, nestled back in abundant foliage, behind a circular driveway. There were four bedrooms and four baths. The view outside the sliding glass doors to the back was stupendous. First, the pool, then an expanse of lush deep St. Augustine grass, then the calm sweet cool of open Tampa Bay reaching all the way to the horizon.

The realtor was like a carnivore, ready to spring. He was originally from New York and he seemed like the kind of guy who could smell a deal. "I'm telling you Doctor. This is a once in a lifetime opportunity. Make them an offer. They are ready to move."

Gosh, was I tempted, but I just didn't have the money. "All right, forty five thousand."

Donald and the realtor were both startled. Donald threw up his arms in frustration and said "This is embarrassing. I'm getting back in the car. I don't want anybody to know that I know you." That said, he stomped off with Christina on his heals, shaking her head with disdain.

The realtor felt his moment, put his arm around my shoulder, and led me away from them, so that he could utter some words of wisdom in privacy. "Son," he said using the full power of his age and experience. "You have a wonderful reputation as a young and up and coming doctor in this community. But it's obvious that you don't know the first damn thing about real estate." With disdain, he added. "Make them a legitimate offer."

Every emotion that I had ever felt, with regard to inadequacy, rose to the surface. I was totally demeaned and embarrassed. But, my pride still had a spark of life left. Besides, I was stubborn and it certainly didn't hurt to be poor. "All right, forty five five."

The realtor went bezerk. "What, are you crazy. I can't bring them that offer!"

I waited for him to calm down, looked directly in his eye and said in a steely, steady voice. "By law, you have to take them that offer. Let me know what their response is." With that done, I turned on my heals and headed back to the car, where I was hit by another barrage of comments.

On the way home, I remained silent, listening to the criticism and disdain. $80,000 would have been a good deal, but I just didn't have the money.

All week long, Donald harassed me with my wife in total support. I couldn't get them to understand that I couldn't yet afford this kind of place.

To make a long story short, I stuck to my guns and, within two weeks, bought the place for fifty one five. My mother gave me ten thousand as a down payment and the seller took back a first mortgage for $40,000 at seven percent. My payments were two hundred and eighty three dollars a month and although we had no money left and no furniture, we had a beautiful place to live.

Knowledge, brilliance and negotiating skills are great to have, but in the art of the purchase, poverty remains supreme. You just can't get water from a rock.

Certain events stand out in residency. Some are serious, some humorous and some are just plain sad. Each though is unique in it's own way and I will relate some of them to you.

One such event surrounded my diagnosis of a probable ectopic pregnancy in a service patient. I brought the news out to her boyfriend who was pacing nervously in the emergency waiting room. I told him that we were going to have to operate on her and he responded with surprise.

"You mean, put a scar on her belly?"

"Yes,' I responded in my most somber tone.

He looked at me menacingly. "You put a scar on her belly, and I'll kill you."

I responded emphatically." If I don't operate, she'll die."

He never missed a beat. "If she dies, I'll kill you."

I turned, walked away, and found a private alcove in the back of the emergency room where I had time to ponder that dilemma and come up with a solution. Finally, a light bulb lit up above my head as the solution hit me. It would cost me a surgical case but it was worth it.

I returned to the waiting room and again addressed the boyfriend directly, if somewhat demurely. "I want to tell you Mr. Err…."

"Warren."

"Before we do anything, I want you to know that I'm just a resident and I think that this kind of case requires a real expert."

He threw his cigarette butt on the floor and squashed out the ash with his foot. "What are you saying?"

"I'm saying that I think that you need a better surgeon and I'm going to refer you off to one over at St. Judes hospital."

"Can it wait?"

"Absolutely," I said with conviction.

"You need a private doctor and I'll refer you to Dr. Merrit over there. He's the expert."

On the way out the door, while getting into the ambulance, he thanked me profusely. Dr. Merrit was gonna be in for a big surprise but he could handle it. He weighed two hundred and seventy five pounds and in his heyday, played 1st string tackle for a big ten school. Warren would meet his match.

The next day, Merrit backed me into a corner in the OB lounge and asked me for an explanation. He was a good guy and he took it good-naturedly. I asked him what happened and he said that he had the same confrontation with Warren.

"How did you handle it?" I queried.

He looked around the room to see that no one was listening and said. "I grabbed the little son of a bitch by the throat and lifted him up off the floor and told him that, ifhe ever threatened me again, I would drive him through the floor like a nail. I had all I could do to keep him from fainting."

I marveled at his eloquence. Two hundred and seventy five pounds says a lot.

The next episode turned out to be a living nightmare for me. I walked in to an exam room at the "New OB" clinic and met Linda Mousey for the first time. She had come in from North Carolina in her ninth month of pregnancy and was obviously near term. After examining her, I decided that the best course of action was to let her go into labor at her natural time, since I couldn't be sure ofher due dates and we were still in the pre ultra sound era. She asked ifI could tell this to her husband and I had the nurse beckon him from the waiting room. In walked Paul Bunyon personified! He was a massive man, his well-muscled physique accentuated by the denim vest and chains he wore on his shirtless torso.

"Hi," I greeted him, indicating a chair right next to the exam table. "My name is Dr. Robbins and I am one of the doctors that is going to take care of your wife until she delivers.

He didn't waste any time. "What do you mean, till she delivers? She's here now to have the baby."

"What did you say your name was?" I asked.

"I didn't say. It's Mike, Mike Mousey. My friends all call me Mickey."

I had all I could do to keep from bursting into hysterics especially since I picked up a muffled snicker from the nurse assisting me. I avoided her gaze and continued. "Well, Mike," I started but he interrupted.

"Something funny?"

"No, no," I answered.

"Good. I said my friends call me Mickey."

"Okay Mickey," I mumbled with a hand over my mouth so he couldn't see me fighting an uncontrollable smile. "This is the first time that I have seen your wife and there is no way that I can be sure as to her due date. Therefore, the safest thing to do is to wait for natural labor to begin since I don't want to make the mistake of delivering her prematurely."

"I don't know nothing about your big words and all, but I do know that our doctor back home said she's to have the baby today and I expect to have it today."

It was like talking to the wall. "I understand your impatience, but I just can't make magic happen at the risk of your wife and baby. I can't confirm her due date."

"I just told you that Dr. Walker back home said that he would give us the baby today if we was still home."

"Mickey, I can't speak for your doctor, but here, we don't do elective inductions."

"What," he interrupted.

"Elective inductions, errrr, deliveries of convenience. They are just to risky."

"Well when do you want to do this? Maybe tomorrow?"

"Mickey, I don't know. When the baby is ready, it will come." He looked up at me and scratched his head.

"Seems to me that you don't know as much as my doctor back home." "What do you mean?" I asked, somewhat peeved and frustrated.

"It's pretty obvious to me. Dr. Walker's smart enough to know when she's supposed to have the baby and you ain't got no idea."

"Mickey," I pleaded one more time, trying as hard as I could not to knock Dr. Walker. "Your doctor had the advantage of seeing Linda over an entire pregnancy. I've only had this one visit and it wouldn't be prudent for me to guess."

Mickey stood up, getting ready to leave. "Well, I don't know, but there's no sense beating a dead horse. You gonna do what you gonna do. But, if anything happens to Linda, I'm holding you responsible."

Shaking my head in concession, I shook his hand and said. "Don't worry, we will all do our very best."

He stopped and looked me straight in the eye, still holding my hand in a vice like grip. "I told you doc, not all of ya! You're her doctor, Something happens to my Linda and I am holding you responsible." He continued to look into my eyes, for what seemed like an eternity, and then, as quickly as he appeared, he dropped my hand, indicated for Linda to precede him, turned around and left the room behind her.

With the door closed, my assistant burst into hysterics. I looked at her and said. "Can you believe it; Mickey! Mickey Mousey! God! What next?"

She shook her head and between giggles mumbled. "Mickey, Mickey Mousey! Mickey, Mickey Mousey! God, I can't stop laughing.

Two weeks went by and, in the throes of chaos, constant activity, constant decision making, and shared patient responsibility, I forgot about Mrs. Mousey.

One night, I get a call from Dr. Krell, at five in the morning. Krell was one of my second year residents, dumped on me by the chief of the department. He was southern born and southern bred and his medical motto was. "If they're not allergic to steel, slide them under a knife." I had already spent half a year controlling his surgical ardor and I was not in the mood to listen to him politic for another case at five o'clock in the morning.

"Dodd?"

"Yeah, it's me," I mumbled in a barely audible voice.

"Are you sleeping?"

"Not now," I said with a hint of sarcasm. He ignored it.

"I got a little girl here who has been completely dilated for five hours. I need to cut this baby out of her."

"Five hours?" I asked, shocked to the core. The rule was that you never let anybody go over two hours after complete dilation of the cervix.

"What happened?" I added, now fully awake. Krell was as honest as he was insensitive.

"I fell asleep at eleven and the nurses never called me." "That's not good enough Krell," I said harshly. "It's your responsibility...."

"Yeah, yeah, I know, but that's water under the bridge. She needs a section right now, and I need you to give it the okay and come on in to help me."

"O.K. Krell. Get her ready and I'm on my way, but you got a lot of explaining to do."

The ride to the hospital took forever. Although the case was Krell's, I was responsible as the chief resident for everything that happened on my service. There was no excuse for letting her go for five hours and the results could be calamitous, from a ruptured uterus to a fetal demise. Fortunately, the heart rate was fine and we would have the baby out within minutes after I arrived. But, I was worried about a paper thin lower uterine segment that had been stretched and stretched with the added hours of labor. I knew that this could create severe vaginal lacerations and that the surgeon had to be extremely gentle with the tissues to hope to avoid rips that were difficult to repair. I toyed with the idea of punishing Krell by not letting him do the case. He should not have been rewarded with the opportunity to do a surgery in the face of negligent care. But I didn't want to face a major blow up at five thirty in the morning and I had been informed by the head of the department again and again that his technical skills were impeccable.

After arrival at the hospital, it took only minutes to get started. Krell was into the uterine cavity and had the baby out in a jiffy. Although there was a lot of blood, I insisted on checking for vaginal lacerations before I let him close the uterine incision, and sure enough there were two that I could identify on my side.

"You better let me change positions with you Krell so I can sew up those lacerations."

"No need to," he bullied. "I can do this."

"You ever do this before?"

"Easy as pie," he responded, while starting to sew.

He seemed so confident, so I let him continue.

"Make sure you can see what your doing, and you get only the mucosa. There's a ureter down there."

"Hey man, stop worrying and just give me a hand."

I don't know why I didn't stop him right there. He had momentum going and he seemed so cock sure of himself. His hands were steady and he sewed so smoothly. No wonder everyone thought that he was great.

When the case was done and the patient was off the table, all personnel, from scrub nurse to nurse anesthetist, commented on the great job that he had done. I left the OR just in time to hear him give the ward clerk at the nurse's station an oral order.

"Better get an IVP and barium enema in the morning."

I hurried down the hall and called after him. "BillyJoe, BillyJoe." He stopped and turned around to hear what I was saying. "What are those tests for."

He shrugged his shoulders and responded. "I don't know. Just making sure I didn't snag one." He turned to start to walk away but I stopped him in his tracks.

"Wait a minute! What do you mean you might have snagged one?" "God man, there was a lot of blood down there. Just a precaution." "I told you to let me do it if you couldn't see. You assured me that you could see. I told you that you could hook a ureter if you couldn't see."

"Listen man, I did the best I could. I couldn't take all day. We got rounds to make and surgical cases coming up."

"If you weren't sure, you should have told me Krell. We'll deal with this later." As an afterthought I added. "By the way Krell, what's her name."

"I don't know, err, Linda, Linda Massey."

My hair stood up on my head as the familiarlarity of the name rang home.

"Massey Krell? Massey or Mousey."

"That's it," he said, snapping his finger, as he turned to leave the room, voice trailing behind him. "Mousey, that's the one."

Sure enough, the IVP revealed a blocked ureter and Linda had to be scheduled with a urologist for surgery to open it up. Upon hearing the news, Mickey Mousey wanted answers. Unfortunately, I was sitting on the toilet, taking care of business, when Mickey burst into the OB lounge and pulled the door of the cubicle open. I was startled by this massive figure looming in the doorway, but did the best that I could to maintain my composure. "Excuse me," I said sarcastically.

He ignored that and asked. "What's going on?"

"I'm sure Dr. Krell explained that to you. Right now, I think you can see that I'm busy. If you'll kindly shut the door, I will be out in a few minutes to talk with you."

He was not to be deterred. "I don't give a damn what you're doing," he said threateningly. "I want some answers and I want them now."

My tone softened in a milieu of fear and empathy. "Listen Mr. Mousey. I understand your concern, but I can't help you like this. If you'll kindly give me a few minutes, I'll be out ofhere in a couple of minutes and answer all the questions that you have."

He hesitated for a second and said. "All right. I'll wait out here for you but you better be snappy about it." He turned and left the room. I reached up and pulled the door of the cubicle closed, feeling thoroughly embarrassed, violated and vulnerable. I did my best to finish up, but my heart wasn't in it. Feeling still stuffed, I got up and walked into the OB lounge, a little uncertain about dealing with this potential volcano.

Mousey was a ball of energy ready to explode. I hadn't taken a full step into the room that he didn't hit me with the first accusatory question. "What happened?" he said, hands raised in the air, eyes peering into my own like laser beams.

"Didn't Dr. Krell bring you up to date. He was in charge of Linda's labor and did the Caesarian section. I only came in to assist at the surgery."

"I told you that you were the doctor and that I was holding you responsible."

"Mr. Mousey, I will be glad to help in any way that I can but you have to understand that we run this service in a way that the OBGYN department dictates that we run it and not necessarily like you want to have it run."

"Now what the hell does that mean?"

"It means that we take turns on call and when Linda came in, Dr. Krell was on call and in charge."

"First of all," he said pointing a finger right in my face. "I asked around here and they said that you were the big MaGilla and that you were in charge. So don't try and pass the buck. I expect you to be on top of this and I expect some answers now."

"All right Mr. Mousey," I sighed. I will do the best I can to help, but you are going to have to accept the idea that Doctor Krell is her primary physician."

"Fine for now. Now start talking."

I tried to ignore the dictatorial tone. "I'm sure that I will just be repeating what Dr. Krell told you, but here goes." I took a deep breath and tried to relay the story without adding fuel to the fire. The damage was already done and there was nothing that I could do about it.

"Linda had what we call cephalo-pelvic disproportion, in the face of a prolonged labor, and because of that "

"Stop man," Mousey interrupted, frustration in his voice. "Don't give me any of that fancy double talk. Just tell me in plain English what happened."

"I'm trying Mickey," I said, with frustration in my tone. Just listen to me and I will try to make this as clear as I can." The man was smart and tenacious, with an obvious gap in the English language, and I wanted to be as careful as I could to tell him what happened, without inciting him to explode. "Linda had a long labor but the baby was too big to come out from below. Do you follow?"

"Of course I follow! Do you think I'm stupid? Now you're talking American."

With that nebulous encouragement, I continued. "Therefore, she required a Caesarian section. At surgery, she had a very stretched out lower part of her uterus as a result of the long labor. This tore as the baby was delivered and necessitated the application of stitches in an area that runs very close to the tube that carries urine from the kidney to the bladder. One of the stitches caught this tube and blocked it and now it is going to have to be unblocked."

"You mean back to surgery?"

"Yes, Mickey, I'm afraid so, but after the surgery, she should recover nicely."

He stomped around in a circle, gathering his thoughts and then shook that ominous finger again in my face. "I knew this would happen. My doctor in North Carolina said that she should have delivered two weeks ago but you wouldn't listen to me."

"Mickey! That has nothing to do with this. She would have had the same problem two weeks ago."

"How come he didn't see where he was sewing?"

"He's got to answer that one for you. It's difficult enough for the surgeon to see let alone the assistant surgeon. I'm sure that he tried to be as careful as he could."

"How come you let him do it? You're above him."

I wanted to say that I would have taken over if I knew that the patient was his wife, but instead, I benignly commented. "Because Dr. Krell is a very capable surgeon," I lied. "What happened to him could have happened to anybody."

"When is this surgery?"

"I don't know exactly. We are going to have to schedule it with the urologist in the next day or two."

"I don't like it," he said threateningly, pointing his finger right in my face. "It smells like something fishy is going on. But I expect," again shaking that finger right in my face, "that you will be in charge this time. I don't like you, but they say you're the best they got. Just don't fuck up again this time and keep me informed."

With those words spoken, he turned and left the room, leaving me to feel like I was a little kid that was almost caught with his hands in the cookie jar. I didn't like the way he spoke to me or made demands with implied threats. Obviously, Mr. Mousey didn't care. He had his agenda and it was going to be followed.

The next six weeks were a living hell. Linda had her surgery and went through a slow recovery with a couple of setbacks along the way. She developed a wound infection early in her post operative period and Mousey went on a rampage, constantly suspicious that there was some kind of conspiracy to do his lady in. He questioned every Dr. who came on the floor and hounded me every place I went. I called security, but they were ineffective. Mousey was a big man and he had the run of the hospital. Nobody was going to stop him and he prowled the halls both day and night, going anywhere he wished to go. There were no safe havens. To avoid him, I had to come in at five thirty in the morning and get my rounds in before he woke up. Then I could disappear in surgery all day and sneak across to the clinic in the afternoon. Occasionally, he was able to chase me down and it didn't matter to him what my obligations were. He was going to talk to me now. One time I told him that I had to get to an emergency and he physically restrained me until I answered his questions to his satisfaction. Another time Krell came into the OB lounge and told me that Mousey wanted me out in Linda's room right now to sign the baby book. "Go tell him that I have an emergency surgery now, but I will be happy to do it when I'm done."

"You go tell him," was Krell's response. "I already signed the book."

I went and hid in a closet for thirty minutes and then sneaked into the surgical suites. After catching my breath, I sauntered out the swinging doors, only to find Mousey hovering there like a vulture.

"I been looking for you."

"I know," I said, "but I've been busy in surgery. What can I do for you?

"I need you to come sign the baby book. Let's go."

Since discretion was the better part of valor, and I felt somewhat puffed up by my classic passive aggressive avoidance ofMousey for the past forty minutes, I decided to follow like a little lamb. We arrived at Linda's room. I asked her how she was doing which was fine by now. Then I signed the book where Mickey indicated and I noticed that every OBGYN on staff had signed it too. "How did you get all these signatures?" I asked.

"What do you mean, how did I get all those signatures? When they come down the hallway, I just tell them to come sign it and they do. They're all not ornery and full of double talk like you."

I didn't want to touch that with a ten foot pole. I turned to leave and Mousey grabbed my arm and added. "I don't expect to have to chase you down the next time I tell you to come. You understand."

That was about all I could take. "Listen Mickey. This hospital does not run for your convenience. I have an important job and a lot of responsibilities. I just can't stop surgery because you have a whim that you have to see me."

"There you go with that northern bull shit again. At least Krell don't bull shit me like you do."

"Okay Mickey. In your terms, just cause you got a stick up your ass, doesn't mean that I have to jump, especially when somebody's life is hanging in the balance." I jerked my arm away and continued. "Oh God, what difference does it make? You'll never understand what I'm talking about anyway." I turned to leave the room, but he had to get in the last word.

"You keep talking like that and I just might have to take you outside and teach you a lesson." His voice trailed off as I continued down the hallway. I never even turned around once so he never knew whether or not I heard him. By now, I was just numb and, after six weeks, I just didn't care.

When Linda left the hospital, four weeks after admission, we had a going away party. It was a wonderful affair and a wave of euphoria washed over us as we waved goodbye at the hospital steps.

"Freedom at last. Oh sweet freedom; let my people go!" I intoned out loud. All the staff around me heard the words and started to clap, louder and louder. They had felt the incessant pressure too and were tired of being under the gun of this unpredictable, semi-rabid mass of humanity.

When Mousey first came, word of his intrusive and intimidating behavior spread quickly. My junior resident and eventual partner had the driest sense of humor of any man I ever met. On the second day of Linda Mousey's hospital admission, he walked up to Mousey and said. "Hi, I'm Mr. Barkin, Marty Barkin. I work here at the hospital and I wanted you to know that your doctors are Dr. Krell and Dr. Robbins. Please don't hesitate to ask me for anything you need that is not medical." With that little statement, he walked away, etching in stone for Mousey that he should come only to Krell and me for medical attention and not to "Mister" Barkin.

Seven months later, I returned the favor. I walked into the exam room for New OB's only to be surprised to see Linda and her mate sitting there as big as life. After her exam, I regretfully informed them that I would not be taking care of Linda since I was leaving the program and I was being replaced as chief resident by another doctor. I did not tell them that I would be staying in town as a private physician, but did ask them to follow me into another exam room to meet the new chief resident. Mousey was his usual obnoxious self, distraught, distrustful, and demanding that I stay. I finally convinced him that I had another life and that staying was not a possibility, so he reluctantly followed me into the new chief resident's exam room. "Mr. Mousey," I said with great formality as the chief to be looked up somewhat surprised. "Do you remember Mr. Barkin?"

"Of course. He was very nice; a lot nicer than you. He offered to help wherever he could."

"Well I have great news for you. He's a doctor now, yes, Dr. Barkin, and he will be in charge of this department when Linda is ready to deliver. I'll leave you guys now to get to know each other just a little better. And don't forget. Now that he's a doctor, he doesn't have to limit his help to non-medical things. Now he can take care of everything." With that said, I saluted Dr. Barkin and left him to his own fate. I'm not sure if he ever forgave me for that, but I do believe that one good turn deserves another.

Tradition and protocol run deep in medical training. No matter what, you were expected to always be polite and respectful to the people that ranked above you. One year, I coached little league football with my mentor, Dr. Walter Phillips. I noticed that the other assistant coaches called him Walt. With fear and trepidation, I approached him and asked him if I could call him Walt, or Uncle Walt under these circumstances, so that as a thirty-year-old, I didn't look absurd to all the twenty to twenty four year olds that were calling him Walt. He looked at me in disbelief and said. "I call Dr. Stone, Dr. Stone," and walked out of the room. Dr. Stone had been his mentor and the message was perfectly clear. In our little medical world, the standards were higher and I was just going to have to live with them.

I was forty-five years old before I tried that again. By that time, he had been through years of therapy and he was now able to give me a surprising, but more reasonable response. "I guess," he sighed. "If it's that important to you that you can call me Walt, then go ahead and do it." He put it across like it was a major concession, and for him, in his changing world, it probably was.

My chief residency year was the greatest learning experience of my life. My appointment did not come without reservations on the part of the head of the department of Ob-gyn. He was a southerner; quiet, reserved and conservative. I was a northern liberal; loud, gregarious, and uninhibited. He dressed in conservative attire. I wore ponchos, chains and tennis shorts. The difference in out dress just symbolized the myriad of differences in our personae.

It took him a long time to realize that, in spite of our differences, I was qualified for the job and that, when it came to patient care, no one was more diligent, more careful and more concerned. But in the beginning he didn't know that and therefore was afraid to give me complete autonomy. He insisted that I give two transfer residents carte blanche and they, if I had left them alone, could have easily destroyed, in one month, the good reputation our OBGYN service had enjoyed for many, many years. I called them Mutt and Jeff, Krell being the tall, lanky one and Nevil Bittner the stockier one.

Krell, I have already touched on. He was brash, direct and honest and his whole focus was on getting as much surgical exposure that he could. He had transferred from another program because our department head, Dr. Larry McKay had promised him that he would not have to turn his cases over to me, but that he could get them staffed with attendings himself.

This was a big obstacle to a chief resident's learning experience. Usually, in most programs, the chief resident has the pick of the surgical cases and then hands down the routine cases that he doesn't want. Reversing the process, the first year resident gets the minor and, if lucky, the easy major cases that the second year resident has already done and is now tired of doing. The second year resident gets the routine abdominal hysterectomies and a few easy vaginal cases that the chief resident has done enough of, and the chief gets to screen and do all the difficult, rare and unusual cases that he wishes to do in order to round out his training. Hopefully, once in practice, he has been exposed to enough situations so that he is never shocked and paralyzed with something he has never seen before.

I was now being told that Krell would be able to keep the cases he had found. Being a team player, I sucked it up and played the game as best I could. Despite his freedom, I still felt responsible for the entire service and, if I took the time to watch after Krell, I might at least get some exposure to cases that I might not otherwise see.

What I saw, made my hair stand up on my head. He tried to clear everybody he could for surgery. Thank god, the attendings wouldn't let most of these through. The one's they did clear for surgery were often in for a rough ride. He had no sensitivity toward pain or pride. One day he called me in to see a breast reduction. How he got that cleared on a gynecology service I will never know. He then proceeded to pull the young ladies shirt apart, exposing her breasts, and said enthusiastically. "Will you look at those babies! Look at them!" He proceeded to put his palms under her sore breasts and bounced them up and down while she winced in pain. "Damn," he added. "Are those babies beautiful or what." He puckered his lips, made a kissing sound, and than took my arm and walked me out of the room, never looking back at the poor young girl, tears streaming down her face from the pain and humiliation.

Krell was also sloppy when it came to pre and post op orders. He would forget vital medications or vital tests and I had to constantly wipe up behind him. I had numerous talks with him, but to no avail. I had no hammer to hold over his head since he was able to clear surgery cases with other attendings without having to go through me. The only time that I had complete control over him was if I operated with him and he stayed away from that as much as possible, fearing that I might take the case away. The only time that he was forced to include me was when I was on second call and he was on first call. Then, any surgery that came through the door that he had to do that night, he had to clear and do with me.

Despite his inadequacies, I wasn't about to rat on him. I resented Dr. McKay's lack of faith in me to control, for lack of a better word, Krell's enthusiasm, and I figured that he would just have to find out for himself. Also, I wanted to divorce myself from any more responsibility for him ifI couldn't control what he did, so that I didn't get identified with his mistakes.

If given enough time, water seeks its own level and, eventually, Dr. McKay reluctantly took over his supervision and began to see the problems for himself. Soon Krell was put back under my supervision and from that point on, most of his actions were controllable. While I faulted myself for the Mousey case for not jumping in sooner, I never again let the fear of confrontation prevent me from doing what I thought was best for the patient. I wasn't here to be liked by the other residents. I was here to do the best job that I could and make sure that the patients received optimum care.

Nevil Bittner was another case. He was in his mid thirties and had held and important diplomatic post before deciding to become a physician. He had a lot of friends and, while in medical school, he was allowed to train for one year in fetal monitoring under the guiding eyes of one of the few national guru's in monitoring technique. He came to our program as the "expert" in fetal monitoring, since we were just about to begin to use monitors ourselves. We were also told that Nevil was an expert in the insertion of epidural anesthesia, which was the latest rage in OBGYN anesthesia, and was just beginning to reach the south.

Our first fetal monitor showed up and we opened the box and set up the machine. Nevil adroitly attached all the belts and wires in the right places, and "presto," we had a reading on our first high risk patient. I went out to read the little book that came with the machine. The book described three types of readings, early, late and variable decelerations.

Once back in the room, Nevil was setting up the patient for an epi- dural. His hand shook as he inserted the needle between the vertebrae. Finally, spinal fluid came back and he was about to inject the medication when I asked him how much he was inserting. He gave me a figure, which was triple the amount that you used for a spinal. "Nevil," I said. "You can't use that for a spinal."

In the most supercilious tone he could muster, he said. "Excuse me, but I am giving an epidural."

"Nevil," I persisted, as I grabbed his hand, preventing the insertion of the medication. "You are in the spinal canal."

"I am not," he insisted."

"Nevil, fluid came back."

"So, what does that mean?"

Boy, did that hit me. He didn't even know what fluid meant. He was a walking time bomb.

"Give me that," I said as I grabbed the needle from him and adjusted the medication in the seringe to meet the dosage for a spinal. I slowly inserted the medication, realizing that I was blessed with another work in progress. He not only wasn't an expert in epidurals. He could not have ever given one safely if he didn't know what spinal fluid looked like. When we left the room, I told him that he was not to give another one without my supervision. He told me that he was going to discuss this with the head of the department and I advised him to do so. I knew, when Dr. McKay heard the story, that he would put a moratorium on Nevil's epidural adventures until he could learn the difference between a spinal and an epidural.

His lack of knowledge in fetal monitoring also became painfully obvious that day. As the day wore on, he pointed out a change as a late deceleration that was clearly an early one. Over time, I realized that, after thirteen minutes of study, I could display about thirteen more minutes of knowledge in fetal monitoring than he could. His year under the tutelage of "the expert" was not spent learning how to read the tracings. Instead, it was spent setting up the machines, after he took them out of the box, inserting the tapes into the machines, calibrating them if they needed calibrations, cleaning them when dirty and trying to repair them when they broke. He was never taught to do an epidural and nobody ever showed him how to read a tracing.

Over the next few months it got painfully worse. The man was inept. He had what appeared to be DT's from alcoholism and we caught him stealing Valium for his own personal use. Unfortunately, the attending staff was slow to pick up on his ineptitude. He cut a dashing figure and since he was older and had the exciting diplomatic background, he got away with calling most of the attendings by their first names, while some of them still reverentially called him Dr. Bittner. He received his Caesarian section privileges after only five months, faster that anyone in the history of the program and set the stage for creating a lot of havoc. With a knife in his hands, he was a walking time bomb and I and Marty Barkin were repetitively called upon to get him out of trouble.

As I said before, this last year of residency was the greatest learning experience of my life. I was a good and careful doctor. I did not get any complications to speak of and therefore I did not get the experience of dealing with complicated problems with my patients. Fortunately, with Krell and Bittner, I was exposed to multiple medical and surgical problems. Without them, I would never have learned to repair a ureter. I would never have learned to repair a hole in the bowel or the bladder and I would never have learned to go back in and stop a post-op bleeder. Ironically, in medicine, show me a doctor who is great at handling complications and I will show you a doctor that has had a lot of them. Conversely, show me a doctor that fumbles with uncertainty over a complication and I will show you a doctor that hasn't seen that problem before, probably because he was too careful to have it. In my most important year, I worked my tail off and, looking back, I had the fortunate opportunity to learn a lifetime of skills from someone else's mistakes. For that I am eternally thankful, for in all my years of practice, no matter what my doubts, no matter what my fears, I never met a case that I couldn't handle.

By April of my final year, I started to feel "short timer's syndrome." I'd been running a marathon for four and a half years and now the end was in sight. In two months I could get off the train. I was a perfectly conditioned machine. I had gained tremendous stamina and tremendous knowledge through this ordeal and I was now ready to go out on my own. I wouldn't have to take orders anymore. I wouldn't have to do anybody's bidding. I could do my own thing, my own way, and I had the momentum and confidence to make it happen.

Tom Norris, the chief resident the year before, was now in practice and he asked me to join him as a partner. I politely said no, explaining that I was getting out of my indentured servant obligation and the rules of engagement would probably have to change too radically to suit him. I just wanted to do my own thing and be beholden to nobody. I just wanted room to breathe.

Unlike other physicians of my time, I approached my choice of practice location in a methodical, scientific fashion. There were approximately five thousand deliveries in the two St. Petersburg hospitals and sixty five percent of them occurred at my hospital. For all intents and purposes, almost all of those patients came from a radius of twelve miles around my hospital, extending mainly to the north and west. When I plotted the deliveries on a map, I was shocked to see that the areas that supplied the most deliveries had the smallest number of obstetricians and gynecologists. I decided right then and there to open my office in the North West end of town and began the long tedious process of finding a professional building to rent in this area. I decided that it must be upscale since the only thing I had to sell was my image, and my image was based on my appearance and the appearance of the office that my patients had to come to. In retrospect, I couldn't have approached it any better.

THE DEVELOPING YEARS

In that "life of dreams" called youth, the greatest pleasure lay in lofty aspiration and imaginative anticipation without regard to reality.

In each of our lives, though, there comes a time, to some early, to some late, in which we must descend from our ivory towers and accept the compromise that the real world has to offer. How well we do this often determines the level of success that we finally attain.

To me, the weight of reality began creeping in the door at age twenty and, finally, announced herself so firmly by my twenty-second year that I could deny her no longer. At least, in my case, she was no surprise, and that, in itself, was enough to permit me to succumb, with only token rebellion.

For that I can thank my father, for he beat the endless drum of reality and its challenges. He laid down the formula for success with insight and brilliance, and I followed it, not because of it's beautiful simplicity and truth, but because of his relentless and tenacious nature. Whenever I began to detour from that guided path, he brought me back with cold, logical and persistent rebuke.

The explanations were always in terms of practicality, never in terms of morality.

I would say, for example. "In school I am just stagnating. The material is boring, inapplicable, and of little use."

And he would retort. "You will learn little in school, but it is required by society that you garner certain labels before you can pursue your own interests and enlist the faith of a following." He would pause and sigh and then repeat himself in different words. "People rely on diplomas. They trust them and are impressed by them. Give them what they want." Assuming that his words were too complex for me, he would usually offer a simple analogy. "Let's suppose you were a laborer and you put in your eight hour day. The boss, though, wished to pay you off in one dollar bills instead of dollars of a larger denomination."

He would pause letting the hypothesis set in. "Would you refuse your wage on the principal that you were expecting larger bills and didn't want to put up with the inconvenience of dealing with single dollar bills?" With confidence he would answer his own question. "Of course not. The eight hours of work are already done and the cost of defiance is much greater than the inconvenience of carrying a large wad of money."

He would lean forward in his chair, straining over his pendulant abdomen, palms outstretched, as if laying the point to me on a silver platter. "By the same token, you have put in X number of years in school. The effort required to complete the few remaining requisite courses for your diploma will be far less than the effort that you have already expended in your studies. Even if the infromation is useless, you must gut it up and complete those courses so that you can get your degree. With it, you are on the road to success. Without it, you may know twice as much as the next guy and still find that road much more difficult to traverse."

He would pause again and relax back in his chair, his tone becoming less argumentative and more conciliatory. "I didn't say that you should not learn. You should, but you will do this on your own. Along the way, for the small inconvenience of memorizing trivia to pass a few examinations, you should make sure that you get that label. That is just good common sense. Only a fool would throw it away. With the label, you may enter a room, remain silent and then leave as a messiah of wisdom in the minds of others. Without it, in the same company, the most eloquent and articulate commentator is disposed of as a loud mouth. Such is the nature of people. Don't fight them. You won't win. Court their predjudices and disillusionments to your own advantage."

And when it came time to choose a final path with regard to what I would do for the rest of my life, he asked me. "What have you selected as a career that you would like to pursue?"

I would have liked to answer; "Politics with the Presidency as the ultimate goal, or acting, or playing ball," but by then I was indoctrinated enough in reality to know that he would consider a response of that nature to be ludicrous and time wasting. "I don't know," I replied.

And then my father expounded again on the cold hard facts of life. Being a fledgling realist, I had to make that great compromise, that is set my goals at a practically attainable position that would reward me with good standing and position in the community, and in so doing, abandon the glamorous, exciting ends that were, for all practical purposes, non options.

With my father, I listed all professions that I would consider and eliminated all those with too many uncontrollable variables. Politics and acting were out, although to me they were the most intriguing. Football and baseball were out, since my size guaranteed to relegate me to professional mediocrity. Business was discarded as too risky and so on and so on until the choice lay between a number of aseptic, but predictable professions.

We placed the assets of each into one column and the liabilities into another and assigned point values to each. Medicine won hands down. Prestige, income and security were guaranteed. The price to pay was a few more years of study and, since finances were no obstacle, the conclusion was obvious.

My personal leanings were never even considered. The facts that the field left little room for imagination, made unreasonable personal demands, and involved an extremely depressing side of life, were brushed aside as minor drawbacks. The fear of death, the nausea evoked by bodily emissions or unpleasant odors, the faintness generated by the sight of blood, were matter of factly discarded as obstacles readily surmountable with repetitive exposure.

And so the choice was made on the basis of cold sound logic and I could not disagree. Accordinly, my approach to my last two years in college were altered. With my father, that plan was drawn and, once on the path toward my goal, I knew that retreat would be difficult, and become even more so the further along the road I traveled. Acceptance of my new role and duties in life was not easy. Required to satisfy the new goal were good study habits, and the ability to sacrifice my immediate pleasures for those that lay ahead.

The concept was entirely new to me for, until that time, my role and duties coincided with my pleasures and there was no conflict at all. I loved to play ball, contribute to social events and interact with people. These had been the ends in themselves. In college though, my play was mediocre, limited, not by desire or cunning, but, by physical size. Since my peers judged my intelligence and attractiveness on the strength of my athletic performance, I found that I had catapulted from a position of central attraction to one of just another guy in the crowd. My altered role in life had come as a shock and surprise.

Confusion, supported by a sense of depression and bitterness set in. I came to realize gradually and reluctantly that I would have to set other goals in life and attain them if I wanted again to stand apart and revel in the glories of success. Unless I achieved fame as an actor, politician or sports hero, I doubted very strongly if I could ever approach those high school years of glory. But the taste of attention and success remained and, in desperation, I was laid ripe for the acceptance of my father's appeals.

As I faced the abyss of mediocrity, my mother's expectations, in spite of the divorce, gave unintended emotional support to my father's logic. Furthermore, she had some lessons to teach me on her own. For a start, she believed that the rules were different for men and for women. Men needed to be abstemious of life's pleasures. Their role was to protect and support their families. They needed to be responsible for their actions and needed to do what ever it took in order to achieve that goal. On the other hand, girls just had to find a husband to take care of them.

When I went to college, I wanted a car. When I asked her for one, she refused to buy it for me and told me in her noxious tone. "A man earns his own money for a car."

That was that. I went out and got a summer job and saved twelve hundred dollars. When I wanted to buy a used sports car, her fear took over and she offered me a six hundred dollar gift if I bought a brand new, boringly safe, Chevrolet Biscayne. It had black floor mats and an AM Radio. Nobody could be less excited about a new car.

At Christmas time, I returned home from school for the holidays.

It was an eleven-hour drive through wet, snowy and foggy conditions from Montreal. I was tired and beat. Despite my fatigue, the first thing I did was enter the house and fly up to my closet of a room, two steps at a time. I opened my clothe's closet inside the hovel they called my bedroom, promptly removed my sister's overflow clothes (from her walk in closet,) that were threatening to break my short closet rod, and threw them out into the hallway. Then, I flew down the stairs into the kitchen, and demanded to know, before I said hello, whose Impala Chevy convertible was sitting out side in front of the house.

"That's some way to greet your mother," came my mother's reply.

"Hello ma," I said perfunctorily. "Now whose car is that."

"You can't even kiss me hello?" she said, a chuckle in her voice. I walked over and gave her a hug and a kiss and then repeated.

"Okay, whose is it?"

"If you must know, it's mine."

"Who drives it?" I pressed.

"Why do you have to deal with that now? Can't you just calm down and ask me how I am?"

"Never mind mom, I know you're fine. Now who drives it?"

"Well, your sister drives it to school to teach." My sister was a science teacher in the Baldwin Junior High School system, soon to be a department head.

"Who paid for it?"

"I did," she stated indignantly. "I told you that it's mine."

"So why doesn't she get her own car?"

"She can't afford it. She's saving for when she gets married."

"She can afford it! That's why she gets paid a salary," I yelled. "Who pays for the gas?"

"I do." She paused for a second and averted my gaze. "She said she wouldn't go teach unless I gave her the car and money for gas."

"Do you buy her lunch too?" I added sarcastically.
Still averting my gaze, she continued.

"Sometimes. Sometimes I make it for her," she responded pitifully.

"Have you ever driven that car?" I accused, somewhat astonished to say the least.

"I really haven't had a chance," she explained. "She needs it so much."

I gave up. There was no way to pierce that armor. My mother was spoiled and protected by a domineering, powerful, and omnipotent father. She expected her daughter to follow in her footsteps and her son to follow in his.

My mother also taught me that I must be accountable for my actions and responsibly deal with both the negative and positive results there from. One summer, I had heard about a "foolproof" system of betting at Yonkers raceway. It was a variation off an arithmetic and geometric progression on the horses in the number one postposition at the track. History had it that the one postposition had never lost more than seventeen races in a row at Yonkers and won, on average, one race in five. The reason for this phenomenon was that it was a short distance to the first turn and the number one horse almost always got there first, forcing all the other horses to fall behind or take a much longer outside circle. It didn't take a genius to figure out that, if you tried to win ten to fifteen dollars a race, you could cover seventeen races with six or seven thousand dollars and average over one hundred dollars a night in income. With twenty seven hundred of my friend Pete's money and three hundred of mine, we set off on the adventure, just after high school graduation. With luck and greed on our side (we didn't always stick to the ten or fifteen dollars a race,) we were able to run that money up to close to fifteen thousand dollars. It became a job and Pete and I would alternate days. Since I had no transportation, Pete would loan me his Thunderbird sports coupe and I would drive up to Yonkers, like a big shot, three times a week. With a girl at my side, I would valet park the car and go into the clubhouse. I'd get a table and order the best of foods and drink, trying to impress the girl that I was with. Being afraid to go to the fifty-dollar window, for fear of the tax collector, I would always place my bets at the ten-dollar window. Sometimes, I would have to bet two to three thousand dollars and I would say to the ticket man when he asked "who?" and "how many?"

"One horse and just keep punching till the bell goes off."

Occasionally, on a Friday night, blue collar guys would be there with their hard earned pay checks and, upon seeing me bet over a thousand dollars, they would jump to another window to lay down their weeks wages on a horse that they thought I had inside information on. Most of the time that horse would lose. I usually didn't care, because there were more races to run and I knew that the one post position would ultimately win.

In the clubhouse, big cigar in my mouth, I was becoming more and more obnoxious. Sometimes, if I wanted to impress the girl that I was with, I would turn to my date and say. "I don't like what you're wearing. Here's fifty bucks. Go buy yourself a new dress." Then I'd lean back in my seat and suck on that big cigar.

One day I went to visit my father and he asked me.

"Where were you last night?"

"I don't know," I responded matter of factly. "Out with the guys or something."

"Were you at the race track?"

I paused, making believe that I was trying to remember. "Er, Yeah. Let me think. Yeah, I believe I was."

"What about the night before?"

Right then, I knew he had me, and I confessed all.

He admitted seeing me on TV a couple of times and then going to the track three other times and catching me twice. I told him about the system, and how much we had made.

"Listen," he said. "Don't you think that I'd be down at the rail in the pouring rain, with a newspaper over my head, yelling ride him home Willie, ride him home, ifI thought you could win." He paused to let that sink in and then added emphatically. "Money is money. It gives you power. But if you go back, you are going to eventually lose. Put it in the bank!"

My mother's thoughts were not so practical. I came home one day and threw four thousand dollars on the table and said. "Go buy yourself a fur coat, and don't ever tell me again that my father never got you one.

"Where did you get that money?" she demanded to know. With the cat out of the bag I told her the truth. "I won it at the track."

"Well, put it back in you pocket," she insisted with indignation. "It's dirty money and I don't want it. A man works for his money. He doesn't gamble for it."

Eventually, Peter and I lost the money. We got too greedy and tried to win thirty and forty dollars a race, and then arrived at the fifteenth loss in a row. We had to bet our remaining few thousand dollars on a horse called Fabricator, who went off at three to ten. While he won, he only paid nine hundred dollars profit on a three thousand dollar bet. We were devastated because we were down to almost where we had started. The money meant nothing to us by this time. It was only paper. We recklessly bet it all on the next couple of races and lost and when it was all said and done, I ended up owing Peter twelve hundred dollars.

My mother saved me and in the process taught me about owning up to my responsibilities and obligations. She softened the blow by saying. "Everybody makes mistakes. You have a responsibility here. You get a job and pay Peter back fifty dollars a week, save the rest of your money for a car, and I will give you fifteen dollars a week allowance that you can spend. That made the problem less daunting and I was able to pay off my obligation to Peter over two summers with a sense of pride. Furthermore, I was able to save enough money to buy a car.

Nothing more was ever said. To this day in my life, I live within my means. I don't gamble and I don't risk money that I can't afford to lose. I never borrow money recklessly and, when I do borrow, I make the payments before I ever consider spending anything on myself.

During my college years, while my mother paid my tuition and room and board, she made me work for my spending money. My summer jobs helped me learn to plan and budget. Not only did they teach me how to take care of my responsibilities, but they also taught me a great deal about people and the real world. When I was done with these experiences, there were no more illusions, and I was street savvy, knowledge that would serve me well later on in life.

After my failure at the track, I got a job for the rest of the summer at a restricted beach club as a cashier in the coffee shop. By restricted, I mean, "no Jews allowed." I got the job because my nose was small and my last name did not definately identify me as a Jew.

Some very important people were members, like Sherman Bartly, the original owner of the famous Bird Club in New York City. Apparently, he was the first one to put up a red velvet rope, making people wait in line before they would be seated. Even if his place was sparsely occupied, you still had to wait and the psychology of this phenomenon made him a rich man. Anything not attainable becomes more desirable, and people would come in droves just to wait behind that red velvet rope.

The prejudicial overtones were not confined only to Jews, but seemed to encompass most immigrants, people of color and all the people that were poor.

The short order cook was a first generation Puerto Rican with an accent, and he was subjected to a daily dose of superiority and disdain.

On Labor day weekend, the club, which usually catered to approximately one thousand people on weekends, and had the facilities to handle about half that many, had to service the needs of about three thousand people. Needless to say, efforts had to be intense and creative in order to pull things off and make the weekend a happy time for all.

Our little Puerto Rican took the bull by the horns. He came in early on Saturday, went into the back storage room, filled a barrel up with tuna fish, celery, onions and mayonnaise, took off his clothes and jumped in the barrel. He then vigorously worked up a lather, until there was a barrel full of tuna salad. He then jumped out of the container and hopped into the shower to clean himself off. Emerging from the shower, he dressed and began to scoop tuna salad into metal containers. He then put some of the containers into the fridge under his short order station and the rest of them in some of the service toilets and surrounded them with ice. He then proceeded to slice tomatoes and lettuce, putting some into his short order station and the rest into wax paper that he deposited into the ice in the toilet bowls. Excess fruit for salad and garnish also found their home in the ice filled toilet bowls, service tanks and service sinks. There just wasn't enough refrigerator space. Then, without a word or a smile, he got on a stool and pissed in the pot of "the soup of the day." Getting down, he turned and commented, with only a wink of the eyelid to let me know that this was his way of getting back. "Adds a little flavor. Don't you think?"

I cracked up and he couldn't keep from smiling. "I don't believe you!" I said with surprise, all the time shaking my head in awe.

In accented English, he retorted. "Beeleeve et amigo. Notheeng but da best for deese assholes."

The day was surreal. About eleven o'clock, they started piling in; the rich and the famous; the wealthy and the self proclaimed elite. For four ninety five, (twenty five dollars today,) they tore into those tuna fish sandwiches like there was no tomorrow, and, for a buck more, they got a hearty bowl of soup.

This was his way of getting back; his way of sticking it to those supercilious assholes who had demeaned and ridiculed him all summer long. It was his way of showing that he was just as worthy of respect as they were and, if they were going to debase him, then he would pay them back in spades. I learned not to underestimate anybody, no matter how poor or stupid they seemed to be. At the very least, I learned to treat waiters and waitresses with respect, and I never send food back, even if it is improperly prepared.

After my first year of college, I needed to get a job in order to save spending money for the next year. My mother was willing to pay for college but, in her words, "a man earns his own spending money."

So off to work I went again. I found a job driving an ice cream truck for a cop that had bought into a business opportunity deal. He bought nine trucks and ran the business along with his gorgeous wife, who used to be a Las Vegas chorus girl. Nightly, before and after I went to sleep, she was always the object of my fantasies. Along with me, they hired eight ex convicts to drive their trucks and a convicted arsonist to manage the operation.

I got an eighteen-percent commission for everything that I sold. I took the truck out about noon and came back at midnight. Sometimes I sold one hundred and fifty to two hundred dollars a day. But, some days, especially when it rained, I sold only twenty or thirty bucks and it cost me more to buy my meals than I actually earned in commissions.

The cop, whose name was Al, had a very inaccurate way to control inventory. He counted the bags of liquid ice cream that he put on the trucks, expecting about twenty dollars a bag. It soon occurred to me that I could stretch the amount of money that I got from the bags by adding a little milk to the mix, by running the ice cream on the inside of the cone, and by using less ice cream and more syrup and whipped cream in the sundaes. This way I could pay for my meals out of the gross income and he would never know it.

After two weeks of stealing my lunch money, I began to feel guilty. I also liked the policeman and loved his wife, and that combination enhanced my sense of guilt. I decided to confess and make amends if he would let me.

I also used the opportunity to try and impress his wife. "Al," I said. "If I'm taking lunch money, how much do you think the other guys are taking?"

"How much more can they take?" he offered with a cavalier attitude, trying to look like the big man in front ofhis wife. Here was my opportunity to impress her.

"A lot!" I said emphatically. "They can vary the amount ofice cream that they put into cones and sundaes significantly and they can even buy some bags of liquid cream at Carvel up the street."

"Supposing they can, which I doubt. What do you want me to do about it? Count the cones?" he said sarcastically, with a sophisticated all knowing grin on his face.

His moment of glory was gone in a flash as I disdainfully replied. "No Al, you don't have to count the cones. Just count the boxes of cones and sundae dishes that you put on each truck, and lock the truck each night. After a six day rotation, recount the inventory and calculate out the amount that should have been taken in."

Trying to recoup, he commented. "That's gonna be a waste of time."

I leaned foward in my chair and grabbed hold of the moment. "I'll tell you what. Let me try for a week, no charge to you. IfI can proove that there is significant stealing, make me the assistant manager and I will be in charge of inventory control. If I can't, I'll go back on the truck."

Al looked at June and with a nod, she gave her tacit OK. "OK," he said. We will give it a try."

Elated, I went right to work. I had unburdened my soul with impunity, and had set myself up for a new job that I knew would bring results. Most importantly, the boss's wife finally noticed who I was, and I was going to show her that I was a lot smarter than her husband.

Work started at midnight, after the trucks came in, and finished at ten AM, when the guys returned to ready their trucks for the day. No longer could they just take supplies, but they had to request boxes of cones and sundae dishes from me. Each truck had an initial inventory taken, and each time the driver was switched, a final inventory was taken and this was correlated against the expected gross. At the end of the week, all nine trucks came up short, ranging from two hundred to four hundred dollars a driver.

When Al issued the paychecks on Friday night, from midnight

until two AM, they were all shoved back on their heels and sent reeling. He had reduced their paycheck by their shortfall and we almost had a riot on our hands. Fortunately, the trucks came in at different times and there were never more than three of the ex convicts there at any time. A couple of the earlier discontents tried to hang around to see what they could stir up, but Al told them to leave if they still wanted their jobs. Both of them got in their cars while cursing under their breath. One of them turned to look at me before he pulled away and pointed his index finger at me like he was shooting a gun. He had a family to feed and his paycheck had just been reduced by one hundred and eighty eight dollars. He deduced that my job was the only thing different and now he was getting fucked. Somehow, stealing one hundred and eighty eight dollars was no part of the equation. Two of the convicts quit on the spot. They figured that their scam was up and that they could make better money some place else. Both of them whispered. "I'm gonna get you you little bastard," as they passed me on my way out the door.

Danny Boyle, the manager, was nowhere to be seen. He knew to avoid these guys. The tension in the air was so intense, it could be cut by a knife, and the time passed by painfully slowly. But Al was resolute and firm. He made it clear that he was not going to put up with any more bullshit and that they better toe the line or else. One guy leaned over his desk and demanded menacingly, "Give me my fuckin' money."

Al stood up to meet him, looked him in the eye and said. "Get the fuck out of here before I decide to take you in."

The driver hesitated for a moment and then turned around and left in a huff. Finally, with the last guy gone, Al locked the door, and then a big grin broke out on his face. He had been losing about twenty three hundred dollars a week in pure profit and didn't even know it. Now the bleeding would stop.

June walked over and gave him a big hug and then came over to hug me too. I could feel her big tits rub up against my chest and it sent a wave of electricity through my loins. They were so soft, and she was so voluptuous, that I wanted to trip her and beat her to the floor. But all I did was hang on a little longer than I should have and let the palm of my hand accidentally slide across the bulging side of her breast when she pulled away. "God," I thought wistfully. "After I saved him all that money, he ought to volunteer to let me fuck her. At the very least, he should let me look at those deliciously succulent mammaries."

But no such act of generosity ensued. Instead, I was hired on a permanent basis for the rest of the summer at three hundred dollars a week and, after thanking him, I returned to the garage to get the trucks ready for the next day.

The summer progressed slowly. Three hundred a week wasn't chicken feed, and, since I was working at night, I didn't go out and spend a lot. I was able to pay Peter off from the debt that I incurred at the track the year before and still save about one hundred and fifty a week. Despite my fears that one of the ex-convicts would take out his frustrations on me, nothing of note happened. I just did my job and kept my mouth shut.

In early August, the manager, Danny, was arrested for arson. Whether he did it or not, I would never know, but I did know that his position was now open. It was no contest. I was chosen by default, and I was now making four hundred a week as a nineteen-year-old manager. By the end of the summer, it was clear to me that Al would never have enough money to carry these trucks through the winter, even ifhe was able to get some decent income by converting them to sandwich and coffee trucks. When the summer ended, he sat down with me and begged me to stay. "I'd really like to keep you on Dodd, and I'm willing to up you to five hundred a week."

The offer was tempting, but I tried to explain. "Al, I love you guys, but I'm going to school. This was only a summer job. I need to go back and finish college."

"Too bad," he lamented. "I figured that we could convert these trucks to mobile luncheonettes and service all the factories and construction sites out here over the winter."

"Al," I said reluctantly. "It won't matter."

"Whatta ya mean?" he asked defiantly. "Me and you. We can make this thing happen."

"Al, the numbers just don't add up. By December, you won't even be able to make the payments on the trucks."

"How do you know that?" he asked incredulously.

"Al, it doesn't take a genius to see the hand writing on the wall. You just need to do a few projections."

Scratching his head, he sat back in his big swivel chair and sighed. "Jeez, it's that bad?"

I just nodded my head.

"You know, for a nineteen year old, you are one smart kid, sort of like my er, what do the Italians call it, er,"consigliere." What do you think I should do?"

I thought about it for a moment. And then, without cracking a smile, kiddingly said.

"I think you'd be lucky if the place just burned down."

Al just nodded. We both stood up and shook hands to say goodbye. June was there, and I made sure that I gave her one last hug before I left, so I could burn the feeling of her pillow soft voluptuous breasts into my brain. As I tearfully walked out the door, I realized that I might never see those breasts again.

Al called after me just as I got to my car.

"Don't forget to stop by to say hello when you come home for Christmas."

"I won't," I called back as I got into my car, knowing full well that this chapter in my life was probably closed.

When Christmas rolled around, I returned home from vacation. One morning I picked up the newspaper and read where the Mr. Swifty Ice Cream Depot burned down. Al was just lucky I guess.

With each experience in life, I learned something new. With Al, I learned the importance of thoroughly understanding what you got

CONFESSIONS OF A GYNECOLOGIST

into and the importance of really understanding the workings of your business. Anything less, usually doomed you to failure.

In the face of all that parental pressure, I succumbed and agreed to make that first monumental compromise. My goal was now set, practical and unglamorous yes, but at least attainable and able to supply me with the sense of importance and worthiness that I needed to be happy.

I regrouped my attack and set about conditioning the actions that would propel me toward my ends. The change was tumultuous. Sports were fun and school was work. Although procrastination and inconsistency forever plagued my scholastic efforts, I was, since I was a quick learner, able to achieve decent results. As time moved forward, my capacity to focus and my study skills improved and so did my grades. As I had taught myself to be a quarterback, I taught myself to be a student.

My high school experience had given me a good foundation in understanding what it took to be a good student. In that arena, I had developed the tools of learning and had sporadically implemented them. In my first two years in college, I had basically coasted along, relying on the skills I had learned in high school along with very little else.

Yet, I knew how to take notes, research information, make an outline, and write a paper with footnotes. I also knew how to read effectively and how to study most efficiently. I just needed to learn how to implement these tools of learning in a more consistent manner, and sensitize myself to each course's professorial preferences, so that I could emphasize material which was more likely to show up on an exam.

The learning process was slow. I saw little relevance in the dull material to be memorized and regurgitated for exams. Accordingly I fell short of my projected study schedule time and time again. My concentration span was poor and this, combined with poor initial study habits, prevented me from achieving the great grades in my junior year essential for a guaranteed acceptance at medical school in this country. But there was hope, for, in fleeting moments I was able to concentrate and imprint rapidly in my mind the text book material. Over the past two years, I had found my ability to assimilate knowledge had improved, and those occasional inspirations became more frequent until, in my final year, I was able to achieve excellent grades.

I applied to numerous American medical schools and had received multiple rejections along with a few interviews, surprisingly at the higher ranked medical schools. After these interviews, I made the waiting list at a few of the better schools, but had been summarily rejected by all the regional or less known schools. By the time that I figured it out, it was too late.

I had gone to college in Canada, at McGill University in Montreal. Despite the fact that I had been sporadic in attendance and concentration, I had reasonably good grades and excellent ones in my senior year. The problem was, that, in Canada, the numbering system was different. McGill was rated as one of the best schools in the world and the competition was fierce. At freshman orientation, the dean stood up and said. "Look to your left and look to your right." Then he paused a moment and added. "Only one of you will be here next year."

He was true to his word. Of the remaining students, most had "C" averages. I had a solid "B." The problem was that a "C" represented a number between fifty and sixty-five and a "B" meant a sixty-five to an eighty. An "A" average was eighty or above and only a very small percentage of students, (maybe three percent or less,) were able to maintain grade point averages over eighty. These were only numbers, and tests were devised so that only twenty five percent of the enrolled students would receive averages over sixty-five. At schools like Harvard, Yale and Cornell etc., they recognized this and therefore recognized that I was a student worthy of consideration, albeit for the waiting list. At the less renowned schools, where I should have been a "shoo in," I wasn't even given consideration, because they didn't understand the grading system. I went to the dean, begging him to send an explanation, but for him, politics prevailed over truth. He didn't want to take the chance of offending the admissions committees of the lower ranked schools by accusing them of provincial ignorance. He said. "I'm sorry, but I can't do anything. They ought to know the difference between the grading systems and, if they don't, it is not for me to instruct them."

Other factors also contributed to my universal rejection from American Medical schools. In most schools, the acceptance process gave weight to the geographical origin and religious background of the applicant. This meant that a white protestant applicant from South Dakota, with a B minus average, had a better chance to be accepted than a Jewish boy from New York City, with a B plus average. This was definitely unfair to the student, but I could really understand the thinking. Ethnic kids from urban areas usually had cultural pressures that pushed them to attain better grades than country kids. Furthermore, they usually attended schools with better facilities and better teachers. This meant, that, if grades were the only criteria, America would be filled with an army of physicians which were truly not representative of the make up ofits population. In all honesty, ifI were running an American Medical school, I would want a representation of students that mirrored the make up of the population. Obviously, to accomplish this, I would have to give preferential treatment to many Americans whose grades were not quite as high as other students that I chose to reject. So I was left out in the cold with regard to American medical school acceptance.

But there still were the European medical schools. Bathed in tradition, and surrounded by a halo of mystique, they held a glamorous attraction for me. I knew, if accepted, I could do the work. When I could concentrate, I seemed to learn much faster than anybody else around me. The only obstacle I would have to face was my own inability to discipline myself on a daily basis and I wasn't ever sure ifI could get that under control. I'm sure that, ifI had seen a psychiatrist in this day and age, he would have diagnosed me as ADHD: that is attention deficit with hyperactivity. But back then they didn't use those words. If you didn't do well, it was just because you were a lazy no-good piece of shit and that label I couldn't tolerate. Every kid on my block, short or tall, skinny or fat, handsome or ugly, or smart or stupid went on to graduate school, and I just couldn't face my family, let alone my neighbors, if I didn't get in somewhere.

The long awaited response came from the Italian Consulate in July. "Nell nome dell grande diretore, Guiseppe Carducci, ci siamo consigli-ato ad informarvi della vostra accetanza alla faculta di Medicina and

Chirugia per l'anno scolastico 1963."

The tension, built up over the months of rejections, broke like an overextended balloon and was replaced by a feeling of relaxed elation. I was finally accepted in medical school, albeit a foreign one.

My choice had come and I was determined to grab it by the horns. With the allure of life in Europe in my grasp, I told my father that this was a great option. My father wasn't so sure. He made contacts with various board members at a number of American Medical Schools. A few feelers came back and, for ten thousand dollars, a commitment was made with a well-known mid-western school.

My father put it to me. In this country, once in, the attainment of my MD would only be a matter of time. Abroad, the obstacles were many. The language barrier, the inferior facilities, the different curriculum and requirements, the lack of practical training, the examinations for entrance into this country and, finally, once in, the adaptation to the American system were often insurmountable barriers. Practically, ten grand was cheap.

But there still remained in me a bit of the romanticist. I liked the idea of living abroad, travelling, meeting new people in different cultural settings and not having to lead a regimented existence. I felt that I could leave Europe as an individual, worldly and knowledgeable, not only in my chosen field, but in the appreciation and interpretation of life. In this country, I knew that I would become a good physician. Nevertheless, I would be a rubber stamp of the guy before me, and, in the game of life itself, I would have no time to progress. I would leave my medical training with great technical tools but the social skills of an eighteen-year-old.

There was also a little idealist left in me. I refused to sneak in the back door, and I turned down the offer and told my father not to pay the "grease money." I didn't like the undercover methods often used in this country to attain what you want. I knew it went on from the college kid buying a term paper for fifty dollars to the great Washington lobbyist offering a senator a multitude of incentives to back one project or another. My father, the pragmatist, fought me tooth and nails. But, for the first time in my life, I stood firmly on my ground, despite all attempts to break down my resistance. Slowly, unwillingly, clawing at every thread, like a wounded bull in the ring, my father gave up. He made one last fleeting attempt as I was about to embark on the "Christopher Columbo" for Italy. With my final "no", he understood. Tears welled up in his eyes as we said goodbye. His last words were not, "I will miss you," but rather, "make me proud."

As I stood by the rail watching him, shoulders slumped and head bowed, I sensed the depression that emanated form his being. He wished to control and direct and he finally had to come to the realization that I was an individual with a will of my own. Most importantly, I know he felt that I was doing the wrong thing. There would be many lonely moments later on when I thought that he was right.

OPENING A PRACTICE

The first year was a whirlwind of excitement, filled with uncertainties and growing responsibilities. The practice of medicine is a business and, if there is one thing that they don't train you for in medical school, it is business. There are no courses on marketing, accounting or, for that matter, any business skills. There are no courses on public speech or the psychology of dealing with people. When a doctor comes out into practice, he is like an eighteen year old getting out of high school, because the demands of his studies for the past twelve to fourteen years have precluded him from participating in the normal social growth process.

But the special skills that a physician acquires in training allows him to surmount obstacles that others just wouldn't dare to contend with. The years of abuse in training taught me never to give up, no matter what the barriers that I had to overcome. "Quit" just wasn't part of the formula.

I found a brand new office complex on the northwest side of town, the area from which the greatest number of pregnant patients at my hospital came from. Furthermore, I knew that cities on the east coast grew toward the northwest, so that I could expect the population to expand in my direction. Since I had no money, I arranged a five-year lease with four months of free rent up front. I also was smart enough to include a five-year option, so that I had the flexibility to move if my practice out grew the space. But, with the option, I couldn't be raped at the end of my first five-year term if I decided to stay put. They agreed to finish the space to suit and I spared no expense, making sure that I had the little things that would set my office apart from other physicians. Today, it is commonplace to set up attractive, well decorated offices, but back then, in nineteen seventy three, it was usual to have just a plain office with standard waiting room chairs, old magazines, and standard equipment. Instead, I put "pass through" doors in the bathrooms and dressing rooms in every exam room. Common sense told me that women were very uncomfortable, getting undressed in a large room with a door to the hallway that could open at any time.

Each dressing room had a mirror, a pillowed bench and a stand with little refinements like perfume and tissues. The waiting room was set up like a living room, with couches and big chairs. There was a TV in one corner, and fresh flowers on the coffee tables. There were the best magazines for women, and only the latest editions. On the tables were pieces of literature that pertained to some of the services we offered in the office. Tapes and videotapes had not yet arrived on the scene, but, when they did, I was the first to get them.

Christina helped with the decorating and the purchase of all the furniture. She had a tremendous flair for interior decorating and she coordinated everything perfectly, from the wainscoting and crown molding in my rich and warm consultation room, to the light comfortable atmosphere of the exam rooms. Attention was paid to flow, so that a patient could go through intake, bathroom, lab, consultation room, exam room and payment center without having to backtrack at all. When we were done and ready to open, we knew that we had a very unique office setting.

Paying the tab was another problem. I had very little money to start with, and I needed cash fast. I went to the bank and was able to secure a loan for twenty thousand dollars. It amazed me how easy this was for me, but the explanation lay in the fact that, at that time, doctors were tremendously safe risks. They never went bankrupt and eventually produced enough of an income flow to easily support payments on the amount the banks would loan them. When I got more fiscally sophisticated, I realized that, up to the level that they thought a doctor's income could support the debt service on a loan, a bank would offer them the money, no questions asked. But after that point, it was a different matter. Doctors were bright and energetic people and were filled with ideas and schemes to make money. But because of their naivete, they were notoriously bad businessmen and bankers had a blanket rule that, beyond the debt service that the doctor's income could support, they would not loan doctors any money. As the years rolled on and my business acumen grew, I would be constantly baffled and confused that, past a certain point, no matter how sound my proposal, I could never get a bank to give me a dime. It was frustrating to deal with bank officers that didn't seem to have the drive to understand what I was talking about and from the start showed no spark of interest. Sitting back, years later, I came to understand the irony of the situation. Once the word "doctor" was introduced, a cap was put on the loan, no matter how good the idea, no matter how potentially profitable. I was of a different ilk, but they refused to give me a chance. While other developers and promoters continued to bilk the system, resulting in a severe banking and savings and loan crisis in the late eighties and a public bail out of billions of dollars, I was never able to use the banking system for a myriad of business opportunities. Most of these resulted in very profitable ventures anyway, making my investors happy campers. How much more profitable or expansive these ventures could have been, I would never know, but I did know that they were much safer ventures for the banks to participate in than the majority of investments that they made in which they risked their stockholder's money and, later, when they went bankrupt, the tax payer's money.

My second source of cash flow was the emergency room. While I completed my office and grew my practice, I worked forty hours a week in the emergency room for six months at fifteen dollars an hour, until the cash flow from the practice was enough to pay the bills, and allow me a meager sum on which to support my family. No matter how hard I worked and no matter how fast my practice grew, I always seemed to have to scrape to pay my bills. In my first year, I charged one hundred and eighty thousand dollars. But I only collected one hundred and twenty thousand by the end of the first year, because there was a three month delay in insurance payments, ten-percent non collectibles, and of course a growing accounts receivable. The fifteen thousand that I earned in six months in the emergency room gave me a gross intake of one hundred and thirty five thousand in cash. My office cost me ninety thousand dollars to run (approximately one half of the gross charges.) That left forty five thousand dollars plus the twenty that I had borrowed. Out of that sixty five thousand, I had paid thirty five thousand on furniture and equipment and seven thousand (interest and principle) on my loan, leaving me with twenty three thousand dollars. From that, I owed fourteen thousand dollars in income tax, since the purchase of furniture and equipment was done with profits and did not reduce my tax obligation beyond the amount that I was able to depreciate. Since I lived on about fifteen thousand dollars, I had only eight thousand left to pay taxes, and had to delay the rest with, of course, their incumbent penalties. By the second year, cash flow got looser, but that first year was a rough one. I was making all that money and still living from hand to mouth like a dog.

Despite the cash flow problems, my practice exploded over the first year and a half. I had hit the nail on the head with regard to location and image. People were awe struck with the office and, once in the door, they stayed. Furthermore, there was a constant buzz about the new Ob-gyn in town and the practice grew exponentially, until I was filled with patients after only one year in practice.

I was overwhelmed with work and tired of being on call every night without relief. I couldn't go out and have a drink, for fear that I would be called in to treat a patient. I couldn't make love to my wife with ease and comfort, for fear that the beeper would go off and I would have to stop what I was doing. I couldn't even go to the bathroom in peace for fear that I wouldn't be able to finish.

My marriage was suffering for a myriad of reasons and, being forced to make love to my wife with a beeper at my side did not help the situation. By the time that I had completed my first year of practice, six years had passed since I finished medical school. We had gone over to Italy after the first, second and third years, each time hoping for a full reconciliation with her family. But not only did Christina's father refuse to see her, but he ordered her mother to do the same. We stayed at the seashore at Rimini and both other sisters came to see her often. Her mother also made clandestine visits whenever she found an excuse to visit one of her other daughters. But visits were often tearful and short, knowing that her mother was on a short leash and would have hell to pay if she was found out. At first, her mother was cool to me, but she softened her attitude, after seeing how well I responded to all of her girls when they came to visit. She never mentioned the Jewish thing and I was never sure how she felt about the issue. At this point, I really didn't care.

On June third, in the last year of my residency, Christina delivered our first born, Dean Andrew Robbins, named, against my better judgement, after Dino Martelli, Christina's father. She pleaded with me with the voice of desperation, hoping beyond hope that this gesture would be the catalyst for reconciliation with her father. As much as I detested the bastard and all he stood for, I had no choice but to cave in. For her, the stakes were too high. He was her father and, despite the fact that he callously discarded her like a piece of soiled underwear, she needed his approval and support. By this time, because I hated him, I was no help, but I reluctantly had to agree that a name was just a name, and if this action could bring resolution to her estrangement and the resultant happiness therefrom, then I was all for it.

Birth announcements were sent out and within a week she received overseas phone calls from her sisters and her mother. Her mother told her that they would be coming to visit at Christmas time, when little Dean would be six months old. Although somewhat cold and stiff, Christina finally had her reconciliation with her father. She cried in his arms as he stood awkwardly there, not knowing what to do to control her sobs. Finally, out of desperation, he held her away and whispered some words of endearment that I couldn't hear but, nonetheless, set off a new round of tears. I said nothing to him directly and vice versa.

They insisted on staying at a hotel and I didn't argue, although Christina begged them twice to stay with us. On the ride home, desperate and impatient for a full reconciliation, she attacked me.

"You could have been nicer," she said, venom in her tone.

"Listen Christina," I responded angrily. "I'm doing all that I can stomach. He's your father and I will not get in the way of you developing whatever kind of relationship that you can with him. But I am not going to make any special effort to befriend a man that hates me because I'm a Jew."

"You don't understand. He's not really like that. You have to give him a chance."

"No Christina," I said pointedly. "You don't understand. In his heart, he's still a Nazi and he'd kill me if he could."

"Stop being so melodramatic," she said with disgust. "He's my father. He's not going to try and hurt you."

"Fine," I said, putting an end to the discussion. "You coddle up to the animal and I'll just continue to watch my back in silence."

She said no more, but it was clear that she was building up more and more resentment toward me. I wanted to make it as easy as possible for her, but I could only go so far. The man had to make some gestures first and he just wasn't about to do that. On my side, I was going to leave the door open for him, but I was not going to help him get through it.

Her folks spent one full week in town and every moment that I had to spend with them was awkward and uncomfortable. Fortunately, the moments were few, as I was busy with work, and Christina smartly chose those times to spend with her parents. What they talked about I was not privy to, but with each passing day, Christina became a little more distant. She was being torn in two directions and I was not attentive enough to actively apply pressure from my side. My workload was overwhelming and we spent very little time together. She was fatigued taking care of the baby and, when I got home, I could think of little else but sleep. We grew further and further apart, and each time we tried to communicate our feelings and expectations, emotional outbursts rather than logical discourse prevailed. Compounding the situation was the fact that Christina was home sick. While she had adapted well to American society, this was not home. The people that she was familiar with and cared about were not here. The food wasn't what she was used to and the humor just wasn't the same. Within a month after her parents had left, she asked me if we could take a trip to Italy.

"I can't go now," I said in a tone that made it clear that I thought that the request was absurd at this time, given the burdens of the new practice. "Not only can't I afford to take off work, but I have no one to cover my patients."

She didn't waste a moment in reply. "Fine, I'd like to go myself for a few weeks and visit my family and my friends."

The request made me feel very uneasy, but I recognized her need for more frequent contact with her Italian roots. I also felt that I could use some time away from the constant tension at home and devote all my energies to my growing practice. After a short pause, I responded. "You know, that might be a good idea."

Christina didn't miss a beat. She had her plane reservations set up quickly for the following week. I took her to the airport and we perfunctorily said our good-byes. I waved one last time as she got on the plane with the baby. Three weeks seemed like a long time. I didn't realize how long it really would be.

Without any distractions at home, I put my heart back into making the practice grow. I volunteered to speak before multiple condominium associations and senior citizen residences about the importance of yearly breast exams, pelvics and pap smears. I knew in my heart of hearts, that, if I told them to eat low fat, exercise regularly, stop smoking and wear seat belts, I would be covering ninety five percent of the things to do for preventative medicine. Therefore, I made sure to touch on those topics before talking about the specific services that I could offer them. I also prepared topics for hospital conferences, hoping to get referrals from the family practitioners that attended, and I joined the American Medical Society and the local Medical Society. In addition, I offered my services to the chief of staff at two different hospitals to participate on medical committees of their choosing.

Furthermore, I gave fifty-percent discounts to nursing staff, hoping to woo them into my practice. People often asked nurses if they would recommend an Ob-Gyn and they usually would refer them to their own personal physician. This worked well for me and, once word got around, my patient load of nurses grew geometrically. This was true because I had a great rapport with many of the hospital nurses and a bedside manner that took into consideration their feelings and concerns. I came out into practice at a time when most gynecologists took a paternal role toward their patients. They made the decisions on the course of treatment and expected the patient to treat their words as gospel and follow their instructions blindly. There were values to that system, because it afforded the physician the opportunity to act as a buffer between the patient and the sometimes horrifying conditions of a disease. But people didn't want that anymore. Ignorance was sometimes bliss, but ignorance was not in vogue. People wanted to know and they wanted full disclosure. They wanted to participate in the decision making process and they wanted the physician to inform them of their options; not select the option for them. I picked up on this early, and I was soon thought of as the gynecologist that you could talk to; the one who didn't make judgements or dictate orders. If they had cancer, I gave them choices. If they were pregnant I also gave them choices. The decisions, well informed ones I hoped, were theirs. I just gave them information, advice and the technical skills to carry out their informed wishes.

Office décor, location, image, skills and bedside manner all contributed significantly to my early success. Judicious advertising helped just as much if not more. Traditionally, it was not considered professional for physicians to advertise their wares and the local medical society forbade it. It didn't take long to figure out why. If a physician had to spend years building his practice, then it had significant value to a new physician who wanted to buy an established one. Furthermore, no advertising guaranteed stability of the older practices, since their refurbishment was a product of patient referral, and they had the most patients from whom new patients could be referred. I broke tradition and upset the apple cart. Other physicians were up in arms, and I was brought up for review by the medical society and warned not to continue. But this was just an empty threat. It wasn't illegal. They couldn't do anything about it except try and come in the back door by reviewing my cases and censoring me for bad treatment. I dotted my "I's" and crossed my "T's" and never gave them a chance. It proved that you could break tradition, but you better be perfect or close to it. Otherwise, they will find a way to devour you.

At the time that I entered practice in nineteen hundred and seventy three, another great change took place in America, flying in on the wings of civil liberties, first offered to blacks and now being made available for women by the United States Supreme Court decision in Roe vs. Wade. This decision opened up the door for all women to have the legal right to abort their pregnancies on an elective basis without being accountable to anyone but themselves. It gave them a choice and no longer did they have to accept being bound and chained by unwanted pregnancies.

Most established physicians were reluctant to do abortions for their patients, for they felt that it would reflect badly on their practices. They feared being labeled as the town abortionist with all its negative implications. Also, many of them had a religious objection to abortion and would not do them under any circumstance. Others were trained in an era when they were illegal and frowned upon by the traditional powers that be. For them, the additional income did not justify the risk.

My attitude was totally different. I believed in women's rights and I believed in their right of choice. On moral grounds, I was willing to make sure that women in my community had the option available to them and, on pragmatic grounds, I certainly could use the money. My door was open and it began to fill up.

Doing pregnancy terminations was a whole new experience. Although the procedure was similar to a regular dilatation and curettage, it was originally done under local anesthesia in an outpatient setting. This required some special skills on the part of the practitioner, not to be discounted because of what he was doing. It required patience and tenderness. It required soft, reassuring speech that coordinated perfectly with the technical procedure and it required stamina, because the physician might be required to do twenty to thirty a day (in large cities that number might reach forty to fifty per day.) It also required a gentle and sensitive touch, for the procedure was done through feel rather than vision.

Because, for the most part, insurance didn't pay for the procedure and Medicaid payments were small in some states and not allowed in others, abortions weren't very expensive. Throughout the seventies and early eighties, for less that two hundred dollars, an individual could get a history and physical, multiple lab work, surgery, post operative exam, counseling and a start on birth control pills if so desired. You couldn't get a tooth pulled or a root canal for that in America, and a conventional D&C in a hospital would cost a patient over two thousand dollars, ten times as much, before they were done.

What this told me was that if patients had to pay most of a bill directly, the cost would then be determined by the rules of supply and demand. In medicine, insurance companies and government (Medicare and Medicaid) got in the way and set the stage for human nature to run rampant. Given the chance, patients, doctors and insurance companies all bared their teeth and showed their inherent greed.

Normally, in the supply and demand system, if you wanted a new suit that you had to pay for and you went to the store to buy it, only to be told by the sales person that you needed three suits and four pair of slacks, you would leave the store and shop somewhere else. But supposing someone else, not involved in the decision, had to pay for it. Then you would listen to the sales person because you had nothing to lose and everything to gain if they could get the third party payer to foot the bill.

Because of government and insurance companies, that's how the system worked in medicine. Physicians would recommend testing, procedures and treatment that would be blindly accepted rather than challenged, because the patient didn't have to pay the bill. The third party payer really didn't care, because they were the insurance company and the government. Rather than fight the expense, the insurance companies just raised the premiums. As long as employers and individuals would pay higher premiums, skyrocketing expenses could be ignored. Government just raised taxes. It was simple and it spiraled upward. Physicians also facilitated the process, for they were rewarded for over testing and over caution and punished for good common sense decisions. Instead of introducing economic feasibility into the equation, they ignored it. No one could fault them for doing an extra test and, in the process, they got paid for it too. On the other hand, if they failed to do a test on someone who suffered later because of the delay, they were subject to a malpractice suit. The fact that they would have had to test one hundred thousand people at a cost of ten million dollars in order to find that one person with the terminal disease is of no consequence in a malpractice case. The only thing in question is whether or not this test could have prevented the eventual calamity in that individual. No wonder most doctors ignored economy, comfort and convenience for their patients. Over testing and over treating protected them from malpractice and lined their pockets. It was clear to me back then that this system could not go on forever. It was also clear what was looming on the horizon.

Only control of volume could reduce medical costs by threatening hospitals and physicians with a sudden loss of a large patient flow, unless they accepted reductions in payment schedules. Only big business and government had pockets deep enough to gather the volume necessary to wield that kind of a big stick. The masses didn't trust government enough to allow for socialization of the system, because history is totally aware of the waste, inefficiency, and abuse that absolute power generates. By default, that left big business and it was clear that the savings that they extorted from the system would not be passed on to the consumer but rather used to line their own pockets. The system would continue to spiral and the only difference would be that twenty five to thirty percent of the money would end up in the pockets ofbig business, and the hospitals and physicians would have to compromise medical care if they wanted to stay in business.

Today, the situation is in sad flux. A physician signs a contract with an HMO, agreeing to indemnify them from any malpractice judgement against them as a result of his negligence. The physician, not being an attorney, doesn't understand that his malpractice coverage, for which he pays dearly, doesn't cover indemnification, so he is totally exposed to losing everything he's worked a lifetime to save. For the most part, he has no choice anyway, because in order to survive, he must be signed on with the HMO's that control the largest volume of patients in his locale.

The HMO's, also, dictate what tests he can and cannot do and, if they don't pay for them, he is often not allowed to suggest them to the patient, at the risk of no longer being a provider for that HMO. Occasionally, he is faced with a choice of compromising what he thinks is good care by not ordering a test an HMO won't pay for, or suggesting the test anyway, and losing his provider status with the HMO. Damned if you do and damned if you don't. You have to be nuts to go to medical school today.

There is an eventual answer to the problem and it's salvation shall be found in the remarkable information that computer analysis can provide. Government must take control of the medical system, at least to the extent of quality assurance, risk management and analysis of costs. Right off the bat, if they never did anything else, they could save ten percent of the cost of medical care by standardized billing. Today, billing is a nightmare in all hospitals and medical offices in that there are a myriad of forms and codes to use, differing from payer to payer, causing tremendous delays and inefficiencies in payment. Of course inefficiency and delay work well for private companies, as they allow them to hold cash longer, and make significant interest dollars on their capital reserves.

Secondly, the game of musical patients could be avoided, with the result of tremendous savings to the medical system. The game is played like this. All physicians have to cover emergency rooms for a certain number of days and nights each month, depending on the number of physicians that practice their specialty at that hospital. When a physician is called in at three o'clock in the morning to see an indigent patient whom he knows cannot pay the bill, he is quite perturbed. If he admits the patient, he will be forced to care for that patient for the extent of their hospital stay, and for a time thereafter, even if he doesn't get paid. Even if the patient has Medicaid, the payment is usually so inadequate, it's laughable. Therefore, if the physician can find any justification to send that patient home and treat them as an outpatient, he does so, knowing that, if the patient returns to the emergency room tomorrow, somewhat sicker, and in need of more extensive care, someone else will be on call and have to take care of them. In the end, this game of musical patients compromises the care of the indigent, and costs the taxpayers more dollars.

Those two being "no brainers," what else can be done? Many things, starting with this. Divide the country up into regions and then districts. Each state can be a region, and each county a district. It really doesn't matter. Monitor quality of performance, frequency of exams and tests, frequency of surgeries, and costs etc. in all regions. Support this by setting up government programs in small districts in which the physicians are government employed and paid extremely high salaries, and oppose that with some districts in which physicians are rewarded for service and see the difference in utilization and quality assurance. The physicians paid by salary are promoted for doing the right thing.

They will be rewarded for low utilization, without compromise of quality of service. The right mix will obviously be established by the promoted physicians who will eventually oversee the system of quality assurance and utilization. With these standards set, guidelines can eventually be laid down for the ninety nine percent of physicians who are paid a fee for service. If their performance deviates too far from the norm of expectation, they are brought into line by review and censor. If they do not adapt, they are eliminated from the program.

The salaried physicians can also determine the reasonable effort required to do a certain procedure, for there is no incentive for them to distort the truth. In this way, a reasonable and fair fee schedule can be determined. The same control system can also be done for hospitals and nursing care facilities, which, by the way, comprise ninety percent of the cost of medical care in this country. The standards can be set and refined and the institutions can be forced to meet those standards.

Enough philosophy for now. Back to nineteen seventy three, it was clear that my practice was growing in two directions, the conventional practice on one hand and the abortion practice on the other. It was clear that each one hurt the other and that they needed to be separated. It was from here that the clinic that specialized in pregnancy termination and family planning was born in Florida.

In order to separate my practice from the pregnancy termination service and to provide a more stabile income base for a partner, I opened up a small facility to primarily service that need. I figured that my partner could do most of the procedures and supplement the practice income flow. I thought, also, that I was going to make this important service more readily available to the segment of the population

that desired it and, in the process, help provide a source of future patients. Never, in my wildest dreams did I expect to do the kind of volume that we did.

THE DEVELOPING YEARS

On the boat over I met Francis, Francis Catrelli. They called him Frank for short. I never wondered why.

Our first encounter came at a bridge table. Two guys and a girl were idly twisting their thumbs and absent mindedly fooling with two decks of cards. I saw a bridge score pad on the table and logically assumed they needed a fourth. Boldly I approached. "I'm a pretty good dummy if you're missing one."

"The chair is open to the highest bidder," Frank retorted, "and since you're the only one asking, set your ass right down in that chair."

The game moved smoothly along. I played with Frank and easily slid into his style of play. He tended to overbid and I accommodated with a conservative game. The cards ran right and we were trouncing our adversaries. During the contest we made small talk. The girl on the left was all mouth and no body. Her voice was rich and resonant, emanating between large white buckteeth and a cannibalistic smile. The rest of her fell indistinctly into the background. I wouldn't have even let her blow me. That's how bad she was.

The guy on the right was a cool French-Canadian. His skin was leathery and tanned, with just a little meat around his chin to hint that he was in his thirties. He supported a one-day growth. Wide shades covered his eyes. His hair was pitch black and slung back in the "Duck's ass" style of the era. The collar from his black leather jacket covered the back and sides of a thick bullish neck and a cigarette dangled from his lips. I couldn't help but see a print ofMarlon Brando sitting in that chair.

"Shit," Frank said as he picked up his hand.

"You," the girl said turning toward Frank, "are vulgar. Must you use that language?"

That moving mouth, when blocked from the body, looked like a barracuda. I winced, imagining that thing surrounding my manhood.

"Fuck you," Frank retorted.

"Boy are you a smooth talker," she said sarcastically.

Frank put down his cards, furrowed his forehead, looked right into her eyes, and said threateningly. "Shut the fuck up and bid."

So as not to seem to fall apart, she mumbled something under her breath, but you could tell by the break in her voice that she was innerved. You could also tell that he disgusted her with his liberal use of the language and, after she regrouped, she refused to give him an inch.

The game moved on long into the night. There wasn't much else to do anyway. Besides, I enjoyed the constant exchange between Frank and the girl. I thought the Canadian did too. He didn't say much. He just listened, responded and attended to his hands. At 5:00 A.M. Frank got up to go to the bathroom for the eighth time. Too much beer I guessed. The Frenchman looked at his watch, yawned and said he had to go.

"Where," I asked.

"To church," he replied.

"What the hell for."

"I've got to say mass." He paused, while a broard smile broke out on his face. "I'm a priest. My name is Father Perreau."

The girl looked startled and so did I.

"Hey," I said excitedly. "I'm not catholic and I've never been to mass. But I am curious. Can I come?"

"Sure, I'll meet you in the church in ten minutes."

Frank walked back into the room just then and I called to him.

"Frank, you wanna go to mass?"

"Fuck no! You'll never catch me there."

"Frank."

"What?"

"I'd like you to meet Father Perreau."

"Oh, hello Fath—," he paused dumbfounded.

Perreau just smiled and then said, "I'll see you in ten minutes."

At 5:15 Frank and I were on our knees side by side. While I watched, he was praying up a storm.

Thank god for Frank Catrelli. Otherwise I never would have made it to Bologna.

From the moment we docked at Genoa, his fluent dialect, sprinkled with some textbook Italian, got us through customs and on the train to Bologna with most of our baggage. One piece of mine was lost, apparently during the loading in New York City, and, with the fervent promise from the Italian lines officials that it would shortly follow on the next boat, I left Genoa for Bologna with excited anticipation.

The last, alas, was to be prolonged for Frank and I found ourselves on an "accelerato" (local) instead of a "diritissimo." Frank apparently asked for the next train to Bologna and the clerk at the station didn't bother to explain the difference. They never did offer pertinent information unless directly asked for. Only irrelevant or wrong information was spontaneously offered. We stopped at every little village along the way and what should have been a four-hour trip on a comfortable train turned into a fourteen-hour nightmare. We arrived in Bologna at 5:07 A.M. in the black of night. Both of us were tired and drawn and the excitement of arrival in our new home was suffocated by our physical exhaustion. We didn't even look around. We toted our luggage to the nearest hotel. Once in the room, I undressed quickly to race Frank to the shower. I won and hopped in under the warm sprinkle. I reached out for the soap but there was none. I later learned that Italian hotels did not supply soap. I lay under the stream of water, relaxed and sleeping, figuring I could rub the dirt and dust off later.

The chill hit me like a knife. The water had suddenly turned ice cold and I jumped out of the shower like a startled rabbit and wrapped myself in a hand towel, the only one I could find. I would later learn that all of Italy was filled with little surprise traps like shingles falling accidentally from a building, flies in the soup, oblivious drivers, ad infinitum. It still continues to amaze me how they remain over populated. You walk out on the street and you take your life in your hands. Somehow, somewhere along the way you lose that incessant and unrelenting feeling of impending doom and assume the attitude of "Que sera sera," ("what will be will be.") And miraculously, with built in radar, you seemed to avoid all the pitfalls. You stopped worrying about inconvenience, waiting, and danger and just enjoyed the zest of living.

We both slept like logs and arose with renewed vigor, anxious to start the day. Our spirit was dampened when we discovered that there was no place to find bacon and eggs for breakfast. We settled for a couple of pastries each, washed down with a cappuccino.

Over breakfast I learned a little more about Frank. He was born Alberto Francesco Catrelli, named after his father, in Naples in 1928. At the age of three he immigrated, with his two older brothers and parents, to the United States of America and they settled in a small coal-mining town in the hills ofWestern Pennsylvania. Life was hard and primitive but full nevertheless for the Catrelli family. His father worked seventy hours a week in the mines from the day he arrived till the day he died at age forty, crushed to death under a mountain of coal. Nevertheless, Alberto's twelve years in America were wholesome and rewarding. While in Pennsylvania they had added three more offspring. Frank's mother, Maria, head held high and smile fixed to her face, ran the household with efficiency and warmth. The small two bedroom wood frame home was kept immaculately clean. A pair of triple layer bunk beds had been built in one bedroom for the seven children. In the other bedroom Alberto and his wife were able to culminate the days labors with a few moments of semi-privacy. The walls were thin and Frank could hardly remember a night when he could not hear whispered endearments escaping between the rhythmic squeaks of coiling bedsprings.

Old Alberto's income was meager, but with resourcefulness and undying spirit his mother always made do. The noodle was the hallmark of the Catrelli table. It took the form of spaghetti, linguini, riga- toni, and tortelloni and on Sundays, for a special treat, lasagna, tortellini or manicotti. There may not have been meat more than once a week, but the meals were wholesome, and no one ever left the table hungry. Before each meal a prayer was always said and each child bowed their head in respectful reverence to God and father.

With regard to clothing, hand me downs were the name of the game. Their pants were made of coarse baggy material, and didn't always fit, but they were warm nevertheless. With skill and patience, his mother darned socks and applied patches to pants as needed. A pair was never discarded until the patched patches themselves wore through. His mother made the girls' dresses by hand.

On Sunday, all bathed, scrubbed and dressed in their best, they attended church. And, during the mass, God help the Catrelli child that shuffled in his or her seat or mumbled a word of discontent. Frank remembered that, if his bladder were full, it was best to wet his pants than incur the wrath of his father.

It was old Alberto's dream that all his children would get the education that eluded him. After dinner they would all remain at the big dining room table and, in silence, attend to their studies. In the early years they all went to Giovanni, the oldest brother, for help if they did not understand a problem or a word, for old Alberto and Maria could not read or write English. But as Frank grew older, it became obvious that he grasped academic ideas more readily than his older brothers did and had an uncanny ability to simplify complex material and explain the concepts in basic tangible terms. The youngsters began to gravitate toward him with their school problems and within the family it was gradually decided that he would be the one to attend college. There was no resentment on the part of Giovanni or his second older brother Fabrizio. It was a decision of practicality and it would be their duty to help old Alberto in the mines to save the money to send Frank to college.

The sudden death of Alberto at age forty delayed those plans. The

Catrelli's, as well as the other fifteen hundred families in town, lived with the constant fear of a mine explosion or a collapsing tunnel. But this fear was continually shoveled into the deep recesses of their minds, only to be agonizingly brought forth with each periodic tragic incident.

On the day of the accident the whole Catrelli male clan, along with a hundred other workers, dug feverishly toward their buried relatives. The mood was silent and somber but the men worked on to near complete exhaustion through the cold icy night and the following day. When all hope was lost, the four boys, Giovanni 18, Fabrizio 16, Frank 15 and little Pino 12, walked home with heads down and shoulders bent, realizing that the rock on which the family was built was no longer there.

On arrival home, their bowed heads and silent frowns told the story in an instant. Maria and the girls tried to remain strong but little Sophia broke the dam of stoicism with a muffled sob and, once broken, the wall burst and the whole family wept in each other's arms. All that is except Frank. The tears that begged to flow freely were squashed unwillingly by enraged bitterness. He knew that his father and men like him had been exploited and that safety conditions had been ignored for the convenience of the profiteers. He made a vow that night that someday, somewhere, justice would be served and he would crucify and then castrate the whole lot of them.

Giovanni assumed position as head of the household quite naturally. After a short period of adaptation, it became obvious to all that he was just as firm and just as determined as his father to provide food, shelter, order, and discipline to their lives. The gay carefree attitude, though, that enveloped the Catrelli household, when Alberto was alive, had been replaced by a cloud of burdens. Maria had not fully recovered from the ordeal and the young girls had to take over a good part of the household chores. Fabrizio had to quit school and help Giovanni in the mines. Frank had wanted to work also, but they insisted that he remain in school, as he represented to them their only hope of crawling out of the pit. Once out, he would pull them all up beside him.

Four months after Alberto's death, Giovanni was drafted into the army and Frank had to go to the mines. Three months after that they received notice that Giovanni Catrelli had died bravely in the service of his nation. The household rained with despair and the dreary hopeless existence that lay in store for them was reflected in the somber expressions of the children. As usual, they all went about their daily tasks with promptness and efficiency but their actions, once colored with gaiety, flightiness, and abandon, were now marked with the cold hard brand of reality. The background of laughter was gone and not one face supported a smile. They had all given up and accepted the cards fate had dealt out to them. All that is except Frank.

By day he toiled in the mines. By night he read and studied and attended classes until he unwillingly succumbed to the sweet relief of slumber. Each day at dawn he coaxed his aching body from the bed, the energy for labor being generated by a core of hatred toward those who coldly exploited the bodies and brains of his fellow miners and exposed them to unnecessary danger.

All his efforts were funneled toward eradicating that injustice. He knew that an education was an important tool in the armament of a crusader. Therefore, after providing the grim necessities, school held the top priority.

By 1948, at the age of 20, he had achieved his high school diploma from night school and along with Fabrizio had kept the family on an even keel. His grades were good. But, because he had not attended a formal day high school, all his applications for university scholarships had been denied.

He decided to work a double shift for two years and save the wages from one of those shifts for his college tuition and expenses. He felt that with that buffer, some state loans, summer jobs and after school employment, he would be able to contribute to the household and still have enough to pay for the cost of college. Those two years were long and dreary, marked by long arduous hours of work deep down in the bowels of a mountain, and clouded by a complete lack of intellectual stimulation and a deep sense of stagnation.

Maria took in day work to help supplement their income and, by the end of those two years, college became a reality.

Frank's excited anticipation of final acceptance to the state university for the fall of 1950 was stamped out by a draft notice from the armed forces. Deep frustration set in as another obstacle had abruptly fallen in his path, while, for the first time since Alberto's death, the road seemed free and clear.

His mother Maria, upon hearing the news, wept, as she saw for Frank only the same fate that had befallen her first born Giovanni. Fabrizio was grim and frightened by the necessity for him to assume full responsibility for the family. Despite the fact that he was titular head, it had come to pass that all decisions were made by Frank and only out of courtesy was Fabrizio consulted for his nod of approval. It was just a rubber stamp though. He never refused.

With a forced smile, and a solemn vow to his mother that he would return and pursue the elusive education, Frank Catrelli, age 22, kissed his mother and sisters goodbye, shook Fabrizio's hand and left his home state for the first time in his life.

A new world and a wealth of experience were opened up to him. His innate curiosity and mental alertness allowed him to absorb it all like a sponge sopping up water.

That which he had read and dreamed about; that which had seemed so distant and intangible now became first hand experience filled to the brim with excitement. At Fort Baker, in New Jersey, he underwent basic training with ease as his body had been conditioned by the years of hard labor in the mines. He enjoyed the intimacy of living with men around his own age, almost all with a different background than he. He listened intently with fascination as most of them, finding a willing listener, unfolded their life stories to him. His serious non-complaining nature, combined with his ability to listen and avoid gossip, quickly installed him as a leader and sought after friend.

After the rigors of basic training were finished, he began for the first time in his life to enjoy the many hours and days of leisure time that belonged to a private in the United States Army. Also, despite the fact that he forwarded half of his paycheck to his mother, he experienced for the first time the power of having spending money in his pocket to use for pleasure and luxury as he saw fit.

His weekends were usually spent in New York, at first just walking the streets, awed by the incessant and overwhelming activity. Later, he began frequenting the museums, art centers, shows, and ballgames with which New York was over endowed.

For the first time in his life he went to the seashore and saw the beauty of the soft billowy waves slapping against the jetties. He slept there that first night just to experience the sensation of the sweeping serenity and freedom that enveloped the darkened, star lit beach. Waking up to the sun bursting over the horizon, bringing a new spark of life to the sandy dunes, was sheer ecstasy. It was there that he met Janet.

Age 22 is not the time to experience your first love, but Frank Catrelli had not had the time or inclination for that before. That morning, while he sat on the beach watching the sunrise, his silent concentration was shattered by a voice behind. "Do you always come here this early or do you sleep here?"

He jerked his head around, startled at the unsuspected intrusion. She stood before him proud and tall, dark black hair flowing down to her waist, the tight knit black suit exaggerating the voluptuous curves of her body. She quickly shifted her body to a point where the sun shone behind her and Frank, looking up at her face, could see no more than the silhouette of her form. Standing there, with the sun outlining her shape and her soft long hair blowing in the light breeze, she looked like a goddess to him. "I slept here last night." He placed his left hand over his eyes trying to shield them from the glare reflecting off the perimeter of her figure.

"I've been watching you for a quarter of an hour. You seemed so intent in observing the sunrise. I'd never seen anybody so involved in anything before."

"I've never seen it before."

"The sunrise?"

"No, the beach." They both laughed.

"What's your name?" she asked.

"Frank, and yours?"

"Janet."

"Hi Janet."

"Hi Frank."

"What are you doing out here so early?"

"Spying on you. Besides I like to swim at dawn. It refreshes me."

"What are you waiting for?"

"You," she turned and ran toward the crisply breaking waves.

Frank jumped and followed her into the water.

From that point on he spent all his free weekends with Janet. He had always been shy and withdrawn with girls before. They had made him feel worthless and awkward, but with Janet he felt comfortable and wanted. She showered him with attention and affection. She taught him the act of lovemaking and, when he fumbled, she overlooked his ineptitude. His body, though, was lean and strong; his basic nature empathetic. It didn't take him long to learn the movements that aroused her and stimulated her response.

A whole new world of pleasure was bared before him and he seized it with abandon and without control. As time passed, the mores with which he was inflicted in childhood became more suspect and open to scrutiny. By church rules Janet was weak, dirty, and immoral, but to him she represented a source of strength, fun and interest. It seemed wrong that one so giving of pleasure should be labeled as evil and hell bound. And as he investigated his past, he discovered other inconsistencies in church doctrine.

No longer was life a series of single instinctive reactions to given situations. It took on, instead, many shades and with it came confusion and anxiety; elation and depression. He left up no armor, and, once freed from the incarcerations of his own mind, allowed himself full exposure to the sensations of life.

Nothing was guarded and when he fell, he fell hard. In the ensuing months he had fallen overwhelmingly in love with Janet. He also felt secure in her singular love for him for, within the framework of his own experience, there was no other way to account for her willingness to give completely of body and mind. His misinterpretation could be accounted for in the column of innocence but, whatever the reason, there was no way to assuage the pain.

The weekend of their half-year anniversary he was scheduled to be on base. On Friday, he received notice that they were shipping out for Korea and that all men in his company were to have weekend passes to go home. He decided right then and there that he would ask her to marry him and bring her home to Maria for final approval. He went directly to her apartment, took the stairs two at a time in his impatience to let her share the good news. The key she had given him went into the lock and he quickly opened the door. There, like a nightmare before him, was Janet kneeling on the floor bent over a phallus, shuddering at the pinnacle of climax. Her head shot up, startled by the intrusion, semen dripping from her lips.

The bottom fell out of his stomach and he slammed the door trying to shut out the scene before him. Shaking, he moved to the corner of the corridor, kneeled to the floor and emptied his gut. Body tremoring, mind churning and ready to explode, he felt the compulsion to run, run, run. The rest of the week was a whirlwind of confusion, just perfunctorily going through the motions, still numb from his tragic encounter with Janet. He refused to take her calls and blocked her out of his mind. When he got on the boat to ship out, he was ready for combat. "After all," he said to himself. "There just wasn't very much worthwhile trying to live for. I might as well go out in a burst of glory."

His body shuddered from the cold as he inched up closer to the corner of his foxhole. Bombs were bursting around him and his body shook, not only in unison with each concussion, but with the anticipation of same. The man to his left, once his friend Joe, was a lump of worthless disfigured flesh. The man to the left of Joe was huddled in the other corner whimpering uncontrollably.

He took a few deep breaths, trying to gain control of his shivering body. Raising himself from the hole, he lunged and crawled for the cover of a large boulder fifty feet in front of him. Rhythmic flashes belched from a machine gun nest on top of a ledge a hundred feet in front and twenty-five feet to the left of the boulder. The brush behind him was cut up by the bullets and a bazooka shell fell off to his left, just as he tumbled behind the rock. A sharp pain shot through his left leg and he saw blood trickle through his pants. The pain dulled and he felt faint. He wrapped a bandana around the wound for compression and huddled at the base of the boulder to catch his breath and regroup his thoughts. He motioned with his hand for his men to follow, but nobody moved from the holes. That machine gun was pinning them down. He lifted his eyes to a level with the top of the boulder so that he could survey the terrain in front. Only that machine gun stood in the way of conquest of hill #42. Suddenly, his eyes drew singular focus on that gun, its long barrel emanating from the dark bowels of a dugout on the side of the hill. He lay his helmet to the right of the boulder and the machine gun responded with rhythmic ejaculations. Suddenly, its image magnified before him and its repetitive bursts became deafening. With each burst a wave of pain shot through him. His hands covered his ears, but the pain bore through them and he knew that the only relief could come from complete annihilation of that gun.

Ignoring his helmet, he shot off across the open plain, diving into a small cave at the side of the hill, miraculously avoiding enemy bullets. Without hesitation, he pulled out the pin on a grenade and tore out toward the machine-gun, still twenty-five feet to the left and fifty feet up the hill. As he drove his body toward the gun, muscles tensed, face contorted in agony, a shriek of incredible pitch and intensity emanated from the very depths of his soul.

The gunner spotted him just as he sprung from the cave. Somehow, though, that shriek left him startled and paralyzed, for just a second or two perhaps but, nevertheless, enough to allow Frank to launch that grenade into the nest. The explosion made the earth before him tremor and the world spin around relentlessly. The pain had peaked and, suddenly, he was gratefully relieved as the world around him turned black.

He woke up in a field hospital, head thumping and eyes squinting to avoid the light. The initially hazy image of a man focused into that of the commander of the division, Col. R.J. Brown. Frank had never met Brown before in the six months he had spent in his company and his countenance expressed confusion. "How do you feel Sargent?" Brown said leaning over the bed.

"Head hurts a little but I think I'll be alright."

"What about the leg?" he said pointing toward the bandaged limb.

Frank looked down surprised and suddenly became aware of the dull ache in his calf. "Funny," he said half-surprised, "I didn't even think of it. Is it bad?"

"No, just hit the outer part of the calf. We were mostly worried about your head."

"Don't worry sir; I'll be alright. Just a little shock I guess."

"Fine Catrelli. Now rest easy." He patted him on the good leg as he turned toward the door. Then, as an afterthought, he turned again toward Frank and said, "By the way Catrelli, your action out there speaks for itself. I'm recommending you for a Congressional Medal of Honor."

The president stepped before him and the room fell to a hushed silence. "For courage above and beyond the call of duty, I am proud and honored to award the Congressional Medal ofHonor to Francesco Catrelli. It is on the shoulders of men like Frank that the strength of America lay."

Tears welled in the corner of Frank's eyes, as the President stepped forward to pin the medal to his chest. In a life of dull miserable toil, this was his moment of glory and he was going to bask in the moment. "Thank you, Mr. President."

"You're welcome Frank and I mean every word." The President turned toward Maria, standing to Frank's side and congratulated her on raising such a fine son. "You raised a real fine American boy Mrs. Catrelli. You should be very proud." She stood awestruck and hung on every word said by the great man before her. She had faith in her son Frank and knew that he would be a credit to the Catrelli name. But in all her life, she had never expected to stand face to face with the President of the United States, on equal ground, as he praised her for her efforts in raising her son. Her face mirrored the pride she felt and, with all the inner courage she could muster, she uttered a reply meek in intensity perhaps but rich in content and meaning.

"I am filled with joy to have him home with me Signore Presidente." The tears rolled down her reddened cheeks as she continued almost inaudibly. "If only his papa were here to share this moment with me. Then he would know that all that work has been for something."

The President nodded understandably and excused himself from the banquet on the plea of urgent business.

That night they partied and the following day Frank was bombarded with phone calls, well wishes, girls looking for husbands and business opportunities. He was overwhelmed with his own self-importance but, as the day wore on, all the interruptions became a nuisance. Finally, he had to have the hotel clerk screen them, limiting incoming calls only to family or army officials.

The following day he was given his new assignment. He still had one year to spend in the armed forces and for that period of time he was to work with the division of recruitment as a traveling procurer for future army personnel.

He traveled around the country first class and gave a patented speech, previously prepared for him, to a variety of groups ranging from Boy Scout troops to Spanish American war veterans. Barnstorming offered him a rare opportunity to see the country from top to bottom, on his own terms, with time to spend and people to cater to his needs.

Job offers kept streaming in over the year and he began to screen them carefully. Eventually, he settled on a position with International

Fuel Corporation, a company whose home base was in Pittsburgh, close to his hometown. The job paid well, fourteen thousand dollars per year, but many of the other offers were financially more attractive. He chose this position though for they promised him the directorship of a new division dealing with the improvement of working conditions for company personnel.

He started the job with enthusiasm and laid the groundwork for a number of effective and practical methods to improve overall safety and comfort at work. Although costly, they might, in the end, result in a sense of renewed spirit, loyalty, efficiency and, most importantly, augmented net profit. But at every turn he met repetitive obstacles. "The time was not right" or "the funds were too low" or "next month we'll look into it." It took him almost a year to realize that he was being used as a figurehead; that as a Congressional Medal of Honor winner with a coal miner's background, he was admired and trusted by company employees. As long as token improvements were made, the companies could continue to delay implementing strong but costly safety measures. But to be sure, he continued to bang his head against the wall for another year. Finally, in a moment of complete frustration and anger, he told the company vice-president, to whom he was directly responsible, to shove the whole works up his ass and quit.

During that year, though, he had come upon problems, common to the miner, that thoroughly fascinated him; silicosis and lung cancer. In order to combat these miner's enemies, he had spent numerous hours with company doctors and observed their frustration in trying to treat these diseases that were best combated by prevention. But he admired their undying spirit and tenacious ability to rebound from failure and try again to fight the problem on all fronts.

Furthermore, he found the basic science of the disease process fascinating and, as that year wore on, he found himself spending much of his leisure reading time involved in articles on medicine and disease. When he quit his job, he had already determined that he was going to be a physician. It was just a question of time as to when he would begin.

With a part-time job, the GI bill and twelve thousand dollars in savings, he was able to continue to help support Maria and the girls as well as attend college.

Upon completion of his degree, he applied to medical school and, on the basis of good grades and the Congressional Medal ofHonor, he was accepted at numerous universities in the country. But tuition was steep and not one would supply him with a full scholarship. He could see no way to meet expenses and still send enough money to Fabrizio to help support their mother. He still had eight thousand dollars of savings left and felt that he would have to contribute at least this much to Maria over the next five years. Fabrizio had gotten married and, although now an assistant supervisor on the morning shift, could not support Maria alone. His oldest sister was married and the younger two were still going to school. He wished not to put too much pressure on them and he knew that, if he could send thirty to thirty-five dollars a week, Maria could live with her daughter or son and still contribute her share to the household.

Without a scholarship, there was no way to make it in this country. Frank had given up all hope of attending medical school when his mother approached him with the idea of going to medical school in Italy. Learning the language would be no real problem. And total expenses could be kept to less than twenty one hundred dollars per year. He would also be able to spend as much time as he wanted in the U.S. in order to make extra money, as there was no requirement to attend classes and examinations could be taken during any of three examination periods in the year. All in all, the program seemed attractive. Frank applied and was accepted. He was on his way.

Frank and I had to search for a week before we found adequate housing. Availability, not price was the problem. Apartments were dirt cheap, but it was difficult to find one. There just weren't enough to go around. For some reason, the laws of supply and demand just didn't seem to apply in Italy.

Finally, we ventured into the most luxurious buildings in town. They had a penthouse apartment available. The cost was one hundred and ten dollars per month for three bedrooms, dining room, kitchen, and two baths. It was a split-level layout with double level balconies.

We were amazed at the rent. The sum was enormous for most Italians, but more than reasonable for me. Even Frank was overwhelmed and agreed to taking the apartment if we took in a third roommate.

With the lease signed and a two month deposit put down, we then found out that there was a two hundred and forty dollar per year cost for heat, elevator and cleaning the halls. The sum was payable on a monthly basis. It was irritating, not because of the twenty dollars per month, but because we had been mislead with regard to rental.

What is more, we were told that we had to pay a seventy-five dollar fee to the rental agent who had the exclusive right to rent all apartments in the building. We had never seen him before, but he typified the method of Italian payola. There were always a million hands in the pot. Petty yes, but irritating just the same, like a fly buzzing around your nose.

With the lease signed and the apartment in our name, we then went about the task of utilities and furnishings. Unfurnished apartment for rent was the understatement of the year. Naked would have been more appropriate. The bathroom lacked shower rod, curtain, medicine cabinet, towel racks and, much to our chagrin, a toilet seat. The kitchen needed a stove, fridge, cabinets, and the like. All other rooms needed everything. There wasn't even a light socket in the house, let alone the bulbs. You had to wire your own. Looking on the brighter side of things, I was thankful that the walls were plastered and that they didn't rent just rough shells.

My first attempt at getting electricity for the house ended in total failure. I had found my way to the electric company. You couldn't call and, even if you could, we couldn't speak on the phone. I arrived in the building at ten a.m. With dictionary in hand, I got my message across to the lady at the information desk and she pointed to the line in front of window nine. I stood in line for forty minutes, until my time came, and then presented the clerk with a letter from my landlord stating that I wanted electricity turned on. He replied to me in Italian, nodding his head up and down, and I spit out the only sentence I had memorized.

"Non capisco (I don't understand.) Sono Americano (I am

American.)

This only enticed him to speak with greater intensity. For some reason people think foreigners will understand better if you yell at them. Well, loud or soft, the words are the same. You either understand or you don't and I didn't have a clue. Again I repeated my practiced phrase. "Non capisco, sono Americano."

Not to be dismayed, he tried once again and then his face lit up. He held up his index finger, indicating in international tongue to wait a minute. All that lacked was the yellow bulb over his head signaling "idea!" He called over his friend who nodded affirmatively and then approached me. His mouth formed a circle and the word "hello" emanated between his lips. My heart sung for joy. From out of the twilight zone back to the real world. "Excuse me sir." I let the words rush like water over a dam. "All I want to do is register for the electricity so that it can be turned on in my apartment."

"What?" came the reply between a grimace that indicated confusion. "Please talk more slowly."

I regrouped my thoughts, paused and spoke more slowly, enunciating every word in exaggerated fashion. "I want to have electricity."

"Ah," shouted the voice of understanding.

"It says so right there," I said pointing at the paper. The first clerk spurted in with a few Italian phrases and my savior again nodded his head.

"Yes, but we want to know what type, industriale o normale."

"What?"

"Industriale or normale."

"I still don't understand." My face registered my confusion.

"Industrial. It is for those things that are necessary. Forno—er— stove, refrigerator ecetera. Normale, it is for the lights, the television, and so on."

"I guess I need both." "Guess?"

"I need both," I repeated eliminating the word guess. When speaking to a foreigner, the KISS rule applies. Keep it simple stupid.

"Good." He picked up two application forms and handed them to me. "Go over to that desk and do these forms."

He went down the application form with me, rapidly telling me what went where and, with vague understanding, I thanked him in Italian and walked over to the desk. My confidence was thin but at least it was buoyed by the dictionary in my hand. I was wounded and I needed that crutch.

I labored for an hour until the forms were complete and I had learned a number of Italian words such as address, citizenship, name, etc. and returned to the line. It moved quickly but, with only three people to go, the clerk closed his draw and hung up a sign that said, "chiuso." The two people in front of me threw up their hands, shook their heads and appeared to be arguing with the clerk. Reception was poor however as he paid them no mind, then turned his back and disappeared into the building. I walked to the information desk and frantically looked up the word open. I knew how to say when.

"Quando apre?" I said in Italian.

"Alle quatro"

With face contorted I repeated, "quando? No capisco."

"Alle quatro."

I got the word quatro all right. That was four o'clock. I had four hours to blow. That was my first real agonizing exposure to the Italian midday break. It took me a good year before I could acclimate myself to it and arrange my plans so that it would not interfere with my day.

I could never make them appreciate the common sense in a short lunch break and early dinner at home. No matter what the inconvenience, they enjoyed the four hours of their mid day siesta. The extra commuting trips on crowded buses and a workday that began at eight and ended at nine or ten at night didn't seem to phase them. But, then, making love for your lunchtime desert is a difficult habit to break.

At four p.m., I returned, and braced myself for another offensive. The big doors swung open at 4:06. It was my first exposure to Italian time. I bulldozed my way in to be the first in line. No luck. My window didn't open and so I was number seven in the line to the left. It moved slowly as the clerk withheld nothing from his daily chatter with his clients.

My turn came and I silently gave my application to the clerk. He held out his hand for more. I looked dumbfounded.

"La carta ballotta," he said in Italian.

"Non capisco, sono Americano."

He began to rant in Italian, hands waving all over the air. Finally he gave me some sort of warning accompanied by the manual "disappear sign." Before I left, I put in a desperate plea yelling "English, English" while I pointed toward the back. He could have cared less. He didn't even try to find the interpreter and I was now out in left field without electricity and without any idea what to do next.

Later on, with time obscuring the pain and improving the perspective, I could appreciate the gross humor of the situation. But at that time, I was totally destroyed. A creeping sense of uncertainty began to gnaw at my adventurous instinct, as I became more acutely aware of my inability to cope with even the simplest of problems.

I became aware of a schism in my personality. To the Americans I was confident, capable, intelligent, interesting and independent. To the Italian, I was a meek and frightened foreigner, insecure in action, slow of step and indeterminate of decision. As I was categorized, so was I treated? And as I was treated, so I reacted, until a pattern was formed. Once having attained fluency, my most difficult task resided in the destruction of those habit patterns and the attempt to incorporate what I thought of as my true character within the framework of the Italian language and its culture. I found that I could attain only partial success, for a personality is really only a conglomeration of actions and reactions to the set on which one plays his role. With the set changed, and the significance of my actions interpreted differently, the reactions to me had to be altered. These altered stimuli naturally initiated different responses on my part. And so in Italian I remained a different personality, felt differently, thought differently, and responded differently.

During this period of the development of the "Italian me", I finally did get the electricity and the phone while Frank handled the other utilities. It took four weeks for the former and nine months to get the phone. Thank God that water wasn't a problem.

Every simple task was a major crisis until, after a few weeks, I became aware that the little things were no longer dreaded but handled matter of factly, almost instinctively.

Progress was being made. Frank and I registered at school in late October, four weeks after we had arrived. This was also an ordeal, the basic inefficiency and redundancy of the procedure being again further complicated by the language barrier. But through it all we learned. Words and phrases were repeated again and again under strain as well as under relaxed conditions. By the time school started, we had at least one hundred words at our command, and within the confines of limited exposures, restaurants, grocery stores, and cigar stores, etc., we could communicate quite easily.

Each night we went to the bar, which was a café of sorts. Hard liquor was sold but the term bar did not hold the same connotation as it does in this country. It was a place where men gathered to play cards, billiards, and pinball or mostly just to gossip and exchange views on whatever topic hit their fancy.

Frank and I would spend hours just listening and, as we grew more fluent, we began to appreciate the quality of knowledge that these men displayed. Most of them had, at most, an elementary education, being forced by war and by the rebuilding years to forgo their education in order to provide food for their stomachs and shelter for their bodies. Nevertheless, most of them were well read with regard to the issues of the day. They were keenly aware of the political problems that beset their nations, and were practically skeptical about the intentions of all their great politicians. They interpreted actions, not in terms of morality, but in terms of expediency for a particular nation at that time. To my surprise, they were not in love and piously indebted to their great white American benefactor. Rather, they thought of us as simple, hard working, bumptious buffoons, totally void of sophistication. They saw us, in the face of success based on circumstance more than design, as being totally but wrongly convinced that our way of life was the best and only system by which to live. They liked our basic honesty, but they were annoyed at our insistent dogmatism. It was easy to be righteous when things fell your way and you could afford it. It was another matter when the price of survival was pride.

So, in those first months Frank and I were methodically stripped of our foundation in nationalism. Things were no longer black or white but gray. We began to see the flaws in our nation's character and the wisdom in that old Italian saying, "Tutto il mundo e un paese", (All the world is a country), meaning that people are the same wherever they are, no matter what disguise they wear. Sometimes we argued vehemently but, more often than not, we had to agree that most Americans were filled with propaganda and had a warped and fairy tail appreciation of our role and intentions in foreign affairs. In the same way, though, the Italians had to agree, if somewhat reluctantly, that some of our actions in war and in post war years had to be based on morality and not on pragmatic ulterior motives alone. During these daily debates, we added depth to our characters in the ability to understand and tolerate different ways of life and in the ability to reason with control and objectivity.

GETTING A PARTNER

My new partner's name was the infamous Mr. Marty Barkin, by now known as Dr. Marty Barkin. He finished his residency in late nineteen seventy four and joined me in practice immediately there after. We fit together well. He was serious, quiet, hard working and reliable, and he helped in the development of the clinics and the practice. He was always there when you needed him, and he always took care of his responsibilities.

With a partner in place to share call, I was now free to travel to nearby cities and, on my day or afternoon off, look for sites for new clinic facilities. After the first clinic, I could gather demographics that were extremely useful in evaluating any new location. The limiting factor was of course money and physicians to provide the service locally. We could not borrow from banks for this purpose, (it would not have been politically expedient for banks to loan money to abortion clinics even if they were profitable loans,) but we were frugal enough and able to generate enough cash flow in the practice to open up at least one new facility every year. Finding a doctor who was skilled in pregnancy terminations and wanting to do them was another task. Our trump card was that we would do the procedures in any new facility, until we found a physician who wanted to do them. All we needed to do, for my comfort, was to find a local Ob-gyn who was willing to cover the few complications over the year that might require hospitalization. This would guarantee a continuity of care and an easy transition in case the patient developed complications. Securing a covering physician of equal qualifications was not an easy task, but occasionally we would find one with a political conviction or a profit incentive that would motivate him or her to cover.

In one medium sized Florida City, the demographics were perfect, since there was no competitive clinic, and I eagerly searched for an office to rent. Although there was available empty space, all the initial feelers sent out by our realtor were rejected, until we decided to soften our explanation when they asked about use. Instead of saying abortion clinic, we just put down medical practice and, all of a sudden, we had some places to see. When they found out that we would be doing some abortions there, they all adamantly refused to rent us the space. The last rejection came from an accountant and his brother that had a small medical office to rent on a main thoroughfare. That office would have fit our needs perfectly. At least he had the courtesy to call. "Hello," I intoned hopefully. Maybe this was it.

"Dr. Robbins?" he queried with his southern twang. "Is that you?" I always marveled at that statement. He asked for me and I had picked up the phone. Who the hell did he think it was, Dracula?

"Yes it is," I responded.

"I'm sorry but I have some bad news for you." My heart dropped, but I let him continue. "After reviewing your application with my brother Bill, we have decided that we would not look kindly at, nor consider it the Christian thing to do, if we rented you this office for the purpose of providing abortion services."

"Mr. Jenkins," I pleaded. "The purpose of the office is to provide obstetrical and gynecological care to patients. This includes delivery, surgery, office care, and in a few cases abortion, as is their constitutional right."

"I hear ya, but we just don't think it would be the right or fair thing to do. I called because I just wanted to tell you directly."

This was my last hope. I thought quickly and took a chance, playing what I thought might be a trump card. "Fair!" I stated loudly in my best southern accent. "Well do you think it's gonna be fair, when in twenty years you got ten million more male niggers walking the streets, armed and dangerous."

"What?" he asked, somewhat confused.

I didn't let up. "You talk about fair. Well this ain't a great answer, but it's the only answer we got. These niggers and spics are reproducing like rabbits, and we gotta do something about it, or this won't be America no more. At least, let's keep the ones nobody wants off the streets."

"I never thought of it that way before."

"Well you need to think of it that way Mr. Jenkins. You need to think about your own kids and your own grandchildren."

"Well, let me speak to my brother Bill, and I'll get back to you." "Sounds fine to me Mr. Jenkins. I'll be lookin forward to your call." It took all I could do to keep from puking, but sometimes the end justifies the means. The words "nigger" and "spic" were anathema to me and their use contradicted every tenet I believed in. Nevertheless, the right of women to choose had to supercede any distaste I had in utilizing whatever means were necessary in order to get the brothers to rent me the facility. Whatever it took! That was my new motto. Within the hour, Bob Jenkins called back. I forced myself to wait thirty seconds before I picked up the phone. "Dr. Robbins here."

"Doctor?"

I shook my head and answered.

"Yes Mr. Jenkins. It's me."

"I just discussed the information you gave me with my brother Bill and I have some good news for you."

"Yes," I responded with excited anticipation.

"We considered what you said very, very seriously and we both feel now that it would be the Christian thing to do to rent you the place, as long as you didn't have any big signs saying that word out there. Can you do that."

"Of course I can Mr. Jenkins and I want to reassure you that you are doing the right thing for God and country."

"I believe we are too. I'll have my attorney send over the lease and you can take possession at the beginning of the month. Is that okay?"

"That will be perfect. Thanks for calling," I added and hung up the phone. I sat back in my chair and took a deep breath. I couldn't believe that they took the bait. Worse, I couldn't believe that anybody thought like that. How could the color of one's skin have anything to do with an individual's humanity? It made my hair stand up on my head, but if that's what it took to rent a facility that would offer a service that all women, black or white or green, had a constitutional right to have, then that's what I'd had to do. One thing was clear though. Civil rights for blacks as well as women had a long way to go.

Over the years, we were able to provide a needed service to that Florida community, but providing that service was not without turmoil and danger. In the first year, I serviced the clinic and had to walk through picket lines to get to the inside of the facility. The atmosphere outside was loud and freighting. Many times I was threatened, and occasionally I was physically pushed or blocked from entering so that I had to do an end run to the back of the building to get in. Soon, I secured a license to carry a concealed weapon. There was something wrong with this picture. Here I was, a doctor, traveling to a community to perform a much-needed medical service and I had to pack a weapon to protect myself. In the beginning, I wasn't making any money. I was traveling three hours by car, each way, taking my life in my hands with each trip. Sometimes, when I left town, I was followed out by a couple of pick up trucks, honking their horns loudly, as I would leave the city limits. I was close to giving it up, until a set of events took place that cemented my resolve to continue, no matter what the risk.

Before I would do a procedure in another city, I wanted to make sure that there was clear cut continuity of care for the patient. This certainly was not required by law, since specialists were always on call at area hospitals to take care of complications from outpatient procedures. But it was good, traditional medicine for the same or an informed doctor to deal with most postoperative complications, because the original surgeon obviously would have "inside information" that could be helpful. Operating on an individual outside of your home city, and, then disappearing, leaving the patient to fend for herself was considered itinerant surgery. Itinerant surgery was not illegal, but it was frowned upon by local medical societies, and physicians that performed itinerant surgery usually were subjected to reprimand by their medical societies. Reprimands often resulted in local hospitals beginning investigations of doctors and the process often steam rolled into expulsion from the medical staff.

Therefore, to offer the best care possible and to avoid reprimands,

I made sure that I found a covering physician in each city where I opened a clinic. In this clinic my covering physician was an Indian lady, Indira Nehri, well-trained and new in practice. It was a marriage made in heaven. She had great credentials and could offer wonderful continuity of care for the few complications and hospital admissions that may occur in any year at a busy clinic. In turn, we could supply her with some extra pay and patient referrals to help build her young, developing practice.

After we were open for one week, she called and told me that she could no longer cover the clinic. When I asked why, she responded evasively, with fear in her tone, and quickly got off the phone. Fortunately, I found another doctor to cover, or I would have been forced to close the clinic. Fearing that Dr, Nehri was bullied somehow into backing out of coverage, I gave instructions not to give out the name of our new covering physician. Three weeks later, I saw a post operative patient that told me that she had some cramping after one week and went in to see her regular gynecologist, Dr. Nehri. She related to me the information that Dr. Nehri agreed to see her that one time, but under no circumstances was she going to see patients that were treated in my clinic.

I asked the patient if she gave her an explanation and the patient said that Dr. Nehri told her that she was told by the chief of the department of Obstetrics and Gynecology that she would not get full obstetrical privileges at his hospital if she dared to have anything to do with my clinic.

That made me irate! There was only one hospital in that area that did obstetrics and, if Dr. Nehri did not get privileges there, she would not be able to practice obstetrics. The department of obstetrics and gynecology had only seven practitioners and the chief of the department was the senior member of a three man group of Ob-gyn's. Essentially, he was able to control the department and control the vote. He was a catholic and vehemently opposed to abortion.

Effectively, he was conspiring to prevent the women from his county from having access to a procedure that was their constitutional right. Now, I was caught between a rock and a hard place. This man was conspiring against the constitution of the United States ofAmerica and there was nothing that I could do about it. When I confronted Dr. Nehri, she confessed to me, but stated adamantly that she was going to have to practice in that community, and, if deposed, would deny that any pressure was exerted to force her to stop coverage. "Nothing," she said, "was going to interfere with me practicing my chosen specialty. I've spent too many years training for this."

"Dr. Nehri," I begged. This man is breaking the law. If you tell the truth, we have recourse."

"I'm sorry," was all she would answer. "I'm just too scared," she declared with conviction and hung up the phone.

There was nothing I could do because, without her testimony, I couldn't prove anything. Further more, Dr. Shaw was a well respected member of an ultra consevative southern community and the district attorney who headed up the federal district, in which the clinic was located, was a professed anti abortionist. At one time he had stated privately that, ifhe caught an anti abortionist violating the law, he would do all he could to turn the other cheek. I was incensed. This was America, and there was nothing I could do.

I continued to operate the clinic, refusing to reveal my covering physician, but I knew that it was just a matter of time until they found out who it was and pressured him to quit. Furthermore, I expected that, while he was philosophically in my corner, he didn't have the stomach for an all out fight and would eventually quit, forcing me to close the clinic.

While I kept operating, Dr. Shaw and his cohorts kept up the pressure. Since I wouldn't disclose my coverage, (and fortunately I didn't have any complications over the next six months that I couldn't handle over the phone, or at my next visit to the clinic,) Dr. Shaw filed a complaint, through his medical society, with my medical society that I was practicing itinerant surgery, and they called me in for a formal investigation.

I found myself sitting before a committee of seven physicians. One of them was the president of the medical society, Dr John Devers, who practiced at a hospital where I had worked in the emergency room for two years during my training. Three of the other doctors were on the staff of Saint Andrews's hospital, where I had not applied for privileges. The questioning was intense and biased. "Tell me doctor," asked one of the physicians from Saint Andrews with a condescending tone. "Do you always abandon your patients after you operate on them."

"Absolutely not," I responded defiantly. "I have coverage."

"We'll get to that later. For now, don't you think that, if you operate on a patient, it's your responsibility to follow up on that patient and care for any problems."

"I do follow up on these patients and I do give them post operative care."

"Come on doctor!" shouted another one of the Saint Andrews physicians, leaning menacingly across the table. "From one hundred and twenty miles away?"

"I have coverage when I am not there."

"What does that mean?" said the first doctor.

"The same thing it means when you leave town and let your partner cover."

"We don't need any smart answers," jumped in the third.

"Excuse me," I said.

"You know that's not the same thing," doctor number two offered.

"To the contrary," I rebuffed. "It's exactly the same thing. I am providing a physician with equal qualifications to cover complications when I am not in town, in exactly the same way that you have another physician cover you when you leave town on vacation or for the weekend."

"He's got a point," the president intoned.

The three Saint Andrews doctors all looked at him as if he was interrupting the flow. They looked back at me in unison and continued their bullying tactics. The first doctor continued the questioning. "At this so called clinic, who answers your phone at night?"

"My clinic director, who is a nurse, screens all calls."

"Don't you think that you're being negligent by not answering your own phone?"

"Who answers your phone at night doctor?" I said, answering a question with a question.

"I do," number one retorted snottily, silently scoring one for himself.

"Who answers your phone during the day?" I asked innocently.

"My receptionist of course," he responded as his colleagues nodded their heads in approval.

"Well," I replied as I sat back in my chair. "It seems like the only difference in my procedure and yours is that I can afford a nurse to cover calls twenty four hours a day, while you can only afford a less qualified individual to cover calls eight hours a day."

A small chuckle emanated from the president's lips and the other three silent physicians on the board.

At halftime (recess,) the president of the medical society took me aside and spoke to me privately. "Dodd," he said. "I don't understand all of this or why you're doing it, but you got these people pretty much up in arms. I remember you as a damn decent emergency room physician. You always took great care of my patients, so I am talking to you like a father." He paused to see if I resisted, but I just stood there silently, listening intently. "We have certain issues in Tallahassee (the state capitol) that we need to lobby on and, in order to get them effected, we need the support of Dr. Shaw's medical society."

"How do I figure into that?" I asked.

"Simply put, they told us that they would not support those issues if we didn't get you to close your clinic or, if you refused, punish you severely."

My blood pressure rose sharply and I thought I was going to burst. I had all I could do to control myself and I responded in a cold, intense and hateful voice. "Dr. Devers. I have been going to this clinic for six months now, driving three hours down and three hours back, sometimes after no sleep the night before. I have to fight my way into the clinic and they follow me out of town, honking their horns when I reach the county line. I'm half scared out of my mind and I pack a weapon for protection. So far, I haven't made a dime. When I walked into this meeting, I was seriously thinking of closing this clinic." I paused for a second and looked daggers right into his eyes. I needed to finish quickly, before I blew my top and hurt someone. "Now, it will close over my dead body!"

That said, I turned around and stormed defiantly out the door.

Riding home, I had all I could do to concentrate on the road. All the events kept churning around in my head. I couldn't believe that this was happening in America. Suddenly I felt frightened and all alone. I was not playing a game anymore. I was playing for keeps.

After a fitful night of unrest, I woke up tired, but anxious to fight back. I was pragmatic enough to know that I wasn't going to win going through the legal system. I would just have to gut it out and hope that my covering doctor stuck it out.

Three weeks later, the medical society wrote me and informed me that they would be canceling my medical malpractice insurance. They were able to secure phenomenal rates for physicians because they brought volume to the carrier. Without them, I couldn't afford to pick up new insurance and pay for the tail coverage on all the prior years. Basically, I was left bare and exposed and, again, I had no recourse, even though they had no legitimate justification for canceling me. This was the final straw.

The following day, I called Dr. Shaw on the phone and made an appointment to see him at the end of his morning office hours on the next day that I was in town. I figured that, if I couldn't convince him, I would scare him. I had nothing to lose, since it was illegal to tape conversations in Florida without the permission of the one being taped. Whatever I said would be his word against mine.

I showed up at his office promptly at noon, and was kept waiting a full hour. I gave him the benefit of the doubt, crediting the delay to the fact that he had just run late with patients. When I was ushered into the office, he didn't even apologize.

Indicating a chair, he stayed seated at his desk and said. "What did you want to speak to me about."

I sat down slowly, crossed my legs and delivered my words deliberately.

"Let me save both of us some time Dr. Shaw and cut to the chase. You don't like what I do and you have a right not to like it or do it. But the women of this county do have a right to have access to abortion, and you have no right to prevent them from having that access."

A big smile crossed his face as he spoke. "I'm not preventing anything," he said innocently. Then, in a deeper tone, he added. "I abhor what you do and the way you do it. You're not interested in these women. All you care about is money. You do your dirty deed and skip town, leaving us with the mess."

Inside I raged and wanted to lash out and hit him. Instead I controlled myself and continued in my icy measured tone. "None of that is true. My charges are extremely reasonable, my service is excellent, and continuity of care is available. I have had no major problems to date and would expect very few."

"Yeah," he cut in. "Who is your coverage?"

"If I tell you that, you'll try the same thing to him that you did to Dr. Nehri."

His interest peeked when he heard the name Nehri.

"Let me tell you this Robbins. I really have no interest on what you think or have to say. What you are doing is morally wrong. It is disgusting, and I promise you that I will do everything in my power to prevent you from continuing your abortion mill here in my county."

Sitting square shouldered, with legs still crossed, I stayed perfectly still in my seat. My tone was soft but menacing. Al Pacino couldn't have done it better.

"Do you know that I have nineteen clinics, Dr. Shaw?" I lied.

"No, and I don't care. You are not going to have one here."

I continued in my eerily soft matter of fact tone.

"You know of course that I couldn't have put them all together myself?" "So, I'm not interested in your partners."

"Maybe you should be."

Shaw looked a little confused for a second and hesitated before he spoke.

"And why is that?" he said defiantly.

I stood up, walked slowly over to his desk and leaned over menacingly. I contorted my face and through gritted teeth, I hissed, keeping my voice to a whisper.

"Because your life may depend on it!" He sat back in his chair, startled, as the pieces started to fall together. I didn't let up.

"Do you understand what I'm talking about Shaw?" Then, just a little louder. "Do you understand who is backing me?" Finally I let him have both barrels.

"You think you're playing a game Shaw? Do you think you're playing a fucking game? They're gonna find your gonads in a garbage can." Leaning further over the desk and seeing Shaw plastered back in his massive desk chair, I delivered the "coup de grace."

"If I ever hear your name again, incidentally, accidentally, socially or professionally, I will put a fucking contract out on you."

Then, mouth to mouth; eyeball to eyeball; I said with all the intensity I could muster.

"You'll be a dead mother fucker you asshole; a dead mother fucker."

I stood in silence, looking down at him with nausea and disdain, as he squirmed in his seat and avoided my gaze. After thirty seconds, I turned on my heels and strode confidently out of his office. I never did hear his name again.

As my skin got tougher and tougher, the practice and clinics continued to grow, taking more and more time. I felt like I was on a merry go round and I couldn't get off. Christina extended her first trip to Italy to almost six weeks and, as her rapport with her parents improved, she spent more and more time abroad. In the beginning, I almost welcomed the separation, but as time wore on, it became crystal clear that we were growing further and further apart. When at home, she dutifully performed her chores, but there was no joy in Mudville. Little Dean was growing rapidly and talking a blue streak. I loved every minute I had with him, but all and all, with all my obligations and his mother's schedule, it was little time indeed. Although I was off call every other night, I used most of that time to do clinic business and, on the rare occasion that I was free, Christina almost always seemed to have things to do. To make matters worse, she was pregnant again and prone to emotional extremes and periods of depression. One day flew in to the next and we really didn't have a chance to catch our breath. Before I knew it, our second child was born in August of nineteen seventy-five, just after Dean's second birthday. We named him Darren Emilio Robbins; Darren with a "D" after my maternal grandfather and Emilio after Christina's paternal grandfather. Christina's mother came over for the delivery and helped enormously with the babies. The four of them functioned very well and it seemed like I was external baggage. My folks came down for a visit, but the time spent together with her mother was as awkward as it could be, since her mother didn't speak English and my folks didn't know a word of Italian. We had a couple of dinners together, with Christina and I acting as translators, but the majority of time we spent with our own respective parents in order to avoid having to be a go between. After a week, my parents left, having spent most of their time on their own waiting for me to be free of work. They got to spend very few precious moments with the babies. When they left, I felt somewhat empty, thinking that opportunities like this would be few and far between. Christina's mother left when the baby was six weeks old and she asked if we could go to Italy for Christmas. I agreed to go if Marty would cover for the holidays, hoping the trip would help rejuvenate my marriage.

Marty would have covered. He was that kind of guy. But he had just undergone some routine laboratory tests and come up with some odd results on the profile. The results indicated that he had to follow up with a bone marrow exam and underwent the test. The results showed that he had a disease called myelofibrosis. The hematologist was very evasive when asked for a prognosis. We went to look up the disease in the library and were shaken by the results. "God, there is no justice," was all I could say. I felt horrible and helpless.

Marty was stoical. "Can you believe this shit!" was all he said.

The literature said that, once diagnosed, individuals with this disease usually lived two to three years. We were devastated. He was just beginning to enjoy the fruits of his years of sacrifice. For the first time, he had enough money to live like a human being and start to provide for his family's security. Now, in one fell swoop, it would all be taken away. Now was not the time to ask him to carry the practice and clinics through the holidays, when we didn't know how many holidays that he would have left. Furthermore, he had a lot to do for his family and he had to act fast. He had been in the process of securing life insurance and rushed to sign the papers. With the help of sympathetic hospital personnel, he was able to get the dates changed on the bone marrow exam, so that it appeared to occur after he had signed the insurance application. All was going well, when he got slapped in the face by a threat from a vindictive and hateful competitor. The competitor, the same Dr. John Walden that had been my chief resident in residency had heard rumors about the steps that Marty had taken in order to secure his life insurance coverage. He resented Marty, because Marty had turned down his offer for partnership and had chosen to go with me instead. He also feared our competition in the clinic community, and he was going to do whatever he could to dilute our strength. Marty called Dr. Walter Phillips, our mentor in residency, and asked him if he would set up a meeting with Dr. Walden. Walden respected Phillips and received a great number of referrals from him. He would not refuse to meet.

Marty went to the meeting carrying an innocent little box. They were all civil and sat down to discuss the issue. Phillips told Walden that he didn't think that what he was going to do was right and Walden responded with a nauseatingly self-righteous tone. "I think that what he is doing is disgusting. It is fraudulent and, as a citizen, it is my duty to report it."

Phillips pleaded with him but to no avail. Through the bulk of the discourse, Marty never said a word. Finally, he just opened up the box to reveal a thirty-eight Smith and Wesson. He looked up at Walden and spoke in a cold monotone. "I'm going to die sometime in the next two or three years. I plan to go alone, but if you make trouble for my family, I am going to take you with me." He stood up and looked over at Phillips. "C'mon, let's go. I'm done here." Without another word, he turned and left the room with Phillips hurrying up behind. Walden never called his bluff. I never wondered why.

Marty miraculously is still alive. What we never understood when we examined the literature back in those early days was that the text book was written before it was common to get chemical profiles in the practice of medicine. The literature had described a two or three year prognosis after diagnosis of the disease, expecting that investigation and diagnosis would follow the onset of symptoms that resulted from a diminished red cell, white cell or platelet count. Generally speaking, these symptoms didn't show up until almost all the marrow was replaced by fibrous tissue and that could take many, many years. What Marty discovered on the chemical profile, that made him pursue the bone marrow test, he never would have discovered under normal circumstances until symptoms showed up twenty or twenty five years later. But Marty didn't know that and, for a long time, he altered his life style, living every day like there was no tomorrow. It even effected his style of practice, often saying to a patient who wanted a screening laboratory test. "Don't do it. You'll just be asking for trouble."

THE DEVELOPING YEARS

The first lecture of my medical career was in Histology on the fifteenth of November at nine a.m. We arrived early in order to get a front row seat.

We entered the lecture theatre as you enter a ballpark, walking up the peripheral staircase until we reached the top row in the building, when the inner sanctum became visible.

We were hit by a shock. At 8:15 a.m all five hundred seats were filled and we had to jockey for decent standing room only positions.

There we stood, amid a room full of Italians, whistling and calling to each other as they renewed old friendships and exchanged gossip about their summer vacations. They could have been Americans, except for the way they wore their coats about the shoulders, with sleeves empty, and the way they used their hands to support their comments. Time flowed by and Frank and I became restless. The Italians paid no attention, but I became acutely aware as the minute hand passed twelve and continued its trip forward. By 9:15, the professor had still not arrived.

I rolled my thumbs, one over the other, as Frank swayed from leg to leg. In younger days his mother might have thought this to be an ominous sign of imminent micturition, but I had firm confidence in

Frank's ability to control his bladder. At least, I knew that he couldn't lift his leg to pee, because the theatre was so packed that he might find it impossible to put his foot down.

At 9:32, the side door at the bottom of the lecture hall swung open and a sudden hush spread through the hall, as all students rose to face the front.

Like a peacock, in strut the professor, resplendently garbed in white robe, the train of which was carried by six assistants; the greeting was deafening as the applause and shouts rebounded from wall to wall.

For two minutes there was no sign of cease-fire, until the professor indicated silence with a gallant sweep of an arm. The arena fell silent as his staccato shrill cut through the room. As he spoke, he took a little jump forward like a cat springing out onto the floor. "Today we will speak about the cell. The cell is the unit of organization of the body, just as it is the unit of organization of the party."

The cheers again rung throughout the hall as I jabbed Frank and strained to hear the translation. Bologna was a communist town and the histology professor was a commie leader.

Although, you would think that the two were mutually exclusive, the entire lecture was a combined politico-histological rally, as if such a combination was remotely possible. Furthermore, it ran three quarters of an hour late, precluding the possibility of attending the lecture that followed.

After two weeks of classes, I was to learn that each institute was autonomous and, that so many conflicts existed between them, that it was impossible to fulfill all the requirements of each. The substitute for this was the payoff. Classes and labs missed were kept track of by the bidello, the so-called non commissioned officer of the institute. For a minimal fee, attendance records could be brought up to date to the student's satisfaction. When it became obvious that the subject matter covered in the classroom only comprised a small percentage of the material for which we were responsible, that the professors were usually late and occasionally missed lectures, and that conflicts were unavoidable, we began to make more and more use of the bidello. By the time the first month was over, the classrooms became vacuums with five hundred to six hundred students dwindling to twenty or thirty.

The quality of the individual lecture though remained excellent as each professor sought to impress rather than instruct. The descriptions were flowery, detailed, exact and often allegorical, even if little or no continuity existed between back to back lectures. Often the material discussed was not applicable to the "tesi," (the list of subjects for which we were responsible.) All in all, the professors seemed more concerned with their presentation as a speaker and the effect it had on students and observers rather than on the effectiveness of their instruction.

Inside of three months, I was never to attend another class or laboratory. I found that most of the material to be covered could be found within the confines of a textbook or two and that I could conquer the subject more efficiently and conclusively using only these sources. Furthermore, a new freedom was opened to me. Because classes did not dictate my physical proximity, I could now choose to travel and live as I wished, making sure only to return to Bologna for examinations.

With our apartment we had made excellent progress. Basic furniture was bought from a variety of local wholesale dealers. The decorative flare was added by Angela Lazari, our Italian neighbor and first year colleague in medical school. As accident would have it, Angela was our next door neighbor and we had met her in rather typical fashion while ascending in the elevator. Our accents were obvious and, with curiosity on her part and desperation on ours setting the pace, we became fast friends. The fact that she was a piece of ass didn't hurt progress either.

Our door was always open and she fell into the habit of just entering and calling out one of our names. Each piece of used, battered furniture that we brought home we would proudly display for Angela and hang on the edge of our seats for her judgement. What an actress! In between bouts of nausea, she reacted with feverish enthusiasm, at first just applauding our selections with a string of Italian adjectives and,

later, adding her own suggestions with regard to location and accessories.

Soon she took an active part in the selection of pieces and ingeniously placed those that we had bought on our own inconspicuously throughout the apartment. Each room took on its own decorative theme and what might have been an obviously makeshift abode turned out to be a home marked by warmth, comfort and style.

With Angela as hostess, our first party turned out to be a bomb. Ten American guys were mixed with six Italian teenage giggling girls, two chaperones and our procurer, Pino Bertilli, who worked in the bar downstairs.

Pino, at twenty, was a real swinger within his group. The group, though, consisted of a bunch of "nowhere to go" people. The guys in his crowd either didn't work or held menial jobs such as custodian, soda jerk, grocery clerk, etc. The girls were seamstresses, hairdressers, etc. All had small ambition; to be free for the weekend, to buy a new dress or shirt next week, to attend a movie, and to participate in the mating game with all its frills and fancies. None of them could think beyond Friday or Saturday night. Those were their concerns and Pino was an integral part of it. Nobody worked hard and nobody stayed ten seconds past quitting time. They paced themselves in work and in life and would in all probability perfunctorily perform the same jobs and enjoy the same pleasures weekly, monthly, and yearly until their retirement. Their ambitions were few and they seemed to be content or at least resigned to their lot in life.

Pino was a cut above his peers. Despite his lack of good family and formal education, he was keenly aware of his station and the prognosis for his future. Being innately curious and restless, he strove to learn about the outside world and the exciting experiences in the life of other people, in other places, in other times. Despite the fact that he reigned as leader of his group, he became intensely disenchanted with his role in life, and aspired to greater things. He resented the system as it existed, for he felt that it suffocated the aspirations of a majority of the poor, and permitted the rich to exploit them. He saw his out with the Communist Party and became an active member. In Italy, though, that was not a crime, and he never let his political views interfere with his social convenience.

Whatever we represented to him, whether a new experience, a contact with the outside world, a stimulus to break the drudgery of every day life, or a source to confirm his staunch dogmatic Marxist views, I do not know. But he was interested in spending time with us and supplying us with girls in return for our companionship. We were happy to accept. We needed the friend and we needed the experience in Italian. Most of all though we needed the girls. To a foreigner, they were always a scarce commodity and, therefore, infinitely more necessary than they would be if the supply were abundant.

At the party we all struggled to make conversation, but even when we succeeded with words, we failed in the content. We just had nothing in common. We tried dancing with lights low and stereo blasting, but the chaperones well placed coughs put a damper on the festivities. One of them stood conveniently in the hallway, eliminating the bedroom as a possible refuge to work up a relationship.

The party ended at six p.m. and the girls filed out with their friends and chaperones, all probably relieved to be on their way. My friends left with a sense of frustration and Pino departed with a firm resolve to offer future invitations restricting the accompaniment of a chaperone.

Frank walked out with Pino, leaving Angela and I alone. We sat on the floor Indian style, facing each other over a low coffee table. The few minutes of silence that passed seemed surprisingly natural and not at all uncomfortable, almost as if Angela and I were such good and long time friends that we had no need to communicate verbally. She looked pensive and after a few minutes I asked her, "Cosa pensi." (What are you thinking?)

"Niente." (Nothing.) She spoke such a perfect Italian and enunciated so clearly that I had very little difficulty understanding almost everything she said.

"It's not possible to think of nothing."

"I don't know, I guess I'm thinking about my boyfriend."

"Giovanni?"

"No Paulo," she retorted sarcastically. "Of course Giovanni. How many do you think I have?"

"No need to be so curt. I'm only interested in listening and trying to help."

"I'm sorry," she sighed. "It's just that I'm so lonely."

"For his body or his mind," I asked pointedly.

Angela angled her face so as to avoid my eyes. "For both I guess."

"There's nothing wrong with that."

"I know. Now speak to my mother."

We both laughed. My voice brought the tone of a serious discussion.

"Do you love him?" I wasn't sure if my curiosity to delve deeper into her problems was based solely on the altruistic interest of a friend, or on the fact that I found her pleasantly arousing and that she represented a new form of that age old challenge, man against woman.

"I think so."

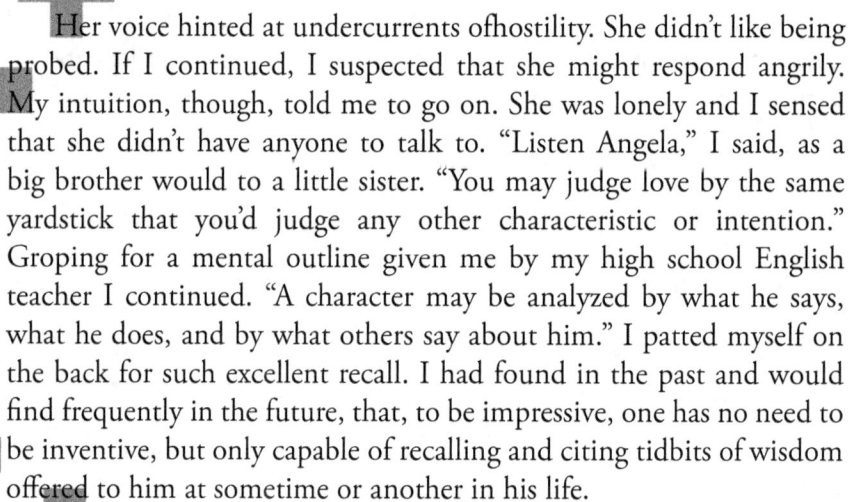

"Does he love you?"

"I don't know."

"What does that mean?"

"Just what I said, I don't know."

Her voice hinted at undercurrents of hostility. She didn't like being probed. If I continued, I suspected that she might respond angrily. My intuition, though, told me to go on. She was lonely and I sensed that she didn't have anyone to talk to. "Listen Angela," I said, as a big brother would to a little sister. "You may judge love by the same yardstick that you'd judge any other characteristic or intention." Groping for a mental outline given me by my high school English teacher I continued. "A character may be analyzed by what he says, what he does, and by what others say about him." I patted myself on the back for such excellent recall. I had found in the past and would find frequently in the future, that, to be impressive, one has no need to be inventive, but only capable of recalling and citing tidbits of wisdom offered to him at sometime or another in his life.

"Go on," she said, more attentive to what I had to offer. "First of all, does he say that he loves you?"

"He has," she said defiantly, almost as if she was afraid that I would think less of her if he hadn't.

"Okay then, does he demonstrate it?"

"What do you mean by that," she challenged.

The time was ripe for a little gentle scolding. "Angela, I'm not criticizing you. I am only trying to help you understand your relationship with Giovanni and to analyze it accurately. Only then can you describe what you can practically expect from the relationship and, then, and only then, can you choose a course of action that will improve your chances of corralling him."

"Now I'm confused," she said jokingly.

"Well if you'd stop interrupting and let me continue you'd see what I'm driving at."

"I'm sorry," she apologized. "Go on."

"Again then," I said with determination. "How does he demonstrate the fact that he loves you? Does he write you, does he call you?"

"He's written me."

"How often?"

She looked contrite and embarrassed. With a sigh, she responded. "Once since October."

"Once in four months!"

"He's busy," she retorted defensively. "He's in his third year of law at Rome and he's buried under the curriculum."

"An individual in love Angela is not that practical. Throughout history, man has sacrificed kingdoms, fortunes and even their lives in the pursuit of their loved ones. Surely, with only a few hours of study hanging in the balance, Giovanni should find time to return home for a weekend, or at least write."

I paused and let that logic seep in and then resumed the questions. "Has he asked you to marry him?"

"No."

"Why not?"

"Because he is a student and he feels that it is a man's obligation to support the woman he loves."

"How noble," I replied sarcastically, "and how convenient."

"Now look" she snapped. "All the things that people say do not have to come under the headings of ulterior motive and dubious intention."

"No," I agreed. "Not when their actions correspond to their words. Don't you see Angela," I pleaded. "You're useful to him when he's at home and I'm sure he likes you. But he's not totally involved and will use any sensible excuse to avoid commitment. What's more, I don't blame him. When he's at home you're available. To make matters worse, you've probably professed your love for him a thousand times in a vain attempt to get him to confess his."

"How do you know that?"

"How do I know," I said shaking my head. "It fits the picture. It's a set scene and it's repeated a million times a day. The characters may be different and settings may vary but the parts they play are the same. You on the one hand overload him with affection and security. For him you represent no risk, only a frequent source of pleasure. The only inconvenience for him is that you don't disappear when he tires of you. This of course tends to make him pull away; he offers more excuses, more reasons for not seeing you, except when his own desire is aroused. The fact that he is less available to you makes him more desirable, thus the vicious circle continues. Simply put Angela, you need him more than he needs you and as long as you demonstrate that need, his will grow less intense."

"Supposing that were true," she asked, resigning herself to the injustice of the enigma. "What can I do?"

"Play the game. Make yourself unavailable to him at his convenience. Stop writing and calling him, make him wonder."

"And what if he doesn't respond?"

"Then he would have very shortly rejected you anyway. At least you could leave the scene with pride. But if you do mean a little something to him; if the time he has spent with you in the past has generated a habit pattern, then he will feel some sense of disruption in the comfortable order of his life. He may begin to chase you a bit on the basis of combined curiosity and prior need and this will of course reverse the cycle and set it going in your favor."

"You think you can control love like that?" she asked, somewhat annoyed that I would make such a supposition.

The confidence in my reply startled her. "Given the spark of arousal and some habit patterns, without doubt. I have seen it happen repetitively in the past. The outcome is perfectly predictable."

"And how long does it take?"

"Six weeks, three days and four hours," I replied mockingly. "What do you want, a timetable? It varies. Sometimes weeks, sometimes months or years. Sometimes never, but then, as I said before, you were too far gone in the first place and the trend was irreversible."

"And how do you propose I get through it? I am tempted every night to call him. When he comes home for intercession, I want to be at the station waiting, so as not to waste a second."

"I don't propose that it will be easy. But I can offer a number of suggestions that might assuage your moments of depression as well as reduce their number."

"Go on, I'm still listening."

"To begin with you must keep active. The more you do, the less time you have to meditate and reflect on your love life. Secondly, you must find a substitute to at least partially fill some of the needs that Giovanni ordinarily satisfies for you."

"What needs?" she asked accusingly.

"For example sex," I said looking her straight in the eye.

"Just like that," she said snapping her fingers simultaneously. "You Americans never cease to amaze me," she added, a note of anger in her voice.

"First of all," I interrupted, "don't categorize me with all Americans. I have suggested this before to many of them and they were just as startled and annoyed as you appear to be."

"No wonder," she said shaking her head.

I continued choosing to ignore her lack of enthusiasm. I had been through this before and knew that, by the very fact that she was listening, the door was not closed.

"Some of them, though, after their first instinctive reaction, chose to think about it logically and sensibly and eventually, on following my advice, were able to control their later affairs almost at will."

"Well," she continued sarcastically. "It all sounds wonderful, except I'm just not used to picking myself up a stud off the street whenever I feel the need."

"Why not?" I challenged.

"Because the whole concept is nauseating to me."

"Why?"

"Because it is."

"For a medical student, Angela, that is one hell of an answer," I said allowing my hands to spread open widely, palms open to the sky.

She paused for a minute and pondered that. Her response was serious and intense.

"I guess it's because of my upbringing. I was taught that sex was taboo except in marriage and only dirty girls participated capriciously."

"You do understand, though, that that's a load of horse shit, don't you?"

"In one way yes, in another no."
"What does that mean?"
Again she paused and pondered pensively before forming her words.

"On a rational basis, I guess, I understand that sex is just a bodily function, to be enjoyed for its pleasure alone and for the purpose of procreation. But the connotation of dirt is so heavily ingrained in me that I just know that I would never be able to satisfy my sexual needs without a deep sense of feeling for the guy."

"Angela come here."

"Why," she replied, fidgeting nervously, unsure of what to expect.

"Because I want to make you feel good."

My gaze fell directly upon hers as I slowly ground my cigarette out in the ashtray.

"What are you going to do?" she said with combined curiosity and apprehension.

"I'm going to give you a massage. If you'll come here I'll show you. When you say stop, I stop. Deal?"

She hesitated for a moment and then slowly slid over to the comfortable pile of pillows at my foot. I moved to her side and placed my hands on her shoulders. I could feel her tremors beneath my touch. I let the pressure of my fingers soften. They began to gently knead the muscles in her back. While I worked, I talked. "Now I want you to concentrate on what I am doing and decide whether or not it is pleasurable. As soon as it becomes unpleasant, I want you to tell me to stop."

My hands continued to knead the muscles of her back; I altered the pressure and rhythm and I could feel the tightness in her back gradually dissipate until the muscles were completely loose and receptive. My hands moved deftly through the muscles of her back, neck and down her arms, stretching and rolling every fiber and joint down to the tips of her fingers. She moaned softly as my hands slid over her waist and buttocks and began to knead the muscles in the groove between her thighs and cheeks. Her legs parted naturally as my fingers rolled over the soft tender flesh of her inner thigh. I bent over her body, pressing my mouth to her ear and whispered.

"Turn over Angela." As she turned, I let her back roll over my forearms and in one sweeping motion picked her up, carried her to my bedroom and laid her down on the bed.

This time I started at her feet and worked my way up through every joint and muscle of her legs until my fingers could sense the warm moistness between her legs through her nylon undergarment.

She began to squirm and then whispered "please stop."

"Okay," I replied and pulled myself away from her. I grabbed a cigarette from the night table, lit it and sucked in a long drag. I sat there silently, smoking my cigarette and sensing the electrical tension between us. I was perfectly relaxed though and in full control. I knew what to expect and, if the mood were not interrupted by Frank returning home, we would end the evening in the full bloom of lovemaking. I'd been through it all before.

"I'm sorry," she cut in.

"For what?"

"For leading you on. I didn't mean to, I really didn't."

"You've got nothing to be sorry for. I told you to stop me when it became unpleasant and it did."

Word for word I could have rolled her answer off my own tongue.

"It's not that," She turned her head to the side, letting her gaze fall away from mine. "In fact it was wonderful. I feel so good and tingly." She sat up and looked directly at me. "But how could I face Giovanni?"

"Just like you're facing me now."

"It's not that easy."

"But it is." I sighed, letting out a ring of smoke. I grasped both her hands and caught her eyes directly. "Angela, if you find me unattractive, if you find my touch distasteful, I can accept that." I paused, knowing full well from her previous response that she didn't. I shifted my position and grasped her hands more firmly. "Angela, don't analyze, just react. Your pleasure is your own. It's got nothing to do with Giovanni. What he does not know can't hurt him. And what you experience with me can at worst be just a source of new insight and at best a moment of ecstasy."

She smiled softly, sensuously, and fell gently back on the bed. My hands began again to caress and massage her body and she responded with moans of pleasure. In that awkward moment of truth, I grasped the elastic rim of her panties and pulled them down over her legs. She lifted her body slightly to facilitate what is, at best, a tense and unnerving moment as I gently removed the undergarment and lay it on the floor. With skirt above her waist I opened her soft white thighs, exposing her succulent moist labia to the stream of light stealing in from the hall.

My tongue found the core of her pleasure and she responded with rhythmic motion and soft grunts of satisfaction. Her total being seemed to concentrate on that one spot of eroticism as her muscles tensed, all channeled into compressing her body against my tongue, all culminating in a series of uncontrollable pelvic spasms accompanied by a soft whimpering cry of relief.

The winter came and the winter went and, then, miraculously, the spring showed signs of following the same fate. June was upon us and June in Bologna is hot as hell. Over the past two months, I had been channeling all my energy in preparation for two exams, histology and biochemistry, and I was fatigued with the tension building up inside me. The exams, I had been warned, would consist of two or three questions and I would pass or fail on the basis of my performance on these and these alone.

Despite the fact that I studied effectively, a cloud of doubt hung heavily over me. For one, I had no yardstick, no previous exams, against which to judge my knowledge. Two, I was told that the exams were short, subjective and grossly inadequate. It was possible to be well prepared and fail on the basis of the wrong question or the mood of the professor. I assumed the opposite was also true, but I felt terribly uneasy about not being able to exert sufficient control over my fate.

Frank and I had begun to study together but we found that we were relatively incompatible. He preferred to learn all he could about a subject and often took off on a tangent. I preferred to confine myself, as best as possible, to the material for which we were responsible; to outline and prepare a response for a given subject. I was practical enough to know that it was impossible to learn everything and remember it for an examination. Hence, the basics had to be understood and committed to memory first. The detail could be picked up later and easily woven into the rough meshwork.

It irritated me to hell when Frank would take the time to research out some minutia, when we had a study schedule to follow. It became obvious to me that we would never finish the curriculum and have time to review, if we continued at that pace. Despite my objections, though, Frank would not adhere to the strict and rigid study program that I had set up. So, when it came to studying, we chose to go our own separate ways.

Studying alone, if much more efficient, was also much more depressing. Without knowing how you were doing or how much you knew, the stimulus to plod on was removed. It was difficult to keep up a consistent effort without yardsticks and without reward. Without anyone or any event to discipline me, I found that I was doing less and less each day. Angela came to the rescue. She was having similar problems and we decided to hold a review session each night. In these we would attempt to simulate the exam situation, asking each other questions and listening to the answers. These acted as a stimulus to study. Each day, I had a definite amount of material to cover. Each night, I would be rewarded with a sense of accomplishment, if I responded well, and an empty uncomfortable gut ifI drew a blank. Within days, I was back into the routine of four to five hours of a daily concerted effort.

My personal relationship with Angela was phenomenal. Over the months, I had trained her to use me as a friend and a source of pleasure but never to become dependent on me. When she needed me, I was there. When she didn't, I made no demands.

Giovanni, as I had predicted, had followed the course that I had laid out for Angela. When home, he took her out more often and, toward the end of his vacation, became verbally concerned with her rather lais- sez-faire attitude. Through well dropped hints, he learned that she had been dating frequently. When questioned, she was as evasive as I had prepared her to be. Despite temptation, she also ceased to question him. On occasion, she also made an excuse not to see him and his interest and demands grew.

When he returned to Rome in February he called frequently. In March, he made a special trip back to Bologna to ask her to marry him. As fate would have it, she was a victim of the circumstance that I had created for her. The cycle turned the other way and, now, Giovanni was just a lovable puppet, whose actions and emotions were easy to manipulate.

As the exams drew near, Angela and I intensified our efforts. For ten thousand lire ($16) she got us scheduled to be examined first. The ten thousand lire went to the bidello, the so-called janitor of the institute. It was not offered as a bribe. It was offered only as a token of appreciation for a consideration rendered. Angela had approached the bidello and asked. "When will the examination session begin?"

"When it begins."

"I guess you're not allowed to tell me."

"Not yet."

"I know that you can't tell me, but my mother is sick. She lives at the beach and I would like to tell her when I will be home for the summer.

"I would like to help but I can't."

"I know you would if you could. Can you just give me a hint?"

"No, but if I were the professor, I would open the session around the first or second or third of July."

"I know you can't, but would it be possible for my partner and I to be the first ones examined?"

"Such things I can't control."

She slipped 10,000 lire into his hand. "I know that, but I just want to thank you for your kindness. My name Is Angela Lazzeri and my partner is Dodd Robbins."

"It is my pleasure, and I hope your mother feels better."

The exam was obviously the third of July for the first was a Saturday and the second was a Sunday. The ten thousand lire was not a guarantee that we would be the first two in the room on July third, for someone else might slip him more and move up ahead of us. But we could certainly rest assured that we would be examined in the morning, for many students were not aware of the system, and many others could not afford the sixteen dollars for good placement.

The advantages of taking the exam early were numerous. For one, you could set your goals on a given day and expect to answer questions early in the morning, when you were fresh and the days events did not have time to dim the mental picture of your answers. It is a known fact that, overnight, your mind, without the irritation of incessant external stimuli, has time to settle, permitting concepts and ideas to be neatly packaged. Therefore, you are best prepared for an examination as soon as you awaken. Secondly, the ordeal of allowing the tension to build up, only to find out that you will not be examined that day, can become tremendously unnerving. If thirty people had signed up for an exam, the professor might see anywhere from six to all thirty. If he sees six, then you return, not only the following day, but for many days after, to wait again and again. If he sees thirty students and you are not there at the end, then he will cancel the exam session and four months might pass before another opportunity arises. Therefore, it was necessary to come each and every day and try to fight your way into the examination room. If not successful, the nerves that were teased and irritated that day did not provide for the mental calm necessary for study that night. Thirdly, the early exams were more thorough and usually the examiners were more lenient. They were fresh, not yet bored, not yet warm and sweaty from the heat of the day. If you answered badly on one question, they often afforded you the opportunity to make it up on the next. This was not always true as the day and, later, the session wore on. Their tempers would grow short and their desire to overcome the partial language barrier that existed dissipated.

On occasion, an individual would be thrown out and failed because he did not organize his answer in the manner in which the professor thought ofit and the professor was just to lazy and irritated at that time of day to tax his own mind. Next, the professors liked assertiveness. An individual who came into the room early was one who was sure of his knowledge. Therefore, if he responded fairly well in the general aspect of the question, the professor just often assumed that he knew the details and didn't bother asking. Toward the end of the session, the opposite was true. They assumed the attitude that you were trying to put something over on them and delved and delved and delved until they finally nailed you to the wall and could say to themselves. "Ah ha, I got you slimy, sneaking, son of a bitch."

So, all in all, I learned early that the bidello could be an important cog in your success or failure in passing exams. Since it was always best to have the odds working with you, the bidello was always our friend. Toward him we were respectful and reverent.

On the third of July, Angela and I came to face the professor. The bidello corralled us in a hallway with about a hundred other agitated, hyperactive students. There we waited, packed like sardines from eight AM to ten AM, when the professor finally arrived to begin the session.

Like the miracle of the Red Sea, a pathway opened up between the mass of students, as he moved silently, eyes fixed on the floor, toward the auditorium. The exam was to be an open one, that is anyone was invited to watch.

Like cattle, we were all driven into the auditorium to sit and wait for what one student described as the Crucifixion. Open exams were not popular with the students being examined. To begin with, there was the additional pressure ofhaving to perform before a critical audience. There is nothing more embarrassing than to be unsure of your ground and, then, to be browbeaten and insulted in front of a packed house. Right or wrong, your only recourse was to maintain an even temper and speak respectfully. The whole episode was demasculinizing to an American, quite similar in effect to castration. To the Italian it was all part of the game. Only a fool would return insults or worse, physically attack the professor. The end justifies the means and the end was to pass the exam. Secondly, the professor enjoyed playing an all-knowing role in the spectacle. Their mannerisms and reactions were all exaggerated for their theatrical effect. There was little difference between being liked or feared as long as he was controversial. The cardinal sin was to be inconspicuous. Therefore, small mistakes were blown out of proportion, and an error, normally ignored, might be the key to a student's downfall in an open exam.

Angela and I balanced on the edges of our seats, muscles tensed, ready to spring forward if our names were called.

"Catreni e Ricardo."

My muscles relaxed and I slumped back in my seat as Catrelli and Ricardo shot up and scurried to their chairs before the professor. They sat before him, unnoticed for a couple of minutes, as he attended to the paperwork on the table in front of him. Without warning, he looked up quickly and simultaneously said,

"Catreni, speak to me about the Kreb Cycle."

What a question, I thought. Nothing could be bigger and easier. I kicked myself for not having offered the bidello 20,000 lire to insure a position ahead of Catreni and Ricardo. Mentally, I ran through the answer to the question that was mapped out in my mind like the figure out of the textbook.

Catreni began his response slowly, nervously pulling words. As he passed through an acceptable definition and a description of the initial reactions in the cycle, his voice began to exude confidence. The rest of the answer flowed smoothly off his tongue.

The professor, Gian Carlo Di Marco, head of the Institute of Biochemistry at the university, son of the renowned and almost immortal retired Head of the Department of Anatomy at the University of Rome, Guiseppi Di Marco, snapped at Catrelli. "What is the purpose of the cycle?"

"To generate energy that is stored in the form of Adenosine Triphosphate."

"How is this done?"

"What?"

Catreni seemed confused. He had already responded to that in his initial oratory, and probably didn't realize that, at that time, the professor was involved in drawing a flower and hadn't been paying attention.

"I don't understand sir; I have already…."

The professor cut in. "That is obvious Catreni. You have memorized well, but you do not understand. We shall try another soon." That statement seemed ominous. He turned toward Ricardo and asked him to discuss the topic of hormones.

That was a topic that most students prepared superficially for the Biochemistry exam and Ricardo was no exception. His answer was vacuous at best. The professor turned from him and asked Catreni two detailed questions. The first he responded to well, the second he could not answer. The professor reacted adversely. "It seems that you two have not studied very adequately. Nevertheless we shall try once more." That statement was absurd. On the basis of one question, Ricardo was prejudged as a type that prepared superficially and Catreni as a type that memorized but did not understand. It was important that they both answer well now for the professor assumed that students that were examined together, studied together, and knew the same amount of material. That also was ridiculous, as often your partner was determined by accident alone. Nevertheless, it was common practice to try and grab a partner who was well prepared. He, with good response, could pull a poor student through an exam. By the same token, we all feared being examined with a poor student for, even if an individual responded fairly well, a lousy exam mate could bring him under. The next question was on glucose and Catreni gave a well-organized detailed answer. His voice though occasionally squeaked and, as he responded, he pressed his palms together nervously. The professor asked one detailed question and Catreni answered well. With a poker face, giving no hint to Catreni of a job well done, he then turned to Ricardo and asked. "Speak to me about phospholipids."

Ricardo again responded fairly superficially and stopped after only a minute of oratory. The professor said. "More."

Ricardo added a sentence and stopped again.

"E la spugna assuigata? (Is the sponge dry?)" the professor asked sarcastically.

Ricardo smiled, somewhat embarrassed as the hall resounded with laughter.

The professor's countenance remained grim. "This is not a laughing matter. You would do better Ricardo to laugh less and study more." Ricardo quickly wiped the smile off of his face. The professor's hands went to his forehead and he mumbled loudly enough for all to hear. "What am I going to do with them?" Catreni and Ricardo sat nervously in their chairs waiting on the caprice of the professor. The situation was ludicrous and theatrical. The professor, true to form in an open exam, kept the drama alive. Catreni and Ricardo were puppets and he played them unmercifully, tearing at their nerves with the creation of an artificial crisis. "All right, one more question, but I warn you; if you do not answer you will fail." For the last three words his pitch dropped an octave. "Speak to me about, ei," he paused, eking out the last bit of drama, as a tense silence fell across the room, "the water soluble vitamins."

This was a big question, one we all studied well and completely. For thirty seconds nobody responded and finally the professor looked toward Catreni and said "Well, I haven't got all day."

Catreni began his response. It had not been obvious to whom he had addressed the question and I am sure that is why Catreni had not answered earlier. Again, he responded well and, three quarters of the way through the reply, the professor cut him off and asked them to step outside. They both thanked him and left, waiting impatiently for the professor to decide on their grade and to call them back into the

room to return their libretto (little book) with their new grades stamped inside.

This was a trying period, very much like an ice skater waiting for her evaluation after her free skate, knowing that her rating was as much a function of politics and emotion as it was about skill. Time seemingly moved in milliseconds. A second seemed a minute, a minute an hour. Occasionally, because you answered extremely well, or very poorly, you knew that you had passed or failed and the moments of waiting outside the door were purely anticlimactic. Usually, though, your responses had laid somewhere between those extremes and the decision of the professor was not predictable. What one-day might be valued as a "B," on another day may be deemed a failure, depending on his mood and his subjective reaction to the student.

The bidello moved toward the carved, deeply stained, wooden doors to call back Catreni and Ricardo. They walked sheepishly into the room and approached the commission's table. The professor did not look up. One of his assistants handed them back their books and called out loud. "Twenty eight for Catreni and twenty eight for Ricardo." Catreni and Ricardo thanked the professor, who did not reply, and exited smiling and excited. They had both received grades equivalent to an A minus, totally unimaginable from the earlier actions of the professor. Apparently he was pleased with Catreni's last response and judged both of the students primarily on this.

Again Angela and I coiled in readiness, as the bidello stepped forward and called.

"Lazari and Robbins."

My stomach seemingly dropped to the bottom of a bottomless pit, as we sprang forward and moved down the steps to the seats before the professor. We occupied them quickly.

My mind was conscious of my clammy hands, palm to palm, moving nervously in my lap. The waiting was insufferable. Suddenly the professor mumbled a question with his head still bowed in the papers before him. Among the words in the sentence, I could only make out my name. "What professor?"

He looked sternly at me, catching the accent in my voice. "You don't speak Italian?"

That I understood and I responded. "Si professore, I do."

"Then answer," he shouted. "In an Italian school you will speak Italian, or you will fail. I am sick and tired of you American students coming to school in this country, living among your own and never bothering to learn the language." His booming voice was overpowering and I had all I could do to maintain composure and self-control.

"I repeat professor, I do speak Italian. The accent I can't help. But I did not hear the question. Would you repeat it?"

"Excuse me," he rasped sarcastically. "You do speak. How long have you been in the country? Two weeks?"

A snicker of laughter rumbled through the auditorium. I felt like standing up and telling the bastard, accent or not, that I could still converse in his language far better than he could in my own. I wanted to grab him by the neck and choke him until he fell to his knees and begged me in Italian to release him, only to have me respond mockingly in perfect Italian that I didn't understand. "All right," he continued, "speak to me about the monophosphate shunt."

The question was fair and under normal conditions my answer would have been organized and well thought out. But, I was so incensed, that my thoughts were cloudy, as formulas raced through my mind in a disheveled sequence. With a supreme and concentrated effort, the clouds began to clear, only to form anew with the intrusion of the professor's booming voice. "Well, I haven't got all day."

At this point my thoughts were all intertwined and my garbled verbal response perfectly mirrored that state of mental confusion. That knife-like sarcastic voice again cut right into me. "What are you talking about? I don't know whether your trouble is Biochemistry or Italian but one thing is for sure. I refuse to bother to discern the difference."

He looked up toward Angela and said again with sarcasm, "I hope you know a little more."

She began to respond, nervously at first, but then with eloquence and the sum total of her answer was excellent. I followed her every step of the way as my mental images focused into place. She had skipped only three significant facts and two of them lay clearly in my mind. The third eluded me.

"Very good, my dear," the professor intoned softly. They were usually gentle with girls, especially if they were pieces of ass. There was a direct relationship between brassiere size and grades, the former usually running about ten points above the latter. A forty-inch set of tits went with a perfect thirty exam score. Eighteen was a passing grade and any girl with a flat chest lay on tenuous ground.

The professor returned his gaze to me. "All right Robbins. Where is the energy released in the shunt?"

My heart, which I am sure was palpitating, began to slow to a normal rate as the tension dissipated with my response. That question was one of the two I knew cold and I responded in an orderly and confident manner. The professor gave no indication of satisfaction and returned to ask Angela another question. Again, she performed beautifully and, miraculously, the small bone he threw to me I chewed up with perfection. He popped Angela a third question, stopping her in the middle of her response. He didn't ask me to continue, but pinpointed two significant reactions in the last half of the question, and asked me to describe the effect of each. The first slipped my mind momentarily, but the assistant, sitting on his side, stacked three pencils on top of each other trying to give me a hint. Suddenly the concept of building sprung into my mind and I dissertated on the anabolic effect of the reaction. The professor seemed disinterested as he returned his attention to drawing the flower in front of him, but cut in with the second question, when he saw that I knew the first. To that I responded well.

A tremendous sense of relief exuded from my every pore when he finally said,

S accomadi.

We thanked him and left the room, waiting to be called back for our librettos. I knew that we had passed, for from that horrible tortuous beginning, the whole exam had moved steadily uphill. Nevertheless, I had no idea what our grades would be.

The bidello called us back into the room, winking at us as we passed through the doorway. The assistant on the other side of the professor took the librettos and handed them back to us calling twenty-seven to Angela and twenty-four to me. Angela and I both said thank you but the professor didn't even look up. Angela turned to leave, but after such brow beating and insult, I was determined to challenge him psychologically.

"Thank you professor," I repeated in a firm voice. Still no response. The assistant waved to me frantically to exit, but I was determined to get the man to respond. I bent my head over the commission's table, mouth twelve inches from the professor's ear, and repeated in a loud

resonant voice. "Maybe you didn't hear me professor but I said thank you."

Finally he looked up startled to see my face with menacing countenance so close. "You're welcome. You're welcome."

Score one small victory for me. I couldn't help but add, with a congenial sincere smile on my face. "In America, professor, we call people who are as nice as you mother fuckers." The last two words were muttered in English.

"Thank you," he said.

"You're welcome." I couldn't help but hear a few muffled snickers in the auditorium. There must have been a few Americans in the room. Score one big victory for me.

My first exam experience taught me a number of valuable lessons. Most important was the need to accept abuse philosophically and not on a personal basis. I had been lucky and Angela did not think it funny when I translated the words "mother fucker" to her. She thought, instead, that I had acted stupidly. The key was not to antagonize the professor. As a student, you were subject to their whims and mood, but you should never intentionally stir up the breeze. She explained to me that, if he had understood, I would never have passed the Biochemistry exam as long as he remained the head of the department and, in all probability, that black ball would have carried on to the other institutions. Secondly, I understood the importance of maintaining a cool demeanor. More essential than what you knew was how you said it. If, under stress, you could not present material in an organized fashion, then you might fail no matter how much you knew. The opposite was also truc. A confident and well-prepared response would be accepted as a passing answer, despite a conspicuous lack of knowledge with regard to detail. On occasion of course, when the professor was in a bad mood, or when an open exam was in progress, or when you entered late in a session, lack of detailed knowledge would be exaggerated and you would fail. But "the when" was never predictable and statistically you were much better off with a general and skimpy but well memorized response than with a mental file of facts that could not be extracted spontaneously in an orderly fashion.

The session moved on, and Angela and I turned our attention to Histology. I could tell that she was unhappy with the exam grade (A-) that she had received in Biochemistry and attributed that "low grade" to my mediocre performance. Nevertheless, she valued me not only as a study partner but also as a friend and confidant. She knew it was only a matter of time before I adjusted and caught on to the system.

Frank, so far, had not fared so well. He had postponed taking his Microbiology, which he had prepared for first, for he did not feel he was ready. I tried to explain to him that he could never be totallt prepared and that he had to sacrifice both curiosity and security in order to review the major sections of the course frequently enough. Only in this way could he have a ready response for most questions and a statistically good chance to pass.

Frank, though, wouldn't listen. He continued to delve into the depths of a subject as his desire dictated. Finally, out of fear and uncertainty, he chose to avoid the July exam session altogether. Meanwhile Angela and I continued to bang away painfully at Histology.

The daily temperature ranged into the mid nineties and occasionally up to a hundred or a hundred and one. There was no such thing as air conditioning. The heat was so intolerable that I sometimes thought of giving the day an ice bath for its fever. Each movement was an effort, but still we plodded on for six or seven hours every day. Our pace accelerated until the last four days, when we reviewed together sixteen hours a day, leaving only six hours to sleep and two hours to relax. Angela began popping amphetamines for that last week. The ease with which she concentrated, as wall as her boundless energy and interest in the subject, tempted me greatly, but I resisted and kept up under my own steam. On July 28th we entered the building to take our exam. We waited and waited and waited to be called but the day passed on with five couples being taken before us. The professor then closed the session for the day and, with hate and frustration, I went to search out the bidello. Angela pleaded with me to let her handle it and reluctantly I gave in. It took all I could do not to interfere. We approached him while he was wiping down the commission's table and Angela said.

"Excuse me signori."

The bidello turned around and smiled. "Yes."

"Do you remember me?"

The bidello looked confused and for just a fleeting moment uneasy. "Of course," he said emphatically.

It was obvious to Angela that he didn't, but she continued anyway. "Then of course you remember my problem with my mother in Ravenna. I told her that I would be home today and now I must stay for tomorrow to take the exam." Tears welled into the corners of her eyes.

The bidello responded sympathetically. "I am sorry my dear, but it is not my fault. The professors took charge of the list personally. Today, believe me, if I could have put you in, I would have."

What he really meant was that some people had slipped him more money or had promised him some other favor. I wanted to kick him in the face. Angela, instead, continued to play on his sympathies. "What an I going to do? I know it's not your fault, but my mother will be so disappointed. The doctor says she is very depressed and on the brink of a nervous breakdown." She began to sob onto my shoulder. "I'm so afraid."

The bidello seemed really concerned. "Believe me, if it were possible, you would have been in today. I promise you, first thing tomorrow."

Angela turned to him wiping the tears from her eyes. She took out a piece of paper and printed our names clearly on it. Along with the paper she handed him another 5,000 lire. "Thank you, I knew you'd understand."

"Please signorita, I can not accept this." The bidello made a token effort to return the money.

Angela held up her hand and he halted. "No. You have been so kind. I will inform my mother tonight of the unfortunate delay, and tell her that I will be home on the first train in the afternoon."

The bidello nodded in assurance.

As we left, I said, letting my animosity and nausea come out in the tone of my voice. "What a son off a bitch. And you! What an actress."

"But we shall be first tomorrow," she replied innocently. And we were.

I had shot my load with Biochemistry and Histology and all the pent up tension, when released, left me with a tremendous sensation of accomplishment. Angela and I celebrated with a quiet dinner and a gallon of wine between us. We would have fucked too, if I could have found my zipper.

I had no intention of returning home that summer. Instead, I planned to gallivant around Europe, seeing the sights and familiarizing myself with the terrain. I had already said goodbye to Frank, who had left on the Swiss Air charter to return home. He had to work to accumulate funds for the coming year. The parting was somewhat stiff and disappointing. We had roomed together and had been through so many new and often frustrating experiences together. But the one experience that separated success from failure, and was for a long time to maintain a barrier between us, was the exams themselves. Frank left, with a feeling of stagnation and uselessness combined with a touch of resentment toward my obvious accomplishments. Although nothing was said, I knew that he blamed the fact that I ceased to study with him at such a late date on his inability to prepare in time for the exams. Nothing was further from the truth, for I myselfhad prepared for two. He would have to work out that problem in his own way.

Angela and I had parted without an impending sense of remorse, but rather with an anticipation of a renewed friendship come October. We had had a profound effect on each other over the last year. She had facilitated my acclimation to Italian society and to the University situation. I had activated her metamorphosis from a dependent, naive individual to a woman in full control of her emotions and intents. We knew that the sexual part of our relationship might end with her or my own involvement with another individual, but the friendship would always remain. Our intense interaction over the past year was too indelibly stamped on our personae to ever let that go by the board.

My folks had just given me $3,500 to buy a new car. I chose instead to pick up a used Masserati. A unique situation existed with used luxury automobiles in Italy. Each year, an automobile was taxed on the size of its engine. For the 3,580 cubic centimeter engines the tax ran about four hundred dollars per year. Without this registration fee, the car could not be licensed.

Any Italian who could afford ten to fifteen thousand dollars for a car could afford the yearly levy. But the tax remained the same for the life of the car and, therefore, an individual, who could not afford to buy a new Masserati or Ferrari, could obviously not afford the yearly tax.

Therefore, a market for used luxury cars was almost nonexistent, and a three-year-old Masserati, selling for seven or eight thousand dollars in the states, would sell for three to four thousand dollars in Italy if you could find a buyer.

I found the car of my liking, a 3,500 cubic centimeter, sleek, silver gray "Gran Tourismo." The asking price was four thousand and five hundred dollars. I offered twenty seven hundred, take it or leave it. He took it. The car was demolished on paper and registered in the state of

Alabama under Judge S.K. Jones, not for four hundred dollars a year, but for only ten dollars a year (on the basis of weight.)

The engine, at this stage of the game, was burned out by three years of hard driving. For a thousand dollars I had it completely overhauled and, with another couple of hundred dollars of bodywork, the car was essentially new in all but body style.

The day I picked up the car, I went home to pack to prepare for my summer trip. While packing the phone rang. I picked it up and the operator indicated it was long distance.

My father's voice fought the turbulence across the Atlantic Cable. "How are you?"

"Fine dad." I spoke, knowing full well that he would have to strain to hear. "I'm glad you caught me. I was just leaving for Copenhagen. How are you?" He ignored the question.

"You're going to have to change your plans." His voice was rock cold and serious and, for a fleeting moment of unsaid truths, my mind was bombarded with tragedies involving my family.

"Joe Baker was involved in an automobile accident in East Germany."

Unashamed, I felt relieved. Joe Baker was a good friend of mine and I was immediately concerned for his safety. But he was not my mother or father. "Is he seriously injured?"

"I don't know. We haven't been able to get much information."

"What can I do?"

"If you'll listen I'll tell you."

I shut up and listened. "Joe's parents can't get passports cleared for a couple of days and they would like you to get to Joe's side as fast as possible. We've tried all day to get information, but the lines through to East Germany are closed and the only information that we've received is that he is in critical condition."

"Where is he?"

"In a hospital in Burg, near Magdeburg."

"Where's that?"

"A couple of hours west of Berlin."

"Okay dad, I'm on my way. I'll call with some information when I get there."

"Good and Dodd, be careful. Don't be a wise guy."

"I won't, goodbye."

"Goodbye."

With the nature and destination of my journey changed, I called my friend Mark to tell him that I had to alter my plans for the European tour. I offered him the opportunity to accompany me and he jumped on it. He chose to come because he sensed the excitement generated by the cloud of fear, mystery and tragedy hovering over the trip. It didn't hurt that I offered to pay all his expenses for this leg of the trip. With grim determination in place of carefree listlessness, we set out, planning to reach Nuremberg that night. After fourteen hours of hard driving, navigating bumpy, twisted and dusty Italian, Austrian and German roads, we arrived at our destination. After a brief respite to stretch our legs, I decided to push on. Once through Nuremberg we moved on toward the border. Since Joe Baker was only a name to him, Mark's resolve dissolved before my own. He had insisted on frequent stops along the way and, when I decided to drive on, instead of staying in Nuremberg for the night, he got quite upset. "Listen, I told you before I left that I've got to get there as soon as I can."

"That doesn't mean you have to break an endurance record."

My tone was curt. I was in no mood to fool around. "I'm going straight through, Mark."

"No sense driving like a maniac." With palms up he pleaded his logic. "He's in a hospital, he'll be there tomorrow too."

The closer we got to the border, the more narrow my vision. His petty concern for sleep and comfort pissed me off. "Listen," I rasped caustically, "I'm going. You want to get out, I'll drop you."

Sensing my determination, he sighed reluctantly. "Okay, you win, Burg here we come." I thought I heard him gulp.

I was too involved to be afraid. Mark, though, paced nervously around the border station as we waited for our visas. I told the border guards that my cousin was injured near Burg and that we had to get there as soon as possible. I thought that would be influential in permitting us to continue through at night.

The guards, polite, stern, and totally detached, asked numerous questions. Each question was backed up by a phone call to confirm my story. After one and half-hours, they gave us permission to travel on the Autobahn to Magdeburg, where we would stay in a hotel assigned to us. With visas in hand, they warned us that we would be expected to be there at five AM at the latest. Under no circumstances were we to go to the hospital that night. The spy movie overtones made Mark pace all the faster.

Once back in the car he confronted me. "Why did you have to lie. They could put us in jail for that."

I was cocky as hell. "There was no way for them to know that he wasn't my cousin." I sounded overbearing if not convincing. "Nah, how could they know and do you really believe they'd let just a friend through tonight?"

Mark was irate. "They're not letting you through. We have to go to the hotel."

I wasn't sure if Mark sensed that I was going to ignore that rule too. If not, Mark was in for a big surprise. I was going to see Joe that night.

As I turned off the Autobahn at the third exit, Mark's hair stood on end and his cremaster muscles pulled a little harder on his balls. "What are you doing?"

"Getting off."

"Are you crazy? They said we had to stay on the Autobahn." He emphasized the word on.

My determination picked up momentum geometrically at the expense of rational. "Listen, if we stay on that road we have to follow two sides of a triangle. If we take the side roads, we follow the hypotenuse of the triangle. We'll get in much earlier."

Mark's tone was again pleading. "Please get back on the Autobahn." "No," I said firmly. That was that.

The East Germany countryside lay still and bleak, as the thick shadowy pines lining the narrow roads enveloped us in a blanket of unknown hostility. As the Masserati purred deeper into the bowels of the nation, a sensation of vulnerability and helplessness crept through me. I challenged my fears with the thought of Joe lying alone, in pain, in an East German hospital. Mark didn't have that advantage and he was overtly frightened.

The car confidently negotiated the bumps and twists of the East German roads and, in lieu of the threatening countryside, the warmth and luxury of its carriage was comforting. We moved through small towns, all marked by the eerie monotony of darkness and quiet. The absence of people and light was unnerving. Occasionally, we would reach a detour, which forced us onto small, unmarked dirt roads, apparently leading to nowhere. The analogy to the twilight zone was crystal clear. Miraculously we always found our way back to the numbered highways that would lead us toward Burg.

Periodically, Mark would break the monotonous purr of the Masserati's engine with words born of fear. "We never should have left the Autobahn. We should have done just what they told us." I let him talk. For the moment navigating the unlit badly marked roads was all I could handle.

"They could kill us and no one would know the difference."

"Oh will you come off it Mark? This isn't a spy movie." I wasn't sure if I was convincing myself, let alone him.

"If it isn't, you're making it one. We are not supposed to be here, and in this country they shoot first and ask questions later."

"If they catch us." I had no intention of running from pursuing police but I knew that conservative, non adventurous Mark considered me to be unpredictable and wouldn't put that alternative past me. I had stung him with the blade of flippancy.

"Very funny."

He waited for me to reassure him that I wouldn't. None came. To him, this had become an inconvenient ordeal. To me, it was a mission, and I resented his continuous barrage of negativism.

Half way to Burg, a car pulled out on the road behind us and followed at a constant distance as we swept across the countryside. "They're following us."

"Who?" I tried to show lack of concern but I had been nervously glancing in the rear view mirror.

"The police probably." Mark kept turning in his seat, hoping the two lights in the distance were a mirage and would disappear. They weren't. He made an abortive attempt at light humor. It fell like a brick.

"I can see it all now in headlines. The bodies of two American medical students were recovered today in a ditch on the side of an East German road, culminating five years of intensive search. The East German police profess ignorance of any knowledge regarding the deaths of these two young skeletons."

"It's possible," I responded seriously.

That drove him further back into his seat. The Masserati's buckets were almost as protective as a mother's breast.

With adrenaline steadily pouring in my veins and one of my eyes glued to the rear view mirror, we continued on toward Burg. For what seemed like an eternity, we waited for the car behind to accelerate and push us over towards the soft shoulder. Finally it did and, as it pulled up alongside, I thought my heart would stop. The women in the front seat looked toward me and smiled. The other woman, driving, pulled out in front, and zoomed off into the distance. The car looked like a reproduction from an Al Capone movie but its occupants were obviously benign.

With the release of tension, my stomach dropped. The cool sweat evaporated from my forehead, sending a chill through me. With that past, I was able to sense the slowing of my pulse as I relaxed back in my seat, and a wave of exhaustion swept over me. My eyes were bleary and I had difficulty focusing. Oh, how I wanted to stop and crawl into a nice warm comfortable bed. But we were past the point of no return and I forced myself to press onward. The silence between Mark and myself rung with tension. There wasn't much to say. We both wanted to get to our destination as fast as possible. Despite the fact that my offhand bravado had left me, to be replaced by a more sensible concern for our safety, I still intended to go directly through to the hospital. If any questions were asked, I hoped to feign a misunderstanding. Signs indicating directions to Burg came up more frequently. We followed them, each kilometer slowly sliding away in an agony of endless time, each successive kilometer longer than the last.

On arrival, I followed signs to the center of the city. The eerie absence of activity permeated the town from periphery to core. There were no signs indicating the location of the hospital and, with streets barren, nobody to ask. So intent was I to arrive in Burg that the obvious problem never crossed my mind. Frustrated, I mumbled. "Where the hell is the fucking hospital?" We continued to drive aimlessly about, lost, anxious and just a little frightened.

With hope slowly seeping away, I spotted a man garbed in dull gray, collar pulled about his neck, walking briskly down the street. I didn't know if they had curfews, or if he was a criminal or a detective, but I felt compelled to risk asking him directions. Mark gulped as I pulled in along the curb. I yelled across the open window. "Where is the hospital?" The echo of my voice ringing through the silent streets startled me. Apparently it startled him too and, with reflex dominating, he backed up against the wall of a building lining the sidewalk. I asked him again and realized that he, of course, didn't understand. Mark tried in Yiddish. With recognition of a word or two, a smile sprung on the East German's face and he approached the car, offering directions eagerly. Mark halted him with a hand motion and offered him a piece of paper to draw on. The directions were exquisitely precise. Ironically, we were only three blocks away and had been circling the hospital continuously for a half-hour. With a sense of relief, I drove directly to the hospital, pulled up in front and parked the car. Simple when you know how.

Energy and enthusiasm renewed, we entered and found our way to the information desk. A nurse stood to greet us, but she obviously didn't understand our English and Mark's pigeon Yiddish did not suffice. She did get the idea that we were Americans, and, putting two and two together, assumed that we were here to see Joe. She indicated a comfortable old couch in the waiting area, and walked quickly toward the inner aspect of the building. We paced nervously. She returned minutes later with another nurse. At first, the only things about her that impressed me were her big tits. The second thing that impressed me dwarfed the first. She spoke English. "Good evening."

I returned the cordiality and rushed on. "We're here to see Joe, the American in the car accident."

She responded slowly with strain and difficulty. "Please, my English is not so good. Speak more slowly. I do not get much chance to practice you know."

It was good enough for me. She was going to understand if it took all night. "The American, car accident."

"Ah yes, you wish to see him."

"Yes."

"But we were informed that you were to be here in the morning."

"We are a little early. I'm sure that Joe is anxious to see us."

Her English improved as she spoke, but her tone was businesslike. She was obviously well schooled but rusty. "I do not think that it is possible at this time. The order said that you would visit with him in the morning."

"Please," I begged, forcing my best look of disappointment, We have traveled a long way. He is alone and afraid in a strange country."

She looked unsure. "I don't know. It is against the rules."

With pained expression, I appealed to her motherly instinct. "Please, just for a moment."

As she sighed, her breasts seemed to swell and her tone melted. "All right, just for a moment. Then you must go."

I smiled and expressed my gratitude. That old axiom held true. Under a pair of big tits lay a warm heart.

We walked down a number of corridors until we reached Joe's room. On the way I asked about his condition. She was evasive, telling me the doctor would speak with me in the morning, but pessimism rung through every word. She obviously regretted her moment of weakness and wished not to dig her hole any deeper. In East Germany, the less you said and the less initiative you took, the better off you were.

I walked in alone. A small night lamp outlined the shadow of Joe's body. His head turned toward me and his features, spotlighted by the cone of light, registered pain and despair."Joe."

"Dodd." His voice wavered but a smile appeared on his face as he instantly recognized my voice. "That you?"

"Joe." I walked to his side and put my hand over his. "I thought you'd be the first to get here. How did you find out?"

"My folks called. Does it hurt bad?"

"No, but I can't move my legs."

I rolled the sheet back and saw the catheter coming from his penis. The urine was at least clear and abundant.

"How did it happen?"

He ignored my question. "Did the doctor tell you if I'd get to move my legs?"

"I haven't spoken to him. I came straight here." "Will you ask him? I have to know."

He pounded the point home. Joe was a good athlete with a stocky powerful build. Looking at his body bruised and broken made me burn with inner rage.

"How did it happen Joe?"

"I fell asleep at the wheel. Nothing happened to Val; when I woke up I was here and I couldn't feel my legs." Again he asked the same question.

"Do you think I'll be able to move them soon?"

"Sure," I said trying to comfort him, "but for now just rest and get your strength back. I have to go over to the hotel and check in. I'll be back to speak to the doctor a little later and I'll see you then."

"Stay a while longer." His tone was pleading.

A lump came up in my throat and I patted his hand.

"I want to Joe, but I took a chance in coming here first. I have to check in before they find out that I'm missing. You know, East German rules. You don't want to fuck with these guys"

He nodded in resignation, not having the energy to object again. I squeezed his hand and, after reassuring him that I would be back in the AM, I left the room.

The hotel was like an oasis in the middle of the desert. It stood out in sharp contrast among the crowded, gray, drab three story walk-ups surrounding it. The architecture was modern and refreshing; a good billboard for western visitors.

We offered the desk clerk all our papers. With all the red tape, I figured it was best to let her burn her ass figuring it out. She looked up at the clock and them back at us and smiled. With a nod of her head, the bellboy took the keys and indicated for us to follow him to our room. Once inside we were pleasantly surprised. All the conveniences were clean and new. The beds were comfortable and the dresser space ample. But the decor was obviously early motel. Taste was obviously not an East German strong suit.

Mark went to close the door and then called worriedly. "Hey, look here."

I turned to face him. "Where?"

"Here, the door." He was really nervous.

The lock. It's on the outside."

I walked over to the window and pulled the curtains. They were barred.

"It figures," I said without much concern."
"Figures. I'll tell you what figures. We're in a jail, not a hotel."

"Now Mark, calm down. They have no reason to lock us in here."

"You forget," he chastised, shaking his finger at me. "They don't need reasons." His voice dropped suddenly to a whisper. "And by the way, don't say anything too loudly that you don't want them to hear. The place probably has bugs hidden all over." Proud of his insight, he strolled toward the bathroom like Sherlock Holmes. I cut the rug right out from under him.

"I don't care what you say. The communists are not a bunch of nasty bastards."

Fun is fun, but I went too far. He had a temper tantrum and then he wouldn't speak to me for the rest of the day.

Two hours sleep wasn't much. But it kept me going. I drove back to the hospital somewhat mummified but still alive. This time I drove alone. Mark wanted to sleep. The bustle and activity around the wards lay in sharp contrast to the dark silence encountered only hours before. With difficulty, I found my way to the Doctor's hospital office. Fortunately he was there for nobody else spoke English. "Good morning," I said, once I entered the room.

"Good morning," he replied in proud awkward English, standing to accept my hand. "You must be Joe's cousin. The nurse on the night shift informed me of your arrival." He was an imposing figure, tall and blond, completely dwarfing me. His office was bare, except for the basic necessities; desk, lamp, two chairs and crude board bookshelves supported by layers ofblock cement. The East Germans obviously did not believe in comforts.

"Please sit down," he said indicating the straight back chair in front of the desk. Tired, I took him up on his offer.

"Thank God you speak English," I said with relief. "It makes things much easier."

"Even under these unfortunate circumstances, it is a welcome opportunity to practice my English."

I spoke directly, getting to the point.

"I appreciate all that you did for Joe. What is his prognosis?"

He laid it on the line without flinching. "Not good. I believe his spinal cord is severed. He will never walk again. Nor will he be able to exert control over his bladder, bowel, and sexual functions."

"Boy, you don't pull any punches."

"What was that?" he asked straining to understand.

"Nothing, just an expression." "Oh."

"There is no hope then?"

"I'm afraid not. Does his mother have any other children?"

"Yes, three, a boy and two girls."

"Then things will be alright," he said with a sense of righteousness.

"What does that mean?" I challenged.

"What about Joe?"

"Oh well, when you fall asleep at the wheel, driving at 75 miles per hour, you can expect that sort of thing." With a sense of justification he added. "He deserved what he got."

"Black and white," I said sarcastically. "Just like that?"

"If you put it that way."

"I don't, but Hitler did."

He frowned. It was no longer convenient to admire Hitler. I took that as my cue and stood up to leave. I decided that I didn't like the man. Just like that.

Joe was happy to see me. He started where he had left off. "Did you speak to the doctor?"

He caught me off guard.

"Yes." The moment the word came out, I knew I should have lied.

"Will I be able to walk again?"

I tried not to let the agony in my throat seep through.

"I don't know Joe. For the meantime, let's concentrate on getting your breaks healed."

"Didn't you ask?"

This time I lied.

"No, I only asked if you were going to die and he assured me you wouldn't. One thing at a time."

His tone was anxious and pleading.

"Listen, I don't care about death. I want to know If I'll be able to walk and fuck. Can you understand that?"

"Yes Joe." He struggled to sit up, but the pain from his crushed ribs forced him back supine. His breath was heavy and he paused while the pain subsided. His tone was controlled, but more intense.

"Will you ask him for me?" He looked directly into my eyes. I didn't turn away. "Please?"

"Yes Joe, I will. But for now rest." I turned my back and walked slowly from the room. He never saw the tears.

Joe's father arrived the following day. He rushed through the swinging door at the end of the corridor, chased by another man and a nurse. His head swam from side to side. I was standing outside Joe's door waiting for him to awake. "Mr. Baker."

He looked up and right through me and then continued onward as if he didn't know me. "Mr. Baker," I called to his back. It was almost a command. He turned to face me and recognition hit home.

"Dodd?" he asked in anguish. We had met at least a hundred times in the last five years, but in this moment of grief and desperation that was uniquely his, he had lost touch with surrounding reality.

"Yes, Mr. Baker, it's me."

He approached rapidly. The man and nurse had caught up to his side. "Where is he?"

"Sleeping, he's sleeping now."

"I want to see him. How is he?"

Again a lump caught in my throat. The doctor had conveniently questioned his own English and asked me to inform his father of the extent of the accident. "And you will see him; but for now the doctor wants him to rest."

I indicated a couch at the far end of the corridor.

"Let's talk over there where you can be more comfortable." While we walked he fired questions.

"How is he?"

"His condition is stable and the doctor says he is out of danger for his life."

His father sighed and sat down on the couch. I sat next to him. The nurse, seeing that I had him under control, left us alone. Mr. Baker's movements had now slowed and his voice was more relaxed.

"Is he hurt badly Dodd?"

"Yes, he broke most of his ribs and his back." I paused wanting to stop there. He paused, tensed on the edge of the couch, waiting for the crushing blow, hoping against all hope that no permanent damage was done. I swallowed hard and delivered. Somebody had to. Better now than later.

"He's paralyzed from the waist down."

His voice was just audible, the pitch a piercing shriek.

"Oh my God, oh my God!"

He fell heavily into my arms and began to sob against my chest, My arm fell around him and I sat straight and still.

"Why, why," he asked again and again.

I remained the silent crutch. Words would be blank ammunition now.

After fifteen minutes, Theodore Baker had composed himself. He sat straight and melancholy, alone with his own grief. I stood up and walked to Joe's room and peeked in. He was awake. I walked back down the hall to the couch.

"He's up, now Mr. Baker if you'd like to see him."

Joe's father stood slowly, bracing himself on my arm.

"I'll take you in."

He shook his head as he spoke. "No Dodd, no. Let me go alone." I watched him move steadily toward the door and disappear within. He wanted to share this moment of deepest despair alone with his son. Alone they could cry in peace.

I looked up and for the first time noticed the man who had chased

Mr. Baker down the corridor when they first arrived. He smiled and walked over.

"Hello, I'm Mike Baker, Joe's uncle."

"Hi," I responded smiling. "Nice to meet you."

He returned my smile. "Bad, huh?"

"Yeah, I'm afraid so."

"Poor Teddy, after all he's done for those boys; to have this happen." Mike shook his head in wonderment to support the lack of an explanation for what he had just said.

"I feel so bad for both of them," I added.

"I understand, but there is nothing that we can do, nothing."

A minute passed in silence. There was nothing more to say until Baker cut in.

"What do you think of the town?"

"What?" I looked up. I was in cyberspace, thinking of Joe and his father and his voice was like an intrusion. So close and yet so helpless. "I'm sorry I didn't hear you."

"What do you think of the town?"

"I don't know, I haven't seen much of it."

Mike Baker leaned over so that he would only have to whisper, his red polka dotted bow tie exaggerating his closeness. His tone was knowing and conciliatory.

"Listen, I know that you're distraught, but there is nothing that we can do. We might as well try and have a good time while we're here."

"What," I asked again, incredulously.

"Come on, do I have to spell it out for you? You've been here two days. There's got to be a hot spot in town."

I looked up totally shocked. Joe was paralyzed and this jerk was looking to get laid.

"Listen Mr. Baker. I don't have time for that now." He didn't heed my warning. This was like out of the twilight zone.

"Listen son, there's no reason to get upset. We're gonna be here a while and I just thought we'd try and…"

I didn't let him finish. All I saw was a smiling obscene face sitting on a bow tie. It was blown up like a balloon that kept getting bigger and bigger, begging for a pin to burst it. My fist lashed out, with all the rage and hurt built up inside me since my arrival. I even heard the pop. From my vantage point, looking at Mike Baker, flat on his back and rubbing his chin, it was clear to me that he finally got the hint.

With Joe's father present, there was no need for us to remain at the hospital. Mark and I decided to travel to Berlin for a couple of days. We would then come back and visit with Joe again, before returning to Italy.

The western sector, marked by new construction, bright lights and laughing ebullient people, lay in sharp contrast to the gray, bleak East The two days we spent there were thoroughly enjoyable and offered us a welcome respite from the incessant inner tension, ever present in the communist sector.

With time running out, we reluctantly moved through checkpoint Charlie to the East Berlin border station. From there we would go to the visa office. With visas in hand, we would then have to return to the Western sector and exit to East Germany again through checkpoint Bravo.

Waiting in the border station was old hat to us now. Mark pulled a cigarette pack from his pocket and a startled look fell across his face.

"Hey, I've got some East German money here. I forgot to turn it in at the border when we came into the West."

"So?"

His tone was exasperating. "So, it's against the law to take East German money out of the country. What should I do?"

I just couldn't stand the daily soap opera. "Give it to me," I said curtly. Mark willingly deposited the East German marks into my outstretched hand, happy to rid himself of the hot potato. I felt pretty nonchalant about the whole thing. With the hundreds of tourists passing through here each day, I never expected them to search my pockets.

The marks never got that far. A hand grasped my wrist and squeezed tightly. I looked up startled. The East German officer wasn't smiling. "Would you step into my office please," he commanded indicating the door behind the desk.

I started to speak, but the words caught in my throat. I swallowed hard and tried again. "Certainly, come on Mark."

"Not him, you," he shot back, pointing his finger only at me.

"Alone?"

"Alone," he said with finality, a sadistic smile creeping onto his face.

I followed him into his office and quickly looked for another door. There wasn't any. Silently, I thanked God. If they took me off, they would have to pass by Mark again and at least I would be able to say a few words to him. "Sit down," he ordered.

I saw the chair in the corner of the room and quickly moved to occupy it. I looked up, and there was a desk in front of me. The East German was standing at the side of it, his lips contorted in an angry grimace. "Not there," he yelled, "there."

I looked over the desk where he was pointing. On the other side there was a wooden stool. Upon realizing my mistake, I gulped, and rose quickly in order to walk around to the other side and sit on the stool. My initial response of fear obviously manifested itself with diminished sensory perception. My field of vision had been narrowed and when asked to sit down I saw only his desk chair in the corner. The desk itself never registered.

No sooner had I found my place on the stool than a light snapped on above my head. I looked up with amused disbelief. Humphrey Bogart had nothing on me now.

"Do we need that?" I asked sarcastically.

He let the question slip by and answered with one of his own.

Where did you get the money?"

I tried to be as honest as possible, knowing the truth should be acceptable.

"We were in Burg just a few days ago and we inadvertently took the money out of the country."

"What do you mean we?"

I corrected myself.

"I mean Mark. He forgot that he had the money and just discovered it outside. That's when I told him to give it to me."

He paused, peering directly into my eyes. The gaze was discomfiting and I let my head drop. "What do you think I am, a fool?" His expression showed nothing. His tone remained icy. "You're lying. Now tell me again, this time the truth."

I repeated the story including a few more details. Again he informed me that I was lying. I repeated the story for a third and fourth time. "Again please, but this time the truth. You will save us all a lot of trouble." His face was still expressionless. "Did you buy the marks on the Black Market?"

"Listen," I said exasperated. "I exchanged the money with my friend outside because I saw nothing wrong. Do you think I would have done that if I knew your law?"

His fist pounded on the desk, and his glare was menacing."I want the truth!"

For me, frustration and fear manifested itself in the form of hostility. I slapped the money onto the desk in front of me and replied in anger. "Here, take your goddamn money, I don't want it."

He edged back in his chair slightly. "Put that back in your pocket."

I persisted, pushing the money toward him. "Listen. You don't seem to understand. I don't want your goddamn money. I can't buy a goddamn thing with it that's worth the bother."

He stood up quickly, snapping his chair back against the wall. "Put the money back in your pocket," he commanded.

Suddenly it hit me. The window; the guards. Outside they could all see in. It looked as if I were offering him a bribe. I decided to press my luck and shoved the money all the way to his side of the desk. "Here, take it, it's not worth the paper it's printed on."

His voice exploded as his hand slapped down on the handle of his revolver. "Put the money back in your pocket and get out of here."

I considered the alternatives and decided to accept the offer. You can't out talk a thirty-eight. I reached for the money, placed it in my pocket and walked toward the door shaking my head. Before leaving I turned back, not being able to resist the last barb. "You people don't know what you want, do you?" I left him, back pressed to the wall behind his desk, baffled but obviously willing to let me go.

Mark met me as I came out the door and around the counter. "What happened? You were in there for over a half hour."

I decided to drag him along. "I'm sorry Mark, I had to tell him."

What do you mean?" he asked suspiciously.

"Well he wanted to know why you gave me the money. I had to…"

"What did you tell him?" he interrupted.

Like a priest administering last rites, I slapped a sallow mask on my face. "I told him the truth, that you were frightened to hold it yourself."

"Why did you do that?" he asked, half accusingly and half in fear of the imagined consequences.

"Look, it won't be bad. The trial will be short and all."

He cut me short. "Trial! What trial?"

"Will you let me finish."

"No, what trial?"

"Your trial," I said somberly, the tone of my voice indicating my concern."

His hand slapped the side of his head. "Oh my God, what did you do to me?"

"I didn't do anything," I replied forcefully. "You did it to yourself."

His face paled and his legs began to tremble. Fearing he would faint on the spot, I guided him over to the bench along the wall. I had to make a supreme effort to keep from laughing. "Now listen," I commanded. "All you have to do is admit that you bought the money on the black market and plead guilty."

"Black market?" His face was now completely drained of color.

"Don't worry," I consoled. "The prisons in East Germany are supposed to be adequate and they promised to give you only a year or two. I'll go straight to the embassy when I leave here and they will get right on it. With all his imagined fears suddenly blossoming into cold hard reality, I could swear, if only for an instant, that his hair stood up on his head.

"I can't believe this," Mark moaned as he bent over and buried his face in his hands.

I sat there silently for what seemed like an eternity and then leaned over and whispered in Mark's ear.

"Quick! No ones looking. Get up and follow me." I rose and started toward the door. Mark got up, looked around furtively, and hesitatingly followed me toward the door.

"This is crazy," he whispered, shaking his head in disbelief. "Shut up," I whispered back. "Just walk slowly and get into the car."

I got in on my side while Mark slid in on the other after stealing a glance back to see if anyone noticed. He was shaking uncontrollably.

"God. This is stupid."

"Shut up Mark and pay attention. We're gonna have to break through the barrier. Just duck as we approach so you don't get your head shot off."

Mark began to rant uncontrollably. "What! Are you crazy? They will kill us!"

I couldn't hold it any longer and, as a smile ripped across my face, I began to laugh.

Mark looked confused for just a second and then realization hit him. "You bastard! I can't believe you. God, you are nuts. You are absolutely fucking nuts." He reached the height of his crescendo with "fucking nuts."

We had two hours to blow before the visa agency opened in the late afternoon. As we drove about the streets sightseeing, Mark remained sullen and unforgiving, after his tirade in the car.

"You could have given me a heart attack," he offered with resentment in his voice. He was going to do everything he could to make me feel guilty.

"You're right," I said agreeably. "I'm sorry. It was just too good to let slip by."

He sat there and sulked a bit as we drove and, as we talked, I could sense his resolve weakening. He had to admit, even begrudgingly, that it was a good practical joke.

I related to him the events that had really transpired in the office and I could sense that he gloated in knowing that even I had experienced discomfort and fear. It brought me down to a level that he could understand.

We spotted a restaurant and decided to stop off for a small bite to eat before going to the visa office. The rather indistinct outside appearance gave no hint to what we would find inside. The place was class, real class. Batiste covered the candle lit tables. Silver sparkled in the glow. Waiters and waitresses outnumbered the clientele and a trio of violinists moved from table to table offering musical score that would have sent a surge of pleasure through the Kaiser's ears. "Let's get out of here," Mark said.

Although dress or convention never really fazed me, I must admit that, attired in dungarees and tee shirt, I did feel somewhat conspicuous. "No, I'm hungry."

"But we can't go in here like this."

"No," I offered defiantly. "Watch." I started forward. The head waiter met me before I got up momentum."

"May I help you?" he asked in German.

His eyes quickly assessed our appearance, and his expression registered disgust. Mark answered in broken German. The waiter, recognizing his accent, retorted in English. "I am afraid that you are improperly attired sir."

I cut in. "Please. We are hungry and we have traveled far. All we want to do is sample good German food. We have no desire to insult you. We just didn't know."

"I'm sorry but."

The twenty East German marks that I slipped into his hand changed his mind. "This way sir," he said briskly, with renewed respect.

He settled us in a corner table, inconspicuous and concealed from the front entrance. The menu was loaded with steaks, stews, and shish kabobs, but my stomach was still churning and the thought of filling it with spicy heavy foods was nauseating. I decided to settle on a melon and a small steak. The waitress approached the table. She was dark haired, tall and lithe and seemed to glide across the floor like a ballerina. Apparently we didn't have a monopoly on ass on the other side of the iron curtain. I placed my order. Mark asked for melon and a soft boiled egg. Obviously, his stomach wasn't settled either. "Is that all sir?" she offered with disdain in almost perfect English.

She apparently thought our dress mirrored our budget. I decided to fight her snobbish distance with overwhelming praise. "Where did you learn to speak English so well?"

Her response was terse and showed where her allegiance lay. "In school. We have better schools in East Germany than you have in America."

Either the headwaiter had clued her in to our point of origin or our speech and dress had made that obvious. "That's a blanket statement."

"I don't understand."

"What I mean is that there are good and bad schools in America just as in other parts of the world. How do you know that yours are better?"

She responded almost as a robot would. "I have seen movies of American students. They are disorderly, disruptive and surprisingly uninformed for their level of education."

"Did you ever think that maybe you were shown only the pictures that your officials wanted you to see?"

"Why should my teachers do that? They have nothing to hide."

"Then why can't you travel abroad and see for yourself? I can come here."

"Because they do not want us to be contaminated with Western depravity."

"Don't you think that East German youth is strong enough to resist such temptation, if it is bad?"

Mark cut in. "Will you leave her alone and let her get the food."

I could see that she silently thanked him for the reprieve. I had confused her and stirred up some mental turmoil. East German youth wasn't used to that kind of exercise. She turned and walked quickly away, disappearing into the kitchen.

Mark looked hard at me and admonished. "Don't start anything." "Now what are you talking about?"

"You know what I'm talking about. Don't bait her. Let's just eat and get out of here."

"Listen my friend." I was incensed and leaned threateningly across the table so that my face was only inches away from his. It's easy to pass through life avoiding every goddamn issue. Well I am not going to sit here in this stinking toilet of a country and listen to her spout that goddamn dogma. That may be good for her peace of mind but it certainly isn't for mine."

"I knew I never should have come on this trip. You're crazy."

"Maybe I am Mark but at least on my tombstone it will say that he lived, he felt, and he acted. You may live longer, but your life will be nothing but an expression of vital functions. He breathed, he ate, he slept, and he fucked, but he never felt a thing. He lived in fear of his own shadow. Your whole goal in life is to get through it inconspicuously without the danger of conflicts. Well, you're here with me now Mark and as long as you stay, your rectal sphincter is going to get a little exercise. So hold tight, or you're going to crap in your pants."

Mark responded weakly and we sat in relative silence until the waitress returned with the food. As bland as our order was, it looked delicious. "May I ask you something," she said.

"Certainly."

"Why do you dress like that?"

"Because I like to."

"Do you always do things you like?"

"Usually. In America we're used to freedom."

"Maybe you are a used to freedom because you are rich but what about the oppression of the Negro and the exploitation of the poor?"

"It's not that simple. Certainly some people are exploited and used but all in all there is no country in the world that offers more in the way of freedoms for the masses."

She looked at me askance. "Listen, it's easy to sit there and say what you like but I have seen movies of your slums and of police brutality administered to Negroes and students."

"I have seen movies of East Germany too, most of which I didn't like. But at the risk of being repetitious, did it ever occur to you that my government allows me to come here and judge for myself. We did not build the wall. You did."

For a fleeting moment I saw the marks of anxiety generated by mental confusion. She quickly annihilated it with some positive internal dogma and her expression again took the form of tranquil confidence. "Do you go to school?"

"Yes, I am a medical student at the University of Bologna."

"And your friend?" She looked over at Mark.

"Me too," he said disinterestedly.

"Do you like America too?"

"Yes."

"You must both be rich capitalists."

"I should only wish," sighed Mark.

"But if you are not rich, how can you afford to go to school? I thought, in America, only the rich could pay enough to go."

"What's your name?" I cut in.

"Ingrid."

"Ingrid," I said in my most condescending voice, "There is much that you have to learn about the United States, and unfortunately much that you must unlearn. We belong to that great massive body of people that represent most of the people of our country, the middle class. Yes, there are some that are poor and some that are rich, but most belong to that great amorphous group I have just named. For the most part, we work and we produce on a competitive basis. Opportunity exists for all, even blacks, and the majority of the people realize a fair amount of success. The average American family eats well, sleeps in comfort, and has a good number of luxuries. When we work, we are efficient and diligent, for promotion and success depend mostly on that. But the average workweek is only thirty five to forty hours, so that there is more than a fair amount of leisure time.

"Is that true?" she looked at Mark.

"Yes."

She turned back toward me. "How do I know that you are not lying?"

"Ingrid." I fixed her gaze and spoke seriously. "You don't. But let the proof lay in the fact that we are still permitted to come here and inspect your country for ourselves and make our own final judgements. You are not allowed to do the same. Who do you think has something to hide?"

"I don't know. But now I must get back to work."

She avoided my eyes, turned and walked briskly back to the kitchen. Mark and I finished our meals and waited on Ingrid for the check. She brought it. Twelve marks, the equivalent of a dollar and a half. Now was the time for the crowning blow. I lay my remaining eighty marks (ten dollars) on the table. Ingrid picked up the check tray, started to turn and then looked back at me.

Excuse me sir, you.

I never gave her a chance to finish.

"You know you've got some nerve."

"I'm only trying."

I interrupted again.

"I know what you're trying," I said abrasively. "I've been a waiter too. Unfortunately I can't afford anymore. I'm only a student." I stood up as if to go, acting as if I put a cap on the discussion.

"Please," she pleaded. "You misunderstand.

I turned back toward her, fixing my gaze to hers, voice subtly castigating. "Now Ingrid, once again. You're a sweet girl but I can't afford anymore of a tip."

She smiled and shook her head as she spoke. "Will you please listen?"

"Ok," I sighed.

She continued to smile and shake her head in disbelief as she talked. "I have never received such a big tip. I don't make this much in a week."

It was my turn to act incredulously. "Are you joking?"

"No, the only reason I turned back to you was to tell you that you had made a mistake and left too much money."

We began to laugh together. She caught control and asked. "Seriously, this is not a good tip in America?"

Like an innocent, awe struck pixie I responded. "For a student, yes, it is more than adequate, but to tell you the truth, I was just a little embarrassed. I wanted to impress you with American wealth but practicality got the better of me. I am on a short budget."

"If that money is a reflection of your budget," she said holding up the cash tray in her hand, "then you would be a wealthy man in East Germany."

"Tell me Ingrid," I asked seriously. "How do you manage to live if you make only eighty marks per week?"

"What do you mean?"

"I mean you need your own apartment, a car, clothes, food, etc."

She began to giggle. "Food and clothes are enough of a problem. An apartment of my own and a car are out of the question."

"Do you mean an adult, single girl like you must live with her parents?"

"Of course."

"How do you get to work?"

"Bicycle."

"How primitive," I said, matter of factly, shaking my head and acting more convinced that this was the last place in the world I would want to live in. "To live in East Germany must be a veritable nightmare."

"Oh it's not that bad. We've had a great deal to rebuild and the Russians have been helpful, but certainly not overgenerous."

"C'mon now. They robbed your country of everything that could be moved."

She spouted doctrine again. "That is not true. There were many war reparations to be made. Russia has been patient in demanding what is due her."

"Well Ingrid," I said condescendingly, "keep the money. I have seen enough to know where my utopia is. It has been nice meeting you." I extended my hand. She took it and came close.

"Please, what is your name?"

"Dodd."

"Please I would like to talk with you again."

"Well we must get our visas and then we must leave. I'm sorry but."

"Please, I will be finished at four o'clock. Can you meet me outside the restaurant?"

I paused for a second to look at my watch. A half-hour was not enough time to pick up the visa. Mark kicked my shin. That prompted my answer.

"Yes, but make it four thirty. That will give us enough time to get our papers."

"Alright, now I must go."

We nodded good-byes and left for the visa office. When we were outside, Mark grabbed my arm. "Listen you stupid bastard, you're just looking for trouble."

I smiled mockingly.

"What's the matter, afraid of a little fun?"

"She's going to want to leave the country with you," he said shaking his head in disbelief. "You should have been in Hollywood, not medical school. What an actor," he exclaimed, slapping his forehead with both hands simultaneously.

"Come on Mark, relax. Just a little fun."

"Your fun is going to get me shot." He looked up accusingly, enunciating slowly, right index finger slowly pointing toward my face. "You don't intend to take her out of here, do you?"

"Now Mark," I said sarcastically. "What ever gave you that idea?"

By four thirty-five we had finished with our visas and I hurriedly drove the ten-minute drive to the restaurant. Mark agreed, somewhat reluctantly perhaps, but still agreed to see the girl again. Apparently, curiosity and excitement had overcome his fears. Still, I couldn't help but feel he hoped she wouldn't be waiting. If that were the case, he had reason to be disappointed. Ingrid was perched on the base of a stone statue at the foot of the restaurant, throwing breadcrumbs to the pigeons. I waved and she came toward the car. "Wow," she exclaimed. In East Germany they didn't have any decent automobiles to speak of, let alone Masseratis.

"Get in, you can show us around Berlin."

Mark opened the door and moved accommodatingly to the back seat. Ingrid slid into the bucket beside me exposing her lithe leg up to the mid-thigh. She was totally absorbed in the complicated pattern of instruments on the dashboard. I ignored her obvious awe and asked matter of factly. "What did you want to speak to me about?"

With obvious difficulty she brought her eyes toward mine. "I want to find out more about America."

"Why?"

"Because before today I was content and sure of myself and my country. Now, after speaking with you, I am confused."

"What do you want to know?"

She looked up and sighed. "Oh, I don't know. Maybe I am just depressed. But life is so serious and demanding here. I wondered what it was like for a girl my age in America."

I put the car into gear and started to drive casually without any destination in mind. The engine, used to the tremendous demands of a floored accelerator pedal, strained for oxygen and gas. But I kept my foot light and never shifted out of second gear.

"Well, the typical American teenager"

"What's a teenager?" she cut in.

"A girl between thirteen and nineteen years of age." "Oh."

I let that settle in and repeated. "A typical teenage girl attends school during the day. The demands are not that heavy and her major problems revolve around her social activities and personal appearance. They usually pay a great deal of attention to their clothes, makeup and hairstyles. A lost eyelash or smudged lipstick is a major tragedy. No date on a Saturday night is equivalent to the death penalty."

"But don't they have to work?"

"No, not usually. Growing up is difficult enough for a young girl. For the most part they are allowed to concentrate on their petty affairs.

Really, for the most part, it's pretty silly."

"How nice it would be to afford the luxury to be silly." "What do you mean?"

"I mean I was never given the opportunity to be a little girl. Nobody cared if my doll's clothing was torn; nobody even cared if I had a doll. There was no time for that. When I was ten, I helped my mother wash clothes for the Russian soldiers. When I was thirteen, I made the mistake of bringing the clothes to the quarters of a Russian officer. He made me have sex with him. I did not resist. You did what you were told. I was so scared. He was not gentle and he hurt me but I bit my lip so he wouldn't see my pain. When he was done, he tipped me ten marks. I came home and gave my mother the money. I didn't tell her what happened. I didn't have to. She just placed the money between her breasts and pulled me close to her. There were no words; there couldn't be. They would have been empty. We just stood there holding each other, knowing that the episode would be repeated. Food, clothes, shelter and staying alive were priorities. There was no time for anything else. Self indulgence, self pride, and morality were luxuries we couldn't afford."

The devastating magnitude of her life experience was magnified by the even temper of her tone. There was no plea for self-pity. There were just statements of fact as if it couldn't have been any other way. My heart cried out to her. I wanted only to tell her that life should be different, was really different, and must be different; that there was hope for the future and pleasures to be pursued. Mark also was moved by her story. He sat, propped up in the back seat and, in his own limited way, spoke with sincerity and meaning.

"You deserve a lot of credit just for surviving. The girls at home are spoiled. They could never stand up under that kind of pressure. They would crack."

"What do you mean crack?"

"I mean that they would collapse psychologically. Their whole life revolves around almost meaningless events. They have no idea what survival means."

"How nice that would be," she mused. She turned toward that the back seat for the first time and spoke for the first time with emotion and hope.

"You know Mark, I did not believe the picture you both painted of America. I thought that life must be as dreary or even worse in the rest of the world than it is here. But the sheer innocence in your expressed disdain for American girls makes me believe that life indeed must be full of pleasurable pursuits in America. Only people who deal, on a daily basis, with insignificant problems can not face the real critical ones."

"And therein lays the irony. They have no capacity to appreciate it," said Mark.

"Oh how well I would," she stated matter of factly, resigned to the fact that she would never have the opportunity.

I had remained silent through the last two exchanges, fighting an inner battle within myself. I wanted to reach out and help this girl, offer her hope for a new fulfilling life. The only meaningful offer I could make would be life threatening to both Mark and me, escape through the wall. I had the right to make that decision for myself. I didn't for Mark.

I continued to drive slowly through the streets of East Berlin, observing the bleak gray buildings, set back on bleak gray sidewalks, walked on by people, heads bowed, dressed in bleak gray garb. My inner frustrations, based on empathy for this undefined populace and crystallized in the form ofIngrid, cried out for satisfaction. The words burst forth, pushing past restraints that logic and good sense dictated.

"Ingrid, would you like me to take you out of this country?"

She froze for a second, a startled expression fixed to her face. "What did you say?"

"Would you like me to take you through the wall?"

"Do you know what you're saying?" Mark burst in angrily. "This is not a joke. You're playing with life and death."

The cool detachment of my response unnerved them. "I know, but to live here is to be confined to death." Ingrid buried her hands in her head. "I don't know, I just don't know." And then it was my turn to be amazed as Mark spoke.

"What don't you know?"

"That I would be better off. I'm afraid, not of a border incident, but of starting a new life in a strange country."

Mark lectured with confidence and understanding.

"The question is not whether you would be better off or not Ingrid. That is a foregone conclusion. The question is, is it worth the risk? Up to now I would have said no. But the greatest tragedy of all is not just that you have to live here, but the totality of the subversive effort that has denied you the knowledge of the hopes and anticipations that lay over that wall. That makes the risk worthwhile."

Mark took Ingrid's chin in his hand and brought her face to his. There were tears in the corner of her eyes; fears and uncertainties written on her face.

"Ingrid," Mark said softly, "I'm no hero. I don't want to die. I would like to disappear from here right now, crawl back into my corner on the other side, and forget I had ever been here. But you and what you represent would be a living nightmare to me for the rest of my life. I've been thinking of what Dodd said to me in the restaurant, when I told him to stop baiting you and he told me that I had to risk participation in the lives of others in order to experience the full breadth of living. He was right. I can't turn my back on you now. If you want to come across with us, I will help. My hands may shake and my heart may burn with the fire of fear, but as God is my witness Ingrid, I will help."

Her eyes teared but her tone was final.

"I will accept your offer." And for the first time I saw just a hint of a real smile.

We drove in silence for fifteen minutes; each of us embedded in our own thoughts. I was formulating a plan of escape. The best I could think of was not very original and manifested great risk. It was like playing Russian roulette. Three chances out of four the Russians wouldn't check. Not very comforting odds. I sighed and laid the time worn plan to them.

"Under the trunk space is a compartment for a spare tire. Ingrid can hide there."

"What if they check?" Mark said.

"Let's hope they don't," It sounded empty, but there weren't other alternatives.

"Ingrid, there won't be time to say goodbye. It wouldn't be safe either. If we're going to do it, we must do it now."

Ingrid nodded silently. Whatever conflicts were stirring in her mind, she suppressed them. I don't think any of us wanted to be too analytical. Good sense would have dictated dropping the whole idea. Ingrid had us pull off on a side road and we parked the car in the shade of an empty warehouse. We cleared the trunk and opened up the spare tire compartment, leaving the tire up against the warehouse. We all looked nervously around, but there was no one in sight. With much contortion, Ingrid squeezed into the vacated area. I placed the cover over her body, shutting off the light. Her last expression was that of fixed determination. We replaced the luggage in the trunk. I then ripped a piece of rubber from the trunk cover, so that its airtight seal would be broken. With a sigh, I closed the' trunk and got into the car. Mark moved in on the other side. Both of us remained silent as we moved toward the border station, caught in the momentum of the moment, rationally wishing we had never gotten into this mess, romantically hoping to have the courage or stupidity, whichever it took, to carry it through.

We arrived In ten minutes. Not a word had passed between Mark and myself. There was nothing to say. We were playing for keeps and the game was out of our hands.

I parked the car, got out and walked into the station to present my papers. Mark followed. We tried to make small talk but I felt terribly conspicuous. The station officer checked our passports and told us to wait outside by the car for the inspector. We moved slowly to the car. Mark got in. I leaned up against the fender and lit a cigarette. My pulse was racing, about a hundred and thirty a minute. Each moment seemed like an hour. The tension was unbearable. I felt as if the walls were closing in on us. The inspector moved up the line slowly and finally came to our car. He was very business like. He opened the front door and slid his hand under the bucket seat. He felt along the backseat and tapped it. He then asked Mark to open up the glove compartment. Mark complied and, when the officer was satisfied, he shut it.

"Open the trunk."

My heart palpitated wildly and I thought I was going to faint. I walked to the back of the car and eased the key into the lock. I could swear my hands were shaking. I turned the key and the trunk popped open.

"Take out the top suitcase and open the bottom one."

I complied. The inspector leafed through the contents. I could swear that I could smell Ingrid's sweat through the partition.

"What's under there?" he said pointing at the partition. A spare tire. "Open it."

My heart seemed to stop. For an instant I was frozen. I closed the suitcase and removed it from the trunk. A sense of impending doom passed over me. Suddenly the officer looked up and brushed passed me.

"What are you doing?"

I turned to see Mark, cock out, calmly pissing against the side of the car. "I'm sorry. I had to urinate. I've got a bladder infection."

The incident had caught the attention of another officer and the people parked in the space next to ours. They were all smiling.

"Why don't you use the bathroom?" the officer asked irately. Mark blushed. "I couldn't wait and I didn't know where it was."

The officer moved back toward the trunk, laughing with contempt, while he winked at his fellow officer. A silent understanding passed between them as they shook their heads with contempt. He looked back in the trunk for what seemed like an agonizing eternity, shrugged his shoulders and said contemptuously. "Put those suitcases back in the car and take that animal out of here before I put him in a cage."

I nodded and then slowly, but deliberately, returned the suitcases to the trunk, closed it and got back in the car. Mark was already sitting next to me, beads of sweat prominent on his forehead. The officer handed me my papers and directed me toward the gate. I thought the car would never start, but it turned over on the first try. I put it into gear, pulled up in front of the first gate, and offered my papers to the soldier. He Inspected them, handed them back and opened the cross bar. I moved through and stopped at the second gate. Papers were again inspected, returned and the last gate to freedom was opened. All the cool deliberation left me as I put the car in gear and accelerated toward the American sector. We were doing eighty by the time we reached the other side, and I had never gotten the car out of second gear.

The next few days were filled with excitement and confusion. The curious bystanders at first surprised, then thrilled with their own presence at this daring event. The group of soldiers that surrounded us, and shut us out from the gathering crowd. The drive to police headquarters, the separation from Ingrid and the interrogation by German police and then American and military officials. They were reluctant to accept the simplicity of our stories. Then, once accepted, quick to castigate our foolhardy stupidity in attempting such an escape; then admonishing us to blend quietly into the old routine, that is go back to Bologna and forget all of this happened.

They evaded our questions about Ingrid's safety and location, saying that she was in good hands and would be given the opportunity to start a new life. Both Mark and I were totally disillusioned, thinking that we would be treated as adventurous heroes, rather than child criminals caught with our hands in the cookie jar. They explained to us that, at this time, they wanted no publicity regarding escapes through the wall, and that our reckless efforts could seriously set back months of progress in East and West German relationships. We were also warned that we were to avoid publicity and, if we didn't return quietly and inconspicuously to Bologna, we were in danger of having our passports revoked.

The newspapers stated only that a girl of unknown identification had been driven through the wall at a checkpoint by two unknown youths.

Never, in that week, were we allowed to see or talk with newsmen. In fact we were kept interned on an American base, exposed to nobody but a few top rank, unidentified officials.

I insisted on seeing Ingrid but they told me that it was in our own best interests to forget the whole affair; that if our names became public knowledge, the East Germans might make an attempt on our lives to deter further escape efforts. Seeing Ingrid would just give them the link they needed to connect us to the affair.

For our own good, we were to be kept here for another week and then would be escorted by plane to Bologna. My car was to be impounded and they would give me the money to purchase a new car of similar value but different make. Under no circumstances were we to mention the event to anyone. And again they repeated that we should never make an attempt to inquire about Ingrid. With a bad taste in our mouth and an empty pit for our stomachs, we reluctantly agreed to their terms. Instead of being bathed with praise and public

adulation, we were the recipients of subtle insults and gentle admonishments.

I wondered how Ingrid had fared and whether or not she had misgivings about her decision to come to the West. If our own experience had been any indication, I doubted that she would be very grateful.

FEAST OR FAMINE

Christmas came and went. I spent it alone in the hospital while Marty, under a cloud of doom, passed the time with his family, constantly thinking about how and when to tell them. I wondered how little Dean had responded to his presents. I tried to call, but the Atlantic cable was over taxed and I wasn't able to get through. Then I got busy with two deliveries and an emergency ectopic pregnancy and, for that time, nothing else could matter. Christina stayed in Italy till the end of January and, when she returned home, we picked up where we had left off; nowhere!

In the practice, it was either feast of famine. Days would go by that were relatively easy. I would see patients in the morning, go to conference at lunch, make hospital rounds and, then, if no one was in labor and I had no surgery scheduled, I would go back to the office and work on administrative tasks for the practice and the clinics. Other days were nightmares. I would be overwhelmed in the office by over scheduling. Because of that, I would run late, and the problem would be often compounded by a few emergencies that had to be seen. To make matters worse, that would also be the day in which I got in late, because I had an early morning delivery at the hospital. No matter how hard I tried, there was no way to catch up and patients would be irate over having to wait for their appointments. During that office session, there would always be a couple of phone calls that I had to take and, then, on occasion, there would be someone in labor at the hospital, eighteen minutes away, a short drive, but in the throes of a precipitous labor, an eternity. Since Marty would be at a clinic in another town, it would be my responsibility to cover the hospital.

At these times, it was always a pressure cooker. You could never leave the office with someone in early labor. If you did, you couldn't generate enough income to overcome your overhead. But when you continued to see patients, while somebody was in labor, you were taking a chance. Each an every OBGYN drew the line where he couldn't take the conflict anymore and it was a different line for each and every one. But there was one constant. When you decided to go to the hospital, no matter how fast you drove, and no matter how many chances you took, the drive took forever. Each time you ran up to labor and delivery, your heart skipped a beat, until you saw that your patient had not yet delivered. In all my years of practice, I only missed one delivery, although I agonized over a thousand. For the one I missed, I racked my brain night after night trying to find something I did wrong to make me miss that delivery. I left the house as soon as they told me she was at the hospital and in labor. Although, I never could find a reason, I always felt uncomfortable for missing that one. Maybe I could have driven faster, or run up the stairs instead of waiting for the elevator. Although the patient delivered a healthy and robust baby, there could have been a bad result. Missing that delivery always did and always will make me feel uneasy.

Always, at these times, there would be some emergency that would result in surgery, again calling for you to be in two places at once. But this was the juggling act that the doctor had to face on a daily basis and, when he played the percentages, it turned out right most of the time. The key word of course being "most."

That night, I would be kept awake by another two patients in labor that were facing a collision course of delivering at the same time. To ensure my lack of sleep, I would be bombarded with a stream of well-timed phone calls, most of them unnecessary. It was hard to believe how self centered and ill informed some patients were. It was not atypical to get a call at three o'clock in the morning asking about an itch that had been present for two weeks.

When I responded with a sarcastic, "what urged you to call now," the patient invariably would reply with a sincere comment that she was sitting back watching TV and she just thought she ought to do something about it.

Another time, a patient called, asking if she had to take her pill every time after oral sex. In the beginning, I often responded in a snotty manner, but after awhile I realized that it just didn't pay. They never understood that I had a life too and that, at night, I was available only for emergencies, not for their convenience. I resigned myself to the fact that I would just have to deal with the fatigue those disruptions caused and go on.

The next day, I would of course be busy all day with surgeries, deliveries and office hours since I hadn't slept the night before. And then, just as suddenly as it had started, I would have an easy day, a night off call and, after I was well rested, another miraculously easy day.

It was in my third year of practice that I again met up with Mr. Paul France. He represented a patient by the name ofBarbara Grey who was dying of cervical cancer. He blamed me, and now I would have to defend myself for the first time. To compound the issue, I had no malpractice coverage for the event, since the medical society had stripped me of their coverage, and I had to hire an attorney and pay for him out of my own pocket. I was incensed, feeling that I was being wrongly and personally attacked.

I researched the case and found out that Dr. Walter Phillips had referred this patient to me for a pregnancy termination, her seventh one. She was a well-educated young lady of twenty-seven years of age who was, of all things, a union organizer. She was a demanding young woman, reluctant to follow instructions, but expectant of special favors. She showed up with a class four pap smear, which was indicative of a high probability of cancer cells, and I sent her back to Dr. Phillips for a culposcopic exam, a test that I had not yet been trained to do. Although, as a rule well liked, Dr. Phillips was on her shit list. She refused to go see him, so I referred her on to another physician who did culposcopy. At her request, we even made the appointment for her.

Six months later she called my office and demanded to speak to me. She asked me for another three months ofbirth control pills, a request that she could make through the front office. I reviewed her chart and asked her what happened at the culposcopy, because I had no record of that visit.

"I didn't have time to go," was her curt response.

"Barbara," I pleaded. "You must go get that done, and I can't give you any pills until you do the culposcopy."

"I can't Dr. Robbins," she said curtly.

"Why not Barbara?"

"I can't afford it."

"Barbara," I admonished. "You should have told me. We have a free clinic in town where they do the procedure."

"I can't Dr. Robbins, I'm living in Ft. Lauderdale now. I'm too far away."

Boy was I relieved. I wouldn't have to put up with this resistance anymore.

"Barbara. You've got to see somebody down there. I can't treat you from up here."

"I already told you Dr. Robbins. I can't afford it. Please can I have just a couple of packs of pills."

I kept looking down at my watch. I was falling further and further behind and this patient wouldn't let me get off the phone. It was always a long drawn out conversation with Barbara and we didn't get paid for phone calls. Furthermore, she was way behind in her bills.

"Barbara," I instructed. "There is a free clinic down there at Jackson Memorial Hospital in Miami where I know that they can help you. Get in to see them and they will give you your pills too."

"Please Dr. Robbins, just one pack."

"Alright Barbara," I sighed. "Just one. I'll get the girls to call it in," and as quickly as I said it, I put the phone on hold and transferred the call to my girls up front. I looked down at my watch and saw that I was now ten more minutes behind and there was no way to make it up. The patients would just bitch that much more.

France deposed me with a smirk on his face. I had found out that Barbara had gone to Jackson Memorial Hospital, where they had discovered a large tumor. She was diagnosed as a stage four cervical cancer and was treated with palliation. She started to lose weight and at present was emaciated and weak. France claimed the she was never treated properly in that it was my job to make sure that she had under gone the colposcopy. He was going to assert that it just wasn't enough to refer a patient. It was the doctor's responsibility to make sure the patient got the exam done.

After the deposition, I spoke with my lawyer. It seemed absurd to me that France would contend that it was my job to babysit this girl. I felt terrible that she had a terminal disease, but she certainly had some degree of responsibility for her failure to get follow up treatment expeditiously. He listened attentively and then gave me my first lesson in the law. "The law Dodd is about winners and losers. In a malpractice case, the doctor is always the loser. It is a cost of doing business and you must approach it like that."

"I understand that she is going to have a terrible outcome, but I absolutely have no culpability. I did everything that could be reasonably expected of me."

"Listen and listen well." He paused to make sure that I was paying attention and not just giving him lip service. "You have not been negligent here, but you are vulnerable."

"How can that be?"

"You're exposed! Put this in front of a jury. An innocent looking, white, American girl, who should be overflowing with life, gets up in the witness box, cachectic and emaciated, and talks in a raspy whisper, void of life. She tells the jury how a culposcopy could have saved her life, if only she had the money, and you didn't bother to get it for her. How does that look?"

"That's not the way it happened."

Leaning toward me, with frustration in his voice, he continued. "It doesn't matter if that's the way it happened! It's her story in front of a sympathetic jury." Sitting back in his chair, after giving that a few seconds to sink in, he added. "I would advise that we look for a settlement. What I'm telling you is that, if this goes to trial, you could lose and lose everything you have. France has his problems too. He knows that he has a weak case, and that he has to depend on the emotions, not the logic, of the jury. He also knows that he has to get the trial done before she dies. A dying woman always makes a bigger impact than one who is already dead. Also, in your favor is also the fact that he knows that you have no malpractice coverage and that, being a young doctor, new in practice, you probably couldn't pay off a large award."

"What does that mean?"

"It means that France has to look at all sides of the equation. Usually a malpractice attorney will jump at a case with potentially high damages, if the award is collectible. He will even take a chance if the liability is low, as long as the potential damages are high, because he understands the fears of the defendant and the cost of defending the case. In those cases, he can usually demand a high settlement.

But your case is just a little different. You have potentially high damages, but low liability and low collectibility. He knows that your only pragmatic risk is to the extent of your net worth and, in his mind, that wouldn't be much more than the cost of a good defense. I'm not promising anything, but I think we can get him to settle for under twenty thousand dollars."

"Twenty thousand!" I exclaimed. "That's highway robbery. Doesn't this guy have any morals?"

Getting up from his chair, my lawyer, Steve Avery, added matter of factly. "That's business my friend, and no; he has no morals and he doesn't care. He knows that it will cost you at least fifteen thousand for a trial and alot of turmoil. All he wants to know is how much you will pay to avoid the publicity and save the minimum of fifteen thousand that is out the door anyway."

Taking my arm to steer me toward the door, he added. "Look at it this way. Either you pay him or you pay me and possibly him too. It's the cheapest way out and it never gets in the papers. You have a reputation, you know, that you need to protect."

I nodded my head in agreement. Everything he said seemed to make sense. "Okay," I said. "Whatever you say. Just get it done fast so I can sleep at night."

Steve nodded, shook my hand and was back in his office behind a closed door in nothing flat. I had to give it to him. He was one smooth son of a bitch and he seemed to know what he was doing.

While I knew that I hadn't done anything wrong, I couldn't quite figure out what did go wrong with Barbara Grey's early treatment. Based on a prior abnormal Pap smear, she had a culposcopy with Dr. Phillips with directed biopsies, which revealed Carcinoma in situ. He treated her with cryosurgery and repeated the Pap smear, getting normal findings. My Pap smear, done six months later, was a class five. As I looked into what happened and read up on culposcopy, the error became crystal clear. Dr. Phillips was the first individual to do culposcopy in our area and the learning curve is always the worst with the first. There were standards that had to be met in order to view a culposcopy as a reliable diagnostic tool. One of those standards was that you needed to see the entire transformation zone of the cervix, and the other was that you needed an endocervical scraping as part of the tissue sample. In Barbara's case, there was no description of an endo cervical sampling and it appeared that her primary tumor originated in the endo cervix. The point of negligence was clear.

One day, I received a call from Dr. Phillips to meet him for lunch. He told me that he had just been deposed by Paul France and he wanted to make sure that he wasn't involved in the case.

At lunch, he opened up the conversation. "France seems to be honing in on the fact that she never got a repeat culposcopy because she couldn't afford it. Am I right?"

"It seems so," I responded, not committing myself. "I'm really worried because I have no coverage."

I hoped that the comment on coverage would get Phillips's attention but he ignored it and continued on. "You know what the real problem was?" Phillips asked.

"Yes I do." I took a deep breath, getting ready to elaborate on the fact that it was Phillips's failure to secure an endocervical scraping in the first colposcopy that was the problem. But Phillips cut me off.

"I expect that you won't comment on that," he said with gaze fixed on my own.

I nodded my head in accord. I knew the stakes, and he was pulling his hole card. Because I owned clinics that did pregnancy terminations, I was on the edge of the medical community. Although I was proud of my skills and my record, I knew that there were doctors in the community who were after me. Dr. Phillips had supported me and, given his political power in the hospital, protected me as well. In my hospital, I needed his protection, or I would be food for the vultures. I was being told not to jeprodize that protection. The fact that he had malpractice coverage and I had none did not concern him. He wanted to protect himself against any bad publicity that might come from the case, and the fact that I might lose everything that I had worked for did not concern him. He was only worried about himself and his veiled threat was perfectly clear.

I chose to keep my mouth shut. Talking wouldn't save me from the suit. It would only involve Phillips and give France a deep enough pocket that would tempt him to carry the case to trial. If France couldn't figure out who the real culprit was, then the hell with him. Besides, all in all, Phillips was a very good doctor. He was an innovator and was responsible for bringing the latest and often the best treatments to our area. In being the first, he was going to make more mistakes and, unfortunately, he had made one on Barbara Grey. She was also at fault. She was not a very cooperative or responsible patient. She abused the service and frequently didn't pay, although she had a good job. She didn't deserve to die, but I didn't deserve the misery she tried to bring to me. Phillips made the mistake, she was irresponsible, and I had to pay. By keeping my mouth shut, I was going to keep that to a minimum and keep Phillips in my corner.

It took a year and a half to resolve the case. At first, France held out for a larger settlement, but Barbara took a turn for the worse and died just before he was able to get the case to trial. He did everything he could to move up the date and we did everything we could to delay the date and, fortunately for us, we prevailed.

Realizing that his case had lost value with Barbara's death, and probably in need of money, France finally settled for ten thousand from me and twenty thousand from the pathologist, who he contended had missed a few cancerous cells in Phillips's post operative pap smear. My legal bills were also about ten thousand. Money wise, I got off cheap.

Psychologically, I went through almost two years of hell, not knowing if this ass hole was going to make this melodrama play out and try to take everything I had. The sad thing was, Barbara's family should have gotten more money from a different source, but the combined incompetence and greed of her lawyer created undeserved havoc for her family and me. Often, malpractice suits resulted in unfair settlements (too high or too low,) at the expense of the wrong defendants. Rarely were they fair and just.

If there were some downsides to the practice of medicine, there were some real perks too. Drug salesmen were dependent on physicians for their sales statistics and, because one physician could have such a profound financial impact on their sales, they would do anything in the world to get a doctor to write prescriptions for their medications. For example, a practicing gynecologist could write prescriptions for forty patients per week for birth control pills for an entire year. This amounts to over twenty four thousand packs of pills each year at twenty-five dollars per pack, representing an approximate gross of six hundred thousand dollars. Given the fact that many of these patients stay on the pill for many years, it becomes clear, even in the face of a high attrition rate, that the stakes are very high. That translates into perks, or couched bribes, whatever you want to call them.

The drug salesmen would do anything in order to get a few minutes of a doctor's time. They would give all sorts of gifts and presents to front office personnel to persuade them to put them on your schedule. They would wait around for hours just to get to see you and lavish you with gifts, in the hope of being able to give you their spiel on their latest hot product. A nifty trick was to set up an outing for you and your staff, so that they could have a captured audience, and it wasn't above some of them to set up a special outing for you and your genitals. Lastly, they would supply you with all of their medicines for personal use, and a variety of samples to give out to your patients so as to start them on their medications.

As a physician, you learned fast that you had to take everything they said with a grain of salt. It was not that they were lying. They just didn't know the whole truth. They were programmed by their companies to give a rote speech on a product and it was clear that they really had no understanding of the disadvantages of the medication, or the advantages of their competitors. Therefore, their information was of little use. Most physicians walked a tightrope, doing all they could to avoid the salesmen, while maintaining enough contact to take advantage of the perks.

The pharmaceutical industry was a microcosm of capitalism, representing all that was good and bad about the system. It was clear that profit oriented private industry could do very efficient and valuable research that was of significant valuable to mankind. It was also true, that lobbying power allowed the industry to abuse the antitrust statutes, resulting in excessive profitability at the expense of the public. For a period of a year, I had a contract with a pharmaceutical company to buy birth control pills for sixty-five cents a pack. One month, I went to purchase more and the vice president in charge of clinic sales told me that the price had been changed to "seven twenty." I thought that he meant seventy-two cents a pack, but he meant seven dollars and twenty cents a pack. He wouldn't explain why the wholesale cost had gone up over one thousand percent, but research on my part came up with a very plausible answer.

The company that I was buying from controlled about one percent of the birth control pill market and they were trying to increase their market share by coming in the back door; that is supplying clinics with discount pills in the hope that the clinic patient, once out on their own, would demand the same pill from their private gynecologist, insuring an increase in market share.

Obviously, the companies with large market shares were being burnt and they began to pressure the company that I was dealing with to raise their wholesale price. The wholesale price of the three companies, that controlled ninety three percent of the total sales in birth control pills, was seven dollars and twenty cents. Miraculously, the company, that I was buying pills from at sixty-five cents per pack, happened to change their wholesale price to seven dollars and twenty cents. Obviously, the other companies used some sort oflever to make my pill supply company comply.

When you studied the structure and relationship among the drug companies, the levers became clear. Although there were approximately fifteen large drug companies, only two or three controlled the market in specific medications. Amazingly, the wholesale price of each of these medications was similar to the other competitors. When prices went up, they seemed to go up for all of them. If a company with a small market share of a medication resisted, they were hit hard by the other companies, who lowered their prices in the medications in which the resisting company had a large market share. The fear of counter attack kept them in line and eventually, not a word had to be spoken. Everybody knew what to do and when to do it. If one company got out of line, the hammer came down.

Complaining to the justice department did no good. These companies were so large that they could make large enough contributions to a political party in order to influence the powers that be to turn the other cheek. Price increases went unchecked and the enormous overflow of profits helped fill the coffers of these big drug companies, giving them more money to hold out as a carrot to tempt people in power. It was a never-ending vicious cycle.

In this world of economic conspiracy, control of the physician's prescription writing habits became the key ingredient to enormous profits. This placed the doctor on a pedestal and, eventually, most physicians acted like they were primadonnas and felt like they were entitled to anything that they wanted from drug companies. As long as it spelled profit for the company, these conditions were true, but once the physician deviated from the plan and threatened profits, he became a target. He had to be stopped.

While in practice, Marty was approached by a pharmacist, who offered to buy out all our unused medications for ten cents on the dollar.

We had a storeroom full of medicines, some samples given us by the drug companies whether we asked for them or not, and some medications that we had bought for use in our clinics. For one reason or another, many of these medications would never be used before their expiration date and we didn't know how to dispose of them.

The pharmacist told us that he was going to sell the medications to a large chain that in turn would pass them on to the consumer at a discounted rate. The odd item, that he couldn't sell, he would offer to clinics or third world countries for free.

We thought that this was a great solution, as long as we limited it to non-narcotic and non outdated medications. We could clear out our store room, get paid a little something for our time, and deliver medication to the world at a discount or free that would otherwise have to be discarded. It didn't make me unhappy that the drug companies would have a few less sales, because of the delivery of otherwise unused medications to the public.

But it did make the drug companies unhappy, and before I knew it, the roof fell in on Marty's and my head. The FBI was at our doorstep and threatening to indict us for mail fraud.

Apparently, each time that a drug salesman drops off a sample, the physician is required to sign a chit verifying that he requested that sample. This was proof that he received it and that the drug salesman didn't sell it on the side. The government contended that the sale of those samples constituted mail fraud, since the chit was sent in the mail. They contended that the sample was intended for personal use and that the sale of said samples constituted an attempt to defraud the drug companies. "What's the penalty for mail fraud," I asked the agent innocently enough.

"Five years for each request," he responded tersely.

I gulped. I'd signed at least five hundred chits in my life. That would constitute close to twenty five hundred years.

A little further investigation showed that we had been stung. Apparently, throughout the country, there was an organized effort to procure sample medications, altering their packaging and selling them in retail pharmacies as normally manufacture drugs. This of course cut deeply into the gross sales of the drug companies who only wanted their samples to be used to hook patients on their medications and to get doctors to write their prescriptions. Naturally, they brought their problem to the justice department and the justice department, knowing where their bread was buttered, responded with vigor and certainty.

In district twenty-six, where I resided, there was a federal prosecutor named Schmuckle, "Mad Dog Schmuckle to some." He was an avid foe of abortion; a true zealot. He was a man of select morality; his morality, and he believed that the end justified the means. He was smart, tough, tenacious, and determined. He was willing to do anything to achieve his goals. He was a formidable foe and one to be feared. Although we could never prove it, we suspected that Schmuckle set up the sting with the man who represented himself as the pharmacist willing to buy samples and unused medication. I've named him Schmuckle because he was a real schmuck, possibly the biggest sch- muck of all time. I've used a thousand adjectives to describe him, but the bottom line keeps coming back to schmuck. Schmuck! Schmuck! Schmuck!

In our naivete, all we were trying to do was to clean out our cabinets, get paid something for our time (I made three hundred and fifty dollars,) and deliver good medications to the public at a discount or sometimes for free.

In reality, we set off a chain of events that would have a significant impact on our lives and make me forever fearful of power, no matter how it was camouflaged.

We were indicted with sixty-three other doctors and a host of other individuals involved in drug diversion. That effectively translated as the sale or gift of medications, given to clinics or doctors by pharmaceutical companies, to third parties, because it cut into the drug companies sales.

We hired criminal attorneys and I began my lesson in the dynamics of the justice system in this country. The players had diverse motives; none of them founded on justice. The prosecutor was interested in publicity. A big win, under the eyes of an awe struck America, was a certain boost to political power. That's why prosecutors jump on

Mafia cases or Union cases or Doctor cases. They arouse the public interest. You never hear about a landscaper having his rights upheld by indicting and convicting another landscaper who dumps illegally. But you will hear about a big name actress who uses child labor or a big company that breaks environmental rules. That is because they generate publicity; people who mow lawns don't. Doctors generate publicity and therefore they are held to a higher and more stringent standard. People like to see well-to-do people knocked on their ass.

The attorney for the defense is interested in money. How big is the fee and how deep is the pocket. If the pocket is deep enough and if he can get enough publicity out of the case to market his services, he will go for the trial. If the pocket is shallow and he can get a big hit up front, the plea bargain is the thing to recommend.

The judge is the battle scarred cynical veteran. He's been through it all. He realizes that he prevails over a hall of lies, not a hall of truths and so for the most part he wiles away his day half listening and half bored to death. Many judges are older and tired of the grind. They like the easy life, the ten o'clock start and the long recess for lunch. Otherwise, they would be practicing law.

The jury completes the tetrad. It is supposedly manned by your peers, but, in all practicality, it is manned by the elderly, the out of work, the derelict, and the ignorant, who don't know how to get out of jury duty, and the true patriot, who doesn't want to get out of jury duty. Usually, the topic is too complex for the jury to understand and the lawyers distort the information so much that even an expert in the case can be confused.

Somehow, from this mix, justice is supposed to emerge. Marty and I were frightened to death and we should have been. My lawyer, Marcus Dawson, explained it to us very simply. They would include us in the bottom level of a conspiracy under the Rico statutes. That meant, for example, that if we bought Cuban cigars from an individual, who had bought them through a chain of people ten times removed, the last of which murdered his girl friend's lover, we could be included in a conspiracy to commit murder. "Seems like a democratic country to me," I said sarcastically.

"Don't joke," Marcus responded. "When they get their hands on you, democracy goes out the window."

"What does that mean?" Marty queried.

"It means that you guys did nothing wrong, but, if this goes to trial, you will be tried under the conspiracy statutes in North Georgia. Two Jewish New York doctors who do abortions being tried in the bible belt for conspiracy to defraud the United States government. First, they have to get past your heritage and geography. Next they got to get past what you do. After that, they have to separate you out from the primary people involved in diversion of medications, and fourthly, they have to understand what mail fraud and conspiracy really are.

"How much will that cost?" I asked. "How long will that take?

"One step at a time," said Marcus. If you go to trial and win, it will take at least eight months for the trial and you will each spend close to half a million dollars."

Marty jumped in almost before he finished. "I don't have that kind of money. There is no way that I could pay anything even close to that."

"And we can't take that much time away from our practice and clinics, I cut in.

"Hold it down guys, hold it down," Marcus intoned, emphasizing his command by pushing his palms toward the floor. "Let me finish."

We both nodded and sat back in our chairs, letting Marcus continue. "If you lose, and there is a remote chance that it can happen, then the world caves in."

"God," Marty said smacking his palms against the side of his head. "How did I get us into this?"

"The next option is to make a deal," Marcus said, identifying us as great candidates for the plea bargain."

I looked up with great interest. The fear and uncertainty were killing me. "What would that mean?"

"I don't know, but let me look into it and see if they are receptive."

"What's their stance on abortion," I asked somewhat concerned, fearful that this could interfere with their flexibility.

"Fortunately, the case is being tried in a district where your anti-abortion prosecutor, Mad Dog Schmuckle, is disliked so there is a chance for reasonable treatment." Marcus got up and ambled toward the door. We followed the hint and rose also.

"I'll know more tomorrow," he said, patting me on the back. "Meanwhile, go back to the hotel and get some rest."

"Yeah right," I said sarcastically, as we left the office. I could tell that I wasn't going to sleep at all until this thing was resolved. The weight of the world was just too heavy on my head. I looked down at my hands and they were shaking and I couldn't make them stop. The thought of two thousand years was just too much to handle.

Too much or two little to handle; it just didn't matter. The wheels of justice turned slowly and the agonizing abyss that I was suspended in, while we waited for progress, was unbearable. Still, I had a practice to attend to, clinics to run, and a family to take care of.

The bargaining session began. The prosecutors wanted favorable publicity and less work. Our lawyer wanted a quick resolution after all his money was paid up front. We pressed for a misdemeanor, so that we wouldn't be viewed as felons. Part of the understanding was an assurance that our medical licenses wouldn't be effected. In return, the prosecutors would be able to get miles of good publicity by nailing doctors with the expenditure of very little effort. Meanwhile, I suffered every day for two months, tossing and turning at night, unable to sleep, fearing the worst, tenaciously trying to keep my mind on my patients and my family. Finally, Marcus called with the "good news." We got the plea bargain; no jail time or loss of license. We just had to plea to a misdemeanor, pay a fine, get a suspended sentence, see a probation officer on a regular basis and otherwise not miss a beat. I breathed a great sigh of relief. It wasn't over yet, but the parameters were defined. I was going to come out of this with a few scars, but still whole. Wow!

I went in to my "vomiting interview" where I was instructed to tell the absolute truth. I was accompanied by my attorney's assistant since my attorney was busy on another criminal case up in New York. I walked in the room and was greeted by two FBI agents and by, what had to be, the fattest female federal prosecutor in the world. My hands were still shaking and I was pretty nervous, but I couldn't help but think that I would eat her if she would let me off the hook. Later, when I told Marty, he said that if I wasn't careful, I'd find him burrowing through the back of my head.

When she opened her mouth, the irony of the situation came into full bloom. Here I was, an educated man, being spanked by an attorney half my age and twice my size, who spoke like she came from the back woods of Tennessee, where thirty something is a chromosome count and the courses on sex education and animal husbandry are given by the same teacher at the same time. "Doctor," she drawled, indicating a chair. "Please sit down."

I took the seat she indicated and began to respond to all the routine questions about name, location, businesses etc. Finally, she asked. "Tell me how you mispackaged, mislabeled, altered and adulterated the medications that you sold to Mr. McVey."

"What," I answered, somewhat confused. "I didn't." She never let me finish.

"Don't start that crap with me!" she screamed, while standing up from her chair and pointing a finger in my face.

I was confused and really frightened. I turned to my lawyer for assistance, but he looked as confused as I did so I turned back and spoke. "Listen, you told me to come in here and tell you the truth and that's what I'm trying to do."

She never let up. "Like hell you are!" She again pointed a finger in my face. "So help me god. The first one out of the gate and I have to deal with this bullshit. I have lost my patience with you doctors. Either you own up, or I swear to God that I will throw the God damn book at you."

I was really frightened and confused now. I didn't know what to say or what she wanted me to do.

"Listen ma'am, what ever you want me to say. I thought that you wanted the truth, but if you want me to lie, just tell me."

My lawyer came to the rescue.

"Excuse me," he offered quietly. "I'd like a few minutes to talk to my client in private if I may."

"Certainly," said the prosecutor sarcastically as she whirled away from the table. "Just get your story straight. I got a lot of doctors to get through today."

We stepped outside and the attorney turned to me. "What are you doing?" "Trying to answer the questions like I was instructed to do."

"But that's the misdemeanor that you're pleading to," he said, somewhat confused. "Didn't Marcus tell you that?"

I was mad now. "Marcus didn't tell me anything, and you didn't have time to prep me. You told me to come in here and tell the truth. I didn't alter or adulterate or mispackage anything. Why can't I plea to what I did?"

"Because they couldn't find a misdemeanor to fit what you did." "What?" I said incredulously. "What does that mean?"

"Just that if you want to plead to a misdemeanor then this is the only one they got that has anything to do with diversion of drugs."

"I can't do that. I would never risk anybody's life by adulterating a medication!" I stated adamantly.

"Fine! What about mispackaging?"

"What about it?" I asked still perplexed.

"Didn't you ever give a patient a sample and put it in an envelope or something?"

"Of course, all the time. What does that have to do with anything?"

"That's mispackaging!" he announced enthusiastically as if he had just come upon a world class discovery. "Go in there and tell her that you did that."

"But every doctor does that."

"I know, but it's still mispackaging."

Triumphantly, we returned to the room to continue with Miss Jones' third degree.

"Are you ready to answer that question now doctor?" she said in a haughty tone.

"Yeah fat ass," I wanted to say, but instead a mealy mouthed "yes ma'am, I am," emanated from my lips. "After discussing the legal definitions of the terms used in this agreement, I have to admit that I have been responsible for mispackaging medications."

"That'll do it," she said, slamming her book shut simultaneously. Then pointing a finger at me, she said. "You ought to know better doctor, you ought to be ashamed."

I wanted so intently to tell her what I meant by mispackaging was so much less ominous than her vision of what I meant, but I decided to leave well enough alone. She could think as little of me as she wished as long as I could get on with my life. From that day on, everytime I thought of her waddling around that conference room, all I could think of was "oink, oink." Thank God it never went any further and I was forced to…Never mind; every time I thought of that it made me sick.

During this process, I continued to practice and felt as if I was in a continuous whirlwind, one-day spinning into the next, things flying at me from all directions. Christina was irritated that I didn't spend more time with the boys. At the hospital they were constantly pressuring me to keep my records up to date. In the office, they were overwhelmed with patients and I was constantly late due to distractions with the clinics, emergencies and an inordinate number of deliveries that pulled me away from the office. When it rains it pours and, no matter how hard I tried to concentrate on what I was doing, the remaining cloud of doubt that surrounded the developments in my criminal case, until I was finally sentenced, would constantly intrude upon my thoughts. I found myself thinking about the potential consequences while I operated, while I delivered, while I half-heartedly listened to patient complaints, while I tried to sleep and even when I made love.

I kept asking myself, "What if the judge didn't abide by the plea bargain?" In the throes of all of this, situations would arise that, because of my circumstances, would exponentially magnify my stress levels and negatively reflect on the conditions around me.

One such example, comical today, but excruciatingly frustrating back then, was a visit with what I describe as two JAPS in a row. I'm allowed to tell it because I am Jewish. As a rule, Jewish patients are responsible patients and reliable payers. But they expect very personal and special treatment, and they expect you to be available for their every whim and caprice. Their families are usually very close, and they expect answers and information at their convenience, without regard to the physician's protocols, obligations or privacy. It would not be unusual for a Jewish girl in labor to have both sets of grandparents, brothers and sisters, and aunts and uncles in the waiting room, each expecting updates at frequent intervals. If "Uncle Sol" was downstairs getting coffee, he would expect you to repeat all the information for his personal digestion and commentary. That was all well and good, but when I went home, I would often receive multiple phone calls from different members of the family, expecting answers and updates, without them ever thinking that they should get this information from one family spokesman, so that I wouldn't have to repeat the information four times and deprive myself of much needed rest.

With this background, under pressure and already half an hour late, I walked into the room to see an obstetrical patient named Barbara Ginsberg. After examining her and discussing her progress, I asked her if there were any questions, and after answering a few, I started toward the door, placed my hand on the handle and said. "See you next month Barbara."

As I turned the handle, I heard her say in a slow, monotonous nasal tone that was uniquely her. "Dr. Robbins."

"Yes Barbara," I responded, with my hand still on the door handle, ready to open the door and move on to the next room in a futile attempt to catch up. Nothing made me more nervous then to be con stantly behind, knowing that my patients were bitching in the waiting room, while I was running like a mad man trying to keep up.

"I have a question," she asked with that same slow, monotonous and ghastly irritating nasal cadence.

"Yes Barbara. What is it," I sighed. I had almost made it out of the room.

"Could you please come back so I can see you. You're always in such a rush."

"Certainly Barbara," I said, moving back into the center of the room. "I don't want you to feel rushed."

"Could you please sit down?"

"Thanks, but I prefer standing. I've been sitting all day."

"I'd be more comfortable if you sat down."

"All right," I sighed, hoping to get on with it. "If it makes you more comfortable."

"Give me a minute. It's not easy to ask."

"Barbara," I said impatiently. "You know that you can ask me about anything from witchcraft to anal sex. What's the question?"

"I know! I know. But please don't rush me."

"I'm not rushing you Barbara," I said, trying to conceal my frustration and doing all I could do to keep from pulling my hair out. "Ask me the question."

"All right," she sighed. "I have to get it out sometime. Do you promise not to think that I'm silly."

"I promise, I promise!" I said, somewhat exasperated.

"Do you know my aunt Sarah?"

"Yes"

"You remember?"

"I think so."

"You know, the elderly lady that I brought in last summer?"

"I said I think so Barbara. Go ahead."

"You're rushing me," she accused, gently shaking her index finger at me. I felt like a little boy being chastised for bad manners. Inside, I was ready to explode.

"Barbara, if you would be more comfortable thinking about this and then coming back to the office at the end of the day, when I don't have a schedule to meet and you could feel more comfortable about asking your question, I would be glad to schedule the time."

"No, that won't be necessary. I can ask you now. Just don't think that I'm silly. OK."

"OK," I echoed.

"Anyway, you do remember my Aunt Sarah," she said, looking to me for conformation. I nodded my head, even though I didn't have a clue, and she continued.

"Anyway, she had a sister, my Aunt Sheila, who, by the way, looks a lot like Sarah, except that she is thinner." She paused for a much-needed breath and I nodded my head indicating I understood so she could continue. I concentrated my focus with great effort as Barbara expounded on her story.

"Anyway, Aunt Sheila was married to my Uncle Bill, who she met while she was going to college. He died last year."

"I'm sorry to hear that," I cut in, not really giving a rat's ass, and getting close to committing assault and battery.

"Oh, that's OK. He was really sick for a lot of years and I think that he was really ready to go."

"Barbara," I cut in. "I don't want to rush you, but you have to get to the question. I do have other patients that are waiting."

"I'm sorry. Sometimes I go off on tangents like that. My husband gets mad when that happens."

"Barbara," I said sternly. "The question."

"Well, my Uncle Bill had a sister who was married to a man whose sister had a set of triplets, and I wanted to know."

She paused, bowing her head to avoid my gaze.

"Gosh, this is so embarrassing."

"Go on Barbara, it's fine."

"Well, I wanted to know what are the chances that I will have triplets too?"

"Jesus Christ!!!" I thought. "He wasn't even a blood relative. How stupid can you get." Out loud, I said.

"Barbara, don't you worry. Your chances are very, very slim. I wouldn't worry about it."

"Easy for you to say. You're not having the baby."

"Barbara. Multiple births occur more in people whose blood relatives have a history of multiple births. That woman was not a blood relative."

"Being related by marriage doesn't make it happen more often?"

"No Barbara," I said as gently and slowly as I could, forcing myself to press my hands against my sides to keep from strangling her. "You've got nothing to worry about." I patted her on the shoulder and moved toward the door as deliberately as possible. It seemed like an eternity, but I got to the handle, turned the knob and felt my heart skip a beat as I exited the room, fearful that I would hear that nauseating nasal cry,

"Dr. Robbins," once again.

I stood outside the exam room, hands showing a fine tremor, sweat upon my brow and took a deep breath. I had fallen fifteen minutes further behind. I took a deep breath, gave out a deep sigh, and preceded into the next den of horror, because there, waiting for me, was Janet Starwitz, who made Barbara seem like a gentle and courteous little lamb. She had all ofBarbara's cadence and tone accompanied by a misplaced arrogance. She was loud, offensive and demanding, and totally oblivious to the rest of the world around her. She took five minutes to scold me for being late and of course I apologized profusely while not telling her that her little tirade was making me later. We went through the normal exam and then, she kept me with a long list of questions, most of which could have been answered by my nurse assistant. Obviously, she needed the words to roll off my golden tongue for them to carry the weight of conviction. Finally, about to leave, with my hands on the doorknob, I heard those dreaded words again in that loud, arrogant, supercilious, nasal tone that made me want to puke. The voice was like "The Nanny's" with arrogance and impatience added to the mix. "Dr. Robbins, I'm not finished. Would you please come back here." I sighed heavily and slumped my shoulders as I moved back into the room. I knew that I was in for it again and, when I got out of the room, I'd be an hour and a half behind.

"Yes Janet," I said, resigning myself to my fate.

When I was finally able to escape, I went right to the front office and delivered my proclamation. In sotto voce, so nobody else could hear, I said to the front office staff. "Never again will I see two Jews in a row. If this happens, I will hound you until I find the culprit and I will make your life an absolute misery. Do you hear me; a misery!" It had nothing to do with prejudice. It was just that my heart couldn't take it.

It was also during this period that I was faced with the three most difficult cases that I ever had to deal with in my practice and, it all occurred when Marty was on vacation. A two man practice could be very comfortable when both partners were in town, for if you were up the night before, you usually had office hours the following morning and, if there was nobody in labor, you usually could get offin the afternoon to rest and relax. Even if somebody was in labor, you could go to the hospital, see the patient, catch some rest and, if you were lucky, your partner would come in after office hours and take over.

This was not the case when one of the partners was on vacation, and those few weeks per year could be an agonizing nightmare. You tried your level best to take vacation at a time when there were few deliveries expected, but sometimes the combination of a few premature births, accompanied by a few delayed deliveries, created a heavy burden for the doctor left to hold the fort. At this time, with Marty gone, that was my bad luck and I was overwhelmed with deliveries. On top of that, I got hit with two patients with post operative abdominal abscesses following vaginal hysterectomies, one of Marty's and one of mine, and a third patient with severe pelvic inflammatory disease that developed an Addisonian crisis post surgery. On top of that, I had five major surgeries of my own during those two weeks and, to cover Marty's absence, four sessions a week at our clinics. For almost two weeks, I lived at the office, the clinics and the hospital, as one day ran in to the next. Each day was an agony, as something would occur to keep me from getting one decent night's rest. I was a walking zombie. Somehow, I was able to get through it, although my wife didn't appreciate my absence, and my office patients didn't appreciate the fact that I was often late. Fortunately, I could wear scrubs in both the hospital and office setting so that I didn't have to concern myself with my wardrobe. Never did I see a more welcome sight then when Marty walked into the office on Monday afternoon to take over. Unfortunately, as luck would have it, we had two patients in labor that I had to cover until he was done with his patients, but at least the end was in sight and I could count on a good night's sleep that night. To compound the issue, that's the night that my son Dean chose to have an appendicitis attack, and I was again back at the hospital, sitting up with him all night, trying to assuage his pain as the signs of appendicitis continued to evolve. His mother was no help and in need of consoling herself. She was not only melodramatic, but also totally antagonistic whenever I tried to calm her down. The night was long, and I fought my way through it, ignoring my pounding head and aching back. Dean was scheduled for surgery at eight AM, and I left Christina in the surgical waiting room, while I watched the surgery. The surgery was routine, but on your own son, every step is crucial and frightening. I was exausted by the time it was over. I stopped in the surgical waiting room to bring Christina up to date and, ignoring her demand to keep her company, ran up to make rounds on my patients, while Dean was in the recovery room. I had my own surgery to do at ten and then I had an office full of patients for the afternoon. There was no other time for me to make sure that my patients were progressing normally and getting everything that they needed. No matter how hard I tried, my wife just didn't understand that and I just didn't have any more time to get through to her. I could hear her telling her friends now that I was just too callous to be concerned with Dean, when he needed me most, but there was nothing that I could do about it. I did my surgery at ten, after checking in on Dean who was groggy but awake in the recovery room. Fortunately, my surgery went well, and I wrote my orders, dictated my op note, changed my scrubs and helped the nurse escort my son to his room, picking up Christina from the surgery waiting room on the way. I sat with her and Dean until twelve forty five and then took my leave to go to the office to see my patients. By the time I got through in the afternoon, I was having trouble staying awake on my feet, but I gutted it up and drove to the hospital to see Dean and take care of a lady in labor. I called Marty and asked him if he would change call nights with me and, despite the fact that he had had a rough night on call the night before, he agreed to come in and take over at ten o'clock PM. The lady in labor was progressing well, so I rotated back between Dean and her labor room five times until they called me for delivery at eight thirty PM. Dean was uncomfortable and wanted me to stay but, because his mother was there and I had a delivery, I left despite his protests. Finally, the patient was delivered and I could change my clothes and get back to Dean's room, where I fell asleep on the cot they opened up for me next to his bed. Christina stayed the night too. At seven, Dean was awake and feeling a bit better. I got up, got breakfast, made rounds, stopped back to see Dean and headed for the office, somewhat refreshed from the ordeal of the last two weeks. It was the first time in two weeks that I was able to sleep for six hours in a row, and I swore that I would make a pact with the devil to work sixteen hours a day, seven days a week, if I could be promised six hours of sleep in a row every single night.

THE DEVELOPING YEARS

Following the East German expedition, the rest of the summer slid swiftly by. I involved myself with trips to the Adriatic, from Yugoslavia through Trieste, Venice, Ravena, Rimini and down to Bari. The only thing they all had in common was the lack of waves and an afternoon sun that shone awkwardly down from the land toward the water. Time had dimmed the vivid episode of my East German expedition. I had remained true to my word and discussed the affair with no one. I assumed Mark had done the same. On our return to Bologna, he had left for the states and we had not been in contact for months. Now, the only tangible evidence remaining of our East German episode was the new Ferrari, bought with government funds, that replaced my old Masserati. The whole affair seemed like a cloudy dream, distant, untouchable and no longer recoupable. I still wondered about Ingrld though, more from self-guilt than anything else. Had I done her irreparable harm, or, after all was settled down, was she capable of adjusting to and flourishing under the Western system. I suspected I would never find out.

Angela and I had begun to attack the last course remaining from the previous year, Microbiology. In Italian Universities, maybe one student in twenty five ever completed all the exams of the year in the

June-July exam session. Usually the good students would finish up in the fall session, October and November, that preceded the opening of formal classes. Anything that remained would be cleaned up in the winter apello (exam session in January and February.) At least half of the students didn't even finish by then, complicating matters by completing their first year's exams the following summer or fall. This of course meant that the classes and labs they were supposed to attend involved courses they were not prepared to take. Conversely, the fact that the classes were of no practical value made preparations for the following year's exams that much harder. In this way, a vicious cycle was laid. Once behind, the workload became harder, pushing the student even farther behind. Angela and I were determined not to let that happen. We wanted to be completely free of last year's responsibilities so that we could devote our full efforts to the Anatomy, Physiology, and Pathology courses that comprised the coming year's curriculum. Therefore, we spent the last two weeks of September and all of October in seclusion studying Microbiology. It soon became evident that this was a difficult course that would test not only our mental acumen but also our will power to maintain a concentrated effort on what could be best described as odious subject matter.

There wasn't much to understand but rather one hell of a lot to memorize. The heat of the summer, sometimes reaching one hundred degrees, bore into us and kept us continually fatigued and void ofiner- tia. The material was boring and filled with detailed minutia. Nevertheless, Angela and I suffered through it with persistent determination that culminated in a perfect exam score on her part and the equivalent of an A minus on mine.

Over the past six weeks, our friendship continued to grow. We were not truly platonic in the sense that we did have occasional sexual contact. But we both approached our physical involvement with a sense of philosophical detachment, using each other to satisfy a need, without placing any more significance than that on the act. Surprisingly, with nothing to prove and nothing to be attained, Angela was able to free herself from all her inhibitions and had developed into quite a polished bedmate. Furthermore, she was able to deal with other men in a flippant casual way that made her that much more desirable. She was constantly besieged with date offers and accepted some, but did not demonstrate particular interest in any one male. She was happy in her studies, satisfied with her sex life and patient enough to wait for the right guy to come along. The guy that she finally picked would really be getting a woman. She was bright, attractive, humorous, and inquisitive and, when he was ready for dessert, the fuck of his life.

Frank had returned after a profitable summer doing construction work. More for convenience, rather than love, he decided to move back in with me. It seemed that he still held me partially responsible for his total failure the year before, although he never outwardly voiced his feelings. Somehow, that ability to find an object ofblame and zero in on it is a beneficial characteristic in most successful men. It frees them from wasting time in introspection and self-analysis and spurs then on toward a tangible goal in the name of vengeance and self-righteousness. True, their errors in approach are often solved by blind accident instead of logical planning, but the very intensity of their effort, no matter how inefficient, is usually enough to get the task done. Frank was no exception.

Frank was back then, more serious and somber than the year before and fanatically determined to reverse his momentum. He attacked Biochemistry with a sixteen-hour daily effort for one month, all alone, confined to his room, even studying through the almost unbearable afternoon hours in a steaming Bologna. Unfortunately, he failed the exam, partially from the lack of the right slant on preparation, partially from the subjectivity of the examiner. Only three questions were asked. One total blank usually meant instant failure and so, to insure some sense of security and comfort, it was imperative to cover all fronts at least superficially. Frank, though, still fell prey to his own curiosities and was not able to discipline himself to prepare first, a general answer for everything, and then, once having that under control, pursue the detail that time permitted. Yet, despite his mistaken approach, an error he was to repeat again and again throughout his medical school career, my hat went off to him.

With back against the wall and nothing to show for one and a half years effort, a more sensible man, a less determined man, a less angry man would have packed his bags and, with slumped shoulders, walked away. But, like a safety valve on a furnace, Frank was able to release the mounting tensions and vent his frustrations on the system, the professor and myself. With renewed confidence, he started from scratch with histology, with the same inadequate approach, but with impregnable armor, and in three weeks time walked in on the exam. This time, with luck on his side, and radar on the part of the professor, who somehow avoided the topics Frank had not covered, he passed the exam. Finally, he was on his way. It eventually would take Frank eight years to complete the curriculum and pass the ECFMG, the entrance exam that would permit him to intern in the United States. Never once did he adapt to the Italian system of education, never once did he entertain the thought of quitting, and never once did he permit himself to shoulder anymore of the blame for failure than a healthy man could tolerate.

Mark returned to Bologna in late September, but we saw little of each other. For one, we were both preparing intently for our exam. For two, we really had very few interests in common. Nevertheless, a true bond had developed between Mark and myself that forms only between individuals thrown together with a common goal and a terrible fear of joint calamity. We knew each other at our worst and, yes, at our best.

We had tested our mettle in the face of the other, and come up naked, but unashamed. In the face of our ordeal, we could have nothing of more significance to hide from each other and certainly nothing more to prove. So in each other's company, we felt comfortable and calm. Therefore our friendship and concern for each other's welfare persisted.

The school year progressed and it became obvious that, once again, the classes were of little value. Furthermore, conflicts between classes still existed and, as early December rolled around, I decided to stop attending and concentrate on my studies by reading and outlining. For this, I did not have to confine myself to Bologna. I asked Angela to take care of the bidellos that insure me "la firma," that is the signature necessary for entrance to the exam. The "firma" was based on laboratory and class attendance, but if it was done on the up and up, no more than two percent of the class would be permitted to take the exam. Five or ten bucks in the right hands always could and always did cover a multitude of sins.

I decided to take a room in a pensione in the Dolomites, near Trento, on Mount Bondone. There I would learn to ski well. I would study in the early morning and the evening with skiing sandwiched in between. Most of my friends thought that I was crazy. Criticism was frequent and well intentioned. "That is not the way to attend school," said one.

"There should be more sacrifice," said another.

"You're not serious enough," added a third.

"That's ridiculous," commented a forth and so on and so on.

Those were the statements but, in truth, I knew that the key to completion of my studies was organization and a few hours of daily effort, not geography.

Unable to convince any of my peers that the change would be refreshing and even conducive to concentrated and efficient production, I left alone, planning to spend four months in semi-seclusion, skiing, eating, sleeping and studying in a wholesome and refreshing atmosphere.

The smell of fresh air whipped through my open window, as the Ferrari purred its way along the winding main highway. The roads were clear, but the bumps and tears in the road became more frequent, as I moved into mountainous territory. The elements apparently had taken their toll. The mountain sides, thick with pine trees, were padded with a smooth carpet of glistening snow. I pulled up the winding rode to the pensione perched on top of the hill. The sun, setting over the roof of the building, added to the breathtaking approach. I eased the car into a parking berth to the side of the building and stepped out into the biting cold. A penetrating chill shot through me as I made my way through the brisk wind to the entranceway of the pensione. On the door, the thermometer read minus twenty degrees and humidity was low. Don't let anyone fool you. Dry cold may be better than wet cold but minus twenty degrees is minus twenty degrees. Dry or wet, you are going to shiver.

The clerk looked up from behind the desk. "What can I do for you?" His accent was sharper than what I was used to in Bologna and I had to strain to understand.

"I'd like to see the owner about a monthly rate."

The clerk smiled. "That's me, Giovani Finelli," he said with earthy charm, extending his hand for a friendly shake. I took it with the same spirit of superficial warmth, still aware, though, that we had not yet settled on a price.

"What will It cost per month for room and board?"

Signor Finelli looked through a few pamphlets in front of him, attempting to lend authenticity to the rates he was about to propose. I knew that the figure he came up with would be as high as the traffic would bear, and would have no basis of reference other than my dress, carriage, and automobile which I had purposely parked as far away from the front door as possible.

As he spoke, his eyes strained to try and identify my car through the glass entranceway. "I can give you a room with meals for three thousand and five hundred lire per day."

I was thrilled with the price but masked my feelings with a despondent countenance. "I was hoping to pay less. For a few nights, that would be reasonable, but I will be here for two to three months."

His concern seemed real. "I understand signore but the cost of food and help has risen markedly in the last year. Anything less would be charity and you do not seem to be the type to ask for that."

"No, I would not want charity. But I thought that a monthly rate would run no more than two thousand and eight hundred lire a day."

A big smile crossed over his face as he spoke. "If I could get a room with food for two thousand and eight hundred lire per day, I would take it myself."

My pride was in jeopardy, for he made feel cheap and ignorant. But that was the game and to win you had to suffer embarrassment and play just that part. "I can understand, but I cannot afford more than ninety thousand lire per month, and I will be staying for two or three months."

His hands came down to his sides. His tone was serious and I could tell he suspected I was lying. "Signore. I like you and you look honest. For you I will make it three thousand and two hundred lire per day. So what if I make no money. Your company in my small pensione will be reward enough."

My eyes said, "you are full of shit." My mouth said, "I'll give you three thousand and one hundred lire. I'm stretching a little beyond my limits, but your place seems to be so unique."

His eyes said, "you penny pinching cocksucker." His mouth said, "one hundred lire here, one hundred lire there, what does it matter. Let's compromise at three thousand and one hundred and fifty lire per day (approximately five dollars.) Deal?"

I wanted to call his bluff and stand pat. But I knew that, if I conceded the extra lire, he would think he put one over on me and he would be that much more congenial during my two-month stay. "So be it," I said smilingly putting out my hand to seal the deal. "I will have to do a little magic to come up with the extra money, but I don't think that I will have a problem."

"Done," he said simultaneously crushing my knuckles with his right hand as be slapped me on the back with his left. "Come, I will show you the room."

Once settled in my, if not lavish, comfortable abode, I collected my razor, soap and towel and strolled down the hall to the common bath. I tried the door but it was locked. Knocking on the door, I asked in Italian. "Are you going to be long?"

"Not very," came the soft feminine reply. "Only a few seconds."

Normally, in Italy, that would be hint enough to return to my room for a long night's vigil. But my curiosity got the best of me and I parked myself outside the door. After 45 minutes of making a pest of myself, the signorina strolled from the bathroom. "YouAmericans,(my accent was obvious,) are so damn impatient," she said, accompanying her words with a supercilious sniff as she swished past.

Her robe clung in spots to her still damp body, outlining the voluptuous curve of her rear. My loins ordered me to pursue. My common sense told me to pick a better time. Proving "mind over matter" I decided to wait and disappeared into the bathroom.

With that episode, I had my first hint that even the most simple and common pursuits in life could become infinitely desirous if made almost unattainable. With anywhere from 8-12 people sharing one bathroom, most of them girls, my day began to center around the availability of that facility, and I was constantly preoccupied with a plan to avoid as many waiting periods as possible.

In my first week there, I would venture to say that I passed an average of 2 to 3 hours a day twiddling my thumbs outside the bathroom door, trying to prod its occupant loose from what had to be almost magnetic appeal. Twice I left, totally devastated and certainly frustrated with my own inability to remove the days sweat and grime from my body. When I did manage to pass through that impregnable door, I drew such sweet delight from the small comforts a bathroom, that we normally take for granted, could provide. I learned, though, that there were rush hour periods and slack times and ifI were willing to rise early (6:30 am) and come in early from the hill (3:00 pm,) I could have the facility all to myself. Needless to say, I rose at the crack of dawn and left the hill at the first sign of a fading afternoon sun.

In all fairness, I must admit that there are very few distinguishing features about an ass. I could have been wrong, but the one I spotted swooping down the hill behind a pair of flailing skis could have only belonged to the girl I saw slivering out of the bathroom that first day in the pensione. I am a connoisseur of ass.

For one, they were both wide with curvaceous hips and rounded succulent cheeks. For two, they were both damp. Now the time was ripe. I glided down behind her and grabbed the back of her coat to keep her from a rude appointment with a tree. Once Christina's body stopped shaking from fear, she thanked me in a tone sprinkled with deep gratitude and romantic awe. From medical student, I had been transferred to a knight in shining armor. "Listen," I said smilingly. "If you are going to stay alive you bettor stay off the hill or learn to ski properly."

She blushed and looked down toward the snow. "I thought it would be easy."

"Well never mind," I said placing a protective arm around her shoulder. "I'll teach you enough, so at least you'll have control."

She seemed a little shy and timid, almost awed by my presence, so I went through the basics of the snowplow. I took it easy but she learned quickly and was eager for more. The controlled tumbles and falls that she suffered didn't discourage her, and when we arrived at the bottom of the hill, she was eager to go again.

I held her skis, as she climbed aboard the chariot, and then jumped aboard myself, with four skis in tow, just before the basket began its long ascent up the mountain.

The sun lay bright but distant in the sky, its warm rays weak and ineffective against the biting December cold. We turned our backs to the hill, trying to protect our faces from the wind. There was not a cloud in the sky and visibility was perfect. The full expanse of the

Dolomites, filled with rolling hills and studded with soft pines, painted a picture of sweet serenity, in contrast to the sharp and breathtaking Alps, just to the north. Christina's voice broke the silence. "It's beautiful. Isn't it?"

"Yes."

"Do you come here often?"

"It's my third time," I replied.

"Why do you choose this place? Is it the best for skiing?"

"Actually not. It's fun but not over challenging. Let's say it's relaxing and that it provides me with the opportunity to think clearly and attend to my work with some patience and full concentration."

"What do you do?"

"I'm a medical student. But enough about me. Tell me something about yourself."

"There's not much to tell."

"Why not let me be the judge."

"I promise you'll be bored." She paused, waiting for me to change the subject, but I stared at her so fresh, pretty face with determined resolve. She shrugged her shoulders and continued.

"Okay, here goes, but I warned you."

I smiled encouragement as she spoke. "I was born In Ferrara, the third and last of three disappointments to my father, all girls." My look of confusion silently begged an explanation. "You see in each and every Italian family it is essential to have a male heir. Especially mine, since historically my family has controlled, both politically and economically, a small region near Ferrara. Needless to say, my father was despondent but willing to be patient after the first girl, my sister Donatella, came into the world. After Juliette was born, he began to resent my mother, especially when she expressed a desire for no more children.

"After all," she would complain to her sister, sarcastically mimicking what must have been my father's voice. "Do you have no concern for · v> priorities?"

My mother compromised, agreeing to have one more child. Total devastation. I was born and there would be no male heir, for she had to have a hysterectomy."

Christina looked up at me inquisitively. "How do you say in America, three strikes and you are out?"

I nodded in accord. "Anyway, the relationship between my mother and my father continued to deteriorate, so that, although I lived under the camouflage of a stable and powerful family structure, a real sense of family did not exist. I was always envious of the kids that had much less in tangible goods, but did not lack for laughter and love in the household."

"Did your parents fight?"

"I wish they did. That would have been something; at least an expression of feeling. It was worse. They were always civil, but distant. My father would come home for dinner and we would all sit together. The only sounds usually heard though were the forks and knives hitting the plates."

"How old are you Christina?"

"Seventeen."

"Do you get along with your folks?"

"When I see them, yes, because I avoid confrontation, but for the last few years I've been away at boarding school and, in the summers, they sent me away on tours. This summer I will be going to America."

"You don't seem too anxious."

"I'm not. I would Iike very much to spend some time home with my family, but my father thinks it important that we get as such exposure to the world as possible. He is like a piece of steel, impregnable, and his decisions are final."

"Do you see your sisters very much?"

"Not this year. Last year Julietta attended school with me. Now she and Donatella are at the University."

"Where?"

"Bologna. They stay with my uncle during the week, but at least have the opportunity to return home for the weekend."

I smiled, shaking my head at the coincidence.

"What's so funny?"

"Nothing, just that it's a small world. That's where I go to school."

"Oh."

I decided to leave it there for the time being. She was so sweet, so unpretentious, so refreshing. Despite her world travels, it was obvious that she had been sealed off from real involvement; given her taste of life only in small sterile samplings. She was a soft, sweet, flower bud waiting her moment to burst into full bloom. I wanted to do it gently. Besides we had arrived at the top of the hill.

On a daily basis I met Christina on the hill. She made remarkable improvement, a reflection of her tremendous agility and incessant drive. Soon she was almost able to keep pace with me and day after day we whirled down the hill, refreshed by the invigorating wind whipping by, smelling the fresh pine scented air, thrilled at the speed and the challenge of the slopes.

On the long ride up, we sat huddled together on the floor of the chariot, sometimes in silence, sometimes talking lightly, sprinkling our conversation with laughter and gaiety, sometimes speaking seriously about matters that stirred our emotions.

As I grew to know her, I realized that she was a much more complex and intricate person than I had anticipated. Innocent yes, limited in real life relationships yes, but totally capable of in depth analysis of any situation she was confronted with. Her emotions for the most part were untested, but she had revealed to me a full and almost completely objective understanding of the disintegrating relationship between her mother and father, and was surprisingly compassionate in understanding the character conflicts that made reconciliation impossible. She also understood her own relationship with her parents and knew that in their own non-demonstrative ways, they truly loved her. If she felt mistreated, it was only because they were doing what they felt was best for her. She went along, only because she knew to resist her father's dominance, cemented in years of Italian tradition, would be futile. And so she attended boarding school, returning home only for the vacations, and tried to make the best of a lonely and cold situation. The yearning for love end fulfillment, though, seeped through in our discussions and I suspected she possessed an enormous capacity to love and cherish; that once the dam was opened, she would overflow with emotion and full commitment.

I found also that I opened up more to her than to anyone else is my life. She was so direct, so honest, so unpretentious and so far removed from the daily pressures and challenges that I had become accustomed to, that I no longer had to play a role. I was just myself with her, relaxed, comfortable, and so happy in her presence.

Despite our developing and enriching rapport, there was no physical aspect to our relationship outside of a squeezed finger or a brush ofher hair. For one, she was at the pensione with a group of girls from school and her teacher, who chaperoned her girls like a jealous mother hen, did not permit the girls to date at night. For two, a Catholic upbringing, combined with almost complete isolation from boys in the past, left her with an infinity of internal conflicts to face and conquer. This, in itself, was a major undertaking in the life of any young impressionable girl and would, of necessity, leave a trail of anxiety, uncertainty and periodic guilt. To add a new dimension of pressure on my part would only magnify these depressing doubts and could only lead to deterioration in our relationship. I wanted so much for things to be smooth, relaxed and spontaneous for her. I wanted her to feel secure and protected in my arms; not challenged and frightened and I knew that the only way to accomplish this would be through patience. Eventually, the forces of nature would bring her to me; when she was ready, on her own terms, secure in the fact that I understood her hesitation and conflicts, knowing that I was an empathetic ally and not an antagonist.

Her three weeks at Bondone passed quickly and the following morning she was to return to school. We left the slopes that afternoon, hand in hand, with the sun still straining to peek over the mountaintops and made our way to the small intimate cafe at the bottom of the hill. Once inside, we isolated ourselves at a corner booth near the radiator to thaw faster. The warm radiant heat began to penetrate my clothes, making my body tingle with pleasure and relief. The day had been cold and, as the protective sun began to drop from the sky, the temperature had dropped rapidly. It was good to feel warm again.

I ordered two hot chocolates and, as we waited, we just sat there, silently staring at each other, the pain of imminent departure and unfulfilled needs reflected in each other's eyes. Christina broke the silence. "I don't want to go," she said simply with a hint of desperation in her voice.

"I don't want you to go."

We sat in uneasy silence for only seconds, but they seemed like hours. Again Christina spoke, the words coming with difficulty. "Will I see you again?"

"Do you want to?" I responded with a question.

"Oh yes," she said with open emotion, tears welling in the corners of her eyes. "I've never wanted to be with anyone so much in my life as I want to be with you."

The bars were broken, the defenses were down and I had to admire her courage for I had not yet given her any verbal indication of affection. I reached for her hands under the table and spoke softly, gently. "I love you my princess."

Her cheeks flushed and her face lit up with a wide uncontrollable smile. The tears flowed freely now, but they were happy tears. She had been willing to remove her armor and lay her heart open, bare and exposed. "Oh God, Dodd, me too, me too!" I reached across the table and squeezed her hand. My hand and arm tingled with schoolboy love and all I could think about was grabbing her in my arms, but, with the chaperone present in the room, I struggled to restrain myself.

Our hot chocolates came and we drank slowly. The hot fluid warming our insides, content for the moment in our expressed love to each other. I knew not what made me say that I loved her, except that in that one fleeting moment, I felt an enormous need and desire to make her happy and, with that fulfilled, I could also be filled to the brim with joy. I wanted her and I wanted to be with her now more than ever, now more than with anyone before. If that was love, then I loved her. "I have a surprise for you," she whispered.

"What is it?"

"I won't tell you," she teased. "But you will know tomorrow before I leave."

I prodded and pried, but she wouldn't satisfy my curiosity and I resigned myself to waiting till the morning.

Soon we left and returned to our passions. I wanted to kiss her, to hold her, to caress her soft sandy curls, but there was no place to go; no place to hide. Once inside the pensione, her mother hen was there to tell her to get ready for dinner and to offer me a few meaningless well-mannered words of greeting in the same manner as if she were speaking to a dumb stallion.

From distant tables we watched each other eat, and then, after dinner, we sat in a group with her friends and her chaperone, playing Parcheesi. Those couple of hours dragged on, so very slowly and I rose to take a walk in the cold night air, knowing Christina could not follow without the mother hen to accompany her. The air was brisk and invigorating, and the ache in my chest and loins became unbearable. I walked for an hour and then returned home. Christina, despondent, was engaging in empty conversation with her friends, as I caught her gaze from the other side of the room. I nodded, indicating upstairs and I hoped that she caught the hint. Her gaze fell quickly to one of her friends and I turned to walk up the stairs, so very hungry for her, so frustrated by her physical proximity but so very distant availability.

I took a cold shower in the surprisingly empty bathroom and returned to my room, leaving the door unlocked. I twisted and turned restlessly for over an hour, finally falling asleep in a cloud of pessimistic doubt that Christina had ever thought of the exquisite privacy of my room.

I was lying on a table totally exhausted, the tension in my muscles beginning to ease as the masseuse's soothing fingers kneaded the muscles of my neck and shoulders. I fell into that half sleep, aware at moments of the soft probing fingers, unable though to account for the timeless periods between. Suddenly I awoke, but the fingers, real, were still there pressing, caressing, and soothing. I turned on my back and I felt warm, sweet breath on my face. As her lips touched mine, I sensed so exquisitely the electrifying contours of her soft succulent body pressed against me. I couldn't see yet, but I didn't have to. It was Christina; the Christina I could see so vividly outlined in my dreams. "I love you," she whispered as my arms wrapped around her, squeezing tightly, trying to erase the virtually absent distance between us, making us one.

My fingers explored her back and moved tenderly around to the soft swell of her breast. She began to tremble, oh so gently, but still tremble in my arms, a subconscious protest to something desperately desired but still new and frightening and in direct conflict with principles imprinted on her in her youth. I turned her on her side, my hands holding her face, and kissed her nose. "I love you, Christina." I kissed her full on the mouth and then, pressing her head against my chest, wrapped my arms protectively around her, wanting so very much to explore the mysteries of her body, willing, though, to satisfy myself with the pressure of her soft luscious curves cuddled next to me.

My mind wandered, and I fell into a deep sleep dreaming of an experienced, confident, uninhibited Christina exploding with me in delicious climax, reaching the acme of sexual fulfillment. But that would be for another time and another place.

The following morning, she left for Lugano, transformed again into a schoolgirl, but noticeably apart, for she was not giggling stupidly over silly jokes like all the rest. Over the past three weeks she had taken a giant step from childhood to womanhood with some of its incumbent pleasures and some of its responsibilities and despairs. As I watched from my window, she stepped somewhat solemnly onto the small bus, and took a window seat in the rear, excluded from the others. As the bus pulled away, she turned to look once more at the window of my room, hoping to see my face, knowing that even if the sun's glare blotted out my image, I would be there. She blew a kiss offher hand, as the bus disappeared into the curve of the road and made its way north to Switzerland.

For my part, I felt lonely, empty and tense. I dressed quickly and left for the hill, hoping to find relief in the challenge of the slopes. The trails were packed hard, without powder, since it hadn't snowed for days, and control took tremendous strength and concentration as I plowed my way down the mountainside. By the third run, with sweat soaking my back, as the warm sun rose up to its peak, I began to feel relaxed and slowed my pace. But I stayed on the hill all day, hoping that the persistent activity would keep my mind clear of Christina and those accompanying feelings of loneliness and despair.

The night was different. I lay there twisting and turning, unable to sleep, unable to smother my thoughts of her, mind churning over her soft words and sweet body, again and again, until finally I fell into a light restless sleep.

The days rolled forward in one ill-defined heap. In the early hours I studied, finding that full concentration was an unrealistic goal. Nevertheless, the job had to be done and I found that, as I bit into the material, the task became easier and more fruitful. Christina's image and words kept popping up at inconvenient moments, making me lose my train of thought and waste valuable time getting back on the right track. Still, all in all, work was accomplished and, under the circumstances, I was satisfied. In the late morning and early afternoon I took to the slopes, studying intently the flaws in my style and trying valiantly to eliminate them. Sometimes, day after day would go by without any sign of progress, but I knew that I had just hit a learning plateau and then, suddenly, all of it would come together and I would move up a notch in ability. The evenings were the worst, quiet, dragging and so horribly vulnerable to meditation and imaginative pursuits. Christina kept violating my thoughts, consuming them, and I didn't resist. I wondered continually if it was just a vacation's infatuation, destined to be as flippantly discarded as I was so swiftly beloved. Or was she really serious? Could our multiple barriers, language, religion, culture be overcome? The more I thought, the more I doubted, and the more I realized how deeply involved I was. I needed to be with her, and more than that, I needed to be reassured by her.

The phones in Italy are lousy. I waited fifteen anxious minutes for our connection to go through and then the static disguised the tones and inflections in her voice that were the necessary keys to my own reassurance.

For a few uneasy minutes we spoke of only superficial subjects, the weather, school, et cetra and the knots in my stomach tightened. Finally I put my cards on the table. "Christina, I'm coming up to Lugano in the morning."

"What did you say?"

I yelled into the receiver, certain that she barely heard the words. "I said that I'm coming up to Lugano in the morning."

"You can't, I have school."

"Play hooky."

"What."

"Play, I mean don't go."

I can`t.

"Why not?"

"Because I can't. What would I tell the head mistress?"

My stomach muscles wound tighter. If she really loved me she wouldn't be that practical. "Listen Christina, after school."

"I can't, I must go to drama class."

"And dinner?"

"We eat together in the main dining room."

"Can't you get a pass?"

"I don't know, I never tried it."

"Well try it." "What if I…"

"What if nothing. Get the pass. Tell your head mistress your brother is coming up to visit you."

"I don't have a brother."

"Your uncle then, I don't care."

"I'll try."

"I'll see you at 5:30."

Anxious silent seconds passed and then, "Dodd?" "Yes."

"I love you Dodd and I want so very much for you to come. I'm just, well you know, scared. I've never done this before."

"I know, "I said gently. "But I need you so much I have to come, Ciao until tomorrow."

Ciao.

I could have kicked myself for doubting. But then I never would have noticed how rapidly the right medicine makes a knotted stomach unravel.

The purpose of my isolation at Bondone was to find a serene and healthful atmosphere that would be conducive to studying with maximum concentration. Meeting Christina had destroyed all that. I could think of nothing else and I had to see her, in different surroundings, to see if she was real, to see if there was really a future for us.

I left that night, checking out in a rush, much to the despair of Signor Finelli. I had all I could do to explain to him that my leaving had nothing to do with my dissatisfaction with Bondone or his pensione and, only after repeated promises to return did he relinquish my arm and all attempts to persuade me to stay on.

An ebullient man yes, but so typically Italian. Once our price was set, he did his utmost to make me feel at home, and I truly believed his

sincerity when he wished me well, and hoped that I had been satisfied with the services he had extended to me over the last month and a half.

The roads through to Como, the beautiful Italian Lakeside City at the base of Switzerland, were tough for any car to negotiate. But the Ferrari wasn't just any car and the rough, cracked, twisting concrete that seems to accompany all rustic scenery, represented only a minor challenge to its grasping Pirellis and balanced chassis. Once through Como, there was a short delay at the border station, a routine perfunctory check by the Swiss guards, and then I was on my way.

The back end of the Ferrari sported the red tag of the "Heart of Dixie" (State ofAlabama), no doubt the reason for the cursory border check. All American students in Italy had to take their cars out of the country at 6 month intervals in order to qualify for foreign registration and gas coupons which saved about twenty cents on the gallon.

About ninety percent of all American student cars were registered in Alabama, since proof of residence in said state was not required to get the license tag. Hence the border guards were used to seeing Alabama cars. I often wondered if the Bolognese people ever drew a distorted image of population centers in the United States. Many of them, I'm sure, made the gross assumption that Alabama supplies at least ninety five percent of the American student power abroad.

It was only twenty odd miles to Lugano and, in no time at all, I was whipping over the high tall bridge, the gateway to this picturesque Swiss town. I found a quaint hotel room in a second class establishment, clean but certainly not overflowing with conveniences. That evening I took a walk in the cold night air, a perfect potion for a full night of restful sleep.

When I woke, the room was still pitch black, but I felt so strangely rested. Then I remembered the tamporellas, the Italian window blind that blocked all the light. I pulled the chain and the brightness sprung at me like a flame. Squinting until my eyes adjusted, I glanced at my watch. The time came into focus and I was surprised to see that it was past noon. I probably had five hours to blow until I could meet Christina.

I dressed slowly, giving meticulous attention to choice of colors, and then to my hair, making sure there wasn't a strand out of place. I felt foolish, never having made that petty effort before. Satisfied, after observing myself with a couple of retakes in the full-length mirror on the back of the bathroom door, I went out for breakfast. Eggs were not in style, as I could have expected, and my stomach wasn't in the mood to tolerate anything heavy. I settled on a Cappuccino and a pastry, paid the check and took another look at my watch that read twelve fifty three. Over four hours to go.

I took a long walk out along the lakeside, pulling my suede windbreaker up around my ears to keep out the biting cold. When I could stand it no longer, I returned back to my room, finding to my dismay that the time was only eight minutes after two. I entertained the thought of going to a movie, but there was nothing playing of interest. I went anyway to see John Wayne, against great odds, conquer a gang of cattle rustlers and win the evasive affections of the grateful heroine. He did it all in Italian too, which made the feat appear even greater.

By 4:30, the movie was over and I still had an hour to blow. The best way to make it vanish was to walk the two miles to the school. Two miles is not a long walk, on level ground that is. Two miles uphill is a veritable nightmare. My legs cramped terribly as I took the final strides up the winding driveway leading to the main administration building. My body was at least warm from generation of its own sweat and heat. My hair was rumpled and wet from the snow.

While trying to catch my breath, I asked the secretary for Christina. She directed me to the lounge to wait. I ensconced myself in a soft armchair at the far end of the cozy room, taking advantage of the waves of heat streaming from the fireplace.

Standing in the archway, bundled in parka and scarf, she looked beautiful. I sat and watched as she walked across the room, smile radiant, cheeks rosy, obviously happy to see me. I stood and just looked at her, our finger tips just brushing, and returned her smile. "Can you leave?" I asked.

"Yes, I have a pass. She looked about nervously. "But let's go now. I told them that my cousin came to take me out to dinner and I'd hate to have to explain your accent to them."

"Okay," I said, thinking how petty and juvenile our problem was.

We left quickly and started the long walk down the hill toward town.

"Did you bring the car?"

"No, I walked."

"It doesn't matter, we can build an appetite walking toward the city.

Somehow I was rejuvenated by her presence for I liked the idea of walking back to town. Maybe it was the downhill course that renewed my energy.

As we passed a large clump of bushes to the right of the sidewalk, I instinctively moved into their protective shadow and pulled her toward me, kissing her full on the mouth and squeezing her like there was no tomorrow. At first she resisted, but then she quickly melted in my arms. "I love you, Christina, Will you marry me?" The question seemed so awkward in that setting. She responded without hesitation as if it were the most natural place in the world to propose.

"Yes."

"When?"

"Now."

My mind swam with hunger and love for her. I kissed her again and then led her down the path to the protective warmth of a quiet, cozy little restaurant at the side of the lake. From past experience I knew the cuisine to be excellent and the atmosphere soothing, but we really didn't need it. We had our own heat and, for those few hours, no environment, no matter how harsh or how cold, could have penetrated our bubble. We touched fingers under the table and throughout the meal never took our eyes off each other. We didn't even taste the food.

The time passed quickly and I had to have Christina back by 10:00 PM curfew. There was no chance to culminate our vows with physical commitment but, when I left her at her dormitory, we were both still in a trance of ecstasy.

All bubbles burst under the weight of external pressures and practical applications. Our momentary inspiration was subjected to all the weapons of suffocation. Getting married in Italy or Switzerland was not a simple chore. It required weeks of effort and documentation. The task was monumental. Parental consent on Christina's part would have greatly facilitated the matter. Strange I hadn't previously thought of the problem.

The following evening, standing at her side for moral support, I cajoled Christina into calling her parents. She was pessimistic and with good reason. At first they didn't even consider her to be serious and laughed at and then chided her for acting ridiculously and impetuously. It must have been difficult but she mustered the courage to stand her ground. Her father's voice was cold when he finally realized that she was serious. "Christina, you are acting childishly. We will hear no more of this."

"Papa," she persisted, "I am in love and intend to get married."

Although the intensity and pitch of his voice remained the same, the tone ran ice picks through her.

"Christina, that is enough of this nonsense. I am your father and you will do as I say."

She finally relented, but could hardly keep from crying.

"Yes Papa, goodnight."

"Goodnight," he said firmly, adding. "The next time you call, have the decency not to upset your mother with such idiotic trash." He hung up the phone, not giving her the chance to reply. She fell into my arms in tears.

The weekend came and I convinced Christina to tell her headmistress that she was going to Milano to spend the weekend with a classmate. The classmate joined the conspiracy, vowing secrecy and loyalty, and the two girls left together for the train station. I picked her up at the station and we made our way back to the hotel. Plans had already been laid for Christina to meet Vana's incoming train Sunday night and they would taxi back to school together.

Christina was noticeably nervous on the way to the hotel. This was her first real experience in defying her parents and social controls. She was afraid that her parents might call, although they never had in the past; that Vana might gossip; that someone she knew might see her in town. But this game was old hat to me. The odds in getting caught in any one episode were slight. Furthermore, a tongue lashing from her folks and a little turmoil at school was the worst that could happen. She of course, without the experience of hindsight, exaggerated the probabilities and the potential punishments. I knew, though, that when I got her to the safety of the room, I could calm her down.

She didn't care for the idea of walking into the hotel alone, but I convinced her that no one would know if she had a room there or not and, if she walked in as if she belonged, she could come and go unmolested to my room. I waited for a few anxious moments until she knocked at the door. Once in, she sighed with relief. "Nervous?"

"A   little."
"No reason to be."

"That's easy for you to say." A pouting lower lip made her all the more seductive.

"Listen." I said, sitting next to her, laying my hand over hers. Her palm was damp and clammy and her fingers held a just palpable tremble. I turned her face up to mine and kissed hers softly, sensuously. "I love you Christina."

Her lips slid from mine as she buried her head into the nape of my neck, a steady flow of soft, almost silent tears dampening my chest. I wrapped my arms around her, letting that protective shell speak for words that weren't. I felt so helpless, so inept. Moments that seemed like eons crept onward and my neck cramped, but I dared not move, fearing that the sudden jolt would upset her equilibrium, allowing the dam to burst and throw Christina into a fit of uncontrollable sobbing. God knew how I'd handle that. The tears leaked forth, steadily releasing her tremendous inner tensions, built up on the frustrations, fears and conflict of the past few days. As the pressures ebbed, she began to shake her head slowly, within the protective shield of my neck and shoulder. "I'm so confused," she rasped steadily, gaining control over her body.

"I know." I whispered in her ear, stroking her hair as I spoke.

"I don't know what to do."

"Why don't you do what you want to do."

She looked at me voluntarily, questioningly. "Is that so easy?"

"It can be," I said simply, fixing my eyes to hers.

"How?"

"By realizing that you are no longer just an extension of your parents morality and desires but an autonomous individual, responsible to yourself; owing Christina, and Christina only. You have the right to pursue your own happiness and pleasures as long as you are willing to accept the incumbent conflicts and anxieties that come along with that assertion."

"And what are those?"

"Don't play dumb Christina. If I have to tell you, you're not ready."

"Maybe I'm not," she spurted defensively.

I looked directly at her.

"If you're not ready now Christina, you may very well never be. Your folks, your friends, your sisters, they count; but secondarily. We count most Christina, and if they don't understand that, then it's their shortcoming, not ours. There will also be pressures and pain but if you're going to assert your own individuality, you must be willing to accept that. Otherwise resign yourself to being a rubber stamp to someone else's dream."

"You make me sound so foolish," she said smiling sheepishly.

"I don't mean to," I said seriously. "I love you Christina and I want so very much for you to be happy."

In that moment she just looked at me, trust and warmth emanating from her being. "Love me Dodd, oh please love me," she whispered, her body flowing into my arms. "I'm so afraid, but don't let me turn back."

And I didn't.

Frank's voice leaked annoyingly into the room, disrupting our concentration. "Getting your balls licked is one of the Seven Wonders of the World."

Angela gave a look of disgust and, with venom on her tongue, commented. "He is really vulgar."

I chuckled condescendingly. "Now, now they're only words. They can't bite. Besides, he's got a point."

"Doesn't he have any taste!"

"Why should he worry. He's not the one with the flashing tongue." She fought it but she couldn't help but smile.

"Very funny."

I got up and affectionately rustled her hair. "Come on, let's take a break, we've been at it for three hours now."

"Okay," she agreed reluctantly, knowing that Frank's friends in the other room would keep us from effective study.

It was now April, and the big push had begun. We were confined to that room for 12 hours a day, together, driving ourselves to learn what at first seemed to be an insurmountable mountain of material. Alone, we never would have kept up the unrelenting pace, probably having to resort to speed (amphetamines) for support. Together, we could act as each other's crutch. At first, the heavy hours seemed unbearable but after being in the routine since mid March, we had already built up enough momentum to keep going. We slid past Frank and his Italian friends playing poker at our dining room table. They were so involved, that they didn't hear us go out of the room.

Frank had been procrastinating lately. He had developed a romantic entanglement with a local prostitute and was too involved with her to do any serious studying.

Frank's capacity for lovemaking was enormous. He met her while returning home from a date, three months ago. After having emptied his gun twice that night, he spotted a seductive looking lithe blond standing on a corner of the viale waiting for a pickup. By Frank's standards, the evening was still young and he figured what the hell. Pulling along the curb, he called out the window, "How much?" The prostitute walked up to the car and stuck her head through the open window. She perused his face, smiled and quoted. "For you, two thousand lire for a blow job, three thousand to fuck."

Frank was turned on by that kind of subtle sophistication. "How much to come to my apartment?"

The whore looked warily at him and made a snap decision. Good dress, old but clean car, American accent. He must be honest. "Alright, for five thousand lire."

Frank nodded okay. All month long he struggled to make his budget. But eight bucks in one crack just because he hadn't been laid in twenty minutes. That was a necessary expense.

I don't know what he had that night, but she came back for more. Every night, for two months, she'd ring the bell at 3:30 am (after work of course.) Frank would groan and groggily stagger from his bed to answer the door and let her into the apartment. She would run to take a shower and then struggle with the again sleeping Frank to wake up and make love to her. He would grunt and groan at first but then begin to moan satisfactorily as the pace of the squeaking bedspring would begin to pickup. The episode would climax with her first whispering and then screaming, machine gun style, a stream of endearments at him, as he brought her to the acme of fulfillment. Frank would show me later the nail marks etched into his back that accompanied each and every one of those endearments.

For my taste, most Italian girls were filled with too many false words and actions of love, borne from traditional expectation and not from the heart. But then again, my girls didn't always lick my balls.

For the last month, though, Frank couldn't stand the pace, for it disrupted his whole lifestyle. Despite his ability to waste time, he was by nature a day person, rising early and going to bed by 11:00 PM. He couldn't stand the constant interruption of his sleep and he used to just wander through the day waiting only for it to end, so he could got back to bed. He wasn't up to studying and he eventually stopped trying.

He finally managed to get the visits down to three per week but, even under the present regime, he couldn't function properly. What made matters worse was that this past week he had received a letter from a man alleging to be Juliana's (his whore's) boyfriend. It read as follows:

Dear Franco,

It has come to my attention that, while I am in jail, you have been making time with my Juliana. Within the month I shall be released. If you do not stop seeing her, I will be forced to indulge myself in the pleasure of cutting off your balls.

Sincerely,
Juliana's boyfriend

The past five days had been sheer comedy. Frank was tough but not crazy. He liked Juliana, but not enough to risk his life for her. While sitting alone with her in the living room, he told her the bad news. Angela and I listened intently behind the door to my room. By nature we weren't eavesdroppers, but this was too good to pass up. "Juliana," he said in a serious and somber tone. "You are a woman worth fighting for and your boyfriend wants you badly enough to kill me."

"But Franco, I love you, I don't want him."

With all the subtlety he could muster, he replied. "Tough shit."

What do you mean tough shit?" she yelled.

Juliana took it all the wrong way, inferring that Frank was ready to stand and fight for her. He had to start all over.

"You don't quite understand," he explained with forced resolve. "We have to stop seeing each other."

She paused for a moment, probably startled. From our vantage point, we couldn't see what was happening.

"I mean that we are through Juliana. I like you, but not enough to die for you."

In between the shattering plates, she hurled an incessant stream of insults at him.

"Fag," crash! "Animal," crash! "Pig," crash! "You balless wonder," crash!

When she ran out of plates and curse words, she jerked her nose up in the air and strode from the apartment. Angela and I were now watching through a crack in the door.

Fifteen minutes later the doorbell rang, but Frank just sat there refusing to answer.

From the depths behind the door came a soft, pleading voice. "Franco, I love you, I forgive you, I need you. Franco, I know that you are in there, I know you're angry but I know that you love me."

The melodrama was more than he could take. Not being able to stand it any longer, Frank finally opened the door and Juliana burst past him into the room. "Oh Franco, I'm sorry," she said as she ran back to kiss him.

Holding her arms, he was adamant. "Juliana, listen, please listen." "Yes." "Juliana, this is no good for both of us. It has to end."

At this joint she burst into tears, pounding the floor with her fists. "Juliana, listen," he pleaded. "It's no good."

But she wouldn't listen, drowning out his voice again and again with. "I know you love me Franco, I know it! I know it! I know it!"

He sighed, and not knowing what else to do, he went to bedroom, leaving her there to continue her battle with the floor. Within five minutes, she was at his side, caressing his body and whispering soft words of love. In disgust, he pushed her aside and came to the point. "Juliana, don't you understand? I don't want to see you anymore. Will you get out of here?"

"Why, Franco? Why?"

"Because I'm sick of you."

"I don't believe you."

His voice shot up a decibel in intensity.

"Listen you stinking whore. Get away from me. You're making me sick."

With that Juliana again did a complete about face, filling the air with a barrage of insults, intermingled with threats never to see him again. With arms flailing, legs stamping and breasts bobbing up and down she continued the onslaught for ten minutes, then dressed hurriedly and stormed from the apartment.

Angela and I just looked at each other and shrugged. What the hell. It had been a good show.

But the show wasn't over. Not by a long shot. The following morning, when I opened the front door, there was Juliana sleeping at the doorstep. She stood up and strode confidently into the apartment for another go round with the sleeping Frank.

The siege continued this way with Juliana making rounds twice a day for the first three days and only once a day for the last two.

Frank prayed that the trend would continue. Meanwhile, he got his hands on a 38 Smith and Wesson police special and packed it wherever he went. When we went out to eat together, he continually looked behind him and gazed at every passing car that slowed just a trifle. Turning a corner was a complicated maneuver, with Frank often using a corner sign or post as a shield, while he glanced up and down the street, before letting himself walk out into the open. "Aren't you overdoing it?"

"Not when it's my ass man. You never can be too cautious."

I just snickered and continued with my wry commentary. But the disease was contagious, and I found myself lagging at least three feet behind and to the side of him, whenever we went out together. The weeks continued to drag on, monotonously and slowly. Angela and I were as satisfied with our daily progress as anyone could be with accumulated knowledge not yet tested. Frank was also satisfied with his, having finally kept Julianna completely away for the past three weeks. I had to give him credit, for it took a tremendous amount of fortitude and steel to consistently keep up with the barrage of insults and the refusal of her favors, only to have her return again as if nothing happened. Fortunately he had not yet encountered that mysterious boyfriend, but was not yet ready to give up his gun. Studying was still out of the question.

As the days moved on, we increased the intensity of our study effort, spending half the day reviewing what we had already learned, and the other half attacking new material. The pace was agonizing, and the repetition nauseating, but we plodded on and on and on.

Over the past few months I didn't have much opportunity to see Christina. But I spoke to her twice a week and got up to see her once for a long weekend in Switzerland. She had returned home for spring vacation and come to Bologna ostensibly to stay at a friend's house for a week. We relived our short time together, by day dancing through the woods, laughing gaily at a picnic on the hillside, at night making hungry love as if there were no tomorrow. If anything, these long draughts of absence served only to reinforce our firm commitment to each other.

Christina had matured considerably during our relationship. She was still concerned, of course, with social opinion and her parent's good blessings, but mostly because of their practical value and not their moral overtones. She seemed to believe, quite sensibly, that what was best for us was right, as long as it didn't physically infringe on the right of others. That was healthy and that's the way it should have been.

She had tried, once again, to breech the topic of marriage with her parents, but it was all in vain. Her father again discarded the topic as sheer nonsense, and her mother echoed his opinion. After exams, I intended to go to Ferrara and meet the man face to face. Ifhe agreed to our marriage, fine. If he didn't, he could go fuck himself.

But Christina came up with a better suggestion. This year, her parents would permit her to travel abroad to any place that she wanted to go. She would of course choose the United States, and we could not only see a lot of each other, but get married there as well, even without parental consent. Then, on return, she could present me to them after the fact. At that point, the old man's threats and dictates would hold no water. He would have to like it or lump it.

Finally the day came for Angela and I to take our big exam, Anatomical Pathology. They said in Bologna that once past this exam, you were really on your way. Angela's mother was having minor surgery on the first day of the exam and she felt that she had to be in attendance. We agreed that I would take the exam with another partner on the first day since it was usually a little easier the earlier that you got in.

The morning of the test, my stomach felt too queasy to eat breakfast. I smoked cigarette after cigarette until it was time to leave. Then, like a confirmed killer taking his last walk down death row, I got in the car and drove steadily to the institute of Anatomical Pathology.

I checked in with the bidello who had me eleventh on his list. "You told me I'd be first or second," I challenged.

"There were some unexpected problems," he responded as if that would be enough of an explanation. His only problem was that ten other people gave him more money.

"Listen, a promise is a promise."

"I agree, but I am sorry. What you ask is impossible."

He turned to leave, but I gently caught his hand with mine, a 10,000 lire bill being the only thing that kept palm from touching palm. In the first year I would have hit him. But that wouldn't have solved my problem.

He turned and said. "Don't worry. I'll handle it."

"No later than third," I ordered.

"I said don't worry. I'll take care of it."

On the revamped list I was fifth. But that was a hell of a lot better than eleventh.

I paced and waited as the first two students passed through the door. Their exam was usually the longest and most detailed. I would have preferred going first, since my knowledge was extensive enough so that I could only benefit from a more extensive examination.

My mind continued to run from topic to topic, hoping and praying that under the pressure, the crystal clear picture I had imprinted on it would not become invisible. The tension built and my muscles wound tight. I studied so long and so hard and, with one bad answer, it could all be over.

The next pair went in as thoughts began to swim through my mind, racing faster and faster, warping all that had been so clear and orderly. I was frightened and desperate but unable to regain control. I paced faster, squeezing one sweaty palm against the other, hoping to release some of the tension, all to no avail.

The bidello called my name. I responded automatically and walked into the room taking the seat in front of the professor. My head pounded, but I fixed my eyes on his mouth and fought to concentrate on his words.

"Speak to me about anemia," he said.

I pulled and tugged internally to construct an opening sentence. Each word came forth with an immense effort behind it, but as I began to talk, that crystal clear picture began to reform in my mind. As I swept through the answer, nailing point after point, the printed lines in my mind read more and more easily, until I could almost read right from a book. My muscles relaxed and the pounding in my head began to dissipate. I knew that, on this question, I was home free. It seemed like forever until my partner answered his question and the professor came back to me. His tone was kind and conciliatory due to the excellence of my first response, but that could change in an instant. "Tell me Robbins. What do you know about ovarian tumors?"

For a second, my mind drew a blank and I started to panic. I forced myself to concentrate and the diagram in the text outlining ovarian tumors began to take shape in my head. The professor cut sharply into my focus and I lost part of the visual.

"Now Robbins. We don't have all day."

I struggled to regain my outline as I verbalized the initial generalities by reflex, rather than thought. Slowly, the outline took shape and, as I progressed through the answer, a wave of calm relief came over me as I realized that I was going to surmount this monumental hurdle.

Realizing that I knew the answer well, the professor stopped me in mid stream and directed a few short questions to my partner. Satisfied, he didn't ask any more questions. He complimented us for our preparation and asked us to wait outside for our grades. The bidello came out two minutes later with a big smile on his face. Looking first at my exam partner, he said. "For you twenty eight," and then turning his gaze toward me he added. "For you a perfect thirty."

After the exam, I went directly home and fell into bed, exhausted from the mental anguish of the past few hours and the sleepless night before. Angela came by to congratulate me and pump me for questions. She was to take the exam the following morning. She told me, though, that she would probably go in late, since the professor only saw five couples today and then, for his own reasons, decided to call it quits. Thank God I wasn't still number eleven. I wasn't sure that I could get up again for an exam of that magnitude. It was the biggest one I had taken and I was sure that just a little more delay would have thrown me into a permanent freeze. But as things went, I thawed just in time and that's the name of the game. They don't pay for missed field goals.

After Angela left, I went back to bed and slept through until late the following morning. I hadn't eaten anything for thirty-six hours and began to notice that I was hungry. It was a good feeling. I dressed hurriedly and went out with Frank to eat. He bombarded me with a myriad of questions, still mystified as to why I was progressing so well at school, while he was mired in a perpetual struggle. He never understood that, when you got right down to it, you had to push yourself to the limit for the last few weeks, so that you could cover and review the material as often as possible. That said, you had to be willing to compromise your knowledge in some areas, so that you could cover the massive amount of information demanded of you and, lastly, you had to be willing to walk in and take the exam, knowing that there were spots in which you were vulnerable and exposed. In a nutshell, you had to accept the risk of embarrassment. You had to accept the risk of failure.

With my belly full, I finally began to feel comfortable again. The sun was shining and the outlook was bright. Oh, how sweet the smell of success. There was no stopping me now.

Angela returned home exuberant, but just as hyper as I had been the day before. She had creamed the exam, and we went out that evening to celebrate, culminating the night with savage lovemaking. God was she good but, throughout, I could always maintain full control. With Christina there was something different, not definable, that always threw me over the brink and brought me to the point of sheer carefree pleasure, free at least for that fleeting moment, of all surrounding thoughts. Some call it love. That, I guessed, must be part of it.

The next day we rested and then back to the books we went. It took awhile to get our momentum going, but soon we were again in full swing. But we both carried about us a new aura of confidence. No exam could be more demanding, more exacting and more challenging than the one we had just passed. For this year at least, it was all anticlimactic. We were over the hurdle now and way out in the lead. The rest of the race was downhill.

The summer came and I returned home to the states. I hadn't seen my parents in over a year and a half. Like most reunions, it was charged with inadequate expressions of deeply rooted emotions. But just being together again felt good. I noticed also that my relationship with them had changed. They were more aware of my surging individuality and my acceptance of my responsibilities. They treated me accordingly, like an adult and not like a child still in need of continual guidance.

Christina arrived two weeks before me with a pair of girlfriends from school. They had planned an extensive three-month plus tour of the United States and their parents had consented, under the condition that the full itinerary was presented to them. The plan was for them to fly to San Francisco and then make their way back over a five-week stretch to New York. Hotel accommodations were prearranged, as were train and plane tickets.

They expected to arrive in Washington after two more weeks. The last two months could be spent in New York, where one of Christina's friend's father had gotten them jobs at the Italian embassy. They fully expected to earn enough to pay their expenses over that period of time.

I went down to Washington to meet them when they arrived. They were all excited and amazed at the vastness and breathtaking beauty that was America.

Her friends couldn't stop talking, but Christina and I just kept staring at each other while we paid just perfunctory attention to their discourse. After suffering their company for two hours, a proper enough time to account for courtesy, we took our leave. Christina had already prepared the girls on our planned elopement, and they were thrilled to be partners in the conspiracy. We intended to go to Maryland to get married and then, after a brief honeymoon of three days, she would rejoin her friends in New York.

I had already prepared my parents for the event. They were at first surprised, then skeptical, and then, once resigned to the fact that I was going to get married, intensely curious. I promised to present Christina to them as soon as we arrived in New York. That was enough to get their reluctant blessing.

The marriage was a simple affair and, when we left, with documents in hand, we certainly didn't feel any differently. Strange how the night before, our lovemaking was immoral, while after a few words, a kiss and a stamped and signed piece of paper, intercourse had taken on the character of a totally acceptable and necessary function.

We passed three ecstatic days on the Jersey shore, running in the sand, feeling the cool spray of the ocean waves sprinkle against our bodies, laying on the beach, absorbing the warming rays of the afternoon sun. Life was beautiful, if we could have only cut out the outside world forever.

All good things come to an end. The drive back to New York was nerve racking. I wanted so very much for my folks to like Christina and she was so afraid that they wouldn't. I shouldn't have worried. Her fresh young beauty won over my father. Her unpretentious, uncomplicated, respectful, and non-demanding nature won over my mother. My parents were happy and later my father would tease us that she didn't get the bargain, I did. For Christina it was wonderful to have them in her corner; one more obstacle was out of the way.

We thoroughly enjoyed the six weeks we had in New York together. But always, for Christina, there hung the dark gray cloud of deception, having eventually to return to Italy and face her parents. During the last week she was nervous, fidgety and often depressed, constantly in need of support and reassurance. "How am I going to tell them?" she'd ask.

"You won't, we will."

"Do you think that's best?"

"I know it is. Don't worry, I'll be there with you."

"You don't know my father."

"Don't worry, I will," I'd say trying to make light of it.

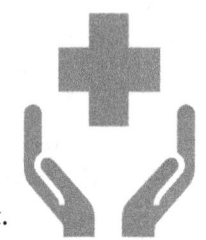

As the day to leave approached, things got worse. I felt helpless and tremendously resentful toward her folks for making her suffer through this conflict. Nevertheless, there was nothing I could do until it was all said and out in the open.

Christina flew home with her friends three days before my flight. On her part, the parting was filled with tears and premonitions of permanent separation, once her father found out. I reassured her and told her to do nothing until I got there; that her folks were powerless to annul the marriage and keep us apart. If they were unreasonable, they might be hostile at first, but eventually they would come around. I hoped and prayed against all odds that they would accept the situation with open arms. I could handle the conflict, but I wasn't sure that Christina wouldn't crack.

The first thing I did on arrival in Milan was to telephone her home. A servant answered and put her through. Her tone reflected longing and depression. "Dodd?"

It's me.

"It's so good to hear your voice. I miss you."

"Me to, when do…"

She interrupted me. "Hold it a second."

"I'm talking to a friend, mother."

I couldn't hear the other voice but I could imagine what she said.

"The American boy I told you about."

There was a long pause and then Christina said.

"No, I won't be long mother."

"Have you told them?" I cut in.

"Of course not," she whispered. "Listen, can you come up on Saturday. Both of them will be home then."

"Of course not," she whispered. "Listen, can you come up on Saturday. Both of them will be home then."

"What time?"
"In the morning. God how I miss you."

"I'll be there at ten. Good bye love." I blew her a kiss. "And don't worry, everything will be okay."

"I hope so."

"Don't worry. I love you."

"Me too," she said, but the "too" was mixed with tears.

The next two days were frustrating ones for me. My wife was unhappy and afraid and I was helpless to do anything for her. I paced the floor, twisted and tugged at my fingers and spent as much time as I could walking from one movie to another.

In between, I'd daydream of riding up to the palace aboard my white stallion, dressed in shining armor and challenging anyone to question my right to my legal property, my wife. Naturally, cowering in fear, no one objected, and we both rode off to live happily ever after.

Saturday came around and I drove up to Ferrara. Somehow, I sensed that my armor might have been made of paper. I found the entrance gate to her parent's estate and, as I rode up the winding dirt road, her massive home sprung into view. Awed, I felt my resolve weaken and my pulse quicken. The home was magnificent and palatial. I thought of her father, eight feet tall, leaning over the third floor balcony, yelling dictums down to his serfs in the valley.

By the time I arrived at the door, my pulse rate could have competed successfully with the Ferrari's Rpm's. Now, I knew what it was like to be on speed. If someone touched me, I'm sure I would have sprung out of my shoes and melted away.

A male servant answered the door and I asked for Christina. In that supercilious, noxious tone, reserved only for butlers, he directed me to the parlor to await her arrival. The room was simple but exquisite, filled with enough antiques to stock a small New York boutique. My mother would have given ten years of her life for a room like this.

Christina rushed in and the room lit up. She walked toward me slowly and we just touched fingers. This precious living beauty belonged to me and I knew then, as God was my witness, that she would be proud of me this day. I would not be intimidated and I would not let them intimidate her. "Are your folks here?'

"My mother is, my father should be home in an hour."

"Would you like me to meet her?"

"In a minute, first let's take a walk," she suggested. "Okay.

We went outside to the late September breeze and walked to the bottom of a small knoll on the other side of the house. "Listen Dodd," she said as she walked. "Maybe we'd better wait a little while, until my folks get to know you better."

I felt relieved; the pressure was off, but I knew, deep down, that I had to stand up for us today. I would not procrastinate and see her torment herself with this silence and deception any longer. "Why Christina?"

"I think it might be less of a blow."

"No Christina," I said firmly, love written all over my face, "I won't let you stay here and eat yourself apart any longer."

"Please Dodd," she pleaded, "let's give it a little time."

"Why?"

"Well because," she paused, trying to pick her words carefully. "Oh Christ, what's the use," she blurted. "My father, not only can't stand Americans, but he despises Jews. This will just crush him."

That just incensed me. I had never considered that aspect of the problem at all. But of course it was so obvious. The son of a bitch was a full colonel in the Italian army during the second world war, an ally of the Germans. His maternal grandmother had been from Bavaria, a true blooded Aryan. Naturally, he harbored resentment toward Americans and Jews, nourished of course by the hard post war years. "Listen Christina," I said, taking her hands in mine and squeezing tightly. "That's not going to change. It's not going to be easy, but we are going to face him, now."

"Oh God Dodd, I'm scared."

So was I, but I just said.

"Don't worry, I'm here." I hoped she didn't detect the hollow ring to those words.

We returned to the house, and sat down again in the parlor making small talk. The air was charged with tension and there was no way to avoid it. My collar felt tight and damp, but I dared not risk loosening it. I wanted everything possible going for me and sloppiness wasn't part of the image. Christina, after some prodding, went out to get her mother. When she entered the room, I stood and introduced myself politely in Italian. "It's a pleasure to meet you, signora," I said smiling.

"Thank you," she replied, "it's a pleasure to meet you too." Ferrara is not a very cosmopolitan province and it isn't everyday that we have an opportunity to get to know an American."

It struck me funny that she was using that old "country boy" routine. But it was equally obvious that she didn't hail from the swamps of South Georgia either; that despite residing in rural environs, she was a woman of background and education. She sat down on the sofa, and I followed to the opposite chair. "Would you like a cordial?"

"Not this early, thank you."

The short silence that followed was awkward. I decided to gamble.

"This is a beautiful home you have. I bet that each and every one of these antiques has a historical story of it's own."

She smiled, apparently happy to dig her tongue into that one. I had hit home with a winner. "That's almost quite true; the little table in front of you was purchased directly from the Kaiser by my husband's grandmother. Many statesmen have been served tea and cakes on it." She nodded her head to indicate the far side of the room. I turned around to look as she spoke. "That breakfront was made hundreds of years ago in Venice and was purchased by one of my husbands ancestors. It was the first one ever constructed with true glass panels and today I'd assume that it's priceless. I would go on and on, but I wouldn't want to bore you."

"No, please do, it's fascinating."

I could tell she wanted to, but she was too much the lady to risk boring me with family history. "No, tell me something about yourself. What made you decide to attend medical school in Italy?"

I had no intention of entering into a long detailed discussion of the rejection system in America. "I felt that a technical education of this nature at home might be terribly limiting; that I might evolve as a competent physician but a very narrow person. I thought Italy would afford me the opportunity to learn, not only to be a fine doctor, but to broaden my base as a person in language and social arts."

'Very good reasoning." she offered and then paused a moment to gather her thoughts. "Tell me, how did you meet Christina?"

"On a ski trail in Italy." I realized right away that that was a slip. This kind of mother didn't go for pickups. She looked harshly over at

Christina who just bowed her head. "It wasn't quite what you think. She had lost control and had been heading toward a tree. There wasn't much time for proper introductions."

"Oh," her mother said, quite relieved. "That is a bit different. I must say that we are grateful that you intruded. Christina is our baby you know."

"Oh mother," Christina said in a snotty tone. Apparently mother/daughter relationships were the same all over the world.

At that moment her father came into the parlor. I wasn't far wrong. His presence was overpowering. He was six foot two at least, well built with sharp, craggy features, topped by a slightly receding dark blond crew cut. Christina stood and walked over to greet him. "Good morning, daddy."

"Good morning, dear," he replied in a deep confident tone.

"Come over. I'd like you to meet someone."

I stood slowly to my full five feet eleven inches, as he seemed to notice me for the first time. His facial features were hard to read, but I guessed he enjoyed observing the uneasy feeling most people have on initial greeting. I wasn't going to give him the satisfaction. I stood until he addressed me. "Welcome to my home, Signor…"

"Robbins." I filled in the last name for him. "Thank you Signor Castrani for allowing me to visit." I replied as confidently as I could.

"Dottore," his wife corrected.

In Italy, all University graduates have the title of doctor. That was faux pas number two. "Excuse me, I meant Dottore." I said as we shook hands. His grip was firm and vice-like. I returned it pound for pound.

I didn't bother to tell him that I was also a university graduate with a major in psychology. In Italy, medicine was an undergraduate degree just like business or engineering and they had assumed that I didn't have my diploma as yet. Christina couldn't let it go. "Dodd is a Dottore too mother," Christina cut in.

"Will be you mean."

"No, is," she corrected. "In the United States you must have a University degree before attending medical school."

"Oh," her mother replied, quite abashed. "Then please excuse me."

"It's nothing. Please call me Dodd. Where I come from we don't place much emphasis on titles, just on the man." I wasn't sure that they knew how to take that one. But the room stunk with snobbery and I didn't much care.

"Tell me Dodd," her father said. "Robbins? Where are your ancestors from?"

"All over Europe sir. But I am a forth generation American on my father's side." I wasn't quite sure what he was getting at.

"You're Jewish, are you not?"

"Yes I am," I answered firmly. If this was going to be a problem, it was better to get it out into the open.

His face showed nothing as he continued to question me. "How did you happen to meet Christina?"

I didn't make the same mistake twice. "I was just telling your wife that I saved her from a rude introduction to a tree on a ski trail in Bondone. We were staying at the same hotel and we became friends."

"Have you skied there often? For me the place is too benign." "I'm not an expert yet. I still find it challenging." "Don't let him fool you father," Christina cut in. "He skis very well."

Her father looked up sharply. "I don't like false modesty. It is a trait of deception."

"There was no deception intended," I said firmly without a trace of apology. "I just see no reason to blow my own horn."

"Forgive me," he offered. "If you weren't so quick to jump to your defense, you would have seen that there was no personal implication intended."

I wasn't sure what he meant. But if he was playing with me, he was succeeding. I felt uneasy. I knew then that I would have to present them now with the fact that Christina and I were married. To delay would only serve to deceive them longer and to offer them more cards to lay on the table of self-righteousness.

"Dottore, if you have a few minutes, I would like to speak with you and your wife about a number of serious matters."

"A number," he said somewhat amused. "What could you and I have in common that is of a serious nature?"

Christina began to move uncomfortably in her chair. My collar felt as if it were choking me and my palms and armpits felt damp. "Sir, Christina and I have known each other for almost a year now. Much better than you may realize."

He sat on the edge of his chair and fixed his harsh gaze on mine. "Yes, get to the point."

I felt weak, and wished that someone would come and open up the windows to let in the fresh air. If only I could loosen my collar. "Then to get to the point sir," I said as confidently as possible, holding my eyes with great effort on his, "Christina and I are married."

His facial features froze and I set myself, ready for the explosion.

Christina's mother broke the unbearable silence with, "Oh my God! What are we going to do?"

Her father ignored me and looked directly at Christina. "What is he talking about?" Christina was frozen to her chair. "I said what is he talking about?"

With great effort, she brought the words up from her throat and whimpered. "We're married papa. I love him."

"You love him," he echoed, mimicking the higher pitch of her voice. Then louder, he added. "Who the hell is he?"

I was proud of her. With all the control she could muster to try and finally challenge the voice that dominated her life, she replied. "He is my husband."

He stood up from the chair, face afire, and leaned menacingly over her. "And where do you think you have the right to choose your husband?"

She began to respond, but his hand lashed out and caught her across the face. She looked up, eyes wide, fear written on her countenance. Momentarily I was transfixed to my seat.

"Antonio," her mother pleaded, "That won't solve."

"Father." Christina started, but his hand lashed out again and then the other one and I was up in a flash, throwing my body across his, ramming him into a long narrow table along the wall. Antique glassware shattered all around us as he grunted and fell to the floor. I stood back, not sure what to do.

He stood up slowly, smiling menacingly, condescendingly, holding in his hand a riding crop that was lying on the table. "I see that the "Jew" has finally learned to fight if he can sneak in the first blow. I must teach you a lesson."

I backed off, trying to reconstruct the pieces, hoping against all hope to prevent something he and I might long regret. "Listen, I don't want to fight you. But you have no right to hit my wife."

"No right," he said cynically, advancing toward me. "Since when do Jews have rights?"

The whip lashed out and struck me across the shoulder, sending a bolt of pain down my arm. I backed away flinching, arm up to protect my face.

"Antonio, stop it." his wife pleaded.

The whip flashed out again and caught me on the top of the head. "Animal," he shouted. "Crawl. Get down on your hands and knees and crawl."

"Father," Christina cried jumping to her feet. "You're crazy."

He turned and snapped the whip across her thigh and she screamed in pain. In that moment, I saw my opening and I sprang at him. The whip again caught me across the ear, sending a searing pain across my temple, but I was already airborne and in the next instant crashing him onto the floor.

Inside me, the combination of fear and hate finally exploded in a rage of fury. I smashed my fist hard into his nose sensing the sweet sensation of splintering bone. The other fist cracked into the depression made by the first, squashing the tip of his nose against the side of his face. I wanted to hurt, hurt so badly, this tormentor, this sadistic oppressor that had intimidated my wife for all of her years; that had supported sympathetically, and maybe even actively, the attempt to annihilate my people. I hit him again and again, drowning out his pleas for mercy with my fists until he eventually fell limp and listless to the poundings.

I seemed to hear the distant voice of Christina calling, pleading and then I felt fingers tearing at my arms. "Dodd, stop it! Stop it!" I tuned in and the words became louder and louder, more and more meaningful. Finally I realized how far I had gone and my arms fell limp at my sides. I stood slowly, bringing my hands up to my temples.

"God," I said, looking down at the blood pouring from his nose and pooling on the Persian rug. "Grab some ice and towels and call a Doctor.

Christina ran to get the ice and her mother jumped for the phone. They were both used to following orders and in times of stress their training didn't fail them. My heart thumped and thoughts of funerals and trials flashed through my mind. "My God I thought. What did I get myself into?" I took his pulse and my heart slowed. It was strong and bounding. Then I turned him on his side to prevent aspiration. Christina brought the towels and, after wiping his face, I filled a clean towel with ice and applied it with pressure to his nose. The bleeding began to slow and he started to moan and move his arms and legs lethargically.

By the time the doctor arrived, her father was sitting in a chair, his wife at his side holding the ice to his face. The hate charged atmosphere was almost unbearable. I despised him and I knew I always would and, because of his imprinted hatred of Jews and his humiliation tonight, I suspected the feeling would always be mutual.

Asking him if he wished for me to take him to the hospital would only be an empty offering. He had played his cards and left us no alternative but to leave. The next play would be up to him. "Come on Christina," I said while standing up. "Your father will be okay.

Let's go. "Can't we wait," she pleaded, obviously torn between her two loyalties. Looking at him I said.

"I don't think he wants us here."

Her father made no reply and I looked back at her.

"See. Let's go."

"Go to your room," he ordered with the same conviction, but certainly not the same resonance in his voice.

Christina looked at him and then at me. "Christina, go pack your things," I said.

Christina left and went upstairs. In ten minutes she came down with her bags, a picture of sorrow and torment, framed by the archway entrance to the parlor. "Christina," her father called in a last desperate effort, "come here."

She looked up at me and I nodded assent, She approached his chair and he looked at her. "Christina, if you leave this house now, you will never step foot in it again."

"Papa, no."

"Antonio," her mother pleaded, "you don't know what you're saying." But he turned away.

"Christina," I said firmly, but with intense feeling, "say goodbye to your mother and get into the car. I'll take your bags."

They both embraced, tightly, and emotionally, probably for the first time in their lives and then, with head bowed and tears in her eyes, she walked from the room not to look back again.

I started out the parlor door, but I felt I must make one last effort. I addressed her father sharply. "She is your daughter and she loves you, although why she does is a mystery to me. Don't do this to her and don't do this to yourself."

"She is nothing to me now," her father blurted out in defiance. "Married to a Jew, I spit on her."

My muscles tensed and I wanted so very much to strike out at him again, to challenge his manhood, to call him the scum of the earth and to grind him into oblivion. I had all I could do to control my hands, but I made up for it with the words that shot out of my mouth.

"Listen and listen carefully," I said, pointing a finger menacingly in his face. "If it were up to me, I would just beat the crap out of you. You may be rich and you may be well connected, but nobody could be more low class than you are. It's people like you, with all their power and all their prejudices that create hatred and violence in this world. It took the Jews two thousand years to learn how to deal with the likes of you. No more religion, no more turning the other cheek. In Israel, we answer manure like you with a shovel. You spit at us, we spit back. You kick us, we kick back. You shoot at us, we shoot back. There will be no more mass murder; no more odds of one hundred to one. And let's face it. One on one, you're just a coward like the rest of you Nazi's."

I paused to let that sink in and then continued. "Your daughter loves you, and I assume, to the extent that you are able, that you love her too. Don't disown her. Don't do that to her, and don't do that to yourself.

With that said, I turned on my heels and strode defiantly out of the house. It was all I could do not to mimic the Nazi goose step.

The next few months of our marriage were difficult ones for

Christina. She was plagued with constant guilt, as well as the frightening challenge of adapting herself to a new lifestyle. I'm sure that she had many moments of remorse.

I tried my best to bend like a sapling in order to make her life easier and free of disappointment. I filled the air with constant praise for every minor accomplishment she made. I listened attentively and sympathetically to all her problems, big and small, and stretched like a rubber band whenever a conflict of interest arose. Yet, a massive vacuum still existed, sucking her back into moments of depression, longing for a piece of what was once so very much a part of her life. My concern for her and my grating sense of helplessness distracted me from my attention toward school, complicating my own feelings of ineffectiveness. I soon realized that I could do little about her depression. Only time or reconciliation with her folks would solve that. I could, though, do lots about school and, for both of us now, it was essential that I get down to tacks and make progress. By working day and night, I finally caught up to Angela and we were off to the races again.

Through the spring and early summer, Christina was left to shift mostly for herself. But she understood the nature of my work and tried so very hard not to complain. She apparently knew that, within the sphere of my work, I would not bend, for if I were to allow myself the luxury of paying primary attention to her needs, then I would lay the seed for my own self-destruction.

For most of that long hot summer we didn't stay in Bologna. Instead, we traveled throughout Italy and then to France, Belgium and all the way to Copenhagen. But that hole in her life kept following her and we both soon realized that we would be just as well off suffering the heat of Bologna, given our preoccupation with internal matters.

The rest of the summer was of course unbearable and I began to think that there was no real hope for us. Her depression had infected me and we sat out the rest of the heat wave bored, frustrated, and sensing, without discussion, an impending doom to our relationship.

My last year of school began, and I was determined to learn my subjects well; to grab the tools that would permit me to function within an

American institution, once I returned home. Little did I know that the tools of learning were not for the taking and, no matter how hard I studied, I could not expect to develop as a clinician without seeing, touching, and suffering over patients.

Angela and I hit the books and Christina was again left alone. While last year I left reluctantly, this year I looked forward to any excuse that would get me out of the house. I did not let my problems at home interfere with my study. Somewhere, alone the line, I had developed that necessary ingredient of all successful men, the ability to catalogue concerns and set them aside for the problem at hand. I had learned to compartmentalize. When I studied, I set Christina out of my mind. I had to or I couldn't survive.

The days dragged and they turned into weeks. The tension built and the pace quickened. I was coming home to the final wire; all I had worked for, for five years, was to culminate in a rash of six exams through late May and June.

Never had the pressure been so great. For each subject I was well prepared, but still unable, no matter how hard I studied, to eliminate all areas of vulnerability. Since the exams were so subjective and so short, the statistical probability was such that there was a good chance I would fail one or two. It was like playing Russian Roulette. The first one, Pediatrics, I just managed to get through. But the pressure didn't let up as I returned that night to review for the Neurology exam in four days. I nailed that one and began the same night to push for Ob-gyn. That I knew fairly cold and I creamed it. My feet were almost cut out from under me in Legal Medicine. I pleaded and begged for a final question and the professor, after twice refusing, gave in. I responded fairly well, and he shook his head from side to side when he told me to leave. My stomach churned while I waited outside the room for the final dictum. Without feeling, I dug my nails into my thumbs, and waited for the final verdict. The bidello came out, for a moment his expression somber and my heart sunk. Then he smiled and held his thumb up. I looked. "Eighteen!" I just passed. The son of a bitch had let me hang for just a few seconds, but they were agonizing. He'd been though it before. Some practical joke.

The last two exams were the most difficult. I walked into Clinical Medicine in a semi-daze, but the first question was simple and I rode home from there. Two days later the last one came. It all boiled down to this, Clinical Surgery. I felt again just on the edge of losing control as I waited outside the professor's door. I fought with my body and my mind to a standoff and, when I was finally asked to come into the room, I still didn't know if I would function effectively. My mind swirled as I took my seat, waiting for my question, one question. That's all they asked. One question would mean passing or failing; one question that would give or deny me my degree; one question, that if answered well, would be my ticket home.

The professor looked pensively at a blank piece of paper before him. The seconds gnawed away with the rhythmic tap of his pencil as he pondered the question he was going to ask. "Speak to me about pheo-chromocytoma."

I fought to clear the haze and scraped the dark recesses of my brain for all the facts I knew about this rare tumor. All the while he stared impatiently at me, as I hastily constructed a mental outline for my answer. Then I began to speak, as my mind continued to scratch for more detail to place into my response.

As I spoke, he began to draw a picture and subconsciously my voice started to fade. He looked up suddenly and ordered. "Go on! Go on!" I snapped back to the problem and continued to talk, still fascinated by the fact that, all the while he was drawing a flower. I had heard rumors that he did this on every exam, carefully attempting to make all the pedals equal in size, attentively coloring each one in a bright pastel, until he was finished. When he was finished with the flower, the exam was over. If he asked you to leave before the last pedal was done, you failed.

I spoke slowly, knowing that I could not expound on that tumor for more than two to three minutes. He never lifted an eyebrow, as petal after petal was colored in with agonizing detail. I began to discuss treatment of this disease as he arrived at the last petal. I knew that it was surgical; Otherwise, he wouldn't have asked the question. But I knew nothing of the technique, and was unsure of the medical management, once the tumor was removed. We were going neck and neck. He slowly filled the last petal in, as I casually mentioned the fact that surgery must be performed. I paused and he looked up. "What do you do after the tumor is removed?'

I didn't understand the question. God, why couldn't he draw faster? "What, sir?"

"I thought I was quite clear," he said coldly. "What do you do after the tumor is removed?"

I still didn't understand the question. Close the incision, take a shit, and eat a ham sandwich? What the hell did he want? "You close the incision."

He started to laugh and shook his head at his colleagues, seemingly conveying the fact that I was a hopeless case. "Figliolo (son)," he offered, sweetly. Then his face turned beet red as he yelled. "What must you watch for when the tumor is removed."

I again started to shake involuntarily, but somehow my mind was insulated by a halo of peace. "How futile," I thought. What a son of a bitch. On what should be one of the most glorious days in my life, he was crapping all over me, not for lack of knowledge on my part, but for his own inability to communicate effectively. Of course I knew what I must look out for. "You must watch for a sudden drop in pressure, professor, and treat it accordingly."

"Va bane (very good)," he said sarcastically, falling gently back into his chair. "You may leave."

I stood up to go, my eye catching the paper on the table. The flower was done.

The rubber stamp of the official committee was anticlimactic. With my good grade in surgery marked in the book, I had completed the course of study and, two weeks after that last exam, I came before the board of medical dignitaries to take the oath, present my thesis and receive my degree in medicine and surgery. Somehow, despite the fact that I had overcome the insults, the abuses, and the obstacles over the last five years, I felt no great elation. I felt only a sense of relief, as the knots in my stomach began to release, and a growing curiosity about what would come next in my life. Unfortunately, it was July 29th, too late to begin the internship year on July 1st. We would take the next couple of weeks to sell our furniture, pack our belongings and start off for Genoa, Italy, where we would triumphantly set sail for the United States.

STRUGGLING THROUGH IT

Finally, the day arrived and we traveled to Atlanta to face our destiny. Since Marty and I had to be there on the same day, we were fortunate enough to have a sympathetic colleague who was willing to cover us for the day, but Marty had to fly back that night to take his regular call. Patients in a two-man practice expected one of their doctors to be there when they needed them.

I had one more problem to face than the other doctors did. When first approached by the FBI, I was asked if there were any records of what transpired. Since I thought that everything we were doing was legitimate, I had kept records. Now though, in the face of a sting, I decided to get rid of the records and deny their existence.

That decision came back to bite me in the face. Because I was limited in time, I had a young woman, who did the administrative management of the clinics, deal with the separation of medications for sale. She was told to exclude any narcotics or outdated medicines, confining herself to things like antibiotics and vaginal creams; things that could benefit people at significantly reduced prices. For that effort, she got to keep half the money. She kept the records and, before denying the existence of records to the FBI, I needed to make sure that our stories gelled and that they were airtight. She was an attractive and articulate woman, who made a wonderful impression on people, but she was not capable of expansive analytical overview. To make matters worse, she was hard headed and arrogant and the combination of arrogance and ignorance was deathly. I tried to review all possible scenarios with her, but she was as resistant to suggestion as she claimed to be loyal to me. She swore that she would say nothing about records, that she was capable of handling it and that she didn't need instruction from me.

On that basis I proceeded, adamantly denying the existence of records. Meanwhile, because she had received a few hundred dollars in monies, I decided to get her a lawyer for her own protection. I knew that they weren't after her, but I felt that I wanted her to have the best protection possible, just in case. I paid up front for her lawyer.

Unbeknownst to me, she told him about the records and, as her lawyer, he told her that, since her secretary had typed the records, she had better own up to their existence or she may end up with a number tattooed on her arm. She collapsed and told the FBI everything, but never told me.

There couldn't have been a worse scenario and this was exactly the type of thing that I wanted to avoid by discussing it with her beforehand. We had moved our office location in the past year and, in the process, a lot of information was lost. The records were kept in a file with three open sides. All she needed to do, when she spoke to the FBI, was to say that she thought that she gave me the file, but, if she did, she never looked inside it. Then she should have added that, since so much stuff was lost in the move, she didn't know if the records were still there. That could have been consistent with a statement from me that admitted that she gave me a file that was empty and that I suspected that the little information that we had was lost in the move. God, she could have at least told me what she was going to do, so that, at the worst, I would have had a chance to go back to the FBI and tell them that I had found some records. Instead, without thinking, she hung me

out to dry, and if she had planned an act of sabotage on her own, she couldn't have done it better.

As a result, I was charged with obstruction of justice and could expect a stiffer penalty than the other physicians caught in the sting. I don't think that she ever understood the full impact of what she had done and it was clear to me that she never understood the concept of team loyalty. It was also clear that, when the chips were down, she was only going to think of herself. She was never going to "win one for the Gipper."

After all was said and done, I tried very hard to be objective about her position. I realized that I had expected extraordinary things from an ordinary woman and, while she was totally self focused, she was certainly not malignant in her intent. Till that point, she had done her job well, and although she had certain limitations, she was entitled to the benefit of the doubt. With some reservation, I let her continue, ignoring my emotional distaste for the relationship.

Now, fifteen minutes away from facing the judge, I asked my lawyer. "What are you going to say about the obstruction of justice charge?"

"What are you talking about?" he asked, some what confused. I was startled. "What do you mean what am I talking about? You knew about it," I said accusingly.

"Jesus Christ, why didn't you remind me?" he shot back, recognition registering on his face.

"Because you said."

"Never mind," he cut in sharply. "I'll handle it! Just let me do the talking in there. You keep your mouth shut."

We entered the courtroom, and the judge asked Marcus for an explanation of the obstruction of justice charge. Marcus responded in an even, matter of fact, tone. "The doctor, your honor, was walking in the pit in his great room. He has a lovely home."

The judge interrupted. "I'm sure Mr. Dawson that we are all able to appreciate the doctor's ability to buy a lovely home, but in the interests of the court and it's packed calendar, could you please stick to the point."

"Sorry your honor," he offered, giving himself more time to think. "Anyway, last summer the doctor was pacing in his pit, reviewing the information and, feeling that he no longer had a need for it, he threw it in the fire."

The judge never missed a beat. "In July Mr. Dawson? In Florida? Can't you do better than that?"

From that point on, I knew that I was at the mercy of the court and that this judge was in no mood for mercy. His statement was terse and to the point.

"Outside of the obstruction of justice charge, it doesn't appear that you did anything so terrible. But I have a public that I need to account to and I cannot let you get away with toying with the federal government and thinking that you can lie to them at will. Therefore, I am sentencing you to a one-year jail sentence, all of which is suspended except for ten days, and a year of community service. After those ten days, I hope that you will be sober enough to stop thinking that you can play games with the law."

And so it was etched in stone. My lawyer "earned" his fee with that display, and I ended up with an experience that I shall never forget, humbling and frightening yes but, more importantly, an experience which would change my outlook on freedom and justice in the United States of America.

My people gave me a going away party, a gay affair, inclusive of a cake with a file hidden inside and a "soap on a rope." They made light of the upcoming event and I played along. Dean was a little apprehensive and kept asking me questions about jail. My answers were evasive and flippant in order to allay his fears. I was ready to go and, without much fanfare, Christina dropped me at the prison in McClenny, Florida, where I expected to serve out my ten days.

After processing, I was put in a cell with three other guys. Nobody said much and we each kept to ourselves. Everything was progressing smoothly when, on the second day, I was outside in the yard exercising. A guard came out and told me to come inside. I followed and he took me to two men that he said were federal marshals. They told me to stand straight and they proceeded to put chains on my ankles and handcuffs on my wrists. "What's going on," I asked, somewhat apprehensively.

One of the marshals looked at me sternly and answered. "Just shut up and do as we tell you."

I turned to the local guard for help but he just shrugged his shoulders and walked away. "Come with me," said the rude marshal, leading me by the upper arm.

I shuffled my feet quickly to keep up and asked. "Where are we going?"

"You're being transferred."

"Transferred? What do you mean transferred?" I asked hurriedly. I didn't understand what was happening and I was frightened that this was some kind of set up planned by Schmuckle and his cohorts to have me killed. I stopped in my tracts, fighting the pressure on my arm and asked again. "Where are we going? I have a right to know."

"The other marshal looked up and answered.

"We're transferring you to Savannah."

"Why?"

"They don't tell us why," said the first marshal.

"Now come on," he said, again pulling at my arm.

I hesitated a moment, but the other marshal chimed in with an explanation.

"This is a county facility and it's common for us to move short stay federal prisoners from one county jail to another, depending on the availability of space."

The explanation seemed plausible for the moment and I felt a little relieved, as I moved slowly toward the door. "What about my stuff?"

"You can get it when you get out. They'll hold it for you here." "Wait a minute! I'm not coming back this way."

"Then they'll mail it to you," said the first marshal, pushing my head down as I got into the back seat of the marshal's car.

I rode in silence for the first twenty minutes, taking in my surroundings, as the marshal's drove toward Savannah. Fear level diminished, but still somewhat on edge, I noticed that they were holding an easy conversation about fishing while they completely ignored me. "Excuse me," I cut in. "Can somebody tell me why we are doing this?"

The first marshal turned around and said somewhat perturbed. "Just be quiet back there."

I couldn't take this illiterate macho slob anymore, but discretion got the better part of valor and I spoke politely. "Listen, I'm not trying to make trouble. I just asked a simple civil question, and I'd like a simple civil answer."

"C'mon Bob," said the other marshal. "Let's give it to him and then maybe he will shut up."

Bob turned around and commented. "You're a short stay federal prisoner. We have contracts with the county jails to house our short stay prisoners, but when they run out of space, we have to move them."

"So you're telling me that it takes two marshals and an automobile for an entire day to deal with transferring me for six and a half more days." A ten day sentence was really eight and a half days since you count the first and last day, and you got one day of automatic credit for time served. I couldn't believe that they were wasting that much money on my transfer.

"That's correct," said Bob. "Now, will you let us get back to our discussion?"

"Certainly. I wouldn't want to strain your brain with anything it couldn't process."

"Whoa!" he said sarcastically. "What's that supposed to mean?"

"It means that you impress me as a low class, uneducated, rude slob. Otherwise I'd say your perfect." The moment that came out I wanted to take it back. My momentary rage made me forget my vulnerable position.

"Stop the car Jim! I need to show this guy some manners."

"Calm down Bob," said Jim. We have been pretty rude."

"Yeah," Bob said, looking menacingly back at me sitting behind the metal screen. I couldn't help but amuse myself with the thought that, from my perspective, Bob looked like he was in the cage.

"Maybe so," said Bob. "But you're the guy in the chains. Not me." Asking what he thought was a rhetorical question, he added. "So who do you think is low class and stupid?" Ignoring Bob, I spoke to Jim. "Do they do this kind of transferring often?"

"Hundreds every day," responded Jim, somewhat matter of factly.

"God," I said, shaking my head in disbelief. "That must cost the tax payers hundreds of thousands of dollars every day."

We drove for the next two hours with very little conversation. Bob sulked in relative silence, my intrusion having upset the sanctity of his fishing camp stories. With the scenery getting more and more familiar as we approached Savannah, I was starting to feel much more comfortable and cocky. "What do we do about lunch Jim," I asked.

"They'll give it to you at the county jail," he responded assuredly.

"Bullshit!" I countered with the jargon of the day. "It's after one and they are not going to give me anything to eat."

"So you'll lose a few pounds," Bob cut in. "Looking at you, it'll do you good."

"Listen, I know my rights. I'm entitled to food."

"Been in two days," commented Bob to Jim, "and he's already a jail house lawyer."

"How about it if I treated you guys to the most best meal in town?"

"No can do," replied Jim.

"Why not?"

"Because it's the rules. But I will stop at McDonald's for you. What do you want?"

"I'll take a quarter pounder with ketchup, onion and tomato. No mayonnaise. I repeat, I am allergic to mayonnaise. No mayonnaise!"

I was a little disappointed with their refusal to have a meal on the town. I figured that I could stay out of prison for at least a few hours that way. But I was hungry, and the hamburger would do. I really wasn't allergic to mayonnaise, but I hated it so much, I couldn't eat anything that had mayo on it.

Jim pulled up to the first McDonalds in Savannah and allowed me to get out of the car to stretch, while he went in to get the hamburgers. I enjoyed watching the people glare at me out of the corner of their eyes, the gazes mixed with curiosity and fear. A couple of times, I made some quick jerky moves and watched two of the nearby thrill seekers flinch. "Gotcha!" I called, until Bob told me to shut up.

Jim returned with the food and we got back in the car. "I'll give you yours at the prison," he announced and I smelled the food and watched them eat until we arrived at the county jail fifteen minutes later.

They gave me my bag, helped me out of the car, and rang the buzzer for entry. An outside door opened and they told me to step inside. The door shut, and an inside door opened up and I stepped through. A guard met Jim and me at the entrance. "What do you have in your hand?" he inquired.

"Lunch."

"You can't bring that in here," he said anxiously.

"Well I need to eat. I didn't have any lunch."

"You'll have to throw it out. You'll get dinner by five thirty."

"I'm a diabetic, and if I don't eat now, I could go into shock."

"You can't make an exception," asked Jim.

The guard thought for a second and then said, "Sorry, you're just going to have to take him outside to eat."

I stepped back behind the inside door and he closed it. Then the outside door opened up and I walked outside with Jim at my side.

"What's happening," asked Bob, a confused look on his face.

"He has to eat it out here," Jim replied, and then, turning toward me, he said.

The guard thought for a second and then said, "Sorry, you're just going to have to take him outside to eat."

I stepped back behind the inside door and he closed it. Then the outside door opened up and I walked outside with Jim at my side.

"What's happening," asked Bob, a confused look on his face.

"He has to eat it out here," Jim replied, and then, turning toward me, he said.

"All right," sighed Jim, and he unlocked the cuffs, leaving the leg chains on.

I opened the package and took one bite of the quarter pounder that was dripping in mayonnaise. "God," I shouted. 'I told you no mayonnaise."

"I'm getting tired of you," said Bob, menacingly approaching me.

"God, I feel dizzy." I put my hands on the side of the car and slowly slid down to the ground, dropping the inedible hamburger to the ground. I rolled to my back and started to moan.

"What's this bullshit now?" asked Bob, somewhat bewildered.

"He said he was allergic," answered Jim as he came over and knelt by my side. "You OK?"

I acted sort of out of it, although I was perfectly fine. "I told you, no mayonnaise," I mumbled, and then acted as if I went unconscious.

Jim called to me, louder and louder, almost as if the intensity of his voice would bring me awake. He slapped me sharply on each side of the face, thinking that that would bring back, but I suffered the pain and let them agonize over this dilemma. "Jesus," Bob said, leaning over Jim's shoulder. "What are we going to do?"

Jim ignored him and started to give me mouth to mouth. That was enough for me and I coughed and shook a couple of times before opening up my eyes, just like I was regaining consciousness.

"You OK?" he asked, somewhat relieved.

"Jesus!" I said. "I told you guys that I was allergic to mayonnaise."

"I told them no mayo," Jim stated adamantly.

"That's not enough," I responded, shaking my head in disgust.

"You got to tell them three times, and then check."

"You feeling better?" Jim queried, probably more concerned for himself than he was for me.

"I don't know? Just give me a few minutes."

"He looks OK to me," Bob cut in, still leaning over Jim's

Shoulder. Jim turned to look up.

"Will you just wait a minute, dammit. Just hold your horses."

Turning back to me, he said.

"Do you think that you can sit up."

"I think so," I said hesitatingly. "But I still need lunch."

"God," wined Bob putting his left palm to his head and turning around. "What is it with this guy."

"You wait here," Jim said to Bob. "I'm going to get him a sandwich."

"Hey, don't leave me here with him," I pleaded. This guy's a Neanderthal."

"What did you call me?" chimed in Bob, malice on his mind.

"A Neanderthal."

"What's that?" he asked Jim.

"Never mind," he said, shaking his head. "Let's get him up and take him in the car." Shaking his head, he added. "I don't know which one of you I wouldn't trust, but one things for sure. I'm not going to leave either one of you alone with the other."

Jim helped get me to my feet and into the back seat of the car. Bob sulked on his way to the front seat. You could see that he was mad and that he'd have liked a chance to get at me with no one looking. But, the bottom line was that they were taking me to lunch, albeit a late one.

All good things must come to an end and, after sating myself with a "whopper," ala Burger King, I was returned to the prison. I said goodbye to my newfound friends, Jim and Bob, and entered the heavy steel door. It closed behind me and, when the inside door opened, I was taken in for processing. This was a maximum-security prison and, after being made to take off all my clothes, I was searched from top to bottom, inside and out. I was then assigned a pod, a large cell that housed twelve prisoners. The cell was fronted by a cage that, just like the front door, had a double entry system so that the guards would never have to be exposed to an entire cell full of prisoners while another one was being removed from or brought into the cell.

I found a cot between two black prisoners and then quickly got in line when they called us for canteen. Apparently, we were allowed to buy twenty dollars worth of goodies, once a week. I bought all I could and came back to the cell and dumped the stuff on my cot. I caught the furtive look of both my black neighbors and figured this was "do or die" time.

"You guys look pretty hungry and I've got more than I can handle here. Pick a couple of things if you want them," I offered.

Both of them looked hesitantly at me and then cautiously approached the cot, leaned over, chose two items each and stepped back to their respective cots. Jerome muttered thanks, but Ben said nothing. He just looked at me suspiciously. I sat down on the cot and put my stuff away on my shelf. After a minute of silence, I introduced myself and said simply to Jerome. "You been here long?"

"Too long. Nine months," he mumbled. "How about you Ben?"

"A while," he said, irritation in his voice as if he was disturbed by the intrusion.

I left it alone. I felt like I was trying to negotiate a safe pathway over shards of glass. I turned back to Jerome and made some small talk as Ben sulked restlessly on his bed. Talk was awkward, until we accidentally found a common interest in sports and, then, from that point on, I got to know Jerome pretty well.

He was the class of the pod. He was six feet four inches tall with a lanky, but strong, build. He grew up in Savannah in a black ghetto. He spoke softly and mumbled his words, obvious testimony to his lack of education and his distrust of his communication skills. But his carriage was awesome. Like a magnificent thoroughbred, he exuded strength in his easy gait. When he turned on a TV station, nobody dared to change it. But, if someone else was watching, he never changed the channel. When dinner came, he slowly rose and got into line, never rushing to get in front of anybody, but never challenged for the place he held. Every other day we were allowed on the basketball court, where he excelled with simple explosive moves. Never did he give a cheap shot; never did he back off from a power move in the post. He had the make up of a leader and, in a different time, in a different place, he would have been a person of significant impact.

We were two people from different backgrounds, with different outlooks, and with different futures, fleetingly crossing each other's life pathway, momentarily sharing common fears and obstacles. Somehow, in that brief time, we were able to surmount the barriers of diverse cultural origins and exposure. Somehow we bonded, and as unlikely as it would seem, we were able to open our hearts to each other.

Jerome disclosed to me that he thought that he was being charged with murder. He said that he worked for a man in construction who supplied him with weed. The man had a reputation for cruelty and was suspected of having killed two other people. His boss came to Jerome's house and they went out to the wood shed to discuss the fact that Jerome owed him money. Jerome said that he didn't have any and the boss pulled a gun and, in a rage, said he was going to kill him. Jerome said that he grabbed an ice pick off the workbench, and lunged at his boss, grabbing his arm with the gun, as he stabbed him with the ice pick. The man fell dead at his feet and Jerome fled. Two days later, a fire started in the woodshed and they found the body. Jerome was arrested and he had been in jail since. To his knowledge, he had not been formally charged and he had no trial date set. He just sat there in the pod awaiting his fate, with no knowledge of habeas corpus or any of his other rights.

He had an attorney by the name of Clay, Henry Clay, just like the famous debater of the nineteenth century. Jerome was paying him one hundred and fifty dollars a month and, since his common law wife had left him, was having trouble raising the money for each payment. In fact, at present, he was two payments behind.

I called the attorney to offer to make up the last two payments, hoping to spur him into action, but as our conversation continued, it became perfectly clear to me that Clay wasn't going to do anything at all.

In fact, for one hundred and fifty dollars a month, he couldn't afford to do anything. When confronted with the facts, he admitted that he was going to be ineffective at best, unless I wanted to be the deep pocket for Jerome to the tune of sixty thousand dollars. I declined, and we agreed that Jerome's best interest lay with a public defender who was over worked and under skilled.

I contacted the public defender and spurred him into action. Weeks later, when I was already back home, safe and comfortable in my own bed, Jerome called and told me that the public defender thought that he could get him a plea bargain for manslaughter with a sentence recommendation of five to seven years. He would probably have to serve two to three years of the five to seven and would be given credit for double his time in the countyjail. Ifhe was lucky, he could be out in a few months.

Before I advised him to take the deal, I wanted to ask the public defender a few questions. After all, this would be Jerome's second felony and acceptance of the plea bargain would put him in a potentially vulnerable position. His first one was for drug possession and, god forbid he made another mistake or got caught in another situation, he could be put away for life.

I asked the public defender why he wouldn't take this case to trial, given the fact that Jerome was the only witness, and the dead man had a terrible reputation. He was known to carry a gun, and was found in Jerome's woodshed with a gun next to his hand with his own fingerprints on it. How, I wanted to know, could Jerome lose.

His answer was clear as he spoke into the phone. "Jerome will be tried in Savannah," he said, "by an all white jury." He continued with a strong sense of conviction.

"He is six four and dark black with deeply recessed eyes. In the witness box, he will bow his head, avoid the gaze of the jurors and mumble his answers incoherently, all body signs of someone not telling the truth."

"But given his background, all those responses have plausible explanations," I rebutted.

"To you and me yes, but probably not to an all white southern jury ready to lynch another nigger. Besides, whatever happened, probably happened over drug money and therefore it's murder."

"Wait a minute," I interrupted. "They won't know that it happened over drug money and Jerome will testify that he was just being asked to pay back a loan."

"I'm telling you, it won't matter. They will find him guilty. Listen, I don't mean to cut you short, but what is your interest in this matter anyway."

"My interest is that I have been exposed to a good man who is being treated unjustly because he is ignorant and poor. It is a real eye opener for me and, within limits, I want to try and help out."

"My best advice to you doctor would be to stay out of it. Jerome is as comfortable in jail as he is out of it. In fact, outside, he has to work for a living. Inside, he gets three squares, a comfortable bed, a dry roof, and recreational facilities. He can do his time easily standing on his head."

"So, you would recommend the plea bargain?"

"Absolutely! Better for him and better for me. It's a no brainer."

I thanked him for his time and returned a call to Jerome. Years ago, I would have told him to stand up and fight, but that was before I knew how decadent and contaminated the judicial system was. Now I wasn't so sure and I knew that it wasn't my right to play with his life. I told him everything that the public defender had said and that he would have to make his own decision. He thanked me for interceding on his behalf and for the twenty-five dollars a month that I was sending him for canteen money and got off the phone.

One month later, after accepting the plea bargain, he was sentenced to fifteen years, not five to seven, in prison. He would have to serve at least six of those years minus his credit of almost two years of county jail time. At best, he would be out in four and a half years.

After sentencing, I was surprised at how even keeled he was when I spoke to him on the phone. It was almost as if he had been numbed by the system; almost as if he had expected worse and was happy to settle for what he got. Maybe the public defender was right. For Jerome, jail just wasn't that bad because, in life out on the streets, he never really had a chance. The cards were just too heavily stacked against him and maybe he knew that. Maybe he knew that three squares and a dry roof was just about all the good that he could expect out of life.

I couldn't help but think, though, that if he had been O.J. Simpson, he would have been acquitted in a trial and lauded for his courage in standing up to the criminal element. After all, it was his word against a dead man's and his version appeared to be not only plausible, but also believable. So much for justice and reasonable doubt.

On my third night in Savannah, after midnight, a new prisoner was introduced into the pod. He was a lithe little guy that looked like a weasel. Once in the pod, he furtively perused his surroundings, and chose a cot diagonally opposite mine. After looking around, he took out a cigarette and lit it with a lighter. For three days, I had been suffering from nighttime, nicotine withdrawal, because they did not allow lighters or matches in the cell. We had to use a wall heater that was turned off at the stroke of midnight. Feeling like a cigarette, I sat up on my cot, took out a smoke, leaned over and asked him for a light. Without a word, he again sneaked a look around and, while cupping the lighter, leaned over and lit my cigarette. In the darkness, the flame from the lighter exaggerated the outline of his wry smile. His white teeth shone brightly in front of me and etched into the right front incisor was a gold swastika. For a second, I was startled, but I quickly forced myself to recover and asked matter of factly. "How did you get that lighter past the guards?"

"Easy man," he replied. I just shoved it up my ass and, when that goddamn gook doctor came to check my ass hole, I screamed like a banshee." He took a drag on the cigarette and continued. "You know these sons of a bitches. They don't want to get sued. So he had the guards put me in a room and told me to stay there till I shit in a pan."

"So what happened to the lighter?"

"It came out and I shoved it back up my ass. These guards are so fucking stupid."

Despite the swastika, the silent boredom of the night, along with the proximity of our cots, lent itself to a natural, interesting and long conversation with a man that would normally make me shiver in my shorts in everyday life. Once he got passed his pseudo machoism, I was amazed with his ability to tell a story, with the way that he postured himself toward the prison system and with his capacity to reason intelligently, even if every third word out of his mouth was "fuck."

"What are you in for?" I asked during the course of our conversation.

"I don't know. They say a man came to repossess my car and I put a shot gun on him and made him lay down and beg for his life for eight hours. I got six witnesses that say I didn't do it."

"You sure seem to know the ropes."

"I ought to," he said emphatically. I've been in and out of prisons all my life. They sent me up for arson the first time for fifteen years but when it was all said and done, I only had to serve five. Shit, if the fuckers would only stick to their sentences, I never would have done it in the first place. I knew I'd get out in five ifI got caught and it was worth the chance for a fucking thirty thousand. Now it's a bitch.

Every time there's a fire, I'm a fucking suspect and they arrest me. It's impossible to keep a fucking job. I've broken my ass to become an electrician and every time I latch on to something good, the cops fuck it up. What a fucking system!"

"Sounds like they fucked you good," I echoed and layed back down on my cot. I didn't want to ask if he was still a Nazi.

The following morning I walked over to another white inmate, Jerimiah Turner, that I had befriended and inadvertantly told that I was Jewish. I told him about the situation and that I didn't need a confrontation. I told him to be careful about what he said. He assured me that he would take all precaution and that I need not worry.

At dinner, that inmate joined me at my table and, much to my discomfort, so did the Nazi. They served sausage and Jerimiah turned to me, not thinking, and said.

"Wanta give me that sausage of yours? You're not supposed to eat them."

The Nazi looked up suspiciously and I responded quickly, without hesitation.

"Just cause I'm a little stocky doesn't mean that I have to watch my cholesterol all the time. You worry about what you eat and I'll worry about me."

Jerimiah said no more, and when we were alone, I read him the riot act telling him in no uncertain terms that if he let out that I was Jewish, I would personally break every bone in his body. Needless to say, he apologized profusely. He was really a nice guy. He just forgot and really felt badly about it, but this was survival of the fittist. To guarantee his silence, I needed him to be afraid so that he would think about it.

On my sixth day, the sheriff came to the pod and called to Jerimiah. "Jerimiah, the judge has reduced your bail to fifty dollars."

"Tell the judge that I already paid my bail and that I'm not paying another goddamn cent."

"Jerimiah," the sheriff pleaded. "It's only fifty bucks. I got half a mind to pay it myself."

Jerimiah got mad. "You can't do that sheriff," he said, pointing a shaking finger at the law officer. "I paid my bail and you can tell that fucking judge that I've been here for five months and I"ll stay another year if I have to, but I'm not paying any more bail."

Apparantly, the bail bondsman went broke after Jerimiah paid his bail and so the judge had to ask for more. Jerimiah just didn't understand the system and thought that the judge was trying to rip him off for more money and, therefore, chose to stay in jail instead. The judge kept lowering the bail, but Jerimiah was going to teach him a lesson. It cost them three hundred bucks a week to keep him there and he was going to make them pay. It wasn't the fifty bucks. It was a matter of principle. When I got out, I spoke to Jerome a week later and he told me that Jerimiah got into a fight with Ben over a bar of soap. Jerimiah almost died of a cerebral hemorrage and ended up with a broken left arm and a dislocated left hip. Jerimiah was in jail for a DUI and with a little common sense, he could have avoided all this trouble and turmoil. So much for principle.

Finally, the day came for me to leave. My lawyer had forgotten to follow up on the paper work but, fortunately, my father had forseen the possibility and made sure that everything was in order for my release. At six in the morning they came to get me and five minutes later I was out on the street, dirty and disheveled, but free, oh so free. Christina greeted me with a big hug and my father followed suit. Soon we were in the car, driving away. The events of the last ten days seemed so incongruous, almost like a bad dream, fading away as the automobile ticked off a mile a minute of separation between me and the maximum security prison. Soon, I hoped, it would seem like nothing happened.

But something did happen. In jail, the minutes had seemed like hours and the hours like days. Fear was always there. You were always edgy and your pulse always ran just a little faster. You never knew when someone would explode with a violent reaction. You slept, almost with one eye opened and you never turned your back on anyone. In all my life, I had never felt so abandoned and alone. I had been in the jungle. I had to stay alive and I did. I learned that it was every man for himself and that there really weren't rules that were fair. The strong dominated and the weak were brutalized. Somehow, for a short time, I was able to portray an image of a guy not to be messed with. It was an illussion and, if I had been there longer, I would have been tested and they would have seen through the facade. In the end, I may have been violated and abused, and I would have had no recourse. I was determined never to be there again. Unlike most Americans, I was acutely aware that there were situations out of my control that could determine my fate. There were people in power, behind the scenes, weaving their web to accomplish their own personal agenda, without regard to casualties that they left on the way. Never again would I be able to go to bed feeling that my well being was fostered, let alone protected, by government. Never again would I trust the powers that be to deliver fairness and justice to all.

As the years wore on, my life became more harried and fragmented. The boys were growing rapidly and I stole as many moments as I could in order to share their experiences. Whenever I could, sleep deprived or not, I coached their teams to try and give them as much support as possible. I'd teach and prep them as well as I could, but they both knew that they would play only if they were good enough. It was hard, in the beginning, watching them ride the bench but, as time wore on, they both developed their skills to a point where they made significant contributions to whatever team that they were playing on. I tried to set a good example and build in them a foundation of good character and, to that extent, I succeded miraculously.

My marriage was another story. Christina and I had grown apart. She resented the fact that I had little time for her and, as the years wore on, she spent more and more time in Italy with her sisters and her parents. The boys were often gone all summer and, for that matter, Christmas and Easter vacations too. When she was home, she busied herself with the mundane affairs of running a household in as perfunctory a manner as possible. She handled me with as much distanced politeness as possible and usually responded to my infrequent advances with abject apathy. Obviously, she was in pain, but I could never get the communication process going without it ending up in a diatribe of accusations against me. IfI were a psychiatrist, I might have been more patient, but it was hard to be an empathetic listener while dodging bullets. As a result, things continued to spiral downward, and I had to find my solace and comfort elsewhere.

The medical community was the obvious place, for I had time for little else. Within the walls of the hospital, there were five to ten nurses to every physician, all of whom could identify and empathize with the hardships and struggles that the doctor had to face on a daily basis. After getting through with a difficult delivery or surgery, it was easy to go out for a drink or two together and hash over the enerving events that, with the outcome in doubt, finally culminated victoriously. The romanticism of that moment often carried through to the wee hours of the morning, resulting in exquisite ecstasy for all. As a result, as time went by, I suffered Christina's rejections less and less.

Just like a good football team, every practice needs a good man in the pits. I found one in nineteen eighty one and brought him into the practice as our third partner. Carl Stern was a nice and decent man. He had the reputation of being a tireless worker who could keep going as long as you had patients for him to see. It seemed to be just what we needed. Academically he was very knowledgeable, but surgically, as we found out in time, he was very timid and fearful.

We had twenty five practicing OBGYN's at my hospital. Although Carl's credentials were impeccable, after watching him deal with surgery and emergencies, I would have to rank him as number twenty one or twenty two in those categories. Since he had a wonderful academic base, I thought that with proper coaching, he could develop into a decent overall practitioner.

Unfortunately, he was also a duck. He walked like a duck, and talked like a duck and they tell me that when you look like one and act like one, you are one. His underbelly was constantly exposed and vulnerable.

In my hospital, their were a group of practitioners that hovered around my practice like vultures, ready to spring at the first sign of weakness. They resented my backgound, my religion, my pro-choice stance and my economic and professional success. They were out to get me, and they felt that Carl afforded them that chance.

I was just too difficult to take on. I had trained at this hospital and knew all it's ins and outs. I followed the rules and dotted all my "I's" and crossed all my "T's." I arrived earlier than anyone else when I had someone in labor, and made sure that all my charts were as complete as possible. I practiced consevatively and got consults whenever in doubt. For the most part, I just didn't take any chances and leave myself exposed.

For the most part, many of them liked Marty. He was very respectful of their seniority and, for the most part, tried to emulate my conservative style of practice. He was never confrontational and did his share of ass kissing when he had to. They weren't sure that they would get the support that they needed if they went after him alone. Besides, they really didn't want to get him in the first place. They wanted me.

On the other hand, Carl, like many doctors, was sloppy and inattentive to detail. Despite multiple warnings from me, he refused to follow regimented protocols of behavior that would help protect him from attack. He opened the door, and they jumped on him like "ugly on an ape." They accused Carl of negligent and substandard practice and, true to form, without eye contact, he mumbled some incoherent explanation for his actions.

Medicine is an art, and there are a lot of ways to skin a cat. With the right posture, you can often explain away a questionable action, and with the wrong posture, you can often look negligent in the face of proper performance.

Once a suggestion for a disciplinary action starts, it will pick up momentum and start to steamroll if left unchecked. Carl didn't have the insight to identify or the capacity to control the danger. It was only a matter of time before Carl was asked to appear before the medical council to explain his actions and defend his right to practice medicine. He was devastated and overwealmed. He didn't understand why he was being attacked and he didn't have the fortitude or strenth of character to stand up defiantly in front of this lynching committee and defend himself. He hired an attorney to represent him and asked me to be present to help explain his actions. I agreed and we went before the counsel on a very warm evening in June. The problem was that they decided not to let his lawyer into the meeting. The same rule did not apply to the hospital's attorney. By default, I became Carl's attorney.

As we entered, the hall was abuzz with conversation. We were directed to two seats at one of the four long tables that made up the sides of a square. The scene was intimidating as I looked out at the thirty men about to take their seats. Most of them were strong willed individuals who had been figures of authority during my years of residency and, now, I was going to have to stand up to them and defend a man that they were trying to destroy. The whole atmosphere was charged with electricity as the chairman, Dr. Larry Mckay, my old department head, called the meeting to order. He got right to the point.

"Tonight, the first matter on the agenda will be Dr. Stern's privlidges to practice surgery at City Medical Center. So that Dr. Stern can be treated fairly, he has been asked to be here tonight with his representative, Dr. Robbins, in order to have the opportunity to defend himself against the assusations about to be presented." McKay paused and looked over toward me with a disdainful glare, almost as if to say. "What are you bothering for?" He did say. "We will take the charges one at a time." McKay paused to get everybody's attention and then delivered the first accusation. "Dr. Stern has been accused of keeping sloppy medical records, despite the fact that he has been warned repetitively to keep his records neat and up to date. Can you explain that Dr. Stern."

Carl cleared his throat and mumbled an answer. "Um, I thought that I was catching up." He had a little tic and kept looking downward instead of up at the counsel.

"Is that your explanation Dr. Stern?"

Carl started to answer with a yes, but I had to cut in. "Excuse me Dr. McKay, but we need to put that charge into context."

"What do you mean by that," he said disdainfully.

"I mean that Dr. Stern offers no excuses for the fact that he has eleven incomplete charts. He is absolutely sorry that he has not brought them up to date, but I am sure that this counsel, particularly, has every reason to be empathetic with regard to that failure.

"And why is that?" McKay cut in.

He had opened the door, as I had hoped he would, and I jumped right in with both feet. "Because all of you have many more incomplete charts than Dr. Stern. Dr. Phillips has eighteen incomplete charts, and Dr. Miller over there has thirty one." I continued around the room with the number of incomplete charts belonging to every man in the room who was sitting in judgement of Carl. Finally, I got to the name of the man that I and everybody else considered "the best surgeon they ever saw," Dr. George Proel. He broke a lot of hospital rules, but boy could he operate, and he brought at least twenty surgical cases to the hospital each week. They weren't about to oust him on a technicality because he was just too important as a revenue source. So I offered the "coup de grace." "In fact," I said in an apologetic tone, with an expression showing complete understanding. "Dr. Proel has one hundred and forty one incomplete charts."

"Dr. Proel is not on trial here," Dr. Miller offered loudly with conviction. "This process concerns Dr. Stern only."

"But how can you judge," I retorted, "if you can't compare Dr. Stern's activities to the standards of the institution?"

"Dr. Miller is correct," cut in Dr. McKay. "This proceding concerns itself with Dr. Stern. He has been warned repetitively and has taken no action to correct the situation."

"He just followed your example," I added, but the statement seemed to fall on deaf ears. It was clear that this was a lynching committe and that they were going to have their show.

Ignoring me, McKay added. "Is there any more comment on this issue before we go on to the next." McKay looked around the room for comments but they were all done on this issue. After an appropriate pause, he brought up the second complaint. "Dr. Stern has been accused of operating on patients without waiting for all the results on pre-operative laboratory and radiology tests." Looking at Carl, he gave tacit approval for a response, but I again jumped in to defend him.

"Can you please give us examples?"

"Certainly," McKay chimed in with a supercilious tone. "He operated on a Janet Smite without a chest X-ray report on her chart."

"How do you know that he didn't have an outpatient report."

"We don't, but, as you know, the hospital standards require a pre-operative chest x-ray report on the chart on all paitents scheduled for major surgery."

He sat back in his chair, comfortable with his position, but I was perched for the attack. I had prepared the defense for his attorney, and now that I was representing him, I was determined to use all of the ammunition at my disposal. I had worked in the bowels of this hospital for three and a half years as a resident, and I knew it's heart, it's pulse and it's soul. I knew where to find all the information that I was armed with and I was going to use it to make fools of this august, but oh so pompous, body. They were used to giving me orders, but that era was over. It was time that they stood up and took stock of their hypocrical posture and pompous sense of self-rightiousness. "Dr. Thayer," I asked, directing my attention to the Chief of Radiology. "How often does surgery occur in this hospital while the preoperative chest x-ray report is still waiting to be dictated in your office?"

Thayer shifted in his seat and turned to answer. "I don't know exactly. Very infrequently, if at all, I would expect."

I pulled some papers from my pile as I formulated my response. "I must beg to differ with you. It is common practice in this hospital for surgery to start at eight o'clock in the morning. For most patients, films are taken after five o'clock on the day of admission and they are operated on the next day. Since the radiology physicians leave at five sharp and don't begin again until eight the next morning, how do you suppose all the results get on the charts before surgery?"

Thayer turned beat red. "Now listen here young man. If you are trying to impugne my department, you are not doing a very good job of it."

"I'm only addressing the facts Dr. Thayer. It is common practice for the pre-operative x-ray report to be delivered to the chart well after the surgery is done. In fact, I have here a copy of the radiology report on the last fifty people to have surgery at eight o'clock in the morning in this hospital. According to the date and time of dictation, as noted on the reports, only seven of these people had pre-operative x-ray reports on their charts before the surgery took place. It is embarrasing to say that one of those patients belonged to my partner, Dr. Stern and I think that he should be properly reprimanded. In fact Dr. McKay, while we bring out the paddle for Dr. Stern we might as well use it on you and seven other members in this room. You had three patients in this group without a pre-operative x-ray report on the chart and your three partners had six more. Dr. Proel had four, probably because he does surgery at eight AM four days a week in this hospital, and Dr. Jones had three. The other five physicians in the room had a total of nine, for a grand total of twenty two. Of the forty three cases, members of this judgement committee have committed over half the abuses."

"How did you get this information?" McKay asked insolently.

"Not important," I snapped in a tone as equally distasteful as his. "What does matter is that we have a standard in this hospital that Dr. Stern has tried to adhere to and, based on the evidence, he exceeds those standards.

"We are not going to let this go Robbins. I want to know how you got this information."

"Why?"

"Because this is a breech of patient confidentiality and it has to be stopped."

"Maybe Dr. McKay. What really has to be stopped is physician coverup and patient confidentiality is a convenient theme to hide behind to keep a lot of information from the public."

McKay squirmed in his seat and cleared his throat before trying to regain control of the meeting. "I resent that implication. Nevertheless, that is not the purpose of this meeting and I'm afraid that we are getting off track. We will deal with this latter Robbins. For now, let's get back to the major issue that we are dealing with today. "There have been a number of instances in which Dr. Stern has operated on individuals with out proper pre-operative laboratory evaluation."

I again jumped in before he could continue. "I think Dr. Landers can save us all a lot of trouble if he tells us all what is common practice for this hospital."

I saw a movie once in which an old time lawyer advised his younger colleague never to ask a question that he didn't already know the answer to. I knew Karol Landers' answer. He was a decent man in a tough position. As a hospital pathologist, he had to play by the "old boy" set of rules. But he had a liberal spirit and a sense of fairness. He couldn't stand the double standard and the hypocritical dictums. He needed to protect himself, but he loved the opportunity to stick it to them without ever appearing too intentful. Besides, I had primed him for this one.

"I'm afraid to say that, unfortunately, there are a lot of surgical cases that go off in this hospital without enough pre-operative laboratory screening," said Dr. Landers, performing true to the script. "I think that this might be a good time to review this matter and set up some protocols that would make all of us more comfortable."

"I'm afraid that we will have to table that discussion for another meeting Dr. Landers," chimed in Dr. McKay. "What I really want to know is whether or not Dr. Stern was particularly irresponsible with regard to not properly evaluating patients pre-operatively."

"The answer to that question is certainly no more frequently than the average physician practicing at this hospital."

"Thank you Dr. Landers. If there are no more comments regauarding this issue, we can get on to our more crucial concern." Dr. McKay paused to see if there was commentary. There was none so he continued. "There has been some serious concern regarding Dr. Stern's surgical skills. Dr. Coleman and Jenkins have both sponsored him on cases and find him to be inadequate and potentially dangerous."

This was going to be a tough one. I had operated with Stern and found him to be somewhat sloppy and undisciplined. He had a fine tremor and sometimes was hesitant in his actions. I wouldn't have put my mother, let alone my wife, in his hands but there were some others that I would have trusted less. During my residency, I had operated with all of the twenty five gynecologists on staff at City hospital, and helped to train four others that followed me in residency. With regard to surgical skills, of the twenty nine, I would have to rank Stern as number twenty five or twenty six. He certainly wasn't great, but there were a few more that were worse, let alone dangerous. Their surgical privaledges were not under review because they had trained at City hospital or they were protected by their partners in bigger and more powerful groups. If Stern was going to go down, then I was determined to bring the whole house down with him. I was feeling my oats now and I was ready to roll.

"Well Dr. Jenkins is not here, but I would certainly like to hear Dr. Coleman's comments."

"Jim, the floor is yours," said McKay.

Without hesitation, Coleman jumped to the task like a leopard ready to spring on to his prey. "I had the, er misfortune, may I say, to scrub with Dr. Stern twice in the last two weeks. I found that he was slow, unsure and sloppy. He continuously used his fingers to manipulate and dissect tissue. Any good surgeon knows that proper technique dictates the use ofinstrumentation for dissection and exposure, not fingers. I fear that he is poorly trained and that, if left alone, he will hurt somebody badly.

"Dr. Coleman," I interceded. "Did you know that Dr. Stern is nationally board certified and that he comes highly recommended by the chief of the OBGYN department at one of the most respected programs in the country, St. Martin's medical center."

"I don't care if President Carter himself recommended him! He's still a lousy surgeon."

Now I had him where I wanted him, with his nuts in a vice, and me ready to turn the handle. "Dr. Phillips," I queried. "Didn't you tell us in residency that you rely heavily on your fingers for manipulation, exposure and dissection; that you couldn't see how anybody could get to the next surgical level without using their hands as instruments?"

Phillips sat up in his chair, trying to calculate all the pros and cons of his answer, sighing as he realized that he had expounded on his philosophy to loudly and too often to take the chance of altering his position and being branded as a liar. "Yes, I guess I did."

"Well gentlemen," I said, pausing to get their attention. "I guess that Dr. Coleman's testimony is not necessarily an indictment of Dr. Stern's surgical skills, but rather a testimony to Dr. Coleman's ignorance with regard to surgical methodology valued very highly by others." I stopped to take a sip of water and contined.

"Dr. Stern has been in this hospital for six months. In that period, he has not had a single patient with a severe complication or calamatous result. He has national certification and the stamp of approval from one of our finest institutions. He has practiced at a level well above the standard expected at this hospital. His surgical skills have been challanged by two community practitioners, one who is not here to explain himself, and the other who has demonstrated an abject

intolerance for surgical technique that differs from his own, even if it is appreciated by others as being superior to his own."

For the first time, Dr. Proel spoke up. "Come on Dodd. Let's cut the crap. You know that he hasn't done enough surgery to have an expectation of finding complications, let alone a negative trend."

"Exactly," I retorted. "He hasn't done enough to make any judgement at all." I expected applause. Instead I got Dr. McKay's sharp tone cutting through my moment.

"Are you through."

"Yes."

"Dr. Stern, do you have anything more to say?"

"No."

"Well then thank you gentlemen. You can leave now and we will inform you of our decision."

Carl and I got up to leave and, as I walked out to the hallway, I tried to study the countenances on all their faces. As I looked around the room, I felt a sense of doom. I sensed that they really didn't hear a word that I said and that they were going to give Stern the "death penalty" and throw him off the staff. Their minds were made up and they just weren't going to listen to anybody like me.

We went home somewhat despondent, although I did all I could to keep Carl's spirits up. He had bought a house, over paid for it and was financially strapped. Ifhe lost his privlages, he would have trouble getting into another hospital in Florida and would probably have to leave the state. The house would have to go in a fire sale, and the equity that he strived so hard to save by working long days and nights would all be lost. At age thirty five, starting over with the stigma of having been thrown off the staff of a hospital, would not be an easy proposition. His kids schooling would be disrupted and his wife would never understand. When we got back to my house, he was almost in tears.

I cursed Marty for not being there to help me deal with this. He had his own agenda. He was intimidated by the powers that be and was afraid to confront them, no matter what the truths or consequences.

He was afraid to stand up for Carl, in fear that he would be the next target if he created too many waves. He prefered to stay in the background and dissassociate himself with anybody out of favor.

The call came three hours after we left the room. "You won't believe what happened!" said Karol Landers.

"Good or bad?" I asked anxiously.

"Good! Good!" he added excitedly, "but I got to explain what happened." As I gave a distessed Carl the thumbs up, Landers continued.

"Initially, they voted him down unanimously."

"You too?," I asked incredulously.

"I had to. My one vote wouldn't have made the difference and I need the job. Now will you let me finish."

"Sorry, go ahead."

"They voted him down unanimously and their lawyer, Stan Barton, stood up and in all his pompous splendor told them this, and I quote as accurately as possible.

"Gentlemen, young Dr. Robbins is a little rough and inexperienced in these matters, but I wouldn't mind having him on my legal team. He did his homework and he set us up beautifully. You can choose to do what you wish, but let me warn you. He destroyed us tonight and, if these procedings repeat themselves in a court of law, not only will Dr. Stern's privlages be reinstated, but each and every one of you will be sued for malicious prosecution."

"God, that's hard to believe," I chimed in.

"What happened?" Carl interrupted.

"Hold on a minute and let Karol finish," I said irritatedly, giving Carl the "keep it down" hand signal.

"Anyway, they were stunned. They didn't understand what happened, so Barton explained how you dissected them by proving that the hospital standards were far below Stern's, so that any disciplinary action could easily be viewed as prejudicial and therefore subject to damages."

"Wow, that's beautiful!" Carl kept asking questions and I had to turn away from him in order to listen to Karol.

"Anyway, Miller stands up and announces to the crowd, quote, unquote. Maybe we thought we had one too many New York Jews down here doing abortions."

"No shit!"

"You got it. At least he had the guts to get it right out on the table."

"Then what happened?"

"They revoted and you won. His privalages are intact."

"Karol, thank you. Thank you so very much."

"You're welcome man. You sure got a lot of guts."

With that, he hung up the phone and I related the events to Carl. He went home, content that he would be able to live in his new house and not have to explain his failures to his wife and his children.

I went off to bed, anxious for the next day, when I would face the powers that be in the hospital. The rules had changed and, ironically, they treated me, not with disdain, but with renewed awareness and respect. I was no longer their boy. From that day forward, they knew that they couldn't step on me or my kind with impunity. They knew that to challenge me meant a fight and, worse than that, a fight that they could very well lose.

Amidst the pressure of everyday practice was the constant turmoil at home. In a place that should have been a refuge, I was constantly atacked for my inadequacies. In a place that should have been a haven, I felt increasingly awkwark and uncomfortable. In a place where I should have been able to find peace and tranquility, I found agitation and conflict.

There was no way to resolve issues with Christina. She was fixed in her beliefs and principles and gave no credence to my feelings or needs if they didn't fit her perception of right and wrong. She had been terribly embarrassed by the notoriety of the medications scandle and by the negative publicity that my partner Marty and I were exposed to.

Image was very important to her. She had worked hard to improve her English and she sounded more like an aistocrat than an "Ellis Island immigrant." She had climbed the social ladder and was accepted into all the charitable organizations that counted and she wanted to keep it that way.

In a way, these organizations served me well. Not only was she able to occassionally send me quality patients through her contacts, but her work kept her and the boys in America for most of the year. She still took them to Italy over Christmas and for two months in the summer, but this served only to solidify my relationship with them more and more.

Their absence allowed me to concentrate completely on my business during the summer so that I could give them quality time when they returned home for the school year. I coached their teams and tutored them in their schoolwork. I even wrote a paper or two for them for which they were eternally grateful. Sometimes, when I was not on call for the weekend, I would take them away to golf or tennis camp where the three of us could pal around doing the things that we loved.

I watched them grow with a heart full of pride. Somehow, we were turning out two wonderful, loving, multi-talented, bilingual boys who would be a credit to their family and their community. Reluctantly, I had to admit that Christina was part of the formula too. She set a wonderful example for them and gave them consistency, discipline and love.

It saddened me to be isolated from that affection and love and, if I knew how to resolve the issues, I would have done it in a heartbeat. But somehow, the cards just didn't run for us. The conflicts were too frequent and too big for us to easily resolve, and neither she nor I knew how to go about taking the first step. We both continued to be civil but cold and distant toward each other and there didn't seem to be an end in sight.

From time to time, I am asked the question. "Why did I become a gynecologist?" My response is usually rational and sensible, but it never explores the real depths of the question. It never confronts the ghosts of my past in relationship to my choices today. I don't profess to be a psychologist, schooled and trained in self anayslisis, but I do know how I felt about situations in the past that must have contributed toward shaping my attitudes and my destiny.

To begin with, I grew up in a semi-victorian era. Female nudity was as exciting as it was mysterious. Never did we see a naked woman on the screen or on T.V. A view of cleavage or a bare thigh could set off a tintilating fantasy. Most sexual satisfaction came at home with a visual fantasy and an adept right hand.

In junior high school and college, most of my sexual experiences with women were wrought with frustration and confusion. Despite my exposure to the sexually sophisticated "group" in high school, most women that I dated gave off inconsistent and confusing signals. Most sexual encounters terminated with frustrating dissappointments rather than exquisite delights. It was not uncommon to indulge in heavy and intense foreplay, only to have the lady stop in mid stream and subject herself to self reproach or, worse yet, turn on you and slap you silly for your "wanton" behavior. The female response was often whimsical, capricious and totally unpredictable and it initiated, in the sensitive male, very tentative behavior.

Sexual initiative was ususally left to the male, but he approached it furtively and uncertainly for he had no idea what kind of response to expect. He took baby steps, expecting the axe to fall at any moment, sometimes sending him home accused of primitive and vulgar behavior and, almost always, sending him home with a severe case of "blue balls." On rare occasion, the event culminated with copulation, but not before the male was put through a series of yesses and nos that sent him up and down like a yoyo and made the act of orgasm an act of relief, rather than an act of ecstasy that topped off a thrilling and pleasurable journey.

In summation, the male of my era was primed and conditioned to feel tremendously vulnerable to the unpredictable behavior of his female counterpart. He desperately needed her, but she had total control over his sexual pleasure, unless he were to take a more aggressive roll and try and control events through manipulation or force. The pursuit of intercourse was no longer just the pursuit of sexual pleasure.

It became a pursuit of control; a challenge of dominance; a chance to score.

With this background, what greater irony could there be in life then to spend half of it begging and chasing women for their attentions, only to find that, with the acquisition of the label "gynecologist," you could matter of factly tell them to whip off their panties and spread their legs. Not only would they jump at this request, but they would also thank you profusely and pay you money to look at their vaginas and put your fingers inside of them.

All of a sudden, the pressure was off. You can could examine vaginas all day long and get paid to do it. What control! What a reversal of fortune!

I'm sure that there are a number of other reasons that motivate a physician to select the specialty of obstetrics and gynecology. Dealing with young and relatively healthy patients has to be a positive. Dealing with positive events most of the time, like delivery ofbabies rather than depressing cancers, has to be appealing. Having a combination of medical and surgical problems to deal with has to be more interesting than just one or the other. But at the root ofit all, putting oneselfin a position of complete control had to be a tempting drawing card.

Leaning in the direction of choosing this specialty didn't require a conscious awareness of the transfer of control. For most of us, the awareness may have only been a feeling of comfort, excitement and interest in the process of taking care of women. Conciously, we never put it into the raw and banal terms of winning the battle of control thirty times a day.

Most men fantasize about being a gynecologist. I lived their dream. Other men always found a way to ask me. "What's it like to look at pussy all day long?"

The cool answer is, "it's hard but somebody has to do it." The truth is much more complicated. In the beginning, it's exciting and arousing. The perverted irony of having, all of a sudden, a license to order women to spread their legs is too much for any man to handle sensibly. All kinds of thoughts run through your head, but there are two constants, that you can't get away from, that smother the sexual flavor. For one, almost none of these episodes end with sexual gratification and for two, all of these exposures are done in harsh light where there are no illusions or secrets. Vulvas and vaginas are clearly uneven and assymet- rical. Often, they are marred by pimples or lesions or, for that matter, little crusts from excretions. On inserting the speculum, even the cleanest vaginas, at best, have mucous similar to your one's nose drippings in cold weather. All the rest have some degree of discharge that range from visually displeasing to outright nauseating. It's very hard to reconcile these events with your sexual fantasies so that, for the most part, they fade from your conscious thoughts and you learn to separate the clinical experience from sexual arousal. It would not be uncommon for a gyneclogist to turn his head twice to look at an attractive girl walking down the hallway and, later that day, examine her bare and exposed genitalia with complete disinterest.

Nevertheless, there are isolated situations that can definitely reawaken your sexuality in the clinical environs. These usually occur when you are confronted with an exceptionally erotic woman or a woman who changes the rules and becomes sexually suggestive.

In the first case, you do all you can to supress your reaction, for it is clear that even fantasizing would be considered deviant behavior. Notice, I have said that you try and supress your reaction; not that you always do. What you can do, is control your behavior and approach this lady in as clinical and divorced a manner as possible, while keeping your feelings to yourself. This set of events does not occur often, for, under the glow of harsh lighting, the illusions of sexual perfection are almost always destroyed. But when these feelings occured, they could be quite disconcerting and they aroused, at least in me, concommitant feelings of guilt and betrayal.

The feelings that are aroused in the second case are totally different. The patients usually make a sexually suggestive move like moaning when you examine their breasts or vagina. Sometimes they even verbalize the fact that they find you attractive and that they would like to sleep with you. If you find them attractive, it is easy, without guilt, to revert to the role of the man, instead of continuing in the role of the doctor. The suggestions bring out your sexuality and, from that point on, the development of the relationship can be left to the imagination. I have been hit with all different kinds of statements ranging from,"that feels good" to "do you fuck around on your wife?" I did everything I could to play the role of the absolute square, ignoring the first kind of statement to answering with an absolute "no!" to the second. I did this, not because of a lack ofinterest, but because of an absolute fear of being prosecuted for taking advantage of a patient and losing my license to practice medicine. On the rarest of occassions, if the woman was gorgeous and I was particularly horny, I was exposed to the most rigorous of tests. I can't say that I always passed with flying colors. In fact, I'm not quite sure which choice is passing and which one is failing. Surfice it to say, that I am human and vulnerable and that my behavior was and is not always predictable, let alone correct.

The archilles heel of most physicians is their arrogance; their abject belief that they are god-like and invulnerable. These beliefs do not come without merit. In the process of trainning, physicians are abused both physically and mentally and the surviving product is an individual with tremendous stamina, skill, control and resilience. The problem is that those fine qualities are not tempered with maturity and humility. Social growth ceases at eighteen and doesn't begin again until the young physician is released from the imprisonment of residency at age thirty to thirty five. Fortunately for my patients, in spite of my training, I always maintained a healthy level of self doubt which allowed me to expose my ignorance in the process of getting my patient the best care possible. Fortunately for most of my patients and for myself, I learned caution, humility, tolerance and self protection early in the game from some very poignant situations.

Linda Sutton was a pretty young lady, pregnant for the first time when she came into my office. She complained of vague intraabdominal pain which was never corroborated with the physical findings. Despite the discomfort, her abdomen was soft to the touch and she had no laboratory evidence of a smouldering infection. Marty and I catergorized Linda as a hypocondriac and a complainer. It was frustrating never to find a physical sign to back up her pleas for pain relief. In the beginning, we sympathetically listened to her story but, as time wore on, we responded with clichés. "Be patient Linda," I would respond. "Get off your feet, lie down and take a few good breaths."

"That doesn't work Dr.," she would reply. "I can't stand it any more. "There is no relief."

"I know, I know. It's just normal for a lot of women to go through this in pregnancy." Walking over and putting an arm around her, I would add. "I'm going to give you a perscription for a pain medication that should take care of it." I would sit down and write her a perscription for a benign medication that would do absolutely no good, but would not harm the baby.

Marty was a little less tolerant. Nothing frustrates a doctor more than the inability to do something about a patient's complaint. Instead of accepting his own inadequacy, most physicians lay blame on the patient and it is evident in their tone. Such was the case when I overheard Marty comment to Linda with biting sarcasm. "Tell me Linda. When the dust in the air falls on the bare, exposed hairs on your arms, does this cause excruciating pain?"

Linda responded by bursting into tears. I was more civil at her visits, to the extent that lip service could prevail. Linda continued to complain visit after visit, phone call after phone call and her words began to fall on deaf ears. Nobody ever told me that hypocondriacs could have real pain too.

When she went into labor, I drew the short straw and reluctantly went into the hospital. Her screams could be heard down the hall. Thank god she was a primagravida breech for I was able to do a caesarian section and avoid a long drawn out miserable labor. I gave her preops and took her into the O. R. for her epidural. Thank god that that shut her up. I opened her belly and saw more thick, almost filamentous adhesions than I had ever seen in my life. It took me an eternity to dissect through them until I got to the bladder flap. How they got there was a mystery but it was a real mess. Linda couldn't make a move without something pulling and twisting on something else.

The following day, I walked into Linda's room bright and early, expecting her to be begging for pain medication. Instead, she was bright and chipper with a mask of relief covering her face.

"You okay?" I asked with concern.

"Okay! I am great," she bellowed. "That horrible pulling pain is gone. Thank you doctor. Thank you so much!"

I mumbled something inaudibly, perfunctorily checked her abdomen and vital signs, looked at her lab work, wrote a few orders and left the room. It was clear now that Linda had been in pain for seven months and, instead of trying to help her, Marty and I had been trying to help relieve ourselves of guilt. We just didn't listen and we should not have ignored her pleas for help just because her symptoms did not fall into a comfortable little box with the usual signs of physical confirmation. It was good for me to be humbled this early in my career. Every physician needed this kind of experiece from time to time, just to get him off his pedestal with the other godly idols.

In my second year of practice, I saw a young seventeen year old girl for a second opinion on a ten centimeter left adnexal mass. After repeated exams, I could not feel the mass. Knowing that the first doctor that she had seen was my mentor, I said to her mother. "I don't feel the mass. It is possible that it has gone away. My suggestion is that you go into see Dr. Phillips early on Monday morning. He is an honest man. If he still feels the mass, I would have to assume that it is still there. Dr. Phillips has much longer fingers than I do and many years more experience. I would go with his call."

Sure enough, on Tuesday, I go into his operating room after finishing up my own case, and there on the table is this young girl with her belly opened. Dr. Phillips was removing her appendix as was often done for prevention in those days. He had opened her belly, only to find a small cystic corpus luteum, which is normal in the luteal phase of the menstrual cycle. Shaking his head, he said. "I really felt it was bigger in the office. She had a little adhesion over the ovary and that probably added to the sensation."

I believed him. He never operated unneccesarily for money. He just felt something that wasn't there.

The following day, the young lady was walking the halls of the gynecology floor and I stopped to ask her how she was doing. "Great!" she said, somewhat elated. "Thank you so much for sending me to Dr. Phillips. He saved my life. I feel so good, and he said that I can leave tommorrow."

Her mother was so much more explicit when she caught me in the hallway. "Doctor Robbins," she said with firm conviction. "It takes a special man to admit his inexperience and refer a patient to someone more skilled. Thank you for sending my daughter back to Doctor Phillips. Not only did he get that tumor, before it became a major problem, but he took out her appendix so that she'll never have to worry about that again."

"So much for candor," I thought. The girl never had a mass and never needed the surgery and I still ended up looking like an idiot. I would never expose myself like that again. From this case, I learned that no one was perfect and that my judgement could be better than the next guys, even though I didn't bolster it up with fluffy bravado.

Another situation that really taught me humility and balance was a case of an abnormal Pap smear taken from the vaginal cuff of an individual treated for cervical cancer ten years before. Again, I called one of my mentors for advice and he was pretty disdainful in his instructions. "God Dodd, it's no big deal. All you need to do is biopsy the cuff under culposcopic exam and freeze the dysplasic areas with the cryo. It's all cut and dry."

I had been really pressured that day and was running late. It would have been easy for me to just accept his judgement and follow his instructions, but something told me that what he said didn't make sense. I decided to call the "guru" in gynecologic oncology, Dr. Sam Naugh. This wasn't easy to do. First of all, I had to take the time to explain the delay to the patient, in essence, telling her that I didn't have enough knowledge to solve the problem myself. Secondly, I had to expose myself to the petty gossip and snide commentary of a man who was as small and narrow in character as he was expansively knowledgeable in gynecologic oncology. I did pregnancy terminations and he was as avid an anti-abortionist as existed in the country. Based on that fact alone, he didn't like me and he looked for every opportunity to make negative, untrue commentary about my skills. Nevertheless, I swallowed hard and got him on the line. "Sorry to bother you Dr. Naugh, but I have a patient with an abnormal Pap smear taken from her vaginal cuff, ten years after being treated for an invasive cervical cancer." With all the bravado that I could muster, I echoed my mentor's words. "I thought that I would biopsy the affected areas and treat them with cryo-surgery, but I wanted to make sure that there was nothing more that I could do.

"What are you trying to do Robbins? Kill her?" came the supercilious response.

With the wind knocked out of me, I fumbled for a retort, but instead, just mumbled. "Er, no, er, that's why I'm calling you."

"You need to treat the lesion man! She's gonna have to be explored." He paused for a second and then added. "No sense in me explaining this to you. Why don't you just send her over here so that she can be treated properly."

"Fine, I'll send her right over," was all I could muster in response. He wasn't being fair, but fair didn't matter. He was her best hope for treatment and it was my duty to send her there. I returned to the exam room and refered her to Dr. Naugh, knowing that he would critisize me in front ofher. I wanted to prepare her for the onslaught, but realized that my petty concerns about my reputation paled in confrontaion to the problem that she was going to have to deal with, so I left well enough alone.

The important thing was that I learned to focus on the patient's problems and tried to find the best solutions for their care, regardless of the effect that it had on my reputation, regardless of the inconvenience created for me. I practiced for almost twenty years, and never had a death. I dealt with only two or three major complications and treated all of them expeditiously. I was only asked to do something brilliant a handful of times in twenty years and I never let my own ego interfere with finding the right treatment for these patients, even if it meant refering them to another gynecologist with more experience in that area; even though it meant exposing myself to someone who might soil my reputation.

In an era where most physicians saw medicine as an art, I saw it as a science, subject to the rules of probability. I removed as much of the romanticism and flamboyance as possible from my practice and substituted standing orders and protocols so that faulty memory could be eliminated from the equation.

I understood the delicacy and skill required for certain vaginal deliveries, but I never let these thoughts prevail over the more mundane concepts of placing myself between the mother and the floor so that the baby didn't accidently fall to the concrete. Once delivered, I held the baby like a football and never once did I fumble.

I understood the need for miracle drugs from time to time but never at the expense of giving someone a medication that they were allergic to.

In summary, I am not without flaws, but I did my best. Almost twenty years of practice and not one death. I leave, without fanfair, without medals, without a farewell dinner, without a parade. I leave, content, even smug, in the knowledge that I helped a myriad of patients and never did anybody any harm; certain that I used the tools at my disposal to the best of my ability; sure that there was no way to better my record. I leave, knowing that my results speak for themselves.

EPILOGUE

Time heals all wounds or so they say. Christina and I never found our equlibrium. It is impossible to be a great doctor, a great father and a great husband at the same time.

In the pursuit of a succesful practice, I came up short as a husband. All marriages require compromize on both sides. The problem is that even if you can intellectually identify your partner's compromize, you can't feel it's intensity. Intensity etches into memory like a branding iron burns into flesh, and therefore, the ledger always seems unbalanced. I kept crediting myself with giving in, without giving Christina her due. Needless to say, the opposite was also true.

I guess that time worn adage, "marry your own kind," is true. There are enough compromises in a marriage without having to add all the differences that span diverse cultures.

It's easy to see how harmonious expectation can alleviate a lot of conflicts, and it is just as easy to see how different expectations on the part of the husband and the wife can evolve into irreparable friction.

With Christina, this was all true. We had many differences and we were both too immature, or too unwilling to bridge the gaps. My pride prevented me from making a real attempt at reconciliation with her father and, his belief system, imprinted on him at an early age, made it impossible for him to accept me as part of the family. Poor Christina was caught in the middle and the principle didn't matter anymore. Because of the conflict, she resented both of us, because it made her life that much more difficult.

Furthermore, the gaps in our exposures widened as we grew older, as our activities had nothing to do with each other. The only thing that we had in common were the children and, even there, protective and passive aggressive mechanisms prevented us from common agreement. We separated in nineteen eighty five, when Dean was twelve and Darren was ten. Surprisingly, Christina stayed on in America. She had become acclimated to the conveniences of life here and would have had an impossible time convincing the boys to move to Italy. Like a religion, though, she did take them back home every Christmas and every summer. In the end it worked out very well. Both boys are bilingual. They understand the need to be tolerant of other cultures, as they have had to tread waters between our two, and they have both had enough exposure so that their interests are many and diverse.

Today, Christina is happily or unhappily remarried. I wish I could add more, but I am no longer included in her inner circle of confidants and the boys would never let on that there was "trouble in River City."

Despite the turmoil of chilhood, Dean and Darren have both been succesful in their professional lives. Dean, despite my misgivings, emulated his father and went into the medical field. He attended a six year program combining college and medical school and graduated at age twenty three, a full fledged physician. He did his residency and practiced Ob-gyn for two years before he quit with the following explanation. "I go to the Emergency room at three in the morning to see a medicaid patient. They treat me like crap, and I get eleven dollars for my effort. I take my life in my hands by going out to my car in that neighborhood at that desolate hour and, for the next two days, I feel sleep deprived. Now I go out as a computer consultant. They buy me lunch, treat me with respect and pay me much more than I made as a doctor. To top it all off, I get to sleep at night."

Inside of two years he has become a wealthy man. He is a computer guru. He writes and sings music and, to date, he has sold numerous songs.

Darren has done many more less traditional things, exploring the arts and the sports world. He worked in the movie industry for many years and put together a comfortable little nest egg. He has been the owner and managing partner of a professional sport's team and has dabbled with computers and the internet. He has traveled extensively and has tasted some extreme life experiences, from exploring the Alaskan tundra, to mountain climbing in Nepal and to safari's in Africa. He has seen Australia and New Zealand, the South Pacific islands, most ofAsia, all ofEurope, and a good part of the U.S.A., from Maine to Florida, from Hawaii to Alaska. He has a zest for living and knows how to make the most out of each hour and each day.

Life is fleeting and, in the pursuit of goals, you cross paths with many individuals that you call close friends. Usually, the frequency of contact is limited by the time that you are actually concerned with common aims and pleasures. Exposure usually wanes, once you no longer have common purpose.

In spite of that tendency, I have tried to keep up with Frank, Angela and Mark although never enough to my liking.

Frank finally got his degree in medicine and settled in a small West Virginia town to practice general medicine. He has served his community for almost thirty years. He remained a bachelor, but has a great relationship with his entire extended family and was responsible for setting up a fund that provided funding for all his nieces and nephews to go to college. Once a year we meet in the "Big Apple" to spend some time together, rehash old stories and dreams and take in a couple of shows and ball games.

Angela went on to specialize in public health and eventually married a wealthy diplomate. As an ambassador's wife, she had many duties including raising a family. Nevertheless, when she was stationed here in America, we made sure that we took many opportunities to spend time together and, when she was stationed in other countries, I made sure that we visited her at least once every three or four years.

Mark got out of medical school only two months after I did and did a specialty in radio therapy. He has practiced for thirty years in a small north eastern city and has been instumental in getting his city hospital to purchase up to date equipment so that he could always deliver the best care to his patients. He has devoted his life to his specialty and is recognized nationally as an expert in his field.

In nineteen eighty seven, I took a sking trip to Austria and, after a hard day on the slopes, I scheduled a massage. I was instructed by the receptionist to take a shower, enter the room, lay face down and cover myself with a fresh towel. I followed her instructions, eagerly anticipating the kneading of my sore muscles. The massage therapist entered the room and identified herself.

"My name is Ingrid. Do you have any sore areas that need work?"

"All over," was my perfunctory response. Lying there, something seemed eeirily familiar, but I couldn't put my finger on it. She spoke English well, but there was a hint of a hard German accent, not the softer variety that Austrians spoke. Then it hit me and I had to look up. "Ingrid!"

Not expecting me to move, she pulled back and then a sudden recognition came across her face.

"Dodd! Oh my God!" Her hands moved toward her face as she covered her mouth, startled, not wanting her voice to interupt the excitement of the moment. I reached up and grabbed her hands and she stood there, radiant and smiling, not believing the moment.

"I can't believe this!" She was so excited, she was jumping up and down like a teenager at a concert being performed by a singing idol.

I sat up and wrapped the towel around me and echoed her words. "I can't believe this." We forgot the massage and hugged for a long, long moment.

"I tried so hard to find you," I said, "but they wouldn't give me any information."

"Me too, but I didn't know your last name and by the time they freed me from processing, I had no idea how to go about finding you to thank you for what you did."

"God, I worried about you forever. I agonized over whether or not I did the right thing by taking you across the border."

"At first I didn't think so but, after they felt comfortable that they smothered the media coverage of the event, they set me up in a sympathizer's private residence. Apparantly, there are a number of private charities that help people like me and one of them came through and paid for my training as a massage therapist. I asked about you, but I had been told to leave it alone and just be grateful that you did what you did. Apparantly there were some delicate political negotiations going on and they didn't want to upset the apple cart."

"I was also warned to leave it alone."

"After I got on my feet, I took a trip to Italy, but I forgot the school that you attended."

"What about you family?"

"After a few months, I was allowed to write them and eventually I did get to speak to them on the phone fairly regularly. After I got my passport, I was able to make a couple of trips back and they were allowed to visit me once. Of course, when the wall came down, we were allowed free access."

"God," I said again, pulling back and holding both her hands out in front of her. "I am so glad that I found you"

That night we went to dinner and tried to catch up on twenty years. We talked about a lot of things and the time just seemed to fly by. The next day we skied together and culminated the day's events with a candle lit dinner. In her presence I just felt so excited and fulfilled and her feelings seemed to be mutual. After a week, we both understood our destiny.

Today we celerated our fifteenth wedding anniversary and they have been fifteen years of relative bliss.

The years have made me mellow. Things always appear much more grey to me than black and white and I am far less judgemental than I was as a young man. Some say that my behavior is much more sensible and mature. Some say that it's more hypocritical. I just think that I have become more concerned with harmonious and pragmatic outcomes rather than righteous pursuits. You can put whatever stamp on it that you want to. I am who I am.

My life today is rich and full of joy. My relationships with my wife, my sons, and my daughter by my present wife are deep and loving. We don't always understand each other's travails or feelings, but we try. Enough money has afforded me the opportunity to pursue my many interests in life, without compromise, and to transcend the mundane economic problems that seem to weigh so many people down.

Looking back, I can see nothing to regret. Looking ahead, I can hope for many years of joyous living, surrounded by the people I love, free of the everday economic considerations that most people have to deal with. Who can ask for anymore? Who would want to?

www.ingramcontent.com/pod-product-compliance
Lightning Source LLC
Chambersburg PA
CBHW060854120626
46553CB00001B/75